Illustrated Encyclopedia of Indoor Plants

Kenneth and Gillian Beckett

Illustrated Encyclopedia
of Indoor Plants

over 800 genera and 2000 species
with 278 drawings, 128 in full colour

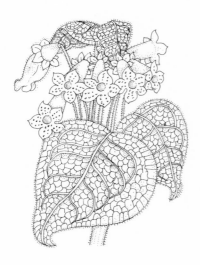

Doubleday & Company Inc.

Garden City, New York

First United States publication 1976 by
Doubleday & Company, Inc., Garden City,
New York.
Copyright © 1976 by Reference International
Publishers Limited.

Phototypeset by Tradespools Ltd, Frome,
Somerset
Printed in the United States of America

ISBN 0-385-12265-9
LCCN 76-1464

Introduction

There must be some basic urge in all of us to have some living greenery around us. Walk around any city area from shopping malls to office blocks and plants are there, living happily in central heating and with artificial light. Go into the smallest of homes and they will be there too. This desire for a little bit of garden indoors seems to have begun last century when people moved from the countryside into the towns and became nostalgic for what they had lost.

At first, with more primitive heat and light, the range of plants which could be grown was very limited, but today an enormous number of plants can be grown quite satisfactorily indoors, far more than most people imagine, and one of the aims of this book is to encourage a bit more experimentation. A great variety can be bought from the bigger nurserymen, but quite a range can be had in most garden centers and many supermarkets. All the equipment needed can be bought so easily too: composts, fertilizers, pest sprays; all these come in handy packs just right for the house. No wonder more and more people are turning to this fascinating hobby.

When setting out to buy a new plant, consider a few points first. What sort of position is it going to have? A sunny window sill will accommodate many plants, but if you have in mind a rather dark corner, something more special will be needed. Will it be grown indoors all the year, or can it spend a few sunny months outside? Again the choice will be different. Look through this book and find what will be your best buy, then set out to see what is available. All plants for sale should be clearly named and those from the more reputable firms will have some instructions for growing as well. If it comes as a gift and has no name then a search through this and other fine illustrated books available today should find the answer.

Once the plant is chosen, make sure it is healthy: one that dies within a few weeks may have been diseased before you bought it. It is not always easy for a beginner to decide what is healthy and wellgrown, but it should be sturdy and compact. Long, bare areas of stem showing between the leaves are a bad sign, as are thin, straggly growths. Leaves should be firm and green, and not hang limply which could indicate not only dryness, but a root rot disease. If the plant is in flower, avoid those which shed petals as soon as they are knocked and those that have no more buds to open, or you may find yourself with a plant that finishes blooming before you get it home. A sign of a plant that has been well looked after is its size in relation to the pot it is in. Tall, narrow plants like the columnar cacti should be twice the height of their pots, while those that are spreading should just be wider than their container. Remember too that cold weather is lethal to many indoor plants which come from tropical countries, and do not buy them in the winter if you have far to carry them in the open.

Once the plant is safely home, check again that its new position is going to be one where it not only looks good, but will thrive too. Points to watch for here are whether it is a shade lover or does best in full sun; how hot or cold a temperature it can stand; and with central heating, perhaps more important, can it stand the dry atmosphere? Many of the shade-loving house plants are from the floor of tropical jungles where temperatures may be constantly high, but so is humidity, and most of these either need, or will do better in a moister-than-normal atmosphere. One easy way of providing this is to stand the pots on a small tray filled with gravel. This is then kept topped up with water, though of course the water level must not reach the bottom of the pot or the compost will become water-logged. The width of the tray needs to be just a little bigger than the spread of the plant. Another method is to use moist peat in a deeper tray and plunge the pot into it. Again the peat must never become soaking wet. Whatever the method used, many of these plants will benefit from a spray of tepid water over their leaves during the hottest periods. This can easily be done over the kitchen sink.

Plants on window sills will enjoy the heat of the room by day, but unless the windows are double-glazed, that heat will be cut off when the curtains are pulled at night and the temperature around them can drop to freezing on a cold winter's night, so move them into the room before the curtains are pulled. Many indoor plants can survive colder conditions than is generally believed and the temperatures given throughout this book are the lowest that should be permitted if the plants are to remain undamaged. Obviously they are far lower than will exist in any living room, but will be useful as an indicator for those in unheated passageways or put outside on the patio for part of the year.

Plants grown around a window frame can be most effective. Put their pots at the side of the sill and train climbers up the sides and even across the top where a most decorative effect can be got when they meet. Making the most of the window space can be achieved in a number of ways. Small glass shelves fitted across the window block very little light, but are ideal places for such light-demanding plants as cacti. Others can be hung from hooks screwed into the window frame. The sill itself can be widened by having a specially-made plant box along its length, overlapping the edge, or a table can be stood in front of it.

For the less light-demanding plants, a darker wall or corner can be made suitable. Trelliswork fixed against it will take many climbers, or one of the specially-built plant growing units, rather like a bookcase with no back to it, can be put either against a wall or used as a room divider where there is space. High shelves can be most effective if they hold plants which will spill over the edges of their pots and hang down the wall. For all plants grown in this way, some extra form of light will be most beneficial and the ideal kind is that provided by fluorescent strip lighting which gives brightness without the heat that the ordinary light bulb gives. Put across the top of a wall above the plants, it will serve two purposes: keeping the plants healthier as well as illuminating them most attractively. The plant growing units already mentioned can be bought with lights already fixed, and these are of course ideal. If ordinary electric bulbs have to be used, be careful not to stand the plants too close as they do give off a surprising amount of heat.

Some plants will need supporting, especially if they are grown in a shady spot. Always remember that the support should be as unobtrusive as possible. Nothing looks worse than a plant tied tightly to a large piece of wood, bigger than itself. Use slender supports, canes, or even loops of wire are fine, and see that they are shorter than the plant. Of course it may grow bigger, but if it does, then get a bigger stick. Use green ties which will show less than other colors, and loop them around the stems, allowing the plant to continue growing upward as it was before, not pulling it to its support. If this is necessary, then the support is in the wrong place and needs moving. One attractive way of growing climbers in an ordinary pot is to make a balloon-shaped structure of loops of wire so that the plant covers them; the loops are best up to four times the height of the pot, not more or it may become top-heavy.

A number of plants really need to be grown in a hanging container. Many orchids come into this category as do the bromels (bromeliads). These are the plants which grow on tree trunks in the wild, a way of reaching the light in the dense forests of the tropics.

Botanically they are called epiphytes, and are also known as air plants. Growing them in the home presents few problems if their requirements are met. As they grow without soil in the wild, getting nourishment from scraps of leaf mold that have lodged in the tree branches and from the abundant rainfall, they thrive particularly well grown on a section of tree trunk or bark. Slabs of suitable bark can be bought for them and the roots of the plant are then wrapped with a handful of moss and a small amount of compost. This is secured to the bark with green, PVC coated wire or a similar, rust-proof and not too obvious wire. The bark can be hung up or laid in a tray of moist peat, and a number of plants fixed in this way on a bark slab makes a very unusual feature. Watering should be carried out with a syringe or a fine-rosed can. The epiphytic cacti such as the Epiphyllums, most orchids, and some ferns and vines are best grown hanging.

After a while, most plants outgrow their original pot and re-potting becomes necessary. If the plant seems to be growing less well or is obviously too big for its pot, see that it is moist, then take it out of its pot by turning it upside down, supporting the weight of the soil on the palm of your hand, letting the plant hang down between the fingers. Hold the pot with the other hand and tap the rim downwards on a hard surface. This should free the edges of the pot from the soil and it should lift off easily. If it does not, the soil may be too dry, so water it and try again. The plant should now be re-potted into a container which allows at least 1 in. of space all around its root ball which should not be disturbed. If you are using an old pot, see that it is quite clean by scrubbing it first in hot water so that no pests or diseases are carried onto the new plant. Plastic pots which have many small holes in the base need no drainage materials in them, but those with a single hole, and this means most clay pots, should have the hole covered with a piece of broken pot or a square of perforated zinc which can be bought for the purpose. The most popular composts to use are those which are peat-based and any of these can be used, but if the plant is large it is advisable to put a little sand or gravel in the bottom first as these composts are very light and the plant easily becomes top-heavy. Also place a small amount of compost in the bottom of the pot, judging it so that when the plant is put into place, $\frac{1}{2}$ in. of soil above its original level will fill it to within $\frac{1}{2}$ in. of the top of the pot, or 1 in. if the pot is larger than 8 in. across. This allows for watering. Fill the sides of the pot, pressing the compost down with a blunt stick, and firm the top with the fingers. Water only sparingly at first until the roots have spread out into the new soil. This will take a couple of weeks.

Watering too much or too little is probably a far more important cause of death in indoor plants than any pests or diseases, but rules are not easy to lay down for the beginner. It is probably safe to say that the majority of house plants are best left to become almost dry between waterings; this applies particularly to fleshy-leaved plants such as succulents and cacti. The easiest test is to scratch the surface of the compost with the tip of the finger. Do not water unless it feels dryish for at least $\frac{1}{2}$ in. down. If it does, give the plant a good soaking so that the water drips out of the drainage holes at the bottom of the pot. If the plant is being kept cool, this may not be necessary more than once a week, but in warm conditions when it is growing vigorously, check every day. Some plants cannot stand getting their roots dry and these need watering more freely, but this does not mean that they should be kept water-logged – far from it, but they do need to be kept just moist and must not be allowed to dry out as the more succulent species can. The two categories are noted throughout this book.

Some plants grow surprisingly well just in water. The popular foliage plants such as most philodendrons, *Dracaena*, *Aglaonema*, and *Coleus* can be used in this way. A shallow container is best so that the water has a large surface area to absorb the necessary oxygen, about 4 in. deep is ideal, and a layer of pebbles in the bottom, or crumpled wire, will help support the plants which are then placed in position. The water is best changed once a week, and a few drops of any liquid feed can be added to the fresh water. These liquid feeds are ideal for use with all indoor plants and most will benefit from their use, particularly those which grow very quickly and soon use up the nutrients in their compost. It is most important to follow the instructions on the label of the pack, as a double dose after forgetting for a few weeks will not exactly help! In fact if feeding has been forgotten for a while and the plants appear to be suffering, the new foliar feeds which are sprayed directly on to the leaves and absorbed at once are most valuable. Generally some form of feed should be given to plants at about two week intervals when they are growing. During their dormant season this is not necessary.

Although it is easy to go out and buy new plants, great pleasure can be obtained from growing one's own from scratch, and a surprising amount can be done on the kitchen window sill, as well as providing extra interest while the chores are being done at the sink! Many species will grow easily from cuttings and these can be begged from friends and relatives, or taken from overlarge plants which could do with being replaced. Relatively little equipment is needed: a large pot covered with a polythene bag supported on a couple of loops of wire is quite an adequate frame, though of course the custom-built propagating trays are ideal and take up far less space if several plants are being raised in this way. Use either pure sand, which is the most successful medium for rooting, or a mixture of peat and sand which will give the plants a little feed once they have rooted. In the sand they must be removed and potted as soon as they are ready or they will starve. A few drops of liquid or foliar feed can however save the day here.

Stem cuttings are perhaps the most easily taken. These are either of soft growths, taken from the growing tips of the shoots, or hardwood, taken from older, firmer stems. The former are usually taken in summer. Remove a length of stem with its leaves attached by cutting just above a bud or leaf to give a piece about 4 in. long on average. Carefully remove the leaves from the lower half of the stem, make a clean cut just below the lowest bud or severed leaf, and place the cutting in the sand or peat and sand to about $\frac{1}{3}$ to $\frac{1}{2}$ of its length. Smaller growing plants will need shorter cuttings than this, but always remove the leaves from the lower half before insertion. As an extra aid to rooting, a hormone powder or liquid can be used. If several cuttings are being taken, and it is always wise to take three or four, space them at a distance equal to about half their length before insertion; only really large cuttings such as those of geranium or x Fatshedera need to be put in separate pots. Water carefully with a fine-rosed can and keep in a temperature of 65°–70°F, but out of direct sunlight. Many plants will have rooted within 10 days, but others will take up to 30 days or even longer. As a general rule, leave them while they look fresh and green, only throwing them away when the leaves brown. As soon as new growth is visible and new leaves begin to appear, carefully remove each plant and set it singly in a pot of ordinary compost as described for re-potting. Water well and keep shaded for a few days while new roots are spreading through the pot.

Cuttings of firmer, harder stems are mostly taken with a "heel." To do this, choose a suitable side shoot and pull it away from the main stem, holding the base of the shoot firmly between thumb and forefinger and pulling it downwards with the other hand. If a long piece of the stem comes away, trim it with a knife or scissors, then treat the cutting in exactly the same way as for soft cuttings.

Many plants root well by using leaves, or even parts of leaves as cuttings. African violets, many begonias and mother-in-law's tongues can be treated in this way, those with smaller leaves like the African violet have the whole leaf removed and the leaf stem inserted as described for stem cuttings. Larger-leaved plants such as begonias and peperomias root from leaf sections. With the first named, small squares of leaf will produce tiny plantlets if laid on the surface of the compost, while the latter is best with a small portion of stem included. Plants with long leaves such as *Sansevieria* can have 3 in. sections cut from a leaf and inserted as described.

Many plants make things much easier by producing plantlets upon themselves. Spider plant *(Chlorophytum)* is perhaps the best known, but mother of thousands, *(Saxifraga stolonifera)* and hen and chicken fern *(Asplenium bulbiferum)* are other examples. In each case let the plantlet produce three or four leaves before detaching it, then treat as a cutting. Bulbous plants frequently produce offsets, that is small bulblets, and these can be separated and potted individually. Other plants which form a tuft of several stems from below ground level can be divided into two, each part forming a new adult plant. Growing plants from seed is always fun, but it must be remembered that the plant from which the seeds were collected may be a specially raised form, not a true species and one that will not produce a new plant exactly like itself. The flowers of the new plant may be a disappointment; on the other hand, there is always the chance, even if only a small one, that your new seedling may be even better than its parents! First fill your box or pan with a seed compost, firming it lightly so that there is $\frac{1}{2}-\frac{3}{4}$ in. of clear space at the top of the box for watering. Sow the seeds thinly, scattering them if they are small, or sowing them evenly with a pair of tweezers if they are large enough to handle. Cover very thinly, the depth of soil above them should be no thicker than the seeds themselves, and water with a fine spray, or by putting the pot or box in water almost to the rim so that the water soaks up through the drainage holes. Allow to drain, then cover with a polythene bag or a sheet of glass and keep in a temperature of about 70°F. Keep out of direct sunlight. A sheet of newspaper is sufficient if they are on a sunny window sill. As soon as seedlings appear, uncover them. The first leaves to appear are usually the seed leaves (cotyledons) which are different from the adult leaves. Once these have opened, remove the seedlings and either pot singly or space out evenly in another box of compost. It is best to fill the box first, firming it gently, then make small holes, just large enough to take the seedlings, using a small piece of wood like a rather thick pencil. Keep shady for a few days. When the new plants are large enough for their leaves to touch across the surface of the box, pot them on to individual pots.

Luckily, plants in the home are not too troubled by pests and those that do appear are usually brought in on new plants, so always look these over very carefully before adding to the collection. If possible, keep them apart as a sort of quarantine period until you are sure there are no aphids lurking among the leaves. If spraying has to be done, always follow the makers' instructions to the letter and if possible either spray outside or over a sink which should be washed down thoroughly afterwards. Aphids are the commonest cause of trouble; they are tiny, soft-bodied creatures that suck plant juices, cripple the stems, and stunt new growth. Spray with derris or diazinon. Leaf miners are particularly fond of chrysanthemums, tunneling between the leaf surfaces, leaving pale, sinuous tracks to disfigure the plants. Diazinon is effective against them. Mites can also be pests, especially in a dry, warm atmosphere. They suck the juices from the undersides of the leaves, often causing the leaves to wither and fall, and stunting growth. Use diazinon, derris, or malathion, though the latter has a smell that many people find obnoxious and it should be applied in the open air.

One of the real problems of a good collection of house plants is what to do with them when you go on holiday. As yet there are no house plant kennels where they can be parked, yet they will need watering while you are away, especially as most vacations are taken in summer when it is hot. The important thing is to find a way of replacing the water the plants lose every day by transpiration (just like perspiration in man). The easiest method is to enclose the plant completely so that the water transpired collects on the inside of the bag and runs back on to the soil. First water the plant thoroughly, then using a large polythene bag, stand the whole plant inside it. Now tie around the base of the plant just above soil level and again, very loosely above the top of the plant, allowing space for aeration. Now place the bagged plant in a shady spot in the coolest part of the house and it should remain moist enough for up to three weeks even in hot weather. If at the end of the period, the plant has some rather pale, soft new growths, these are best cut away. Special watering devices can be bought, ready-made. These usually involve a container of water just above the pots and fibreglass wicks which lead directly to each pot surface. Such a waterer can be improvised, using thick wool for the wicks and anchoring the ends to the pot surface with a hairpin. With a large collection of plants it may be best to invest in a sub-irrigation tray which is filled with sand kept permanently moist from a feeder bottle linked with the mains water supply. Nurseries use these on a large scale. Pots used with this form of watering must not have anything over their drainage holes inside and must be screwed down well into the sand. Indoor gardening, whatever the scale or purpose, is a great hobby, giving pleasure and perhaps most important of all to us these days, something to go on looking forward to from one season to the next as the seeds germinate, new plants come into flower, and some of the curiosities of the plant world carry on their lives on our window sills.

The reader should keep in mind that the line drawings in this book are the artist's impression of the plant depicted and are not necessarily accurate in the finer botanical details.

Glossary

AERIAL ROOTS – roots produced aboveground from stems and branches, often by epiphytic orchids and climbers such as *Philodendron*. They are used by the plant as tendrils and a means of obtaining water and food from the atmosphere and bark crevices.

ANNUAL – a plant which grows to maturity, flowers, seeds, and dies within 12 months.

APEX – the tip of a stem, leaf, etc.

AREOLE – small, cushion-like organs on a cactus which represent extremely reduced shoots. They bear the spines and flowers, and sometimes hairs as well.

AXIL – the angle between the stem of a plant and a leaf stalk growing from it.

BASAL – at the bottom of a stem, bulb, etc.

BIPINNATE – leaves which are divided into a number of leaflets arising on either side of a central midrib, each leaflet then being divided again in the same way.

BULB – an underground storage organ composed of fleshy, modified leaves or leaf bases attached to a short, flattened stem called the base plate. The growing point is in the middle and forms new leaves and flower buds before they appear aboveground.

BULBIL – a tiny bulb which grows on the stems of some plants, particularly lilies, and which will grow into a normal-sized bulb if removed and potted.

BULBLET – a small bulb, usually formed at the base of a larger one, or as in the case of some lilies, on the stem growing from it.

BRACT – reduced and modified leaves which may be colored and act as petals, e.g. poinsettia, or may provide protection to flower buds.

CALYX – see sepal.

CORM – an underground storage organ derived from a swollen stem base, find bearing buds annually upon its upper surface.

CORMLET – a tiny corm borne at the base of a larger one.

COROLLA – see petal.

CORONA – a crown-like outgrowth from the petals, sepals, or base of the flower, e.g. the cups or trumpets of daffodils and narcissi; the stamens of *Hymenocallis* and the crown of filaments in a passion flower.

CRISTOSE – crested. An abnormal form of growth which results in a number of shoots, usually joined, or flower heads arising from the same part of the plant.

CULTIVAR – short for cultivated variety, a man-made or spontaneous mutant or hybrid plant maintained in cultivation.

DECIDUOUS – plants which lose all their leaves annually, usually in late autumn.

EPIPHYTE – EPIPHYTIC – also called air plants, which live on trees or mossy rocks, mainly in tropical or subtropical forests. They are not parasitic (q.v.) using trees only as perches where they can get adequate light.

EVERGREEN – plants which do not lose all their leaves at the same time each year, and are therefore always covered in green leaves.

FROND – another name for a leaf, but particularly the dissected leaves of ferns and palms.

GENUS – GENERA – a term used in classification to describe a group of plants which have a number of characteristics in common. Each genus will contain from one to many species, for example all members of the genus *Philodendron* have a basic similarity, but each separate species within the genus has its own distinctive features. Genera indicates more than one genus.

HERBACEOUS – perennial plants which die back to ground level each year, passing the winter underground, to shoot again the following spring.

HYBRID – HYBRIDIZATION – a plant which is the result of cross-pollination between two different species. Usually it will show characteristics blending those of its parents. Such plants will not reproduce themselves exactly from seed, and in many cases will not in fact produce any good seed (sterile). In some popular plants, breeders have crossed and re-crossed a number of species so that the exact parentage is sometimes in doubt.

INFLORESCENCE – the flowering part of a plant, whether an individual bloom or a large cluster of blooms.

INSECTIVOROUS – a plant which obtains some of its nourishment from the decayed remains of insects which it traps.

KEEL – the lower petals of a flower of the pea family, which are joined to form a boat-shaped "petal".

LAYERING – a method of propagation, by bending a stem so that part of it touches the ground. This part is then slit or notched and pegged down just below the ground surface. It will grow new roots and can eventually be severed from its parent plant.

MOSSING (AIR-LAYERING) – a method of layering (q.v.) with a stem which cannot be brought down to ground level. A slit is made in the bark or hard outer layer of the stem and a tiny piece of wood put in it to prevent it from growing over again. It is best to dust it with hormone powder, then bind the place with sphagnum moss (q.v.) or peat, holding it in place with an outer layer of polythene sheeting. After a few weeks, roots will appear at the wounded place and the rooted top of the stem can be removed.

OFFSET – small plantlets that arise around the base of an old plant. They can often be removed with roots attached, making propagation easier.

OSMUNDA FIBER – a growing medium obtained from osmunda fern and available from garden centers, etc.

OVATE – egg-shaped; leaves, bracts, or petals with an egg-shaped outline, the stalk arising at the broad end.

PARASITE – PARASITIC – a plant (or animal) that lives by robbing another plant (or animal) for all or part of its food supply.

PATINA – a surface sheen.

PEAT – a substance made up largely of semi-decayed, compressed plants remains, especially sphagnum moss. It is used extensively in composts and is available in packs from all garden centers, etc.

PERENNIAL – a plant which lives for several to many years, and once mature, flowers annually. Trees and shrubs are included, but the definition usually refers to soft-stemmed plants only.

PERIANTH – the outer parts of a flower, both calyx or sepals and corolla or petals, which protect the stamens and pistil within.

PETAL – the innermost of the two protective layers or whorls of a flower. They are usually colored to attract pollinating insects, but may be green or non-existent. When fused into a tube, bell- or funnelshaped, they are known as a corolla.

PHYLLOCLADE – a modified stem which has taken on the form and function of a leaf.

PHYLLODE – leaf stalks with the form and function of true leaves.

PINNATE – PINNA(E) – a leaf or frond which is made up of a number of small leaflets arising on either side of a central midrib. The fronds of many ferns and palms are examples.

PISTIL – the female organ of a flower, comprising an ovary and a sticky or hairy receptive surface called the stigma. The latter is often joined to the ovary by a stalk or style. The stigma traps pollen grains from the stamens (pollination), which then grow down into the ovary and fuse with ovules. This is the act of fertilization which results in the formation of seeds.

PLANTLETS – small plants.

PROPRIETARY ORCHID COMPOST – a special mixture of compost which is particularly blended for its suitability for use with orchids. Many different brands are available from any garden center, etc.

PSEUDOBULB – storage organs peculiar to epiphytic orchids. They are swollen stems or stem-sections, sometimes bulb-like but also shaped like clubs, or appearing just as somewhat thickened stems. They bear leaves and flowers.

RHIZOME – a stem which grows underground or at ground level, and sends up shoots at intervals, e.g. *Iris*.

RUNNER – a slender shoot which grows along the surface of the ground and produces roots at intervals, e.g. strawberry.

SEED STRAIN – a particularly desirable form of an annual plant that comes true to seed, providing each generation of parent plants is carefully selected.

SEPALS – the outermost protective layer or whole of a flower, sometimes colored, but usually green. When fused into a tube, funnel- or bell-shaped, they are called the calyx.

SHOOTS – young stems.

SPATHE – SPADIX – the spathe is a large bract (q.v.), often colored, which protects the flowering parts of a plant, usually one with the flowers grouped together on a club-shaped organ called the spadix. Species of *Arum* and *Anthurium* are examples.

SPECIES – the basic unit of plant classification. Each species is a collection of individuals, very closely resembling each other, which breed together and reproduce all their main characteristics from generation to generation. Minor variations (varieties) and hybrids may occur, but these seldom breed true to type.

SPHAGNUM MOSS – a very water-holding growing medium comprising largely the plants of bog moss *(Sphagnum)* and available in packs from garden centers, etc.

SPORE – the reproductive body of ferns, fungi, and other primitive plants. They are dust-like particles consisting of a single cell or small groups. In ferns, they give rise to a small, flat, leafy body called a prothallus, bearing the male and female organs. These, on fusion, give rise to a young plant.

SPUR – a hollow, tubular organ, part of a sepal or petal which contains a nectar and attracts pollinating insects, e.g. nasturtium *(Tropaeolum)*.

STAMEN – the male organ of a flower, consisting of a stalk or filament and two anther lobes which bear the pollen grains or male cells.

STIGMA – see pistil.

SUCCULENT – a plant, usually from arid regions, which has special water-storage tissue making it soft and fleshy. Cacti have swollen stems, succulents have fleshy leaves.

SUCKER – a new growth which rises from the roots of a plant below soil level, and can often be used as a simple means of propagation.

TENDRIL – a leaf or shoot which has become modified into a slender, thread-like organ which will cling onto any suitable support.

TUBER – a swollen, usually underground, storage organ derived from a root, e.g. dahlia, or from a stem, e.g. potato.

TUBERCLE – a soft, nipple-like protuberance, typical of some cacti, e.g. *Mammillaria*.

TUBULAR – flowers with united petals forming a straight-sided tube, though sometimes flared or lobed at the mouth.

VARIETY – a variant of a species which is found in the wild and comes true from seed, e.g. different colored flowers, extra hairy plants, dwarfer or taller forms.

WHORL – a number of leaves, bracts, sepals, or petals borne in a ring all at the same level.

List of plates

88	Opuntia kleiniae	109	Schlumbergera x buckleyi
89	Pachystachyus (Jacobinia) coccinea	110	Senecio tamoides
90	Paphiopedilum venustum	111	Setcreasea purpurea
91	Pavonia multiflora	112	Smithiantha 'Elke'
92	Pelargonium x domesticum 'Kingston Beauty'	113	Sonerila margaritacea
		114	Sophronites coccinea
93	Pelargonium x hortorum 'Mr. Henry Cox' *Geranium*	115	Sparmannia africana
		116	Strelitzia reginae
94	Pentas lanceolata	117	Streptocarpus kirkii
95	Peperomia argyreia	118	Streptocarpus dunnii
96	Pitcairnea corallina	119	Streptosolen jamesonii
97	Plumbago capensis	120	Tacca aspera
98	Plumeria rubra	121	Thunbergia grandiflora
99	Primula obconica	122	Tigridia pavonia
100	Pycnostachys urticifolia	123	Tillandsia lindeniana
101	Rebutia calliantha krainziana	124	Trichantha elegans
102	Rechsteineria leucotricha	125	Tulip
103	Renanthera coccinea		a. 'Blue Parrot'
104	Ruellia macrantha		b. 'Brilliant Star'
105	Saintpaulia ionantha		c. 'Stresa'
106	Sarmienta repens	126	Vallota speciosa
107	Sauromatum guttatum	126	Vanda caerulea
108	Schizanthus pinnatus	128	Zygopetalum intermedium

13

16

14

1

33

36

35

34

55

54

53

56

57

59

58

60

62

63

61

64

66

65

67

68

85

87

89

90

91

92

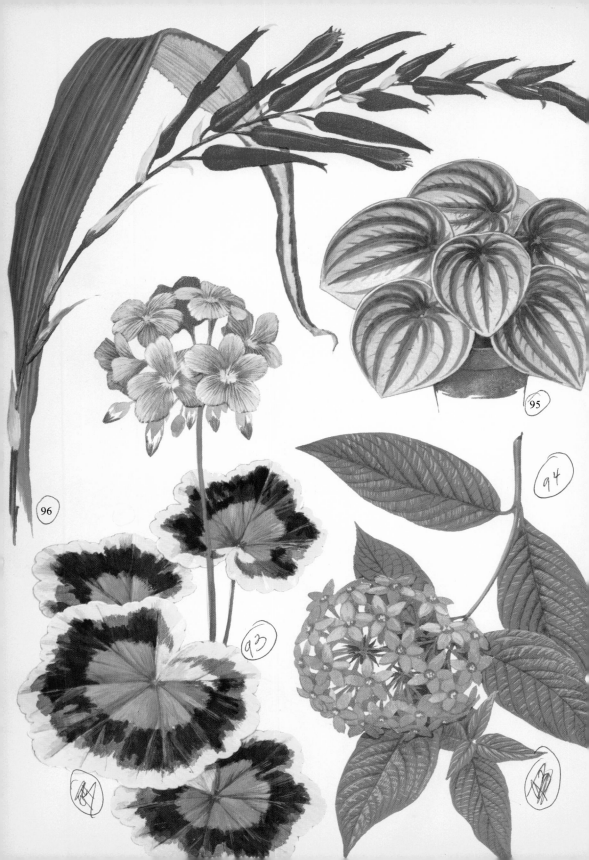

101

102

104

10...

105

108

106

112

110

111

113

116

4

115

121

123

122

124

125

a

b

c

127

126

128

A

Abutilon

Flowering maple. MALVACEAE. A genus of about 100 species of mainly rather large, shrubby plants from the subtropics which make good pot plants where they can be given sufficient room. They are amenable to pruning, and cutting back hard in spring will keep them smaller and more shapely. The leaves are somewhat maple-like and evergreen or semi-deciduous, while the flowers, like lanterns or bells, come in a wide range of shades of red, yellow, and white. They need full sunlight when flowering and the compost must be kept just moist. Propagate between April and August by stem cuttings or by seed sown in spring.

A. x hybridum. A race of robust hybrids raised in cultivation. They can reach 8 ft. if not pruned. The pendant, bell-like flowers are 1½–2 in. long and are borne during summer and autumn. There are many named forms.

A. x h. 'Ashford Red'. Large, dark red flowers.

A. x h. 'Boule de Neige'. Pure white flowers.

A. x h. 'Savitzii'. A much smaller plant with white-variegated leaf margins. In some leaves the green remains only as a small central area. The flowers are orange, veined with red.

A. x h. 'Souvenir de Bonn'. Another variegated cultivar, but a much larger, more robust plant. The salmon flowers are edged with red.

A. megapotamicum. Chinese lantern. An attractive slender Brazilian shrub to 6 ft. which is most effective when trained as a climber, or grown in hanging pots. The flexuous branches bear small, arrow-shaped leaves and the lantern-like flowers are yellow, hanging from a red, balloon-shaped calyx.

A. m. 'Variegatum'. A similar plant with ivory-white variegation.

A. x milleri. Like *A. megapotamicum* in habit, the leaves are marked with yellow blotching, and the flowers are orange-red.

A. striatum. A spreading shrub from Central and South America which can grow to 6 ft. The leaves are deep green and deeply-toothed, and the flowers are like orange bells marked with red veining.

A. s. 'Aureo-maculatum'. A similar plant with yellow blotching on the deeply cut, hairy leaves.

A. s. 'Thomsonii'. Similar to the previous cultivar, but the leaf lobes are less sharply pointed and are hairless. The variegation is yellow-green.

Acacia

Mimosa; Wattle. LEGUMINOSAE. A large genus of almost 800 species of trees and shrubs, mostly from Australia. Some have fern-like leaves which are cut pinnately, others have no true leaves but flattened leaf stalks like simple leaves (phyllodes). The familiar, dense, fuzzy flower heads are composed largely of the long yellow stamens, the other floral parts being relatively insignificant. After flowering they can be pruned to keep them a manageable size. They grow best in full sunlight and need good ventilation. Keep cool over winter in a temperature of 40–50°F (5–10°C). Propagate by seeds in spring or by heel cuttings in early or late summer.

A. armata. Kangaroo thorn. A densely branched, twiggy shrub which can eventually reach 10 ft. In pots it can be kept much smaller and produces globular heads of rich yellow flowers in spring. The phyllodes are small, dark green, and spiny.

A. a. pendula. A variety with laxer growth, the longer, narrower phyllodes and longer stalked flowers giving it a pendulous form.

A. baileyana. Golden mimosa; Fern-leaf mimosa. An attractive tree for tub culture, which, unchecked, can reach 30 ft. Regular pinching out of leading shoots is necessary to keep it suitable for container growth. The drooping branches are clad with fern-like bipinnate, silvery-blue leaves, and the fluffy pompons of bright yellow, fragrant flowers are borne on arching sprays in early spring. It is very popular among florists as a cut flower.

A. cultriformis. A very distinctive shrub, the stems densely clothed with silvery, triangular phyllodes which spread stiffly at right angles to the stems. At the end of the leafy shoot, a spike of stemless clusters of pale yellow flowers emerges in spring.

A. dealbata. Syn. *A. decurrens dealbata.* Silver wattle. A superb species for tub growth which can eventually reach 25 ft. It has graceful, fern-like leaves which are silvery when young, becoming greener as they mature. The fragrant globose flower heads appear in a fluffy avalanche in late winter and early spring.

A. drummondii. A good shrub for pot growth which

can reach 9 ft. It has fern-like, bipinnate leaves and spikes of lemon-yellow pompons which open in spring. It has the advantage of flowering freely when young.

A. farnesiana. Popinac; Opopanax. A fragrant species whose globular, yellow heads opening in early spring are used by perfumiers. It makes a 20 ft. tree, but can be kept much smaller in large pots or tubs. The leaves are bipinnate and ferny in appearance.

A. longifolia. Sydney golden wattle. A 15 to 30 ft. tree, distinctive for the long, narrow phyllodes which are stiff and dark green, and carried almost horizontally on the upright stems. The small, yellow pompons are borne in short spikes, massed together on the long stems in early spring.

A. l. latifolia. Bush acacia. A similar plant with denser spikes of flowers, and wider, more loosely carried phyllodes.

A. l. mucronata. In this variety the phyllodes are shorter and held stiffly, and the flower spikes are looser and a paler yellow.

A. podalyriaefolia. Pearl acacia. A distinctive shrub with silvery-white, ovate phyllodes. The golden-yellow pompons are borne in 2–4 in. clusters, and open in winter. It is worth a place for its foliage alone and can be kept smaller than its final 10–20 ft. in a large pot.

A. retinodes. Syn. *A. longifolia floribunda.* Everblooming acacia. As its popular name suggests, this acacia can be found in bloom at almost any time of the year. It can reach 25 ft., and the 5 in., narrow phyllodes are borne on long stems which arch over the ends and carry loose clusters of pale yellow, fragrant pompons.

A. verticillata. Star acacia. A compact, densely twiggy shrub, the stems covered with narrow, pale green, spine-tipped phyllodes which provide an effective background for the bright yellow flowers which are borne in long spikes and appear in spring.

A. riceana. A 15 ft. shrub or small tree which can be grown as a weeping tree, or trained on to supports as a climber. It has stiff, spine-tipped phyllodes and the yellow pompon heads are borne in spikes during the spring.

Acalypha

EUPHORBIACEAE. A genus containing over 450 trees and shrubs from tropical and subtropical regions of the world. Three of these make attractive pot plants. They require a temperature above 60°F (16°C) and a humid atmosphere and must be kept moist at all times. Give liquid feed at 10–14-day intervals from late spring to early autumn. Propagate in summer by stem cuttings.

A. godseffiana. Lance Copperleaf. A bushy shrub

from New Guinea which is grown for its evergreen foliage. It has bright green, ovate leaves which have a finely toothed, cream-variegated margin. The greenish flowers are inconspicuous. Keep in full light.

A. hispida. Syn. *A. sanderi.* Chenille plant; Redhot cattail. Although a 10–15 ft. shrub, it is often grown as an annual, flowering in its first year from cuttings. The evergreen leaves are broadly oval with slender points, but the attraction of the plant is its long spikes of deep red flowers which hang like 12–18 in. tassels. Warmth and humidity are essential, as well as shade from direct sun. Propagate by stem cuttings in spring or summer.

A. wilkesiana. Copperleaf. A bushy shrub from the Pacific islands grown for its coppery evergreen foliage. Keep in full light. A number of varieties with varying leaf shape and pattern are in cultivation. The flowers are insignificant.

A. w. macafeana. The ovate leaves are finely-toothed and taper to a point. The coppery coloration is overlaid with red marbling.

A. w. obovata. A variety with oval leaves notched at the rounded apex. The center of the leaf is green at first, becoming coppery, while the cream-variegated margins age to a pinkish-orange.

Acanthocereus

CACTACEAE.

A. pentagonus Syn. *A. horridus.* Big needle vine; Thorny cactus. One of a genus of 8 species with long, fleshy stems up to 20 ft. in length, this is the only one commonly in cultivation. The ribbed stems which are 3–4 in. in diameter, have stout gray spines up to 2 in. long on their five angles. The large flowers are 7–8 in. in length, white and funnel-shaped. They open at night and are followed by spiny red fruits. Do not allow the temperature to drop below 61°F (16°C) and water only when the compost feels dry. Propagate by seed.

Acanthostachys

BROMELIACEAE.

A. strobilacea. Pine cone bromeliad. A genus of the pineapple family containing only this one, epiphytic species which makes an unusual pot plant. It originates from South America and has long, narrow, succulent leaves which are covered with a grayish meal and are spiny along the edges and at the tips. The red and yellow flowers are rather insignificant, but are followed by distinctive red fruit clusters rather like small pine cones. The plant will withstand temperatures down to 50°F (10°C), but do not let the compost dry out. Propagate by removal of well-grown suckers in summer, treating them as cuttings.

Achimenes

GESNERIACEAE. A genus of 50 species largely from Central America which contains some very good herbaceous pot plants. They have a curious scaly rootstock, and oval, entire, hairy leaves. Above these the tubular or trumpet-shaped, showy flowers appear in abundance. The tubers should be started into growth in spring and kept in a temperature above 60°F (16°C), with high humidity during the summer when they are flowering. Keep the plants out of direct sunlight. Dry off the tubers in autumn and store over winter in a temperature of 55–60°F (13–16°C). Propagate by separating the tubers when potting.

A. andrieuxii. A very compact Mexican species with rosettes of ovate, dark green, net-veined leaves. From the base of each arise erect 2–3 in. stalks, each bearing a single violet flower with a white throat marked with purple.

A. antirrhina. Scarlet magic flower. A striking plant from Mexico and Guatemala with flared petals of bright scarlet and a yellow tube, marked with red-brown lines. The flowers are borne at the end of the ft.-long upright stalks which are clothed with green, ovate leaves, showing red beneath.

A. candida. Mother's tears. An erect plant from Guatemala, reaching 12–18 in. The white flowers have purple spots inside the throat and are pinkish-buff on the outside of the tube. They are borne in the axils of the long, ovate, somewhat asymmetrical, toothed leaves.

A. ehrenbergii. Syn. *A. lanata.* A distinctive species from Mexico, with pale green, ovate leaves which are covered beneath with soft white hairs. Among the leaves rise the pinkish, purple-streaked flowers which are white inside. The whole plant grows to about 18 in. in height.

A. erecta. Syn. *A. coccinea.* Cupid's bower. A neatly growing plant from Central America, with whorls of bright green, ovate, toothed leaves on lax stems which can reach 18 in. The small, crimson-scarlet flowers are open from late summer to Christmas.

A. e. 'Pulchella'. Has the scarlet flowers flecked with yellow in the throat.

A. e. 'Rosea'. Scarlet with a darker crimson center to each flower.

A. flava. From Mexico. The cheerful orange-yellow flowers of this species are small, but contrast well with the dark green, toothed leaves. The plant is of somewhat loose growth, showing lengths of its buff stems.

A. grandiflora. Kimono plant. A Mexican species reaching 18 in. in height. The ovate, toothed leaves are dark green above and brownish beneath. The flared petals of the large, spurred flowers are red-

purple and the inside of the tube is white.

A. heterophylla. From Mexico. The hairy leaves are ovate, somewhat heart-shaped at the base, and pointed at the tip. They are borne on slender stems. The scarlet flowers are yellow inside. The plant opens in summer and can reach about 1 ft. in height.

A. h. 'Little Beauty'. A shorter, bushier cultivar with rich pink flowers.

A. longiflora. A hairy plant from Central America, reaching 1 ft. The oval leaves are mid-green and toothed, and the large flowers are violet-blue with widely flared petals. *(illus.)*

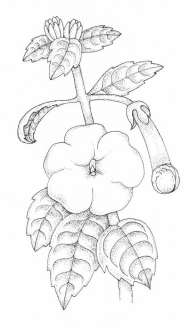

A. l. 'Andersonii'. A cultivar with deeper purple blooms.

A. l. 'Major'. The pale purple flowers of this cultivar can reach 3 in. in length. They are golden-yellow inside the throat and tube, and are strikingly set against the dark green leaves which have a metallic sheen.

A. mexicana. Syn. *A. scheeri.* A dwarf, bushy species with an overall height of only 9 in. The ovate leaves are soft in texture and purplish on the reverse. The large flowers are violet-blue with a paler throat.

A. patens. Kimono plant. A Mexican plant very close to *A. grandiflora* with shining green, ovate leaves and deep violet-purple flowers which are yellow inside the throat and tube, and have a long spur.

Acidanthera

IRIDACEAE. An African genus of 40 species, closely related to *Gladiolus*. The long, linear leaves rise from a corm which should be potted in March for autumn flowering. Keep in a temperature of 60–65°F (16–18°C) while growing, and in full light, then dry off after flowering, keeping the corms at about 61°F (16°C).

A. bicolor. From Ethiopia, it is the only species commonly grown as a pot plant. The flowers are creamy white with a 4–5 in. tube and pointed petals (more correctly perianth segments as these include both petals and sepals) up to $1\frac{1}{2}$ in. in length. At the base they have a red-purple patch.

A. b. murielae. This is a finer form of stronger growth.

Acineta

ORCHIDACEAE.
A. superba. This South American orchid, which is one of a genus of 15 species, makes a good plant for a hanging basket. The pendant spikes of rounded flowers can reach 2 ft. in length and the individual flowers, which never open fully, measure up to 3 in. across. They are a light brownish-yellow with purple markings. The 2–3 leaves are broadly spear-shaped and rise from 3–6 in. pseudobulbs. Grow in a compost of bark chips or equal parts of osmunda fiber and sphagnum moss. It must be kept evenly moist. Maintain a temperature above 60°F (16°C) in a humid atmosphere. Good light is needed, but not direct sunlight. Propagate by division of pseudobulbs.

Acorus

ARACEAE.
A. gramineus. 'Variegatus'. Miniature sweet flag. One of a genus of 2 species of water-loving plants. It has narrow, 8–10 in. iris-like leaves which are held in fan-like tufts and grow from a shortly creeping rhizome. They are variegated with white. The flower is inconspicuous and club-shaped, carried amongst the leaves. Keep the plants moist and out of direct sun. Propagate by division in spring.

Acrostichum

PTERIDACEAE.
A. aureum. Leather fern. One of a genus of 3 species of ferns, found in tropical swamps. Leather fern has thick, tough pinnate fronds which can be from 3–8 ft. in length. They are divided into pointed and slightly wavy leaflets which arise alternately on either side of the stem-like midrib. Constant moisture and warmth are necessary, preferably with a temperature not falling below 65°F (18°C).

20

Propagate by removing the young plants which will be found at the base of the mature fronds.

Ada

ORCHIDACEAE.
A. aurantiaca. One of two epiphytic species from the mountains of Colombia which make up this genus of orchids. This is rewarding to grow, flowering in winter and early spring. The flask-shaped pseudobulbs bear long, tapering leaves and the flowers are borne on arching spikes of up to 15 blooms, each of which is $1–1\frac{1}{2}$ in. across, their brick-red petals narrow and tapered, and often spotted with black. Keep the compost of osmunda fiber and sphagnum moss just moist, and the plants in a cool temperature at all times, a maximum of 65°F (18°C) being suitable. Propagate by division of pseudobulbs. *(illus.)*

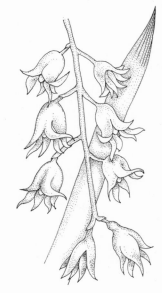

Adenium

APOCYNACEAE.
A. obesum. Impala lily; Desert rose. One of a genus of 15 species of succulent shrubs with a greatly thickened trunk and branches containing a poisonous milky juice. It is native to East Africa. The fleshy leaves are dark green and glossy above, paler beneath. They are borne in tufts at the ends of the branches. The plant is, however, cultivated for its summer borne, showy, deep rose flowers which are 2 in. across and freely produced. Keep in a temperature above 65°F (18°C) during the growing season and do not let the compost dry out.

A cooler, drier spell in winter is beneficial. Propagate from cuttings, allowing the cut end to dry for several days before insertion. *(illus.)*

Adiantum

Maidenhair ferns. ADIANTACEAE. A large genus of worldwide distribution which contains about 200 species. Many of these make decorative pot plants with their elegant, lacy fronds carried on black, arching stalks. They must be kept out of direct sunshine and generally grow best in a warm atmosphere above 61°F (16°C). Keep the compost just moist, never allowing it to become completely dry. Propagate by division.

A. capillus-veneris. Native to warm, temperate, and tropical regions, this dainty species has pale green fronds up to a ft. in length, each divided into many small, wedge-shaped leaflets (pinnae). They are held upright at the base, then arch over to become pendant at the tips.

A. caudatum. Walking fern. The long, narrow, 6–10 in. fronds are pinnately cut into two rows of alternately arranged leaflets (pinnae), each deeply notched on the upper side. If placed on a rooting medium these fronds will root at the tip and will form new plants, providing a ready means of increase.

A. cuneatum. See *A. raddianum.*

A. decorum. The 6–12 in., twice-dissected fronds are triangular in overall outline, each small leaflet (pinna) being fan-shaped, pinkish-red when young, and becoming green as it ages.

A. d. 'Pacific Maid'. A dwarf form with the segments set closer together, giving a stiffer and more compact effect.

A. hispidulum. Australian maidenhair. The erect, hairy fronds are borne on stiff stems giving a distinctive appearance to this fern. The leaflets (pinnae) are leathery, rounded, and stalkless.

A. pedatum. The light green fronds are composed of numerous small leaflets (pinnae) which overlap each other along both sides of the purplish stems. The fronds are forked at the base rather like the rays of a fan. This American and Asiatic fern is hardy in temperate areas, but also makes a very decorative pot plant for a cool room.

A. raddianum. Delta maidenhair. Probably the most widely grown species of maidenhair, it is surprisingly tolerant of poor growing conditions. At its best, the arching, dark green fronds can reach 15 in. in length, each being divided into many wedge-shaped leaflets which are held on slender dark stems. The overall effect is one of lightness and grace.

A. tenerum. The 1–3 ft. fronds arch outwards from the center of the plant, and comprise many deeply-lobed leaflets which have a pink tinge when young. It comes from the Mexico and West Indies area.

A. t. 'Farleyense'. In this form the leaflets are crimped and deeply cut, giving them a crested appearance.

A. trapeziforme. Giant maidenhair. A most distinctive fern with 2 in., bright green, angular, ovate leaflets which taper to a point. It is a tropical species which needs warmth and humidity to produce optimum growth.

A. venustum. A compact, relatively hardy fern similar to *A. capillus-veneris* which grows well in cool conditions. The light green leaflets are pinkish when young and turn a rusty-red in winter.

Adromischus

CRASSULACEAE. About 50 species of intriguing succulents from southern Africa, grown for their curiously colored and patterned fleshy leaves. These are borne on woody stems. The pinkish flowers are small and inconspicuous. They need a cool, dry atmosphere, not exceeding 65°F (18°C) in summer, and if possible between 50°F (10°C) and 65°F (18°C) in winter. Water only when the compost is almost dry. Propagation is best by leaf cuttings.

A. cooperi. Syn. *A. festivus.* Plover eggs. The long egg- or club-shaped leaves are gray-green with dark reddish blotching, more prominent at the top. The spikes of pale pink flowers add little to the attractions of the plant.

A. cristatus. The thickened leaves of this species are green and wedge-shaped, the upper edge crinkled, the lower tapered into a short stalk. The leaf surface is covered with fine hair. The flowers are white with pink-tipped petals.

A. maculatus. Calico hearts. A plant which always

attracts interest by its $1\frac{1}{2}$ in., fleshy, kidney-shaped leaves which are flat above and rounded below, with a light green color, strongly marked with dark red. They have a gray-green, horny margin. The small flowers are pinkish-green.

A. rotundifolius. The roundish leaves which are concave above and convex beneath are borne on upright stems which can reach 8 in., but may become prostrate as the plant ages. Its small flowers are pink.

A. tricolor. Spotted spindle. The 2 in., fleshy leaves, like small, curving cigars, are pale green with brownish-red and silvery markings. They are borne almost erect on stout stems which are densely covered with brown, hair-like roots.

Aechmea

BROMELIACEAE. Among the 150 species in this genus are many, striking in foliage, flower, and fruit, which make excellent decorative plants. Most of those in cultivation are epiphytes, growing in Central and South America above the jungle floor on tree branches. Their stiff, sword-shaped leaves, often spiny at the edges, grow in a rosette which forms a water-holding cup. This cup should be kept full, preferably with rainwater as they dislike lime. The flower spikes are borne on erect or arching stems and stand out because of the colorful bracts which surround the inconspicuous flowers. These are followed by clusters of bright berries which add to the plant's exotic appearance. To grow and flower at their best they need a warm, humid atmosphere, preferably with a temperature between 61°F (16°C) and 80°F (26°C) and some shade from direct sunshine. Most species need a constantly moist, though not over-wet compost. Flowering rosettes die as the flower fades, but new shoots will appear at the base. Propagate in summer by severing these side shoots. Allow the wound to dry for a few days before insertion into 3 in. pots of peat and sand.

A. bracteata. The 2–3 ft. leaves are dark green with prickly margins. The 1 ft. flowering stem grows from the center of the rosette in September and bears a spike of small, yellow flowers, the lower part enclosed by bright red bracts, the upper by green. These are followed by green and red berries.

A. bromeliifolia. Wax torch. The leaves of this species can grow to $3\frac{1}{2}$ ft. in length and are green with a white mealy surface. They curl back strongly at the tips. The 6 in. flower spike has pale yellow flowers which soon become almost black, and the bracts are green or red.

A. caudata. 'Variegata'. The strikingly colored, stiff leaves of this species are deep cream with wide creamy stripes along their length. The spikes of flowers are almost triangular in outline, each floret being orange-yellow, just protruding from the bright red bracts. They are borne on a $1–1\frac{1}{2}$ ft. white, mealy stem.

A. chantinii. Zebra plant. The wide, arching, finely toothed leaves of this species are green, marked with bands and streaks of pinkish-white across the leaf. The dense, branched flower head has colorful yellow-edged, red bracts.

A. fasciata. Silver vase. Probably the most widely grown of all aechmea species with broad, leathery, gray-green leaves, banded with white and arching out from the center. The flowers are blue and the stiff, spiny-edged bracts are light pink; the whole spike is remarkably long lasting.

A. f. 'Variegata'. A distinctive form with lengthwise, silvery-white variegation superimposed upon the normal leaf pattern.

A. filicaulis. When not in flower, this species is not particularly remarkable, with its long, leathery, mid-green leaves which are irregularly mottled with darker green. Its flowering spike, comprising small, white flowers and red bracts, is, however, borne on a long, trailing or hanging flexuous stem, producing an unusual effect.

A. fulgens. Coral berry. Rosettes of gray-green, stiffly-arching leaves which appear dusted with a gray meal and have spiny margins. The flowers are blue and are followed by the attractive, coral-red berries which have given the plant its popular name.

A. f. discolor. Similar to *A. fulgens*, but with a purplish coloration beneath the leaves and violet flowers.

A. lueddemanniana. Rosettes of stiff, blue-green leaves with spiny margins. The small, pink flowers are borne in a branched spike up to 5 in. in length and are followed by blue and white berries.

A. mariae-reginae. A distinctive species with the tight, pink and blue flower spike borne on a long stalk which carries reflexed, boat-shaped, pink, leafy bracts along its length. The leaves form a rosette and are thick and gray-green, up to 18 in. in length.

A. mertensii. China berry. A neat species with a small rosette of green leaves which are spiny at the margins. The small clusters of yellow- or red-petalled flowers form a spike which has conspicuous deep pink, leafy bracts beneath it.

A. miniata discolor. The rosette of soft, dull green leaves which are pinkish underneath, bears a stalk topped with a clustered spike of pale blue flowers and coral-red berries.

A. mooreana. The long, stiff leaves are shining bronze-green, and the branched, flowering spike has vivid green upper bracts and pink lower ones.

A. nidularioides. A species with dramatic leaf

coloration, starting green with white meal, and becoming brilliant red if exposed to sunshine. They are 2 ft. in length and spiny at the margins. The dense, almost rounded flower spike is made up of small white flowers and red bracts.

A. nudicaulis. The stiff, glossy green leaves are borne in a rosette and have small black spines along the margins. The small flowers are yellow with bright red bracts; they make up a loose, short-stalked spike.

A. ramosa. A very leafy species, forming a tough rosette. The yellowish flowers have red bracts and make a loose spike. The berries are yellow.

A. weilbachii. Long, bright green leaves up to 2 ft. 6 in. in length, which are spiny along their margins. The pale purple flowers with their rich red bracts, are borne in a loose cluster on a long stalk.

A. w. leodinensis. A similar plant, but with the leaves flushed bronze above and red beneath.

Aeonium

CRASSULACEAE. A large genus of 40 species of succulent plants from northern Africa and the adjacent Atlantic islands. Most species in cultivation have fleshy, rather flat leaves borne on thick stems almost like small trunks. They produce clusters of star-like flowers which open in spring above the leaves on branched stems.

A. arboreum. Like a small tree, this Moroccan plant has a thick trunk-like stem which can reach 3 ft. in mature, well-grown specimens. At the top of the stem is a rosette of pale green, fleshy leaves, widening at the end, then abruptly contracted to a point. The golden-yellow flowers appear from late winter to spring. Keep in temperate conditions, out of direct sunshine, and water only when the compost becomes dry. Propagate by seeds, leaf cuttings, or by removing a single small rosette and treating as a cutting in late spring.

A. a. 'Atropurpureum'. A decorative form with the leaves purple-flushed.

A. a. 'Cristatum'. A curious rather than attractive form in which the stem is greatly widened, and the tiny, reddish rosettes of leaves are borne along one edge, fancifully resembling a crest.

A. burchardii. A smaller species of similar growth form to *A. arboreum.* The leaves are more triangular in shape at the tips and are gray-green with a bronze overlay. The flowers are pale golden-yellow.

A. canariense. The softly hairy, long leaves broaden at the end, are slightly wavy and can reach 8 or 9 in. in length. They form a wide, flat rosette which is almost stemless. The spring-borne flowers are a light yellow. It comes from Tenerife.

A. decorum. Syn. *A. cooperi.* Copper pinwheel. A

small, heavily branched bushlet, each branch bearing small 2–2½ in. rosettes of shining green leaves, the edges of which are flushed with red-bronze. The pink flowers appear from spring to early summer.

A. x domesticum. A small species with many branches and 2–2½ in. rosettes of fleshy, somewhat hairy leaves. The flowers are yellow.

A. x d. 'Variegatum'. A similar plant with white-margined leaves.

A. haworthii. Pinwheel. The ovate, pointed, toothed leaves are dull green with reddish margins and are borne at the end of branched stems. It can grow to 2 ft. in height. The yellow flowers are pink-tinged, and open in spring.

A. sedifolium. A charming miniature species only 4–6 in. in height. The sturdy branches carry ½ in. rosettes of shiny, brownish-red leaves and yellow flowers.

A. simsii. The strap-shaped, pointed leaves have long, glandular hairs beneath and are stemless. The flowers are pale yellow, borne in clusters on leafy stems well above the rosettes, and open in spring.

A. tabulaeforme. Saucer plant. The closely overlapping leaves form a striking, flat rosette which can reach 20 in. in diameter, like a green plate. The flowers are bright yellow and bloom at the top of a 12–20 in. stem in summer. *(illus.)*

A. undulatum. A single, erect stem of 2 ft. or more bears a flat rosette of dark green, shiny leaves and deep yellow flowers, borne in spring on 1–2 ft. flowering stems.

Aerangis

ORCHIDACEAE. A genus of 70 species of evergreen, epiphytic orchids from tropical Africa. They have sometimes been included in the genus *Angraecum.* The dark green leaves are often cut or notched at the tip into 2 blunt lobes, and the long-spurred flowers are borne in pendant spikes. They are seen to best advantage when the plant is grown in a hanging pan or basket in a compost of equal parts osmunda and sphagnum fiber. Keep the plant at a temperature above 65°F (18°C) and away from direct sunshine. Water freely, and keep in as humid an atmosphere as possible. Propagate by stem cuttings in spring.

A. biloba. The white flowers of this attractive species are 1½ in. across and have golden-brown 2 in. spurs. They are borne in hanging spikes up to 12 in. in length and are fragrant, especially after dark. Flowering season is late autumn to early winter.

A. kotschyana. A dramatic species, the white flowers having twisted pink spurs which can reach 9 in. in length. They are produced in late summer and early autumn.

A. rhodosticta. A white-flowered species, only the tip of the 1–1½ in. spur being green. The flowers are 1 in. across and appear on 8 in. pendant spikes in early summer.

A. thompsonii. A strong-growing orchid, the 1½–2½ in. white, fragrant flowers having 6 in. bronze spurs. The flowering spikes arch over from the top of stout, 2 ft. stems, and blooms can appear at almost any time of the year. This species can withstand cooler temperatures than the others listed here, as it comes from highland areas. A minimum of 60°F (15°C) in winter is suitable.

Aerides

ORCHIDACEAE. These handsome orchids are epiphytic and come from the tropical jungles of southeast Asia. 40 species are known, a number of which respond well to cultivation. They have long, stiff, somewhat fleshy leaves, and the arching, pendant flower spikes bear many fragrant, waxy blooms, remarkable in that their spur curves upward. They grow best in hanging pans or baskets filled with an equal parts osmunda-sphagnum compost. Keep temperatures above 61°F (16°C), shade from direct sunshine, and keep the compost moist at all times. Propagate by removing side shoots with roots attached, or by stem cuttings.

A. crassifolium. King of Aerides. A splendid species from Burma, the large, waxy 1½ in. flowers are royal purple, contrasted with white in the throat. They are borne on pendulous spikes up to 2 ft. in length in summer. The leaves are short and thick.

A. crispum. The 2 in. flowers of this Indian species are white with a pinkish-purple flush, and are borne in branched spikes which are often twice as long as the leaves. They open in summer.

A. falcatum. A somewhat similar species in growth form to A. crassifolium, but the petals are spotted with rose-pink on a white background. They open from May to July. A number of forms are known, all from southeast Asia.

A. fieldingii. Fox-brush orchid. A superb, fragrant orchid with dense, 1 to 2 ft., pendant spikes, so

crowded as to resemble fancifully a fox's brush. Each flower is white and waxy, 1½ in. across and flushed with rose-pink. The strong fleshy leaves are borne on stout stems over 2 ft. in height. It is a native of the mountain forests of the Indian Himalayas and can withstand cooler winter temperatures than the other species—a minimum of 50°F (10°C). Flowering takes place in early summer.

A. japonica. A Japanese species which, like A. fieldingii, comes from cooler regions and will tolerate the same range of temperatures. The short, dark green leaves are borne on 4 in. stems, and the white, purple-marked flowers are carried in lax, pendant spikes in summer.

A. odoratum. As its name suggests, this tropical species, found from India to Vietnam, is very fragrant. The creamy-white flowers are pink-tipped and bloom on their long, pendulous stems in late autumn. A number of named varieties varying chiefly in color are known.

Aeschynanthus

Syn. *Trichosporum*. GESNERIACEAE. A genus of about 80 species of climbing and trailing epiphytic plants of which some make excellent decorative plants either for hanging baskets or for pot growth. They have deep green, evergreen leaves borne in opposite pairs on the long stems, and showy, fragrant, tubular flowers. They grow best in a peat compost, preferably mixed with sphagnum moss. During the summer, keep in a warm, humid atmosphere and water freely, but temperatures can be allowed to fall to 55°F (13°C) in the winter, and at this time of the year they should be kept somewhat drier. Propagate by stem cuttings.

A. boschianus. A Javan species which will attain 1 ft. in height. The leaves are bluntly oval and smooth-edged, and the long, scarlet flowers protrude from a dull purple calyx about half their length. They open in summer.

A. lobbianus. Lipstick vine. Another summer-flowering Javan species with fleshy, elliptic leaves borne on trailing, wiry stems. Each purplish-red calyx holds a brilliant scarlet flower more than twice its length, with a creamy-yellow throat.

A. marmoratus. Syn. *A. zebrinus.* Zebra basket vine. Found wild in Burma and Thailand, this species is grown largely as a foliage plant. It has dark green, slender-pointed, oval leaves which are waxy in texture and contrastingly marked with yellow-green veining. The undersurface is a purplish-red. The flowers are less attractive, being green with brown markings.

A. pulcher. Royal red bugler. This Javan species is an excellent house plant and ideal for growing in a hanging basket. The long, pendant branches bear small, firm-textured, ovate, light green leaves, and clusters of 2½ in., vivid scarlet flowers protruding from a short, pale green calyx.

A. speciosus. Coming from the tropical jungles of southeast Asia, this robust species has 3–4 in., orange-vermilion flowers, shaded yellow at the base and inside the throat, which also has red-brown markings. It has dark, glossy green leaves which are borne on 2 ft., wiry, arching stems.

A. x splendidus. Orange lipstick vine. A hybrid between *A. parasiticus* and *A. speciosus*, the ft.-long stems are clothed with narrow, pointed, oval, dark green leaves, and bear 3 in. deep-red flowers with orange markings. They are borne in large, erect clusters. A striking plant.

Agapanthus

LILIACEAE. A South African genus, now considered to contain 5 somewhat variable species. They form tufts of long, arching, strap-shaped leaves, and the clustered flower heads are borne on sturdy, upright stems. They are best grown in large pots or tubs, and are excellent outside on doorsteps or patios in the summer. Keep well watered during the growing season, but allow to become almost dry and keep in a cool place during the winter. In the spring, start into growth again by increasing the amount of water given. Propagate by division or seeds in spring.

A. africanus. Blue African lily. A striking evergreen species which can reach 3 ft. in height. The globular heads of up to 30 open, funnel-shaped, violet-blue flowers are borne on 1–2½ ft. stalks in summer. The dark green leaves reach 18 in. in length, but arch outwards almost to the ground leaving the flowering spikes standing strongly within.

A. campanulatus. The leaves of this species reach 18 in. in length, but are carried more stiffly, and are deciduous. The wider, bell-shaped flowers are light blue, and open in the summer.

A. inapertus. A tall, deciduous species, the flowering stem often reaching 4 ft. in height. The flower heads are somewhat lax, the individual blue, bell-shaped florets being pendant. A white-flowered form is known.

A. praecox. A similar species to *A. africanus*, but with lighter colored florets which are borne on shorter stalks, giving the flower head a more globular appearance. Many hybrids between this species and the similar *A. orientalis* have been raised.

Agave

Century plants. AGAVACEAE. A large genus from America which contains over 300 species. They are succulent plants, forming rosettes of stiff, often spiny leaves, sometimes of very large size. From the center of the rosette grow the erect, long-stemmed inflorescences, though rarely on pot-grown specimens. These are produced in anything from 8 to 60 yrs., and the rosettes die after flowering to be replaced by offsets or suckering shoots. These form an excellent method of propagation. Grow in full sunlight, in well-ventilated but warm conditions, preferably keeping the temperature over 45°F (8°C) in winter. Most can be kept outdoors in summer. Allow the compost to become almost dry between watering.

A. americana. Century plant; Maguey. In the wild, the gray-green leaves of this Mexican species can exceed 6 ft. in length, but when confined to pots or tubs, 3–4 ft. is more normal. When restricted in this way they rarely flower, but will do so under natural conditions after 10 or more yrs. The cluster of yellow flowers is borne at the top of a stalk 15–30 ft. in height.

A. a. 'Marginata'. One of the most valuable agaves for growth as a house plant, it is very decorative even when small. The gray-green leaves have broad golden-yellow margins.

A. angustifolia. Caribbean agave. A similar plant to *A. americana*, but smaller and neater in growth, thus increasing its value for use indoors. It originates from the West Indies.

A. a. 'Marginata'. In this form, the gray-green leaves have white margins.

A. attenuata. Dragon-tree agave. In this Mexican species, the rosette of 2½ ft., fleshy, gray-green leaves is borne on a thick trunk which can exceed 4 ft. in mature plants.

A. decipiens. Another species from Mexico which, when mature, has a trunk up to 7 or 8 ft., bearing a rosette of thick, stiffly-arching leaves armed with triangular spines on the margins. In spite of its size however, it makes an attractive foliage plant when young, and can be grown for some years as a pot plant before becoming too large.

A. ferdinandi-regis. King agave. A very decorative small species from Mexico with loose rosettes of 6–9 in., dark green, stiff leaves which are white-margined and end with 2–3 spines. They are markedly concave and have a sharp keel on the back.

A. filifera. Thread agave. A Mexican species with a rosette of stiff, narrow leaves which curve inwards. They are bright green with white lines and margins, fibers splitting away from them giving an effect of loose white threads over the plant. The flower spikes can exceed 8 ft.

A. parviflora. Little princess agave. A miniature species from Mexico and Arizona which is very suitable for pot culture. The neat rosettes of dark green leaves are 6–8 in. high, and the leaf margins carry loose white fibers. If given sufficient root room, slender flower spikes up to 5 ft. in height may be produced. Propagation is best by seed as few offsets are produced.

A. striata. From Mexico, this agave has 12–18 in. leathery leaves which are usually less than 1 in. in width. They are blue-gray and striped with dark green, and have fine marginal teeth and a terminal spine. When mature an 8–12 ft. flowering spike bearing green flowers is produced.

A. s. 'Nana'. Lilliput agave. A form which remains small for many years, the leaves at first only 2–3 in. long. They are a yellowish-green and somewhat flatter than the type.

A. stricta. Hedgehog agave. A distinctive Mexican species with stiff leaves up to 15 in. in length and only ½ in. in width. They are borne in a dense rosette looking remarkably like an extraordinarily long-spined hedgehog. The leaf margins are toothed. When mature, a flowering spike up to 7 ft. in height is produced.

A. victoriae-reginae. Queen agave. An extremely attractive species from Mexico with rosettes of dark green leaves, each with a white, horny rib, both at the edges and the center, above and below the leaf. The blunt leaf tip has a sharp, blue-green spine. The flowering spikes can reach 15 ft. but are seldom seen in cultivation. Offsets are rarely produced so propagation is by seed. *(illus.)*

Aglaonema

Chinese evergreens. ARACEAE. A genus containing 21 species, most of which have decorative, patterned leaves. The tiny flowers are clustered into a club-shaped spathe, typical of the arum family, and can be followed by red berries. They are very amenable house plants because they tolerate poor lighting and are, therefore, quite suitable for a position away from the window. Water only when the compost appears almost dry, and maintain a temperature above 61°F (16°C).

Propagate by division, or by taking basal shoots or stem tops as cuttings.

A. commutatum. A long-lived species from the jungles of Malaya and the islands of southeast Asia, with dark green, pointed, oval leaves marked with paler green and silvery-white. The white flowering spathes open in summer. *(illus.)*

A. c. elegans. This form has very finely pointed leaves which are marked with white feathering.

A. c. maculatum. The blunter, oval leaves are more strongly marked with silvery-white.

A. c. 'Treubii'. Ribbon aglaonema. A cultivar with very distinctive, narrow, pointed leaves, dark bluish-green with silvery variegation.

A. costatum. Spotted evergreen. A slow-growing plant from Malaya with glossy, dark green, oval leaves, blunt at the base, and spotted with white, the central vein also being white.

A. crispum. Syn. *A. roebelinii.* Painted droptongue. An erect species from Malaya and Burma with ovate, leathery, dark green leaves which are variegated with a fine overlay of silver, except for a dark central area and the leaf margins. Very tolerant of poor light.

A. modestum. Syn. *A. sinensis.* Chinese evergreen. The first of the genus to be commonly grown under the name Chinese evergreen, and the only species from China. It has firm, waxy, blue-green leaves which are irregularly marked with silver. They are ovate and carried on erect, 6 in. stems.

A. nitidum. Syn. *A. oblongifolium.* A Malayan species with unmarked, green leaves which are long, and taper at both ends. Several cultivars are known.

A. n. 'Curtisii'. A similar plant, but the leaves have silver variegation along the veins.

A. pictum. A slender species from Malaya with bluish-green, ovate leaves variegated with irregular patternings of silver-gray. The yellow-green flowering spathe appears in summer.

A. rotundum. Red aglaonema. A distinctly colored species from Thailand with thick, ovate, dark, coppery-green leaves arising from a short, thick stem. The veins are paler in color, and the underside of the leaf is dark red.

Allamanda

APOCYNACEAE. 15 species make up this tropical American genus, correctly spelt *Allemanda*. They are robust climbing or bushy shrubs with dark green, pointed leaves borne in whorls of 3 or 4, and large, brightly colored, trumpet-shaped flowers. They need a warm temperature, preferably not falling below 61°F (16°C) and flower best in full sun. Water as soon as the compost shows signs of becoming dry, but less frequently in winter. Propagate by cuttings in spring.

A. carthartica. Golden trumpet. The golden-yellow, waxy flowers can measure 4 in. across and have a white marking in the throat. They open from summer to autumn. A good climber when trained to a support.

A. c. 'Hendersonii'. A fine form with rich golden-yellow blooms.

A. neriifolia. A smaller-growing, shrubby species with paler yellow 2 in. flowers which open in summer and autumn. It can be grown in a large pot or tub as a shrub, or as a climber when trained to a support.

A. violacea. An erect shrub from Brazil with whorls of oblong, pointed leaves, and small clusters of large, pinkish-purple flowers opening in autumn.

Alloplectus

GESNERIACEAE. A genus of about 50 tropical South American shrubs, some of which are semi-climbing. They are grown chiefly for their large, velvety leaves, but also have colorful tubular flowers. To produce the finest leaf coloration they require a humid atmosphere, a rich compost which is kept constantly moist, and also some shade. Propagate by cuttings in spring.

A. capitatus. An erect species from Colombia and Venezuela with red stems and olive-green leaves. The late summer and autumn blooming flowers are bright yellow, and each is held within a scarlet calyx.

A. schlimii. From Colombia, the broadly ovate, toothed leaves are dark green and shiny above and purplish beneath. The clusters of small flowers are golden-yellow.

A. vittatus. A very decorative plant from Peru, grown for its ovate, bronze-green leaves, which have a quilted texture and beautiful silver patterning above and red-purple shading beneath. The yellow flowers are borne in clusters, each within a golden-yellow calyx and with small, scarlet bracts.

Alocasia

ARACEAE. About 60 species belong to this Asiatic member of the arum family. They are grown for their handsome shaped and patterned leaves. Their native home is tropical jungle, and they require a warm, humid atmosphere in the summer with abundant moisture and shade. Keep cooler and drier in the winter with a minimum of 61°F (16°C). Propagate by division or offsets in spring.

A. cuprea. The fleshy, ovate leaves of this species from Borneo are heart-shaped at the base and bronze-green above, with a metallic sheen. Beneath they are deep violet-purple. The veins are sunken and conspicuous.

A. indica. A robust Malayan plant with olive-green, arrow-shaped leaves up to 14 in. in length, carried on 15–25 in. stalks. The veins are clearly marked and sunken, leaving the main areas of the leaves with a somewhat ridged appearance.

A. i. 'Metallica'. In this form, the leaves are purplish-red with a metallic sheen.

A. lindenii. A decorative species from New Guinea with shining green, heart-shaped leaves having creamy-white veins.

A. micholitziana. From the Philippines, this species has arrow-shaped, dark green leaves with wavy margins and paler veins, the central midrib being white.

A. sanderiana. Kris plant. A species from the Philippines with leaves as remarkable for their shape as for their patterning. They are narrow and arrow-shaped, with a metallic silvery surface, the leaf edge being deeply lobed around the end of each of the white-ribbed veins. The underside is purple.

Aloe

LILIACEAE. There are 275 members of this genus, ranging from plants only a few inches across to trees. All those described are South African in origin unless otherwise stated. Most are succulents and rosette-forming, with long, undivided leaves, usually stiff and often spine-toothed. The flowers are brightly colored and tubular, and are borne in long-stalked spikes. Give plenty of light and sunshine, and maintain a temperature above 50°F (10°C). Allow compost to become almost dry between waterings. Propagate most species by offsets or stem tips taken as cuttings.

A. africana. Spiny aloe. A slow-growing plant, compact when young with spiny-edged, blue-green leaves on a short, thick stem and with yellow, green-tipped flowers.

A. arborescens. Candelabra aloe; Octopus plant. Although a tree in the wild, this species will remain small in a pot. The fleshy, blue-green, tapering leaves are edged with horny spines and curve downwards at the tips. The orange-scarlet flowers are produced in the winter.

A. aristata. Lace aloe. This attractive species forms a dense ball of 4 in., slender, dark green leaves, each covered with white bristles and ending in a flexuous white point. The orange-red flowers are borne in summer on a 12 in. stem. A rewarding house plant.

A. brevifolia. The fleshy, gray-green leaves are almost triangular and have short, white, horny spines along the margins. They are borne in dense, flattened rosettes about 8 in. across, and the red flowers are carried on an 18–20 in. stem.

A. b. depressa. Crocodile jaws. In this form, the leaves are broader and more markedly concave, giving the center of the plant the appearance from which it derives its vernacular name.

A. ciliaris. Climbing aloe. Although reaching 30 ft. .in the wild, this species makes a decorative pot plant, the flexuous stem bearing spirals of 3-6 in., dark green leaves, bordered with fine teeth. The flowers are scarlet. When growing too large, the tip can be removed as a cutting.

A. eru. A species from Ethiopia having narrow, fleshy leaves which are shiny green and can reach 2½ ft. in length. They have marginal spines and are carried in dense rosettes. The small flowers are yellow.

A. e. maculata. A variety with creamy-white spots on both sides of the leaves.

A. ferox. Ferocious aloe. When grown in open ground, this species can reach 10–15 ft., but it makes a distinctive pot plant when young. The bronze-green, concave leaves have strong, spiny margins, while scarlet, candelabra-like, flowering spikes appear on mature specimens.

A. humilis. A small species, only 8 in. across the rosettes of thick, gray-green leaves. These have white, wart-like spots on the undersides. The flowers are orange-red.

A. h. echinata. Hedgehog aloe. The narrower leaves have pale spines on their upper surface.

A. h. 'Globosa'. Spider aloe. Distinct for its bluish leaves, the tips of which darken to purple in the sun.

A. marlcthii. A strong-growing species, similar to A. ferox, but larger and with a more dense covering of brownish spines.

A. nobilis. Goldtooth aloe. A small species with a rosette which eventually reaches 10 in. across. The fleshy leaves have lighter, horny, tooth-like spines, hence the popular name. The flowers are orange-yellow.

A. saponaria. Soap aloe. The rosettes of 6–8 in., blue-green, sometimes red-flushed, broad leaves are borne on short stems and are marked with

bands of yellowish variegation. The edges are spine-toothed, and the orange-yellow flowers occur in spring.

A. x spinosissima. Torch plant. A hybrid between the tall A. arborescens and the small A. humilis echinata, it has blue-green leaves up to 1 ft. in length, with small but tough spines on the margins and bright red flowers.

A. striata. Coral aloe. A spineless species having attractive, broad, blue-green leaves, with darker markings and reddish margins. The coral flowers are carried in spring and summer on arching spikes.

A. variegata. Partridge-breasted or Tiger aloe. A favourite house plant rarely exceeding 12 in. in height, with 3 tiers of stiff, triangular leaves which are dark green and banded with white spots. The red flowers are borne on 12 in. spikes in winter and spring. *(illus.)*

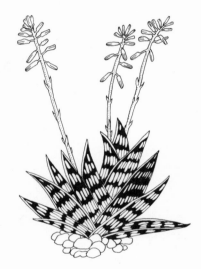

Alpinia

Syn *Renealmia*. ZINGIBERACEAE. 75 species make up this tropical genus of ornamental foliage plants which can carry spikes of showy flowers when given ideal conditions. They are not easy for indoor cultivation as they must have both warmth – a minimum temperature over 65°F (18°C) is best – and high humidity to thrive. Keep the compost moist and the plants in a shady position. Propagation by division.

A. sanderae. Variegated ginger. A small species from New Guinea reaching about 18 in. in height. The pale green leaves are long and narrow, and are patterned lengthwise with white variegation.

A. speciosa. Shell ginger. A large, clump-forming plant from China and Japan with long, leathery leaves. If grown in tubs and allowed to grow large, it will produce its striking, pink-flushed, white flowers in long, pendant spikes.

A. s. 'Variegata'. A somewhat smaller form with the leaves banded and feathered with deep cream.

Alsophila

CYATHEACEAE.

A. cooperi. Syn. *Cyathea* or *Alsophila australis*. One of almost 300 species belonging to this genus. All are tree ferns, and this species, the Australian tree fern, makes a most decorative plant when young with its finely dissected, arching fronds. When mature it can reach 30 ft. It requires a temperature over 61°F (16°C), shade, and most important, abundant moisture at its roots which must not be allowed to become dry. Propagation is from spores.

Alternanthera

AMARANTACEAE. Of the 200 species of this tropical genus, a number are grown for their colorful foliage which can be used as a background for more distinctive plants. The flowers are insignificant. Give full sun, water freely, and keep at a temperature above 55°F (13°C) in the winter. Propagate by division or stem cuttings in spring. All three described are from Brazil.

A. amoena. Parrot leaf. A small plant with reddish-brown, 1 in. leaves shaded with lighter red and orange. Many named cultivars are grown.

A. bettzickiana. Red calico plant. The yellow to orange-red leaves are spoon-shaped and twisted, giving a multicolored effect.

A. versicolor. Copper leaf. The rounder, waved leaves of this species can be a brilliant coppery-red in full sunshine. If kept shaded, the green in the leaf shows through giving a bronzy effect.

Amaranthus

AMARANTACEAE. A widespread genus containing 60 species of annuals some of which are very decorative. The large leaves are undivided and the flowers, though individually very small, are clustered into large spikes. Sow seeds in April and keep in a warm place, over 65°F (18°C) if possible. Once large enough to pot, keep in full sunlight, and water freely.

A. hypochondriacus. Prince's feather. The stout stems of this tropical American plant reach 2–5 ft., bearing ovate, pointed, red-tinged, purple leaves. The plume-like flower spikes are deep crimson.

A. tricolor. Syn. *A. gangeticus.* Joseph's coat. A smaller East Indian plant reaching 1–3 ft., with very variable foliage color in greens, reds, and yellows. Several named cultivars are grown. The flowers are inconspicuous.

Amaryllis

AMARYLLIDACEAE.

A. belladonna. A striking, lily-like species from southern Africa, the only one of its genus, with a cluster of fragrant, rose-red flowers borne at the top of an 18–30 in. stem. They open from August to October and are followed by the strap-shaped leaves which last over winter. A temperature in the low 60's F (15°–18°C) suits them best, and they need watering only sparingly. Keep in full sun. Keep cooler through the winter. Disturb the bulbs as little as possible. Propagate by bulblets.

Amomum

ZINGIBERACEAE.

A. cardamon. Cardamon ginger. Of a genus containing 150 species, this one from Java can easily be kept to 2 ft. in pots, although attaining 10 ft. in the wild. The long, narrow leaves are dark green and give off a spicy scent when bruised. The flowers are borne in a yellow, cone-like cluster. Keep at a minimum temperature of 61°F (16°C), shaded and well-watered. Propagate by division.

Anacampseros

PORTULACACEAE. A genus of small, succulent plants, of which 70 species are known. Keep in full sun, with a temperature always above 50°F (10°C), and allow the compost to become almost dry between waterings, particularly in winter. Propagate by stem or leaf cuttings.

A. buderiana. Silver worms. A curious southern African plant making a network of prostrate, silvery stems, the tiny leaves covered by fine, silver-white scales. The greenish-white flowers are not conspicuous.

A. rufescens. Love plant. The 3 in., upright stems of this southern African species bear fleshy, ovate, pointed leaves which are green above and purplish beneath. White, cobweb-like hairs grow from the axils of the upper leaves. The 1½-in., deep pink flowers are short-lived.

Ananas

BROMELIACEAE. A genus of only 5 species, amongst them the familiar pineapple which makes an impressive house plant. It has rosettes of stiff, spiny-margined leaves, with a central flowering spike topped by a tuft of leaves. Keep in a temperature above 65°F (18°C), in full light. Allow compost to become moderately dry between waterings. Propagate by suckers or the top of a mature fruit with its leaf tuft.

A. bracteatus. Wild pineapple. From Brazil and Paraguay, the broad, deep green leaves are spine-edged. The lavender flowers are followed by red-brown fruit.

A. b. 'Striatus'. The form commonly cultivated, with coppery-green leaves, edged with creamy-yellow margins.

A. comosus. Syn. *A. sativus.* Pineapple. The pineapple of commerce with rosettes of graceful, arching leaves. If kept in large pots, it will produce clusters of violet flowers followed by its edible fruits.

A. c. 'Variegata'. More frequently grown than the type, this form has cream-margined leaves with a red center to the rosette.

A. c. 'Nanus'. An exact miniature of the normal form, excellent for pots.

Aneimia

SCHIZEACEAE.

A. phyllitidis. Flowering fern. A tropical American fern, one of 90 species, getting its name from the fertile fronds which have leaflets in the lower part, then a bare, stalk-like midrib bearing a cluster of flower-like, spore-bearing bodies at the top. The non-fruiting fronds are up to 1 ft. in length. Keep in a minimum temperature of 61°F (16°C), and allow the compost to become almost dry before watering. Propagate by division if possible, or by spores.

Angelonia

SCROPHULARIACEAE. A genus of 30 shrubby plants from Central and South America. They are erect, usually reaching 1–2 ft., and have pairs of long, ovate leaves, and spikes of attractive, purplish-blue flowers. Keep in a warm atmosphere with a minimum temperature of 60°F (15°C) and water freely. Propagate by cuttings.

A. angustifolia. A compact species from Mexico only 15 in. in height, having deep violet flowers opening in summer. *(illus.)*

A. gardneri. Coming from Brazil, this 3 ft. plant has narrowly pointed, bright green leaves. The

spikes of purple flowers, with red dots in the white mouths, are carried abundantly from late spring to summer.

Angraecum

ORCHIDACEAE. A large genus of tropical orchids comprising 220 species. They are epiphytic and grow well in pans or baskets. Their strong stems carry 2 rows of thick, dark green leaves, and the starry-white flowers are remarkable for their prominent spurs. Grow in equal parts osmunda and sphagnum or a bark compost, and keep well watered. Temperatures can fall as low as 55°F (13°C), but warmer, humid conditions are preferred. Propagate by stem cuttings or offsets in summer.

A. distichum. Syn. *Mystacidium distichum.* A central African species with 8 in. stems clothed with 2 rows of flat, overlapping and bright green leaves. The small, white flowers which are carried upside-down, open from July to October.

A. eburneum. A strong-growing orchid from Malagasy with thick, strap-shaped leaves and pale green, inverted flowers with a marked spur and a white, rounded lip. They are fragrant and open in winter.

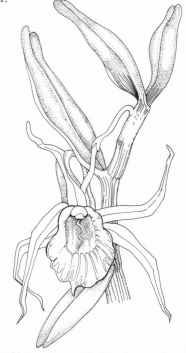

A. infundibulare. A good basket plant, native to Uganda, this species has large, white flowers up to 6 in. across, and a 5 in., funnel-shaped lip which merges into the long spur. *(illus.)*

A. sesquipedale. Star of Bethlehem orchid. A superb orchid. The 2 ft. upright stems bear strap-shaped, blue-green leaves. In late winter and spring, on these stems emerge ivory-white, starry flowers, 5–7 in. across and fragrant. Each flower has a remarkable, foot-long, green-tinted spur, like the tail of a comet.

Anigozanthus

Kangaroo Paw. AMARYLLIDACEAE. A genus of 10 species all from Western Australia. They have long, narrow, upright leaves and tall, branched stems with brightly colored, furry, tubular flowers which sit inside a cup-like calyx. They require full light and water when the compost begins to dry out. In winter keep at a minimum of 45°F (8°C). Propagate by seeds or division.

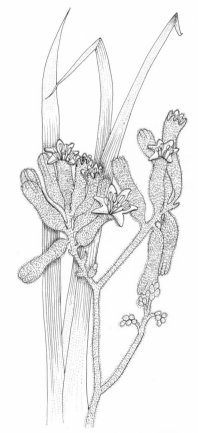

A. flavidus. An iris-like plant which can reach 5 ft. if given root room. It has yellow-green, red-flushed, long, tubular flowers opening at the mouth to give 6 petals. They bloom during summer. *(illus.)*
A. manglesii. Of similar growth to *A. flavidus* but somewhat smaller, rarely exceeding 3 ft. In summer, the velvety-red stems bear clusters of green, furry flowers within a red calyx.

Anguloa

ORCHIDACEAE.
A. virginalis. Cradle orchid. A small, ground orchid from Colombia and Ecuador, one of a genus containing 10 species. It has narrow 12–18 in. leaves and firm-textured, pink-flushed, white flowers, rather reminiscent of an old-fashioned cradle. They open in spring and summer. The plant needs humidity, a minimum temperature of 61°F (16°C), moisture, and shade to thrive. Propagate by division.

Anoectochilus

Jewel orchids. ORCHIDACEAE. An Asian genus comprising 25 species. They are rare among orchids in that they are grown for their foliage, the flowers being relatively inconspicuous. Grow in a mixture of equal parts osmunda and sphagnum, and provide high humidity and plenty of water in summer.
A. roxburghii. Golden jewel orchid. The ovate leaves are bronze-green with a golden center and a red net of veining. The red and white flowers can bloom throughout spring and summer.
A. sikkimensis. King of the forest. In this species the broad leaves are bronze-red and the network of veins is a red-gold. The small, greenish-white flowers occur in autumn

Ansellia

ORCHIDACEAE
A. gigantea. Leopard orchid. One of a genus containing only 2 species, both from tropical Africa. They are epiphytes with tall pseudobulbs bearing long, tapering, light green leaves. The starry-shaped, yellow flowers have brown markings and are borne in long clusters. Grow in an equal parts osmunda, sphagnum mixture or a proprietary orchid compost, keep well-watered when flowering and in full sun. When resting, keep drier and in a minimum temperature of 61°F (16°C).
A. g. nilotica. This form has larger, more brightly colored flowers which can measure $2\frac{1}{2}$ in. across.

Anthurium

Tail flower. ARACEAE. A very large genus belonging to the arum family and comprising 550 species all from tropical America. Many are grown for their ornamental foliage, others for their waxy, flowering spathes. Most species need a temperature above 61°F (16°C), high humidity, and shade. They can be grown in a room for short spells only, though daily spraying with tepid water is a help.

Propagate by division, stem cuttings, or freshly gathered seed.

A. andreanum. Tail flower. An epiphyte from the tropical forests of Colombia, it is an erect plant, 1½–2 ft. in height, with dark green, heart-shaped leaves, and waxy, scarlet-red spathes up to 5 in. long. These protect the creamy-white, tail-like spadix which is yellow-tipped and composed of tiny, petalless flowers. High humidity is essential.

A. a. album. A form with a pure white spathe, contrasted by the spadix which is flushed pink-purple.

A. a. rubrum. This form has deep crimson spathes.

A. clarinervium. A Mexican plant which needs less humidity than the other species. It is grown for its dark green, heart-shaped leaves which are tough but velvety in texture, and marked with ivory-white veins. The small spathe is reddish-green and borne on a long stalk.

A. crystallinum. A very attractive foliage plant from the forests of Colombia and Peru. The heart-shaped, dark green, velvety-surfaced leaves are strongly marked with creamy-white veining. They can be 15 in. long. The narrow spathe is green.

A. digitatum. From Venezuela, this species has its dark green, leathery leaves divided into 5–7 separate leaflets arising from the central stalk. The small spathe is greenish-purple with a purple spadix.

A. imperiale. This species has long, wavy, leathery leaves held upright from a central rosette, fancifully resembling a bird's nest. The spathe is deep brown inside and green on the reverse, and the spadix is also brown. They are borne on short stalks and are almost hidden amongst the leaves.

A. lindenianum. The arrow-shaped leaves of this Colombian plant have rounded side-lobes and a pointed tip. The small, greenish-white spathes are slightly fragrant and borne on long stalks.

A. magnificum. Also from Colombia, this species is similar to *A. crystallinum* but has rounder, duller, green leaves.

A. pentaphyllum. A climbing species from the northern forests of South America, having leaves deeply cut into finger-like lobes, with lighter green veins. Spathe and spadix are green.

A. podophyllum. A Mexican species in which the stiff leaves are deeply dissected into many segments and are borne on long stalks.

A. scandens. Pearl anthurium. A small climber from the highlands of northern South America and the West Indies. Its leaves are oval and a glossy green, and borne on long, slender stems. It has a green spathe and spadix and the tiny flowers are followed by pearl-like fruit with a violet tinge.

A. scherzerianum. Flamingo flower; Flame plant. The most familiar member of the genus, it comes from Costa Rica and is remarkable for its brilliant scarlet spathe from which the golden-yellow spadix spirals upwards. The leaves are spear-shaped and dark green. Many named forms are known with the spathes in shades of red from flesh color to crimson-purple. The best species to try as a house plant.

A. warocqueanum. Queen anthurium. This Colombian species is grown for its foliage – the long, ovate, velvety leaves tapering to a point. They are dark green with ivory-white veining. The small spathe is yellow-green.

Antigonon

POLYGONACEAE.

A. leptopus. Coral vine. One of 8 members of this genus, this Mexican climber has small, arrow-shaped leaves, and pendant clusters of dainty, rose-pink flowers. It needs full sun, a minimum temperature of 55°F (13°C), and plenty of moisture. Propagate by stem cuttings or seeds.

Aphelandra

Zebra plants. ACANTHACEAE. A large genus of 200 tropical American species. They have large, ovate leaves which are glossy and often variegated, and many have brightly colored flowers and bracts. In cultivation they must never be allowed to dry out, and need to be shaded from hot sunshine. A short, cool period in winter is beneficial. Propagate by stem cuttings.

A. aurantiaca. Fiery spike. A shrub-like species from Mexico which can reach 3 ft. The 4–6 in. leaves are dark green with a paler patterning, and the margins are wavy. Above them from October to December rise the large, brilliant, orange-scarlet flower spikes.

A. a. roezlii. Scarlet spike. A smaller variety with twisted leaves which have silvery markings between the veins.

A. fascinator. A dainty Colombian species, the narrow, oval leaves having a shiny surface with a silvery vein pattern on an emerald-green background. The flower spike is scarlet.

A. squarrosa. Saffron spike; Zebra plant. A popular and striking Brazilian species, the dark green, 6–10 in. leaves having clear, white veins. The flower heads comprise golden-yellow bracts which are red-margined at the base forming a long-lasting pyramid from summer to late autumn.

A. s. 'Brockfeld'. A form with more stiffly-held leaves and the veins picked out in cream.

A. s. 'Dania'. A compact form, creamy-white veining and orange-yellow bracts.

A. s. 'Leopoldii'. A robust plant having shiny green leaves with very fine, silvery veining. The small, yellow flowers protrude from the loose spike of red bracts.

A. s. 'Louisae'. Perhaps the best form with wide, white veining on the narrower, rich green leaves. The golden-yellow pyramids of flower are up to 6 in. long.

Aporocactus

CACTACEAE.

A. flagelliformis. Rattail cactus. One of a small genus, comprising only 6 species, all from Central America. The rattail cactus is epiphytic and grows well in pans of proprietary orchid compost. The long, slender stems are bright green at first, graying with age, and are covered with clusters of tiny spines. In late spring it bears showy, 3–4 in., rose-pink flowers followed by red berries. Allow compost to become almost dry between watering, and keep in a temperature above 55°F (13°C). Propagate by cuttings in summer. *(illus.)*

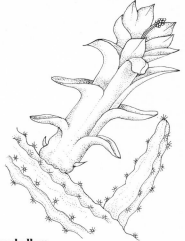

x Aporophyllum

'Star Fire'. CACTACEAE. A hybrid between *Aporocactus* and *Epiphyllum* which makes an excellent hanging plant for a pan or basket. The pendant stems are ribbed and bear large, red flowers, pinker inside and nearer scarlet outside. They flower spasmodically through the year. Give some shade in summer. Propagate by cuttings in summer.

Aptenia

AIZOACEAE.

A. cordifolia variegata. Syn. *Mesembryanthemum cordifolium.* An attractive succulent plant for a hanging pot, having small, heart-shaped leaves which have cream variegation and a scattering of small, wide-open, purplish-pink flowers. Keep moist

in full light, at a minimum temperature of 50°F (10°C). Propagate by cuttings.

Araucaria

ARAUCARIACEAE.

A. heterophylla. Syn. *A. excelsa.* Norfolk Island pine. One of a genus of 18 species of southern hemisphere trees, the Norfolk Island pine makes an extremely decorative pot plant when young. In the wild it can reach 200 ft., but confined to a pot it grows slowly. It is an elegant, almost ferny plant with soft green, curved, awl-shaped leaves set on horizontally borne whorls. A very tolerant plant preferring some shade in summer and a moist compost. Propagate by seed or stem-tip cuttings.

Ardisia

MYRSINACEAE.

A. crispa. Coral berry. One of a very large genus comprising some 400 species of shrubs and trees. Coral berry is an evergreen shrub eventually reaching 4 ft. It has shining, dark green leaves and clusters of fragrant white, red-flushed, or spotted flowers. These are followed by brilliant scarlet berries which will last throughout the winter. Keep moist and in a minimum temperature of 50°F (10°C). Prefers some shade in summer. Propagate by tip cuttings or by seed.

Arenga

PALMAE.

A. engleri. Dwarf sugar palm. An attractive, dwarf palm from Taiwan which can be grown in large pots, it is one of only 5 members of the genus and never exceeds 10 ft. The fronds are divided to the midrib into many narrow leaflets, each jagged at the end. Keep a minimum temperature of 61°F (16°C), provide some shade in summer, and water freely. Propagation by seeds.

Argyroderma

AIZOACEAE. A genus of some 50 species of succulent plants from southern Africa. The thick, almost pebble-like leaves are borne in pairs, and the daisy-like flowers are stemless. Give full light and a minimum temperature of 60°F (15°C). In summer, water freely, but keep almost dry in winter. Propagate by seed.

A. aureum. Silver jaws. The pairs of pebble-like leaves are smooth and almost white. From them rise golden-yellow flowers, 1 in. across.

A. octophyllum. In cultivation often incorrectly called *A. testiculare.* The smooth, blue-white leaves have a flat inner-surface, like an oblong stone which has been cut in half. The flowers are usually yellow, though purple and white forms are known.

Ariocarpus

CACTACEAE. A small genus comprising 5 species from Mexico and adjacent areas. They are round, spineless plants with flat tops and horny tubercles. The large flowers open wide by day. Keep in full sun with a minimum temperature of 50°F (10°C). Water sparingly, allowing the compost to become almost dry. Propagate by seed.

A. fissuratus. Living rock cactus. This small species is remarkable for its beautiful, purplish-pink flowers which are 1½ in. across.

A. trigonus. This plant is 2½ in. in height and covered in triangular tubercles. The yellow flowers are 2 in. across. *(illus.)*

Aristolochia

Dutchman's pipe. ARISTOLOCHIACEAE. A very large, widely distributed genus containing about 350 species, many with attractive foliage and curious flowers. Most are forest species and prefer shade in summer. Keep moist and in a minimum temperature of 61°F (16°C). Propagate by cuttings.

A. elegans. Calico flower. A graceful, climbing species from Brazil. The 2–3 in., kidney-shaped leaves are glossy green above. The freely-borne flowers have a yellowish tube which opens into a 5 in., purplish-brown, shallow cup marked with irregular, white patterning.

A. grandiflora. Pelican flower; Swan flower. A climbing species from Guatemala, having heart-shaped leaves and large, purplish flowers, the long tube bent over, giving the effect of the body and neck of a swan.

A. leuconeura. Ornamental birthwort. The glossy, yellowish leaves of this climber from Colombia are heart-shaped with rounded lobes and variegated with creamy-white veining. The purple-brown flowers are borne on the stems of older specimens.

A. sempervirens. Dutchman's pipe. A hardier species from the eastern Mediterranean which can withstand winter temperatures to 45°F (7°C). It is largely prostrate with small, dark, glossy, heart-shaped leaves, and 1½ in. olive-brown, flushed-purple, euphonium-shaped flowers.

Arthropodium

LILIACEAE.
A. cirrhatum. Renga or rock lily. One of a genus of 9 Australasian species, the New Zealand renga lily makes a striking pot plant. The strap-shaped leaves are tufted and arched, and the starry, white flowers are borne in widely-branched spikes in summer on 1–2 ft. stems. Give full light, frequent watering in summer and a minimum temperature of 45°F (7°C). Propagate by seeds or division.

Arundina

ORCHIDACEAE.
A. graminifolia. This southeast Asian orchid is the only one of its genus. It has tall, reed-like stems, and narrow, grassy leaves. These bear in succession throughout the year loose clusters of 2–3 in., showy, pinkish-purple flowers. Grow in an osmunda-sphagnum mixture or a proprietary orchid compost in shade, and water frequently in summer. In winter, keep drier and in a minimum temperature of 55°F (13°C). Propagate by division.

Arundo

GRAMINEAE.
A. donax. 'Versicolor'. Of the 12 species of this genus, this cultivar of a south European plant is the best for pot or tub growth. It is smaller than the type, its reedy stems reaching 6 ft., and the grassy leaves which are up to 1½ in. across are grayish-green, ribboned with white. The plume-like, flowering spikes open a reddish color and fade to whitish. Water freely and keep in a minimum temperature of 45°F (7°C). Propagate by division.

Asclepias

ASCLEPIADACEAE.
A. curassavica. Blood flower. One of the genus of 120 species of mostly herbaceous plants. Blood flower bears rounded clusters of orange-red flowers through summer and autumn on stems up to 3 ft. in height. The glossy leaves are long, oval, and pointed. Grow in full light, and water only when the compost feels dry. Keep a minimum temperature of 50°F (10°C). Propagate by seed or cuttings.

Ascocentron

ORCHIDACEAE.
A. miniatum. Syn. *Saccolabium.* A small, epiphytic orchid from southeast Asia, one of 5 species

34

belonging to this genus. Its attraction lies in the 4–5 in. spikes of flame-colored flowers which open during spring and again in autumn. The leaves are long and narrow and the whole plant is only 6–9 in. in height. Grow in shade in a proprietary orchid compost. Water freely and keep a minimum temperature of 61°F (16°C). Propagate by side shoots or rooted stem sections.

Asparagus

LILIACEAE. A large genus containing over 300 species of perennial plants. They have no true leaves, but modified leaf-like branchlets called phylloclades. The flowers are insignificant, but are often followed by conspicuous red berries. Grow in light shade and water only when the compost feels dry. Keep a minimum temperature of 50°F (10°C). Propagate by seed or division.

A. densiflorus. A southern African species which is encountered only in its cultivar forms, both of which make excellent pot plants.

A. d. 'Meyersii'. Syn. *A. meyersii*. Plume asparagus. A compact form with 1–1½ ft. plumish stems and fine, needle-like phylloclades.

A. d. 'Sprengeri'. Syn. *A. sprengeri*. A familiar plant with 1–3 ft., arching, feathery fronds on wiry stems. The needle-like phylloclades are bright green, and red berries are sometimes formed.

A. medeoloides. Syn. *A. asparagoides; Smilax asparagoides*. A large species from southern Africa which can reach 10 ft. It has oval, glossy, bright green phylloclades which are carried on zig-zag stems. The florists' smilax.

A. m. 'Myrtifolius'. Baby smilax. A very dainty form, smaller in all parts.

A. setaceus. Syn. *A. plumosus*. Asparagus fern. The "fern" commonly used in bouquets is a southern African species with frond-like, young stems covered with bristle-like phylloclades. When older, they will begin to twine and climb. Red berries are occasionally produced.

Aspasia

ORCHIDACEAE.
A. variegata. An epiphytic orchid from tropical America, one of 10 members of the genus. They have oval pseudobulbs from which grow one or two 6 in., broad, strap-shaped leaves. The long-lasting, fragrant flowers have narrow, green petals with red-brown markings, and a three-lobed, violet-spotted, white lip. Grow in a proprietary orchid compost in a minimum temperature of 50°F (10°C) when resting. Water freely and shade from sun. Propagate by division.

Aspidistra

Cast iron plant; Parlor palm. LILIACEAE. Frequently grown house plants because of their ability to withstand draughts, poor light, and general neglect. There are 8 species in the genus, all from Asia. They have ovate to oblong, pointed leaves, narrowed into a short stalk rising from the base of the plant. Keep moist and partly shaded with a minimum temperature of 45°F (7°C) for best growth. Propagate by division.

A. elatior. Syn. *A. lurida*. The glossy, dark green leaves of this Chinese species reach 18 in. in length. Small, fleshy, dark purple, bell-shaped flowers are borne at ground level on mature specimens.

A. e. 'Variegata'. An attractive form, the leaves having lengthwise stripes of green and cream in varying widths.

Asplenium

ASPLENIACEAE. A large, worldwide genus of about 650 species. They have a tufted form of growth, and generally firm textured fronds which vary in shape from long and undivided, to deeply cut and feathery. Keep shaded from sun, give plenty of moisture and maintain a minimum temperature of 50°F (10°C). Propagate by division, spores, or plantlets.

A. bulbiferum. Hen and chicken fern. An Australian and Malayan species with arching 2–3 ft., feathery fronds borne on black, wiry stalks. Small bulbils appear on the mature fronds, which grow into small plantlets and provide an easy means of increase.

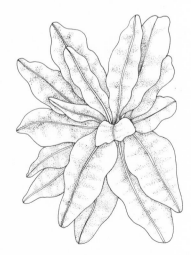

A. nidus. Bird's nest fern. An epiphytic fern from southeast Asia and tropical Australia, which forms a large rosette of shiny, stiff, undivided fronds curving upwards from the centre to a length of 2–3 ft. on adult plants. *(illus. prev. page)*

A. viviparum. Mother fern. A tufted fern from the islands of the Indian Ocean similar to *A. bulbiferum* but with smaller, more finely dissected fronds.

Astrophytum

CACTACEAE. A Mexican genus comprising 6 species of small, compact cacti with a firm, globular shape, broken up by prominent ribs. They have few or no spines. The yellow, daisy-like flowers are relatively large, opening in late spring and summer. Grow in full sun with a minimum temperature of 61°F (16°C), and allow the compost to become almost dry before watering. Use a compost containing some sand or limestone grit. Propagate by seed.

A. asterias. Sea-urchin, or Sand-dollar cactus. A spineless species which makes a dark green dome, 3 in. across, with a scattering of white scales and tufted, white, woolly areoles. The pale yellow, 1 in. flowers are flame-red in the center.

A. capricorne. Goat's horn cactus. A strongly-ribbed, green globe, up to 8 in. across, with silvery scales and a few scattered areoles bearing long, curved, horn-like spines. The yellow flowers are red-brown in the center.

A. myriostigma. Bishop's cap; Star cactus. The surface of this 5–6 in., globular cactus is almost completely covered with white scales and the usual 5 ribs are very prominent and spineless. It can become taller and broader with age. The 1½ in. flowers are pale yellow. *(illus.)*

A. ornatum. Star cactus; Monk's hood. Globular when young, with silvery scales and prominent, spiny ridges, this cactus will become cylindrical

with age, reaching 1 ft. in height. The flowers are lemon-yellow.

Athyrium

ATHYRIACEAE. A genus comprising some 180 species of fern. Many are hardy and minimum temperatures of 40°–45°F (5°–7°C) are acceptable. Give some shade and water freely. Propagate by division.

A. filix-foemina. Lady fern. A species of worldwide distribution having graceful 1½–3 ft. fronds cut into small, pale green leaflets, giving a feathery effect. Many named forms are grown.

A. goeringianum. 'Pictum'. Japanese painted, or Miniature silver fern. A tufted species from Japan, the 12–18 in., arching fronds are made up of deeply dissected leaflets, each being green with a silvery-gray, central band, and borne on a deep red stalk.

Aucuba

CORNACEAE. 3 or 4 species of *Aucuba* are known, all shrubs from Asia which carry male and female flowers on separate plants. The large leaves are undivided and the female plants, if hand-pollinated from a male, produce attractive berries. A tough species withstanding minimum temperatures of 40°F (5°C), requires some shade and moderate watering. Propagate by seeds or cuttings in late summer.

A. japonica. Spotted laurel. A large shrub in its native Japan, this very useful plant can be kept at 12–15 in. in pots. It has leathery, shiny, dark green leaves, and small, olive-green flowers. The glossy berries are scarlet.

A. j. 'Crotonifolia'. A male plant with larger leaves.

A. j. 'Gold Dust'. A female form with the leaves heavily spotted and blotched with gold. Also has red berries.

A. j. 'Picturata'. In this attractive form the leaves are pale yellow-gold except for an irregular, dark green margin. Shade is essential for good color.

B

Babiana

IRIDACEAE. An African genus containing 60 species. The leaves are long and narrow, borne in fan-shaped form, and the upward-facing flowers have 6 spreading petals which open flat to reveal their bright coloration. Give full sun and a minimum temperature of 45°F (7°C). Water freely from winter to spring, but keep completely dry while dormant in summer. Propagate by offsets.

B. stricta. Baboon flower. The leaves of this South

African species are 6–10 in. long, and the fragrant flowers, 1–1½ in. across are borne in a dense spike in late winter. Their color is very variable and two forms are commonly found in cultivation.

B. s. rubrocyanea. The petals of this form are deep blue-purple with a bright crimson center.

B. s. sulphurea. A form with creamy petals, marked with blue at the base.

B. hybrids. A number of fine hybrids have been raised. They have somewhat pleated leaves, and flowers up to 2 in. across.

B. 'Purple Sensation'. The petals are bright purple, and the 3 outer ones are marked with yellow.

B. 'Tubergen's Blue'. A large, flowered form with petals in shades of lavender-blue, darkest at the center.

B. 'Zwanenburg Glory'. The flowers are lavender-purple, and the 3 inner petals are marked with white.

Barleria

ACANTHACEAE.

B. lupulina. Hop barleria. One of a genus comprising 230 species of tropical and subtropical shrubs. It comes from Mauritius, has evergreen leaves with spines in the axils, and makes a compact, 2 ft. plant. The pinkish-yellow flowers are borne in a spike of overlapping bracts very like those of the hop. Keep in full sun and a minimum temperature of 50°F (10°C). Water freely. Propagate by cuttings or seed.

Bauhinia

LEGUMINOSAE.

B. variegata. Orchid tree; Mountain ebony. A widely distributed tropical genus of some 300 species of which the orchid tree is a good specimen plant for a large pot or tub. It has curious, rounded leaves which are deeply notched at the tip, and spring-borne flowers which are very like a carmine-red, cattleya orchid. To flower well, it must have full sun. Water freely and keep a minimum temperature of 61°F (16°C). Propagate by seed or summer cuttings.

Beaumontia

APOCYNACEAE.

B. grandiflora. Herald's trumpet. An attractive woody climber, one of a genus of 15 species from East Asia. The oval leaves can reach 8 in. in length, and in winter the showy, 5 in. flowers, which are like white trumpets with a darker marking in the throat, are borne in terminal clusters. Shade from the hottest sun, keep well-watered and in a minimum temperature of 61°F (16°C). Propagate by cuttings.

Begonia

BEGONIACEAE. A worldwide genus containing over 900 species. Many of these are grown, but so also is a wide range of hybrids and cultivars, new names appearing annually. Almost all have ear-shaped leaves, wider on one side than the other, and 4-petalled flowers. In growth form they vary from low, dwarf plants to climbers, and in color from white through yellows to red. Most prefer some shade, plentiful watering especially when in flower, and a minimum temperature of over 50°F (10°C). Propagate by seeds, leaf or stem cuttings.

B. bartonea. Winter jewel. A small, Puerto Rican species with oval, green leaves which have a darker sheen in the center, and sprays of small, pink flowers in winter.

B. boweri. Miniature eyelash begonia. Originating from Mexico, this charming species rarely exceeds 6 in. in height and the oval, waxy, green leaves are folded and chocolate-spotted along the margins. The flowers, of a very pale pink, open from late winter through spring.

B. x cheimantha. Lorraine begonias. This name covers a large group of hybrids which take their name from 'Gloire de Lorraine', the first cross made between *B. socotrana* and *B. dregei*. They have clusters of small flowers which bloom abundantly from mid-winter into spring. Many cultivars are grown.

B. x c. 'Lady Mac'. Christmas begonia. A bushy form with a profusion of small, pink blooms.

B. x c. 'Marina'. A late autumn-flowering cultivar with deep pink flowers.

B. x c. 'Red Marina'. ('Dark Marina'). A similar plant with deeper red blooms.

B. x c. 'White Marina'. ('Snow Princess'). A large-flowered form with shining white petals just tinged with pink.

B. coccinea. Angelwing begonia. A tall, Brazilian species with woody, cane-like stems which will exceed 10 ft., but can be kept at less than half this height by cutting out old stems each year. The coral-red flowers are borne on pendant stems and are open from spring to autumn.

B. corallina. ('Corallina de Lucerna'). Spotted angelwing begonia. A tall, bamboo-stemmed plant, now considered a hybrid between *B. teuscheri* and *B. coccinea*, the dull green leaves are marked with silvery-white spots and are reddish beneath. The pendant clusters of pink flowers are borne from spring to autumn.

B. cubensis. Holly-leaved begonia. A small, Cuban plant with 2½–3 in., deep green, shiny leaves with sharp teeth rather like those of holly. The white flowers are borne in winter.

B. daedalea. A striking foliage plant from Mexico,

the leaves starting a pale green, becoming darker with age, and marked with red veining which matures to a deep purple-brown. Pale pink flowers borne in summer.

B. dichroa. An attractive foliage plant originating from Mexico. It has wavy-margined, oval, pointed leaves which are silvery-spotted when young, becoming a clear, shining green as they mature. The small flowers are orange.

B. dregei. Miniature mapleleaf begonia. A South African species with somewhat fleshy, red stems which can reach 1 ft. in height and bear maple-like leaves – bronze above, red flushed beneath. The summer-borne flowers are white.

B. x erythrophylla. Syn. *B. feastii*. Beefsteak begonia. A hybrid between *B. manicata* and *B. hydrocotylifolia*, it has large, leathery, rounded leaves, deep, shiny green above and red below. The clusters of pink flowers are carried on long stems above the leaves. A tough house plant.

B. x e. 'Bunchii'. Curly kidney begonia. A curious form with ruffled and crested margins on the leaves.

B. x e. 'Helix'. Whirlpool begonia. Another unusual form, the leaves spiralled from the center.

B. evansiana. Hardy begonia. This species from China and Japan is hardy in mild areas and makes a good plant for a cool room. It has glossy leaves, purplish-flushed above and veined beneath. The flowers are pale pink, and are borne in the summer. This species forms small, red bulbils which can be used for propagation.

B. feastii. See *B. x erythrophylla*.

B. foliosa. Fernleaf begonia. A slender Colombian species with small, rounded, bronze-green leaves borne on drooping stems, giving a somewhat ferny effect. The small flowers are white, tinged with pale pink.

B. fuchsioides. Fuchsia begonia. A shrubby species from Mexico with slender stems which reach 3–4 ft., they are arching and carry a dense mass of shiny, oval leaves, 1½ in. in length. The fuchsia-like flowers are pink or red and nodding. They are borne in winter and spring.

B. haageana. Syn. *B. scharfii*. Elephant's ear begonia. A shrubby Brazilian species with large, dark green leaves which are red beneath. They are borne on 2–4 ft. upright stems and the plant is notably covered in white hairs. The pinkish-white flowers, opening from summer to autumn, have conspicuous soft, red hairs *(illus.)*

B. x hiemalis. Syn. *B. x elatior*. A group of hybrid begonias raised from *B. socotrana* and other species. They are bushy in growth, reaching 1½–2 ft., and have rounded, glossy leaves with a waxy texture and flowers in a wide range of colors which open in autumn and winter. They do not last well in

temperatures over 65°F (18°C).

B. x h. 'Apricot Beauty'. Semi-double flowers of orange-pink, flushed with red.

B. x h. 'Avondzon'. A bright pink cultivar with double flowers.

B. x h. 'Man's Favorite'. An attractive plant with single, white flowers.

B. x h. 'The President'. A rich colored cultivar, the brilliant red, double flowers reaching 2 in. across.

B. incana. A Mexican species with rounded leaves, covered with dense, short, white hairs, and rising from erect stalks. The pendant flowers are white and open in winter.

B. leptotricha. Woolly bear. From Paraguay, this low-growing species has firm, oval, slightly wavy leaves covered with a felting of hairs which are brown on the underside. Small clusters of white flowers appear through the year.

B. luxurians. Palm-leaf begonia. An unusual species from Brazil with its leaves deeply cut into about 17, finger-like leaflets. These leaves are carried on upright, bamboo-like stems which can reach 6 ft. or more. The small, ivory-white flowers open in spring and summer.

B. manicata. This species from Mexico has ovate, fleshy leaves, 6–8 in. long, with a ring of red, bristle-like scales at the top of the leaf stalk. The profuse clusters of pink flowers grow well above the leaves, appearing in winter.

B. m. 'Aureo-maculata'. Leopard begonia. A form having the leaves spotted irregularly with creamy-yellow.

B. masoniana. Iron-cross begonia. A superb foliage plant from southeast Asia, with large, rounded leaves having a quilted surface, marked with a dark brown, central pattern very like the iron cross, hence its popular name. As the leaves mature, they develop a silvery patina and a fine, red hairiness. The small, greenish-white, waxy flowers are borne in winter and spring.

B. metallica. Metal-leaf begonia. A somewhat bushy plant from Brazil, up to 3 ft. tall. It has broadly ovate, green leaves which have silvery hairs and a metallic sheen. The slightly sunken veins show red beneath. The autumn borne flowers are pale pink.

B. olbia. Bronze mapleleaf. A bushy, Brazilian plant having 4 in., lobed leaves which are a dark, bronze-green and covered with fine hairs. The small clusters of white flowers are winter-borne.

B. rex. Hybrids. Painted-leaf or Fan begonias. The original Indian species is now rarely seen, being largely replaced by cultivars with even more showy foliage, making 1½ ft. plants with leaves patterned in greens, reds, pinks, purples, silver, or white.

B. r. 'Helen Teupel'. A hybrid between *B. rex* and *B. diadema*, this fine cultivar has deeply toothed, pointed, oval leaves which are pink with deep red in the center and at the margins, the veins being silvery.

B. r. 'Merry Christmas'. The pointed, ovate leaves are marked with clear-cut colors, deep red at the center, then bands of rich red, silver, pink, and green with a narrow, dark red margin.

B. r. 'President'. The oval leaves of this sturdy cultivar are basically dark green, but are a silver-white over much of the surface.

B. r. 'Silver Dollar'. A small cultivar, its markings rather like a superior form of 'President', with the dark green edges and veins more evenly marked. The reverse is purple-red.

B. richardsiana. A distinctive, almost succulent, South African species, the pale green leaves like deeply-lobed maple foliage. It makes a neat plant and bears small, white flowers in summer.

B. scharfii. See *B. haageana.*

B. schmidtiana. A small, Brazilian species, rarely exceeding 12 in. The heart-shaped, toothed, green leaves are hairy, as are the small clusters of large, pink flowers.

B. semperflorens. Wax begonia. A 6–15 in., bushy species from Brazil which is extremely free-flowering. From it have been raised many strains which are used especially for bedding, but they also make fine pot plants. They all have fleshy, lustrous leaves, usually pale green but sometimes bronze-tinted, and pink, red, or white flowers. These open at all seasons of the year.

B. serratipetala. Pink-spot angelwing. A beautiful foliage plant from New Guinea, with arching stems up to 1 ft. in height, and deeply-lobed and toothed leaves which are a shining olive-green with pinky-red markings. The pink flowers which have toothed petals are open from spring to autumn.

B. sutherlandii. An almost hardy, South African, herbaceous species with shiny, light green leaves on red stems and orange flowers in summer and autumn.

B. x tuberhybrida. A large range of hybrid, tuberous rooted begonias which fall into two main groups. The rose- or camellia-flowered cultivars are robust, erect, fleshy plants with stems to 2 ft. and pointed leaves. Examples are:

B. x t. 'Diana Wynyard'. A double, white-flowered cultivar.

B. x t. 'Guardsman'. An orange-scarlet sort with double flowers. The forms with a pendant habit are more slender, and are ideal for hanging baskets.

B. x t. 'Golden Shower'. A deep yellow form.

B. x t. 'Roberta'. Double, bright red flowers.

B. x t. 'Sunset'. An orange, double-flowered cultivar.

B. vitifolia. Grapeleaf begonia. A handsome, Brazilian species having pointed, leathery leaves like those of a grapevine. The clusters of small, white flowers are borne in winter.

Beloporone

ACANTHACEAE.

B. guttata. Syn. *Drejerella.* Shrimp plant. One of a genus of some 60 evergreen shrubs, this popular Mexican species has ovate, soft-haired leaves and arching spikes of small, tubular, white flowers which are almost hidden within the pinkish-brown bracts. Ideally, keep in a temperature over 50°F (10°C), water only when the compost feels dry, and give full sun. Prune to half-size in late winter and propagate by cuttings in spring. Plants are best replaced every 2–3 yrs. *(illus.)*

Bertolonia

Jewel plants. MELASTOMACEAE. A small genus comprising 10 species of herbaceous plants, some of which are cultivated for their decorative foliage. They require a minimum temperature of 65°F (18°C), humidity, plentiful watering, and shade. They are very suitable for growing under a glass or plastic cover. Propagate by seed or leaf cuttings.

B. hirsuta. Jewel plant. An 8 in. species from South America. The soft, round to oval leaves are bright green with a red-brown, central stripe. The spikes of small flowers are white.

B. marmorata. A 6 in., tufted, Brazilian species with oval leaves which are softly hairy, rich green with silvery-white streaks above and purple beneath. The flowers are violet-purple.

B. m. aenea. A form without white marking on the leaves which have a rich, coppery sheen.

B. 'Mosaica'. A very attractive hybrid, the oval leaves being a quilted, velvety green, with bands of white curving along the length of the leaf.

Bessera

ALLIACEAE.

B. elegans. One of three species which make up this genus of bulbous plants. It comes from Mexico and has narrow, linear leaves and a cluster of 1 in., bell-shaped, scarlet or scarlet and white flowers, borne on a 1–2 ft. stem in summer. Keep in a temperature above 45°F (7°C), water freely while in growth, dry off during winter. Propagate by offsets or seed.

Bifrenaria

ORCHIDACEAE.

B. harrisoniae. Belonging to a genus of 10 epiphytic species, this Brazilian orchid has a single 1 ft., narrowly ovate, pleated leaf rising from each oval pseudobulb. The waxy, creamy-white flowers are 3 in. across, and have a purple-red lip with a yellow center; a beautiful long-lasting bloom. Grow in bark chips or equal parts osmunda and sphagnum, and keep just moist at all times. Give shade and maintain a minimum temperature of 61°F (16°C). Propagate by division of pseudobulbs.

Bignonia

BIGNONIACEAE.

B. unguis-cati. Syn. *Doxantha*. Cat's claw vine. One of a genus of about 150 species now mostly included under other genera. The cat's claw vine from Argentina is a climbing species with pairs of leaves composed of two elliptic leaflets and small, hooked tendrils which cling to any rough surface. The summer-borne flowers are like bright yellow foxgloves. Grow at a minimum temperature of

45°F (7°C) and water only when the compost appears dry. Propagate by stem cuttings.

Billbergia

Queen's tears. BROMELIACEAE. A genus of 50 epiphytes with urn-shaped rosettes of long, narrow leaves and clusters of showy flowers and bracts usually borne on arching stems. All those described come from Brazil. They are tough house plants, doing best in temperatures over 50°F (10°C), with some shade. Water when the compost appears dry. Propagate by offsets or division.

B. x 'Albertii'. Friendship plant. A hybrid between *B. distachya* and *B. nutans* having narrow, dark green leaves with grayish-white scales. The pendant, blue-margined, green flowers are carried within pinkish-red bracts.

B. amoena. This species has a rosette of long, narrow, gray-green leaves, crossbanded with silver. The blue-edged, green flowers and pinkish bracts are carried on arching stems.

B. x 'Fantasia' Marbled rainbow plant. A hybrid between *B. saundersii* and *B. pyramidalis* it has bronze-green leaves with pink and white variegation. The blue flowers and pink bracts are borne on erect stems.

B. horrida. The brown-bronze leaves have strongly prickly margins, and the flower spike is blue with red bracts.

B. h. tigrina. Tiger-urn plant. A form with white-banded leaves.

B. lietzei. The gray leaves are spine-edged, and the pendant spikes of blue and yellow flowers bear pink bracts.

B. leptopoda. A plant with apple-green, recurved leaves, having pale marking and grayish scales. The pendant flowers are green with blue margins and the bracts pinkish-red. Keep a minimum temperature of 61°F (16°C).

B. macrocalyx. Fluted urn. The tubular leaves of this species are green with silvery markings and are held erect. The large, blue flowers and pink bracts are borne on an upright spike.

B. nutans. Angel's tears; Queen's tears. A very popular plant from Uruguay and Argentina, the dark green leaves borne in tubular rosettes and having a bronze-silver overlay. The green, violet-edged flowers and pinkish bracts arch over, and a bead of moisture like a tear drop frequently hangs from the stigma.

B. pyramidalis. Summer torch. This species has wide, dark green leaves faintly gray-banded, and blue-tipped, scarlet flowers with rose-red bracts on upright stalks.

B. p. concolor. A form with apple-green leaves.

B. x 'Santa Barbara'. Banded-urn plant. An

attractive variegated hybrid, the gray-green leaves strongly banded with ivory-white. It has greenish-white flowers and pale pink bracts.

B. saundersii. Rainbow plant. The narrow, bronze-green leaves are purplish beneath and borne in tubular rosettes. They are marked with pink and white. The blue flowers and red bracts are carried on erect stems.

B. vittata. Syn. *B. calophylla.* Showy billbergia. The upright, purple-bronze leaves have silver crossbands and are carried in erect, tubular rosettes. The flowers are dark purple and the bracts red.

B. x windii. The green leaves of this showy plant are gray-scaled and arch outwards from the urn-like rosette. The yellow-green flowers with blue-tipped sepals and large, pink bracts are borne on long down-curving stems.

B. zebrina. Zebra urn. The bronze-purple, spiny leaves have silvery-white crossbanding. The flowers are violet and the bracts a bright rose-red. A very attractive species.

Biophytum

Sensitive plants. OXALIDACEAE. A genus of about 60 species of tropical plants with leaves divided into many pairs of leaflets. They are remarkable for being sensitive to the touch, the leaflets folding back when disturbed. Maintain a temperature over 65°F (18°C), keep moist and in partial shade. Best grown annually from seed.

B. sensitivum. A widely distributed species about 6 in. high when mature, and then looking like a mini-palm tree, with 6–15 leaflets to each leaf. Small, yellow flowers open in July.

B. zenkeri. A smaller plant from the Congo, 2–4 in. high, otherwise similar to *B. sensitivum.*

Bischofia

BISCHOFIACEAE.

B. javanica. Syn. *B. trifoliata.* Toog tree. One of a genus containing a single tree species from tropical Asia. At maturity it can reach 75 ft., but when small is very decorative, having large leaves divided into 3 ovate leaflets which are bronze-green. Maintain a temperature above 65°F (18°C) and give good light. Water only when the compost appears dry.

Blechnum

BLECHNACEAE. A large genus containing over 200 species of ferns in a variety of forms from small, creeping plants to those with a tree-like trunk. They are widespread in temperate and tropical regions and some plants from the latter areas make attractive pot plants. Keep in a warm, humid atmosphere in shade, and water frequently. Propagate by division.

B. brasiliense. Ribfern. A decorative species with long, deeply cut fronds, eventually reaching 2–4 ft., the separate leaflets (pinnae) with wavy edges. When young they have a coppery tinge, becoming green at maturity. The compost must at all times be kept moist.

B. capense. A neater, tufted species from the southern hemisphere, having smaller fronds than *B. brasiliense*, the leaflets being more widely spaced and crimped. It is less demanding and hardier than that species.

B. gibbum. A handsome fern from New Caledonia which has a trunk-like stem when mature. The arching fronds are 2–3 ft. in length, and are made up of narrow, pointed leaflets.

B. moorei. Syn. *Lomarea ciliata.* A New Caledonian species which forms a short trunk when mature. The 8–12 in. fronds are leathery and have broad, lobed leaflets. Those which bear spores have very narrow segments. Must be kept moist.

Bletilla

ORCHIDACEAE.

B. striata. Syn. *B. hyacinthina.* One of a genus of 9 ground orchids, it has 1–2 ft. wiry stems which bear 3–5 pleated leaves at the base, and a spike of purple flowers, 1–2 in. across which are held on an erect stalk and open in summer. Keep in a minimum temperature of 45°F (7°C), water freely, and keep shaded from the hottest sun. Propagate by division.

Bomarea

ALSTROEMERIACEAE. A genus of climbing plants from South America of which 150 species are known. The leaves are strap-shaped, and the bell-or lily-like flowers borne in dense clusters at the end of long stems. Maintain a minimum temperature of 50°F (10°C), water only when the compost feels dry, and give full sun. Provide support for the twining stems. Propagate by seed or division.

B. caldasii. From Ecuador and Colombia, this species has orange-yellow flowers – the outer 3 petals (sepals) are green-edged, the inner 3 have red spots.

B. kalbreyeri. This species from Colombia has striking, 2-colored flowers – with brick-red outer petals and yellow and red spotted inner ones.

Boronia

RUTACEAE. A genus of 70 shrubs, all from Australia. Most species have finely cut leaves. The four-petalled flowers are small, but are carried in abundance. Grow in sun in a minimum temperature of 50°F (10°C), and keep well-ventilated. Water when the compost feels dry. Propagate by cuttings or seeds.

B. elatior. A densely twiggy shrub reaching only 2 ft. The stems are silver-gray, and the leaflets narrow. The solitary purple and yellow flowers are richly fragrant.

B. megastigma. A smaller, more slender shrub, but otherwise similar to the *B. elatior*.

B. pinnata. This 2–3 ft. shrub has very pinnately divided leaves with up to 9 narrow segments and clusters of flat, pink flowers, borne in late spring. **(illus.)**

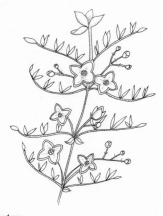

Borzicactus

CACTACEAE.

B. humboldtii. Peruvian candle. One of a genus of 17 South American plants of which this cylindrical, Peruvian species makes a good house plant. Its 2 in. wide stems can reach 3 ft. at maturity, but grow slowly. They have spiny areoles which are yellow-woolly, contrasting with the white-dotted, green stem. The pinkish-red flowers open at night. Maintain a minimum temperature of 50°C (10°C), water only when the compost feels dry, and keep in full sun. Propagate by seed and cuttings.

Bougainvillea

NYCTAGINACEAE. 18 species are known, all originating from South America, but now widely cultivated in warm countries. They make large, scrambling or climbing shrubs, but can be kept a manageable size by pinching out leading growths. The ovate leaves are small, and the flowers are borne within brightly colored bracts. Grow in full sun in a minimum temperature of 61°F (16°C), and water only when the compost feels dry. Propagate by cuttings.

B. x buttiana. A hybrid between *B. peruviana* and *B. glabra* with strongly spiny, climbing stems and branched spikes of bright crimson bracts in spring.

B. x b. 'Kiltie Campbell'. A form with orange bracts becoming red as they age.

B. x b. 'Milleri'. A form with yellow flowers.

B. x b. 'Mrs. Butt'. ('Crimson Lake'). A colorful form with large, magenta bracts.

B. glabra. Paper flower. A Brazilian species having narrow, pointed leaves, and purple-pink bracts which last through summer.

B. g. 'Sanderiana Variegata'. A variegated form, the leaves bordered and marked with creamy-white.

Bouvardia

RUBIACEAE. A genus of some 50 shrubs almost all of which are from Mexico. They have ovate leaves in twos or threes, and clusters of brightly colored, tubular flowers which bloom in winter. Keep in full sun in a temperature above 50°F (10°C), and water when the compost feels dry. Propagate by cuttings in spring.

B. x domestica. This hybrid name covers a number of different crosses largely represented by cultivars.

B. 'Christmas Red'. A fine plant with rich red flowers.

B. 'Fire Chief'. A form with bright scarlet flowers.

B. 'Mary'. This form is a pretty, pale pink, the tube a shade darker.

B. 'President Cleveland'. A crimson-scarlet form.

B. 'Rosea'. A beautiful, rose-pink form, flushed with salmon.

B. longifolia. Syn. *B. humboldtii*. Sweet bouvardia. A slender 3 ft. shrub having delightfully fragrant, pure white flowers which open to a flat star at the mouth and have a 2–3 in. tube. They are shown up by the dark green, glossy leaves.

B. ternifolia. Syn. *B. triphylla*. Scarlet trompetilla. A rather lax shrub with hairy, ovate leaves, and superb clusters of bright scarlet flowers which are carried from summer through to the end of winter.

B. t. 'Alba'. A white-flowered cultivar.

B. versicolor. A wiry shrub, 2–3 ft. in height, with arching stems bearing clusters of 1½ in. orange-yellow, tubular flowers in summer and autumn.

Bowiea

LILIACEAE.

B. volubilis. Climbing onion. One of two species of bulbous plants from South Africa, and grown largely as a curiosity. The bulb reaches 5–8 in. across and is planted with the top half free of the compost. From it, in late autumn, a single, bright, glossy green climbing stem rises bearing small leaves which soon fall, and greenish-white, starry flowers. Dry off from early summer to mid-autumn. Keep a minimum temperature of 50°F (10°C), place in sun, and water when the compost feels dry. Propagate by seed or offsets.

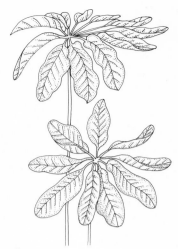

Brassaia

ARALIACEAE.
B. actinophylla. Syn. *Schefflera macrostachya.*
Queensland umbrella tree. One of a genus of 3
species, it comes from the tropical forests of N.
Australia, New Guinea and Java. In the wild, it
can reach 100 ft., but confined to a tub remains
under 10 ft. for many years. The leathery, shiny
green leaves are made up of 3–16 leaflets held like
the ribs of an umbrella. Keep above 61°F (16°C),
preferably in good light, and water only when the
compost feels dry. Propagate by seed. *(illus.)*

Brassavola

ORCHIDACEAE. A genus of 15 epiphytic orchids,
all from Central and South America. The long,
narrow pseudobulbs bear a single, fleshy leaf and
the light colored flowers have narrow sepals and
petals, and a conspicuous lip. Grow in bark chips
or a spaghnum–osmunda mixture, and maintain a
temperature over 50°F (10°C). Keep in shade and
water freely when growing. Propagate by division.
B. cordata. A small species with pale green sepals
and petals, and a white, heart-shaped lip which is
marked with purple. A good plant for a hanging
basket or pieces of bark, flowering in summer and
autumn.
B. cucullata. An arresting species with narrow,
creamy-yellow sepals and petals up to 4 in. long.
The three-lobed lip has a 3 in. long, central lobe
and side lobes fringed and curved back. They are
very fragrant, and are borne singly on short stems,
mostly in winter.
B. digbyana. The 4-6 in. spring- and summer-borne
flowers have greenish-white sepals, petals with a
purple flush, and a creamy-white fringed lip.
B. nodosa. Lady of the night. A striking species
with single or clustered flowers, each with narrow,
pale green to cream sepals and petals, and a large,
white lip, sometimes purple-spotted inside. They
are markedly fragrant at night, and open most
freely in late autumn and early winter.
B. perrinii. The fragrant flowers are 2–3 in. across,
and have narrow, yellow-green sepals and petals,
and a pure white lip, sometimes green-marked
within. They open in spring.

Brassia

Spider orchids. ORCHIDACEAE. A genus
comprising 50 species of orchids from tropical
America. They have somewhat flattened
pseudobulbs and large, leathery leaves. The flowers
have remarkably elongated petals, sometimes up to
12 in. in length. They are surprisingly easy to grow
in an osmunda-sphagnum compost. Keep moist
and shaded, and in a minimum temperature of
50°F (10°C). Propagate by division.

B. caudata. The many-flowered spikes of this West
Indian species are pendant and bear greenish-
yellow flowers barred with brown, and with petals
up to 8 in. in length. They are fragrant and open
mainly in autumn and winter.
B. gireoudiana. A similar species to *B. caudata*, with
larger flowers, the petals sometimes reaching 12 in.
It comes from Costa Rica and Panama and flowers
from spring to early autumn.
B. longissima. This Costa Rican species has spikes
of very fragrant, yellow flowers with reddish-brown
markings. It is most remarkable for its petal-like

sepals which can reach 12 in. in length. They open in autumn. *(illus. prev. page)*

B. maculata. Coming from Central America, this species is also similar to *B. caudata* but has larger, paler leaves. The petals are barred with purple and are 6–8 in. long.

B. verrucosa. A Central American and Mexican species with long, wiry, arching stems bearing spikes of greenish-yellow flowers, purple-marked, and a white, brown-spotted lip. The petals are 5–8 in. long. A very attractive spring- to summer-flowering species.

x Brassocattleya

ORCHIDACEAE. A hybrid group raised from *Brassavola* and *Cattleya*. Many attractive named cultivars have been raised, most combining the features of the two parent genera, having the fringed lip of the best Brassavolas and the vigor of the Cattleyas. They require plentiful moisture and shade, an osmunda-sphagnum or bark orchid compost, and a minimum temperature of 50°F (10°C). Propagate by division.

x Brassolaelia

ORCHIDACEAE. Hybrids of *Brassavola* and *Laelia*, these also blend the characteristics of the parents. Many named cultivars are raised every year. For cultivation see under *x Brassocattleya*.

x Brassolaeliocattleya

ORCHIDACEAE. This group is derived from species of *Brassavola*, *Laelia*, and *Cattleya* and new, named cultivars are still being raised. Cultivate as for *x Brassocattleya*.

Breynia

EUPHORBIACEAE.

B. nivosa. Snow bush. One of a genus of 25 shrubs from the tropics and subtropics, this species originates in the Pacific Islands. It makes a lax bush 3–4 ft. in height and has frond-like branches, the leaves of which are variegated with white. Keep in a minimum temperature of 61°F (16°C), in light shade, and water freely. Propagate by cuttings.

B. n. 'Roseo-picta'. Leaf flower. A form with the leaves marbled with pink and white, and looking like small flowers.

Brodiaea

ALLIACEAE. A genus of 30 bulbous plants from North America. They have narrow, strap-shaped leaves and clustered heads of flowers on long stems. Keep in full sun in a minimum temperature of 45°F (7°C), and water from late winter until the

leaves die off. Keep dry from late summer to late autumn. Propagate by seeds or offsets.

B. coronaria. Syn. *B. grandiflora; Hookera coronaria*. Trumpet lily. The 8–20 in. stems bear purplish-blue, trumpet-shaped flowers, expanding at the mouth to 6 flat petals in late spring.

B. ida-maia. Syn. *Dichelostemma ida-maia*. Fire cracker. In spring, the 1½–2 ft. stems carry clusters of drooping, blood-red, tubular flowers, each yellowish-green at the tips of the petals.

B. laxa. Syn. *Hookera laxa; Triteleia laxa*. Ithuriel's spear; Grass nut. A species with 1½ ft. stems which, in summer, bear clusters of deep blue-purple, funnel-shaped flowers.

B. lutea. Pretty face; Golden brodiaea. In this species the 1–2 ft. stems carry tight clusters of bright golden, starry flowers in late spring.

Bromelia

BROMELIACEAE. Dramatic plants with rosettes of stiff, narrow, pointed leaves with strongly spiny margins. Their bright green coloration turns to red at the center of the rosette at flowering time. The spikes of small flowers have conspicuous, bright, often red bracts. Keep in sun or light shade, in a minimum temperature of 61°F (16°C), and water only when the compost feels dry. Propagate by offsets.

B. balansae. Pinuela; Heart of fire. The leaves of this South American plant have sharp spines facing in two directions and must be kept in a safe position. The long spike of small, white flowers is followed by deep yellow fruit.

B. serra. Heart of flame. An equally spiny species from Argentina with gray-green leaves, and rounded heads of maroon flowers with red bracts, followed by orange fruit.

B. s. 'Variegata'. A similar plant with broad, creamy-white margins to the leaves.

Broughtonia

ORCHIDACEAE.

B. sanguinea. The only one of its genus, this orchid is found in its native Cuba and Jamaica, growing epiphytically on rocks. The small pseudobulbs have stiff leaves and 18 in., wiry stalks carrying clusters of 1 in., bright crimson or yellow flowers from autumn through to late spring. Grow on pieces of bark in some shade. Water freely and maintain a minimum temperature over 50°F (10°C). Propagate by division.

Browallia

SOLANACEAE. A genus of 6 bushy, perennial plants which are best raised annually from seed. They have dark green, ovate leaves, and tubular flowers opening flat at the mouth to resemble violets. Grow in shade in a minimum temperature of 50°F (10°C), and water freely. Propagate by seed or cuttings.

B. speciosa. Bush violet. A Colombian species with rich violet flowers measuring 1 in. across and borne on 1½–2 ft. stems.

B. s. 'Alba'. A white-flowered form, contrasting well with the dark foliage.

B. s. 'Major'. Sapphire flower. A smaller-growing form with larger flowers to 2 in. across.

B. viscosa. A sticky-haired species, similar to *B. speciosa* but more compact. The flowers are purplish-blue.

Brunfelsia

SOLANACEAE. A genus of 30 species of evergreen shrubs of which the following make attractive plants for large pots. They have glossy, firm, dark green leaves, and clusters of fragrant flowers, the long tube bearing 5, flat, spreading petals. Not the easiest of house plants. Shade only from the hottest sun and provide a minimum temperature of 50°F (10°C). Keep the compost moist, but not wet, at all times. Propagate by cuttings.

B. americana. Lady of the night. A West Indian species with white flowers which become yellow as they age. The tube is 4 in., and the flat petals over 2 in. across. They open in spring and summer.

B. calycina. Yesterday, today, and tomorrow. A low-growing shrub from Brazil and Peru with 2 in. wide, lavender flowers which have a white eye, paling to pure white as they age. They are borne abundantly from January to mid-summer.

B. c. 'Floribunda'. A form with deep violet flowers.

B. c. 'Macrantha'. This form has larger flowers up to 3 in. across.

B. latifolia. Kiss-me-quick. A similar species to *B. calycina* but with deep lavender blooms with a white eye which changes to pure white. The plant bears abundant flowers through winter to early spring.

B. undulata. White raintree. A large shrub or small tree in its native Jamaica, this species can be kept to 2–3 ft. in pots, and flowers well when small. The white blooms are long-tubed and fade to pale yellow. They are open in autumn. Ideally keep temperatures above 61°F (16°C) for this species.

x Brunsdonna

AMARYLLIDACEAE. A hybrid between *Brunsvigia josephinae* and *Amaryllis belladonna,* it has strap-shaped, dark green leaves and a cluster of fragrant, trumpet-shaped, pink flowers, yellow in the throat. They are borne on 15 in. stems in summer. Grow in full sun with a minimum temperature of 50°F (10°C). Water freely. Propagate by offsets.

Brunsvigia

AMARYLLIDACEAE.

B. josephinae. Josephine's lily. A South African species which produces large, rounded heads of scarlet flowers on a strong, 1½ ft. stem in late summer. They are followed by the broad, strap-shaped, green leaves. Maintain a minimum temperature of 50°F (10°C), and water freely while the plant is growing. As the leaves die off, water less, and keep quite dry in winter. Propagate by offsets.

Bulbophyllum

ORCHIDACEAE. A large and widespread genus of 900 epiphytic orchids. They have pseudobulbs bearing single leaves and complex flowers, with the outer sepals joined and larger than the petals and slender lips. They are best grown on pieces of bark with an osmunda-sphagnum compost. Keep in a temperature above 61°F (16°C) in shade. Water freely. Propagate by division.

B. dayanum. A Burmese species with short, fleshy leaves and small clusters of flowers rising in spring and summer almost directly from the egg-shaped pseudobulbs. They are 1½ in across, and green with red-purple markings. They sway with the slightest movement.

B. grandiflorum. From New Guinea, this remarkable late autumn-flowering orchid has 4–5 in., pale green, hooded sepals almost covering the small petals and red-brown, spotted lip.

B. medusae. Syn. *Cirrhopetalum medusae.* Coming from the islands of southeast Asia, this decorative plant has 8 in., arching stems which carry a rounded cluster of blooms. These are creamy white and 6 in. across, with red spotting and a yellow lip tapering to a fine point.

B. pulchellum. Walnut orchid. From Malaya, this orchid has small, spring-borne flowers, each with 2 long, rose-pink sepals, twisted upwards to reveal the rounded, dark brown lip and striped petals.

Burchellia

RUBIACEAE.

B. capensis. Syn. *B. bubalina.* This evergreen shrub from South Africa is the only one of its genus. It will reach 5 ft. or less in a large pot or tub and has dark green, ovate leaves, and small clusters of inch-long, bright scarlet flowers which open in spring. Grow in light shade with a minimum temperature of 50°F (10°C). Water freely. Propagate by cuttings. *(illus. fol. page)*

Caladium

ARACEAE

C. hortulanum. This group name covers many plants of hybrid origin, derived largely from the South American *C. bicolor* under which name they are sometimes listed. They have beautifully marked leaves held on long stalks. Maintain a fairly even temperature around 65°F (18°C), and keep the plants free of drafts. Avoid direct sun which may damage the leaves, and water freely except for a rest period in winter when the tubers can be dried off. Propagate by division. *(illus.)*

C. h. 'Ace of Spades'. Rose-pink and white, arrow-shaped leaves with red veining and a dark green margin.
C. h. 'Candidum'. A favorite form with shining white leaves, bordered and veined with dark green.
C. h. 'Lord Derby'. The long, tapering, arrow-shaped, green-margined leaves are wavy and almost transparent. The pink surface is marked with green veins.
C. h. 'Marie Moir'. White leaves marked with green

46

veins and margins, with blood-red spots between. *C. h.* 'Seagull'. A dark green-leaved cultivar with broad, white veining.

Calamus

PALMAE.

C. ciliaris. Lawyer canes. One of a large genus of 375 species including the Rattan palm. The lawyer palm has deeply divided leaves, up to $2\frac{1}{2}$ ft. in length, carried on a stiff, upright, cane-like stem. It makes an attractive pot plant while young. Keep a minimum temperature of 61°F (16°C), give some shade, and water freely.

Calanthe

ORCHIDACEAE. A genus of some 150 species of orchid, both evergreen and deciduous in habit. Most prefer a minimum temperature of 61°F (16°C), a normal potting compost, light shade, and frequent watering. Propagate by division.
C. x bella. A long-established, deciduous hybrid with broad leaves carried on conical pseudobulbs in winter, it bears clusters of $1\frac{1}{2}$–2 in. flowers with white sepals, pink petals, and a long crimson and white lip. They are carried on long, arching stems.
C. striata. Syn. *C. sieboldii.* An evergreen species from Japan with small pseudobulbs, and in spring and summer, with erect spikes of yellow-gold flowers with a crimson-marked lip. A minimum temperature of 50°F (10°C) is sufficient.
C. vestita. A winter-blooming, deciduous species from Burma, the spike of white flowers with a red-marked lip, is carried on 2 ft. arching stems.

Calathea

MARANTACEAE. A South American genus of some 150 species many of which are superb foliage plants. They have oval, firm-textured, patterned leaves. Maintain a minimum temperature of 61°F (16°C), shade from sun, and water freely. Propagate by division.
C. argyraea. Silver calathea. The ovate leaves are silvery-gray with bright green veins, the pattern repeated in purple-red beneath.
C. insignis. Syn. *C. lancifolia.* Rattlesnake plant. The long, narrow, wavy leaves are yellow-green above, and patterned with dark green ovals, alternately large and small, on either side of the midrib. The leaves are deep red on the reverse side.
C. lietzei. A distinctive plant, the long, ovate leaves banded on either side of the midrib with alternate stripes of dark green and silver. The leaves are borne on upright stems and the plant produces young plants from runners.
C. louisae. The ovate leaves are rich, dark green,

with a paler feather pattern in the center, echoed in red-purple beneath.

C. makoyana. Peacock plant. Perhaps the most beautiful of foliage plants with its ovate leaves held upright on stiff stems. They are a silvery, yellow-green above, with dark green veining, and a pattern of alternately large and small ovals like the "eyes" of a peacock's tail. The reverse side has the pattern in deep red. *(illus.)*

C. ornata. The dark green, ovate leaves have pairs of narrow stripes from midrib to the marginal band. This is the juvenile phase of a species, which when adult can reach 8 ft.

C. o. 'Roseo-lineata'. In this form the stripes are rose-red.

C. picturata. The true species has ovate, pointed, green leaves with a white line inside the margin. It is purple below.

C. p. 'Argentea'. A striking form with only the margins green, the rest of the leaf silver.

C. p. vandenheckei. A juvenile form of *C. picturata*, with paler, silvery feathering on the green leaves, and white stripes inside the margin and along the midrib.

C. zebrina. Zebra plant. A beautiful species having velvety leaves with light-green veins and midrib, purple beneath.

Calceolaria

Slipperworts. SCROPHULARIACEAE. A very large genus comprising 300–400 species, most from the South American Andes. All have colorful, pouch-like flowers. They grow best in cool conditions, preferably with a maximum temperature of 65°F (18°C), shaded from hot sun. Water when the compost feels almost dry. Propagate by seed or cuttings.

C. x herbeohybrida. A large group of hybrids and cultivars best grown as annuals or biennials.

C. x h. 'Grandiflora'. A race of large, flowered plants, the 2–3 in., red-spotted pouches in shades of yellow through orange to red. Spring flowering.

C. x h. 'Multiflora Nana'. A group of smaller, bushy plants with 1–2 in. flowers in similar colors.

C. integrifolia. Syn. *C. rugosa*. A shrubby, perennial plant covered in summer with small, yellow to reddish-brown pouches.

Callisia

COMMELINACEAE. A genus of 12 species of creeping plants closely related to the more familiar *Tradescantia*. They have long, ovate leaves, and small, 3-petalled flowers. Keep in partial shade with a minimum temperature of 50°F (10°C), and water freely. Propagate by cuttings or plantlets.

C. elegans. Syn. *Setcreasea striata*. Striped inch plant. A pretty species from Mexico, the pointed, ovate leaves are green with fine, white striping and purple beneath. The flowers are white.

C. fragrans. Syn. *Tradescantia dracaenoides*. A large Mexican species with 8–12 in., broadly ovate leaves, shining green, becoming purplish-red in good light. The white flowers are very fragrant and borne in long, arching spikes.

C. f. 'Melnikoff'. Syn. *Spironema*. The 8 in. leaves of this form are green with yellowish striping.

Callistemon

MYRTACEAE. A genus of 25 Australasian shrubs with slender leaves and striking red or yellow spikes of flowers with no petals, but long stamens like the bristles of a colorful bottlebrush. Keep in full sun in a minimum temperature of 45°F (7°C), and water only when the compost feels dry. Propagate by cuttings.

C. citrinus. Syn. *C. lanceolatus*. Crimson bottlebrush. A slender shrub up to 6 ft. in tubs, bearing red, bottlebrush flowers in 2–4 in. spikes in summer and autumn, even when young. *(illus.)*

C. speciosus. A larger plant with deep scarlet spikes of bloom, up to 5 in. long in summer.

Calocephalus

COMPOSITAE.
C. brownii. Syn. *Leucophyta brownii.* One of 15 species of Australian plants, it is a small, wiry shrub, from 1–3 ft. in height, and is grown for its narrow leaves and stems which are covered with white, woolly hairs. The small, yellow flowers are insignificant. Maintain a minimum temperature of 50°F (10°C), give full sun, and water only when the compost is dry. Propagate by cuttings.

Camellia

THEACEAE. A genus of 82 species of evergreen trees and shrubs from Asia. They have glossy, oval leaves and stemless flowers in reds, pinks, and whites. Keep in a cool temperature, preferably between 40°F (5°C) and 65°F (18°C), in shade, and with the compost just moist. Propagate by cuttings.
C. japonica. Although a tree in its native Japan and Korea, this is easily kept to 3–4 ft. in pots, making a beautiful specimen plant. From the original species over 3000 named cultivars have been raised, with double and single flowers from 2–5 in. across. They open in early spring.
C. j. 'Adolphe Audusson'. Large, semi-double flowers with deep crimson petals, on an erect plant.
C. j. 'Alba Simplex'. The large, single, white flowers are saucer-shaped. The best of its kind.
C. j. 'Drama Girl'. A strong-growing plant with somewhat pendant stems and large semi-double flowers which are rose-pink with a salmony flush.
C. j. 'Elegans'. Syn. 'Chandleri Elegans'. A handsome plant, the large, double, carmine flowers, with some white striping, reaching 4 in. across.
C. j. 'Haku-rakuten'. A strong grower with large, semi-double, white blooms.
C. j. 'Magnoliiflora'. A semi-double, pale pink form with pointed petals rather resembling *Magnolia stellata.* The plant is bushy with paler foliage.
C. j. 'Mathotiana'. Syn. 'Grand Sultan'. A deep crimson, double form, the petals darkening with age.
C. j. 'Tomorrow'. A form with pendant branches and semi-double, rose-pink blooms.
C. j. 'Yours Truly'. A fine, slow-growing plant having pink, semi-double flowers, the petals lined with darker pink, and white-edged.
C. reticulata. A Chinese species having net-veined leaves giving a matt texture and a more sparse, upright growth form. The 4–6 in. flowers are open in early spring. The wild type has single, rose-pink flowers, but many cultivars have been raised.
C. r. 'Buddha'. The waved petals of this rose-pink

cultivar are held upright. A fine, vigorous plant.
C. r. 'Captain Rawes'. The original form, introduced from China in 1820, has large, semi-double, bright rose-red flowers.
C. r. 'Noble Pearl'. A fine plant with large, very deep red, semi-double flowers.
C. sasanqua. This attractive, slender-stemmed shrub comes from Japan. It has ovate, toothed leaves, and pink or white flowers which are single or double. They open through winter.

Campanula

CAMPANULACEAE.
C. isophylla. Belonging to a genus of 300 herbaceous plants with bell-shaped or starry flowers, this species from northern Italy is excellent for hanging baskets. It has pendant stems up to 1 ft. long, with neat ovate leaves, and from summer to autumn, dainty, starry, lavender-blue flowers. Keep in full sun, but well-ventilated, giving a maximum temperature of about 65°F (18°C). Water when the compost feels dry. Propagate by division or cuttings.
C. i. 'Alba'. An attractive white form.
C. i. 'Mayii'. A form with white-variegated, hairy leaves, and larger, more saucer-shaped flowers, up to 1½ in. across.

Campelia

COMMELINACEAE.
C. zanonia. 'Variegata'. Syn. *Dichorisandra albolineata.* One of a Central and South American genus comprising only 3 species. Only this one cultivar is generally available. It has long, ovate leaves which are striped with green, white, and red, and are borne on a stiff, erect stem up to 3 ft. in height. The clusters of small, purple flowers add little to the plant. Keep in good light, but not full sun, with a minimum temperature of 61°F (16°C). Water only when the compost feels dry. Propagate by division or cuttings.

Canistrum

BROMELIACEAE.
C. lindenii. One of a genus of 7 species of Brazilian epiphytes. This plant has a rosette of yellow-green, darker mottled, strap-shaped leaves up to 2 ft. in length. The central flowering stalk carries a head of small, rounded, white flowers, surrounded by creamy bracts. Grow in shade in a minimum temperature of 60°F (15°C), and water freely. Propagate by removing offsets in summer.
C. l. 'Roseum'. Syn. *C. roseum.* A similar plant with rose-pink flower bracts.

Canna

CANNACEAE. A genus containing 55 species of tuberous-rooted, herbaceous plants mostly from the tropics. They have long, ovate, bright green leaves, carried on stiff, erect stalks, and showy spikes of colorful flowers. Grow in full sun with a minimum temperature of 50°F (10°C), and water freely. Propagate by division.

C. coccinea. Scarlet Indian shot. A species from Central and South America reaching 4 ft. in height with small but colorful flowers, the petals scarlet and the lip marked with yellow. They are borne within green sepals.

C. x hybrida. Syn. *C. generalis.* A hybrid name which covers the many large-flowered cultivars now available.

C.x h. 'Di Bartolo'. A form reaching 3 ft. with bronze-purple leaves, and large, deep pink flowers.

C. x h. 'President'. Reaching 3–4 ft., this green-leaved cultivar has bright scarlet flowers.

C. x h. 'Richard Wallace'. A green-leaved cultivar up to 3 ft. in height, having clear yellow flowers.

C. x h. 'Striped Beauty'. A variegated form, the green leaves having ivory-white midrib and veins. The large flowers are a rich scarlet.

C. x h. 'Wyoming'. A purple-leaved form bearing orange-bronze flowers which make a fine contrast in color.

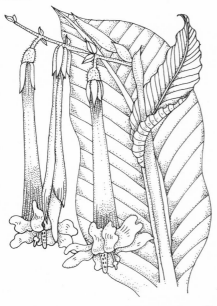

C. iridiflora. This tall species from Peru has spikes of rose-pink flowers which form a 5 in., pendant tube, opening to reflexed segments at the mouth. They are borne in late summer. *(illus.)*

Cantua

POLEMONIACEAE.

C. buxifolia. One of a genus comprising 11 trees and shrubs from South America. It makes a clambering shrub up to 8 ft., and grows best trained to a support. The leaves are small, and the clusters of 3 in.-long, pendant, trumpet-shaped flowers are red-purple with yellow markings. Grow in sun with a minimum temperature of 45°F (7°C), and water only when the compost feels dry. Propagate by cuttings in summer.

Capsicum

SOLANACEAE.

C. annuum. Red and green peppers. Belonging to a genus of some 50 species, this plant, though a shrubby perennial, is usually treated as an annual. It is widespread throughout the tropics. Individual plants reach 9–18 in. in height and have clear green, long ovate leaves, and small, starry white flowers followed by colorful fruit. Keep in full light with a minimum temperature of 50°F (10°C), and water freely while growing. Propagate by seeds.

C. a. 'Birdseye'. The freely-borne, white flowers are followed by the globular, waxy berries, at first green, then becoming scarlet.

C. a. 'Bull-nosed Red'. This 12–18 in. plant has 3–5 in., oblong fruits which are bright red and edible.

C. a. 'Bull-nosed Yellow'. A similar form with edible, yellow fruits.

C. a. 'Christmas Greetings'. The 12–18 in. plants bear cone-shaped fruits in a wide range of colors – from purple, through red and yellow to green.

Caralluma

ASCLEPIADACEAE. A genus of 110 succulents found through much of the Old World. They have curious, leafless stems, and rather starfish-like flowers frequently with a foetid smell. Keep in full sun in a minimum temperature of 50°F (10°C), and water only when the compost feels dry. Propagate by division or cuttings.

C. europaea. A Mediterranean species with 6 in. gray-green, grooved, and 4-angled stems, often spotted with red, and pale yellow, purple-banded flowers borne at the ends of the stems erratically through the year. *(illus. prev. page)*

C. lutea. From southern Africa, the 4-angled, 2–4 in. stems are toothed, and are light green with purple mottling. The striking flowers are yellow, with long, narrow, red-fringed arms.

C. neobrownii. Spiked clubs. The 6–8 in. plump stems are 4-angled, toothed, and dull green with maroon marbling. The 4 in. flowers are dark brown and fleshy with purple hairs.

Carex

CYPERACEAE.

C. morrowii. 'Variegata'. One of the 1500 to 2000 species of sedge which are found throughout the world, it is only cultivated in its variegated form. It has 6–9 in., grassy leaves, which are green with white margins, and small, brownish, flower spikes in spring. Coming from Japan, it prefers a cool temperature with a minimum of 40°F (5°C), and the compost just moist. Propagate by division.

Carissa

APOCYNACEAE.

C. grandiflora. Natal plum. One of a genus of 35 species of shrubs and small trees. The Natal plum is a South African species which reaches about 4 ft. in pots if the leading growths are removed. It is spiny and has toothed, deep shining green leaves. The 2 in., starry white flowers are fragrant and are followed by red, edible, plum-like fruits. Grow in sun with a minimum temperature of 50°F (10°C), and water freely. Propagate by seeds or cuttings.

Carludovica

CYCLANTHACEAE.

C. palmata. Panama hat plant. Of the 3 species belonging to this tropical American genus, this palm-like plant makes a good, decorative pot plant. The leaves are made up of long, narrow segments which are grouped together in 4 sections rather like a damaged fan. They are carried on slender stalks which can eventually reach 8 ft., if grown in tubs. Give good light and a minimum temperature of 61°F (16°C). Water freely but do not let the compost remain wet. Propagate by division.

Carnegiea

CACTACEAE.

C. gigantea. Giant saguaro. A giant cactus, the only one of its genus, reaching 60 ft. in its native North America. The stems are ribbed with spiny areoles, and the white flowers are up to 4 in. in length. It grows well in pots when young. Give full light, a minimum winter temperature of 50°F (10°C), and water only when the compost feels dry. Propagate by seeds in spring.

Caryota

PALMAE.

C. mitis. Dwarf fishtail palm. One of a genus of 12 attractive palms with the long leaflets cut into fishtail-shaped segments. This species reaches 25 ft. in its native southeast Asia, but grows slowly and is a very effective plant for a pot. Keep a minimum temperature of 61°F (16°C), and a humid atmosphere. Water freely.

Cassia

LEGUMINOSAE.

C. corymbosa. One of a large genus of 500–600 species, this tropical American shrub makes a decorative pot plant. It has finely-divided leaves, and golden-yellow, bowl-shaped flowers which open in summer. Although it normally reaches 5 ft., it can be kept smaller by annual pruning. Keep in sun, provide a winter minimum temperature of 45°F (7°C), and water when the compost appears dry. Propagate by cuttings.

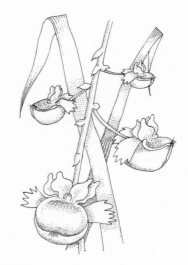

Catasetum

ORCHIDACEAE. A genus of some 70 species of epiphytic orchids from tropical America with long, fleshy pseudobulbs, large, plaited leaves; and flowers on arching stems. They grow well in baskets, requiring a temperature above 61°F (16°C), a position in shade, and frequent watering. Propagate by division of pseudobulbs.

C. bicolor. The arching stems carry male flowers which are 3½ in. across and have brown and green sepals and a white lip with purple markings. The small, green, female flowers sometimes appear. They have a hooded lip and are borne on short, upright stalks on the same plant.

C. longifolium. Both leaves and flowering stems of this species are pendant. The 1½ in. blooms are greenish-yellow with red markings, and have a deep purple, hooded lip. They open in autumn. *(illus.)*

C. warscewiczii. A small species, with egg-shaped pseudobulbs and 12 in. pendant spikes of flowers. These are white with sepals, petals and lip striped with green, the central lobe of the lip being distinctly bearded.

Catharanthus

APOCYNACEAE.

C. roseus. Syn. *Vinca rosea*. Madagascan periwinkle. One of 8 species which make up this genus, it is a fleshy, perennial plant which can reach 1–2 ft. in height. The dark green, glossy leaves are oval with a distinct white midrib. The rose-red flowers, darker in the center, bloom throughout summer. It requires a minimum temperature of 50°F (10°C), full sun, and water when the compost feels dry. Propagate by seed or cuttings, annual replacement producing neater plants.

Catopsis

BROMELIACEAE.

C. morreniana. A neat bromeliad from Central America, one of a genus of 25 species. It forms a rosette of narrow, shiny green leaves up to 8 in. in length. From its center rises an erect stem bearing a branched spike of small, white flowers and pale yellow bracts. Maintain a temperature over 50°F (10°C), keep in shade, and water only when the compost feels dry. Propagate by offsets.

Cattleya

ORCHIDACEAE. A genus comprising 60 species and an immense number of hybrids, probably the best known of all orchids. They have creeping stems from which rise club-shaped pseudobulbs. These carry 1–3 fleshy, strap-shaped leaves, and the superb, showy flowers. Each bloom has 3 sepals and 2 petals, usually the same color though varying in shape, the third petal forming a strikingly colored or patterned, often frilled lip. They occur in a wide range of shades from purples to reds, yellow, and white, and most flower in autumn and winter. Grow in bark chips or a sphagnum-osmunda mix, with a minimum temperature of 50°F (10°C). Keep in shade and water freely. Propagate by division.

C. bowringiana. Cluster cattleya. From Central America, this species has 2 leaves and spikes bearing up to 15, rich rose-purple flowers, each 2–3 in. across.

C. citrina. A Mexican orchid with small pseudobulbs bearing gray-green, pendant leaves, with single, bright yellow, waxy flowers which never open widely. They are very fragrant.

C. intermedia. Cocktail orchid. A neat plant from Brazil with long stem-like pseudobulbs bearing short leaves and clusters of pale pink flowers up to 5 in. across, having a magenta-marked lip. They open in summer.

C. i. 'Alba'. A form with pure white flowers.

C. labiata. A very variable species from Brazil with long, club-shaped pseudobulbs, single leaves, and short spikes of rose-pink flowers which can be 7 in. or more across. The large, frilled lip has red-purple markings with a yellow central spot.

C. l. dowiana. Syn. *C. dowiana*. Queen cattleya. From Costa Rica, this form has very fragrant flowers with yellow petals, sometimes flushed with red, and a very large, crimson, frilled lip, veined and streaked with golden-yellow. Summer flowering.

C. l. lueddemanniana. Syn. *C. lueddemanniana*. A Venezuelan variety with a single, grayish leaf. The sepals are very wide, wavy petals, colored white to purplish-pink, and the similar colored lip has yellow and purplish markings.

C. l. mossiae. Syn. *C. mossiae*. Easter orchid. A favorite spring- to early summer-flowering variety from Venezuela. The 5–6 in. flowers are borne in clusters of 3–7, and are light rose-pink and frilled, while the very large lip has red-purple markings and yellow streaks.

C. l. trianaei. Syn. *C. trianaei*. Christmas orchid. A robust, winter-flowering variety from Colombia, the sepals and crimped petals varying from white to rose-pink and often fully 7 in. across. The frilled lip is narrow, deep crimson with orange markings.

C. loddigesii. A robust species from Brazil and Paraguay, with long, narrow pseudobulbs and 2 leathery 4–6 in. leaves. The 4½ in., waxy flowers are pinkish-white, the petals sometimes waved and deeper in color, and the lip rose-pink with a creamy-yellow marking. They are borne in 2–6 flowered spikes.

C. skinneri. A widespread spring- and summer-flowering species found from Mexico to Venezuela. It has 2-leaved, long, cane-like pseudobulbs and spikes of 4–12 flowers, each 2–3 in. across and a bright rosy-purple. The lip is darker in color with yellow markings. Often recommended for beginners.

C. walkeriana. A spring-flowering Brazilian species,

51

with small pseudobulbs and 5 in. stiff leaves, often red-flushed. The $4\frac{1}{2}$ in. fragrant flowers are pinkish-purple, the petals twice as wide as the sepals, and the lip frilled darker in color with white or yellow markings.

Celosia

AMARANTACEAE.
C. argentea. Of the 60 species belonging to the genus, this annual from southeast Asia is grown for its plumes of colored flowers. The original white-flowered species is no longer seen, two cultivar groups replacing it. Grow in full sun with a minimum temperature of 50°F (10°C), water freely, and pot-on regularly. Propagate by seed.
C. a. 'Cristata'. Cockscomb. Reaching 1 ft. in height with green, or bronze-green leaves, the heads of small yellow, orange, and red flowers make up a solid cockscomb-like mass of color. *(illus.)*

C. a. 'Pyramidalis'. Syn. 'Plumosa'. An erect plant with light green leaves and feathery plumes in reds, golds, or yellows.

Celsia

SCROPHULARIACEAE.
C. arcturus. One of a small genus now included in *Verbascum*. This Cretan species is a shrubby plant from 1–4 ft. high. It has large, lobed leaves, forming a basal rosette the first year and branched spikes of flat, yellow flowers with purple stamens in summer and autumn. Keep a minimum temperature of 45°F (7°C), water freely, and keep in full sun. Best grown annually from seed.

52

Centrantherum

COMPOSITAE.
C. intermedium. Button flower. One of 20 species, this bushy Brazilian plant has light green, ovate, toothed leaves and 1 in., tight, powder-puff clusters of lavender flowers. Grow in full sun with a minimum temperature of 50°F (10°C), and water freely. Propagate by cuttings.

Cephalocereus

CACTACEAE. A genus containing 48 species of columnar cacti. The stems are angular with woolly areoles. The small flowers, which are borne on the top or side of the column, are usually only seen on large specimens. Give full sun, keep a winter temperature of 40°F (5°C), and water only when the compost, which should be half sand or grit, feels dry. Propagate by seed.
C. russellianus. The long stems of this species from Colombia and Venezuela are 4–6 ribbed, and also deeply grooved horizontally, dividing them into small sections. Each section has an areole which has both spines and short, white hairs.

C. senilis. Old man cactus. The gray-green column is ribbed and spiny, the whole covered with silvery, matted hairs giving the entire plant a shaggy look. Its annual rate of growth is about an inch, so takes many years to outgrow its welcome. It is native to Mexico. *(illus.)*

Cereus

Torch cactus. CACTACEAE. A genus of columnar cacti now considered to contain 50 species. Many of these become of tree size when full-grown, but remain small in pots for many years. They require full sun, and a minimum winter temperature of 40°F (5°C). Water only when the compost feels dry. Propagate by seeds or cuttings.
C. hexagonus. South American blue column. A Colombian species, the blue-green, slightly spiny,

ribbed columns being branched near the base. White flowers are borne on large specimens.

C. jamacaru. A Brazilian species which is slow growing, remaining below 3 ft. for many years. The ribbed, blue-green stems have long, yellowish spines.

C. peruviana. Column cactus. From Argentina and Brazil, not Peru, a fine species which has fleshy, blue-green stems with 6–9 ribs. The areoles are set with brown spines. Some authorities consider the plant in cultivation under this name to be a hybrid.

Ceropegia

Lantern flowers. ASCLEPIADACEAE. A genus comprising about 160 species of shrubs and climbers, some of which are leafless, and all are succulent and somewhat fleshy. They have petal lobes which are joined at the tips, giving a lantern-like effect. In spite of their exotic appearance, they are not difficult house plants. Keep away from direct sunlight with a minimum temperature 61°F (16°C), water freely when in growth. Propagate by cuttings in summer.

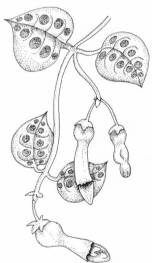

C. caffrorum. Lamp flower. A good hanging plant from southern Africa, the pairs of oval, red-veined leaves borne on wiry stems. The small flowers are green outside, striped with purple, and all purple inside.

C. debilis. Needle vine. A central African species having curious, needle-like leaves, grooved above on long, twining and arching stems. The 1 in. flowers are green with a red flush, and all red inside.

C. haygarthii. Wine-glass vine. A South African species grown for its remarkable cream, maroon-

spotted flowers joined into a curving tube, widening upwards to the mouth where the joined petals appear like the ribs of an umbrella. Above the flower, carried on a red stalk, is a small, white-hairy, red knob.

C. sandersonii. Parachute plant. A curious, twining species from southern Africa, only the young stems bearing leaves. The funnel-shaped flowers have a parachute-like top and are in shades of green. A temperature of 50°F (10°C) is sufficient for this plant:

C. woodii. Heart vine. An excellent hanging plant having dark-purple stems, with heart-shaped, blue-green leaves which have silvery marbling. The small flowers are pink outside and purplish-brown inside. Small tubers sometimes appear on the stems and can be used for propagation. It will stand winter temperatures down to 45°F (7°C). *(illus.)*

Cestrum

SOLANACEAE. A genus of about 150 shrubs many of which look best trained as climbers, particularly around a window. They have long, ovate leaves, and tubular flowers. Maintain a minimum winter temperature of 50°F (10°C), keep in full sun, and water freely. Propagate by cuttings.

C. aurantiacum. A Guatemalan species which can reach 8 ft., but if pruned can be kept much smaller. The leaves are pale green, and from summer to autumn it carries clusters of bright orange flowers.

C. nocturnum. Queen of the night. An evergreen shrub from the West Indies having deep green leaves, and summer-borne, creamy-white flowers

53

carried in dense clusters. Remarkable chiefly for their superb perfume.

C. purpureum. A Mexican, rambling, evergreen species with pendant shoots bearing long, narrow leaves and long, hanging spikes of red-purple flowers, borne through summer and autumn. Red berries often follow the flowers. *(illus. prev. page)*

Chamaecereus
CACTACEAE.

C. silvestri. Peanut cactus. The only species of its genus, this is a very small cactus, with narrow, cylindrical branches which are green, and set with small, white spines from the areoles. Full-grown, the stems rarely exceed 6 in. The flowers are orange-scarlet. Keep in full light with a minimum temperature of 50°F (10°C), water only when the compost is dry, and propagate by removing small branches and rooting as cuttings. *(illus.)*

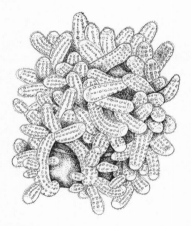

Chamaedorea

PALMAE. A genus of about 100 species of palms, all from America. They are relatively dwarf in growth and many are extremely ornamental. They require warmth, with a minimum temperature of 61°F (16°C), partial shade, and moist, but not wet compost. Propagate by seed, or, with suckering species, by division.

C. costaricana. Showy bamboo palm. This Costa Rican species is suckering, producing a cluster of bamboo-like stems, eventually reaching 18 ft. in height. The graceful green fronds are borne at intervals along these stems.

C. elegans. Syn. *C. e.* 'Bella', *Neanthe bella*. Parlor palm; Dwarf mountain palm. This species, native to Mexico and Guatemala is one of the best for indoor decoration. It has a cluster of erect stems with dark green fronds which take many years to

reach their full 8 ft. It sometimes bears whitish flower spikes, themselves insignificant, but followed by round, yellow or white fruit.

C. erumpens. Bamboo palm. From Honduras, this suckering species has slender, bamboo-like stems and arching, dark green fronds which have unusual well-spaced, broad, drooping leaflets. A distinctive plant for decorative effect.

C. glaucifolia. Blueleaf palm. The bamboo-like stems of this Guatemalan species can reach 22 ft. at maturity. The 4–6 fronds have well-spaced, slender, blue-green leaflets. A decorative plant where space can be given.

C. siefrizii. Reed palm. A small, Mexican species with clusters of upright stems, clear below and bearing arching fronds above. These have long, narrow, almost grass-like leaflets.

Chamaerops
PALMAE.

C. humilis. European fan palm. Two species comprise this genus, this plant being the only palm native to Europe. It is normally a small, bushy species, the many stems rising from ground level, and has fan-shaped, slightly gray-green fronds up to 3 ft. in length. It makes slow growth in a pot or tub, requires a minimum temperature of only 45°F (7°C), and will tolerate some shade. Water freely. Propagate by seeds or suckers.

Chameranthemum

Syn. *Chamaeranthemum*. ACANTHACEAE. A genus containing 8 species of low-growing plants. All are from South America. They have decorative foliage, and yellow or white tubular flowers. Keep in shade with a minimum temperature of 61°F (16°C), and water freely. Propagate by division or cuttings.

C. gaudichaudii. A prostrate plant from Brazil with mats or wiry stems bearing oval, 2–3 in., dark green leaves with silvery-gray veins. Small spikes of lilac flowers with a white center open in summer.

C. igneum. Syn. *Stenandrium*. A low-growing Peruvian species, the dark green, velvety leaves having a wide, golden midrib and veins. The yellow flowers are borne in small spikes in summer.

C. pictum. From Brazil, the oval leaves of this species reach 9 in. in length. They are dark green, with a golden margin and silver blotches.

C. venosum. A small species from Brazil, the 3–4 in., rounded, oval leaves, firm-textured and gray-green, with silver veins.

Cheiridopsis
AIZOACEAE.

C. candidissima. Victory plant. A curious South African succulent plant, one of about 100 species belonging to this genus. It has pairs of silver-gray, boat-shaped leaves, each 3–4 in. long which are joined at the base creating a fleshy letter "V" for victory, hence its vernacular name. In autumn it has large, pink-white flowers. Keep in full sun with a minimum temperature of 50°F (10°C). Keep dry during the summer, and for the rest of the year, water when the compost feels dry. Propagate by seed.

Chirita

GESNERIACEAE. A genus of some 80 species of handsome plants from southeast Asia. They have large leaves and small, foxglove-like, tubular flowers. Keep in shade with a minimum temperature of 61°F (16°C), and water freely. Propagate by seeds or leaf cuttings.

C. lavandulacea. Hindustan gentian. A 1–2 ft., erect plant from Malaya having pointed, 8 in., oval, green leaves, which are softly hairy and have toothed margins. The summer-borne, lavender and white flowers are carried in whorls.

C. micromusa. Little banana. An unusual species from Thailand. The large, pointed, heart-shaped leaves are softly hairy yet glossy, and the 1 in., bright yellow flowers are borne through summer.

C. sinensis. Silver chirita. A very decorative plant from China, forming an almost flat rosette of 3–4 in., dark green, fleshy leaves which are heavily variegated with silver, and thinly white-hairy. The clusters of lavender flowers are carried on short, red-hairy stalks in summer.

Chlidanthus

AMARYLLIDACEAE.

C. fragrans. The only species of its genus, this bulbous plant from South America has 3 in., yellow, fragrant flowers borne in upright clusters on a 10 in. stem. They open in summer after the strap-shaped leaves die down. Keep in sun and maintain a minimum temperature of 50°F (10°C). Water when the compost feels dry, until the leaves die down, then keep dry. Propagate by offsets.

Chlorophytum

LILIACEAE. A genus containing about 215 species. The cultivated forms of one of these are commonly grown. They have long, arching leaves like wide grass blades, and small, starry white flowers on longer stalks. The tips of the flowering stems produce small plantlets which can be removed for propagation. Keep in a minimum temperature of 45°F (7°C), and away from hot sun. Water freely.

C. comosum. 'Mandaianum'. Syn. C. capense or C. elatum 'Variegatum'. Spider plant. A South African species with the center of each leaf having a yellow-cream, longitudinal stripe. The small flowers and plantlets are produced through the year. Much confused with C. capense which does not have plantlets.

C. c. 'Variegatum'. A form with creamy-white leaf margins.

Choisya

RUTACEAE.

C. ternata. One of a small genus containing only 6 species, this decorative 4–6 ft. evergreen shrub is worth growing for its aromatic, shining foliage alone. The leaves are divided into 3 oval leaflets and provide a splendid foil for the clusters of white, fragrant flowers which are only borne on sizable specimens, in spring and summer. Keep in sun in a minimum temperature of 45°F (7°C), and water freely. Propagate by cuttings.

Chorizema

LEGUMINOSAE.

C. cordatum. Syn. C. ilicifolium. Holly-leaved glory pea; Flowering oak. A small Australian shrub, one of 15 members of this genus. It has glossy green, holly-like leaves on wiry branches, and many red-orange flowers with purplish wing-petals. Grow in sun, with a minimum temperature of 50°F (10°C), and water only when the compost feels dry. Propagate by cuttings.

Chrysalidocarpus

PALMAE.

C. lutescens. Areca palm. Of the 20 species in this genus, this dainty palm makes a good pot plant when young. When mature it can reach 10–20 ft. It forms a suckering clump, and bears long, finely divided fronds which arch downwards. Maintain a minimum temperature of 61°F (16°C), and preferably some shade. Water freely and regularly. Propagate by seeds or division.

Chrysanthemum

COMPOSITAE. A genus comprising over 200 species and many hybrids and cultivars. The florists' chrysanthemums are mostly derived from C. morifolium, an Asiatic species, and are among the most popular pot plants. For indoor cultivation they must have cool temperatures, preferably plenty of fresh air, and a maximum of 65°F (18°C). If kept warmer than this by day, they should be put in a cool place each night. Keep them well-watered throughout the growing season, especially when the flower buds are developing. Propagate by cuttings taken from new shoots at the base of each plant in spring. When about 6 in. high, they should have the tips pinched out to promote bushy growth.

55

Many cultivars are available in a wide variety of shapes and colors, new ones being introduced every year. This selection includes some of those which are well-tried.

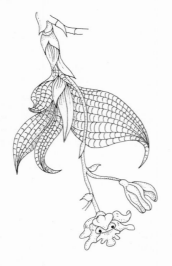

C. m. 'Delaware'. A popular florist's plant having double, bronze-red flowers, the center petals curving in to form a domed head and show the paler backs of the petals. November flowering.
C. m. 'Firecracker'. A striking cultivar with brilliant red petals, the backs of which are yellow and conspicuous as the blooms open.
C. m. 'Golden cascade'. A single-flowered form, the whole plant smothered with yellow daisies in late October.
C. m. 'Golden Lace'. The thread-like, quilled petals are golden-yellow and droop slightly from the center. Classified in the spider group. October flowering.
C. m. 'Loveliness'. A lilac-pink cultivar with double blooms. November flowering.
C. m. 'Maylen'. A beautiful cultivar, forming a tight, 6–7 in. head of pure white, incurved petals in November.
C. m. 'Mermaid'. Sprays of small, pink, semi-double blooms in October.
C. m. 'Yellow Delaware'. A bushy plant with 4 in., semi-double, yellow flowers in November.

Chrysothemis

GESNERIACEAE.
C. pulchella. An attractive, 1½ ft. species from Trinidad, one of 6 belonging to this genus. It is somewhat fleshy and has glossy, ovate, bright green leaves. In spring, clusters of small, yellow, tubular flowers appear, each carried within a brilliant

orange-red calyx which lasts longer than the flowers. Maintain a minimum temperature of 61°F (16°C), and keep in shade. Water freely. Propagate by cuttings or seeds.

Chysis

ORCHIDACEAE.
C. aurea. One of 6 species, this small, epiphytic orchid has long, spindle-shaped pseudobulbs often reaching 1 ft. in length, and long, ovate, ribbed leaves which are folded at the base. The 2–3 in. fragrant flowers are golden-yellow with red markings, and carried on short spikes. Grow in an osmunda-sphagnum or bark orchid compost with some shade, and a minimum temperature of 50°F (10°C). Water freely while in growth, allow to become almost dry between waterings when dormant. Propagate by division. *(illus. left)*

Cibotium

DICKSONIACEAE.
C. schiederi. One of a genus of 10 species of tree ferns, this Central American species can reach 12–15 ft. when mature, but remains smaller in pots. The pale green fronds are deeply dissected, and blue-green, lacy below. Give some shade and a minimum temperature of 61°F (16°C). Water freely. Propagate by spores.

Cissus

VITIDACEAE. A genus of 350 species of succulent and climbing plants presenting a variety of forms. The climbers, which look well framing a window, or on a wall trellis, require a minimum temperature of 61°F (16°C), some shade, and if possible, moderate humidity. Water freely. Propagate by cuttings or layering. The succulent species are best treated as for cactus with more light and less water. Propagate by cuttings.
C. adenopoda. Pink cissus. An African climbing species having shining, bronze-green, toothed leaves divided into 3 ovate leaflets. The leaf surface has markedly sunken veins and a scattering of purple hairs. They are purplish-red beneath. The loose spikes of flowers are yellow, and open in autumn.
C. albo-nitens. Silver princess vine. An attractive Brazilian climber, the arrow-shaped leaves, green beneath, with a brilliant silvery-white patina above.
C. antarctica. Kangaroo vine; Kangaroo ivy. A woody climber from Australia with short, hairy branches and 6 in., shining green, toothed, oval leaves. It is hardier than most species, tolerating temperatures as low as 40°F (5°C).
C. cactiformis. Cactus vine. A curious succulent climber from East Africa, requiring cactus

treatment. The 3–4 angled, winged stems are green and fleshy, and can reach 10 ft. in length. They carry a few ovate leaves which, however, soon fall. The small, green leaves are followed by red berries.

C. discolor. Rex begonia vine. A beautiful tropical climber from southeast Asia, this species must have high humidity to flourish. The long, reddish climbing stems which can reach 10 ft. are clothed with heart-shaped, pointed, quilted leaves superbly patterned. They are velvety in texture, with a purplish sheen, and silvery markings between the sunken green veins. The reverse is maroon-red.

C. juttae. A strange, succulent plant from southwest Africa, the swollen stems like blue-green bottles with a flaky, papery wrapping. It takes many years to achieve its 5–6 ft. The shining, pale green leaves are large and fleshy, and are shed in winter when the plant should be kept quite dry until growth is started off in spring.

C. rhombifolia. Syn. *Vitis* and *Rhoicissus rhomboidea*. Grape ivy. A slender, climbing, evergreen vine from Central America with 3–4 in. leaves divided into 3 ovate leaflets, each a lustrous green and slightly toothed. The veins are sunken and brown, and young leaves and stems are white-hairy.

C. rotundifolia. Arabian wax cissus. An East African climbing species with 2–3 in., rounded, waxy leaves, somewhat saucer-shaped, densely clothing the stems. This species can easily be kept low-growing, by pinching out the leading shoots.

C. striata. Syn. *Vitis striata.* Miniature grape ivy. A slender, evergreen climber from Chile, with reddish stem covered in small, 1½-3 in. leaves, each divided, hand-like, into 5 small leaflets. They are bronze-green above and purplish-red beneath.

Citrus

RUTACEAE. A genus of 12 species which includes all the citrus fruits. Apart from the small calamondin, they need far more room than is available in the average home to grow into fruiting plants, but are fun to raise from pips and while young make decorative foliage plants. Grow in full light in a minimum temperature of 50°F (10°C), and water only when the compost feels dry. Propagate by seeds or cuttings, but remember that cultivars have to be grafted onto prepared rootstocks, so must usually be bought.

C. aurantium. Seville orange. Coming from Vietnam, this spiny tree will fruit well when grown in containers. It makes a small tree up to 30 ft., with oval, slender, pointed, glossy leaves, 3–4 in. long and small, white waxy flowers. It is one of the hardiest species, and will tolerate temperatures down to 45°F (7°C).

C. a. myrtifolia. Myrtleleaf orange. A dwarf form having 1 in., stiff, glossy green leaves on crowded, thornless stems. The white waxy flowers, opening in spring, are followed by bright orange fruits.

C. limon. Lemon. A small tree from Asia reaching 8–10 ft. It can be grown in large containers. The long, ovate, toothed leaves are deep green and borne on thorny stems. The white, starry flowers have red-flushed buds and are followed by the familiar lemons.

C. l. 'Ponderosa'. American wonder lemon. A hybrid form producing enormous fruit, up to 2½ lbs. in weight, but grown more for appearance than flavor.

C. x 'Meyeri'. Dwarf Chinese lemon. Originally raised in China, this widely-branched tree will eventually reach 12 ft., but is slow-growing when kept in a pot, and will produce its fruits freely when little over 1 ft. in height. The white, lavender-tinted flowers are fragrant, and the lemon-like but orange-colored fruits are 2½–3½ in. long, and ripen in late winter and early spring.

C. mitis. Calamondin. A very popular pot plant from the Philippines which bears its abundant ½–1½ in. orange fruits when very small, though eventually reaching 8–10 ft. The oval leaves are dark green and glossy, and the small, white flowers are very fragrant. Both flowers and fruit are borne throughout the year with a best showing very suitably around Christmas.

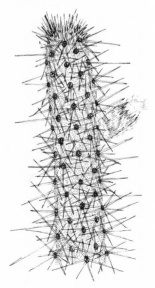

Cleistocactus

CACTACEAE. Of the 30 known cacti of this genus, 3 handsome, columnar species make good house plants. They have erect, ribbed stems with spiny areoles and long, tubular flowers. Maintain a minimum temperature of 60°F (15°C), give full sun, and water only when the compost feels dry. Propagate by offsets or by beheading old plants and using the top as a cutting.

C. baumannii. The stout stems of this South American species can reach 3 ft. in mature specimens, but are much smaller than this in pots. The areoles have sharp, yellowish-brown spines. The 2–3 in. flowers are a brilliant scarlet, and are borne in summer with a tuft of white hairs at the base. *(illus. prev. page)*

C. smaragdiflorus. Firecracker cactus. A similar plant to *C. baumannii* from the same area, but larger with sharp but flexible spines up to 1 in. long from the many areoles. The 1½–2 in. tubular flowers are orange-scarlet with emerald-green tips.

C. straussii. From Bolivia, this handsome species makes slender, erect, many-ribbed columns, covered with delicate white spines and tufts of silvery-white wool. The tubular, red flowers are 3–3½ in. long and slightly curved.

Clerodendron

VERBENACEAE. A genus containing some 400 species of shrubs, climbers, and trees with a worldwide distribution. Many have clusters of brightly colored flowers and are highly decorative in large pots. If there is room for only small specimens, raise plants of *C. fragrans* and *C. speciosissimum* annually from cuttings in spring. Grow in light shade with a minimum temperature of 61°F (16°C), and water freely. Propagate by cuttings in spring and summer.

C. fragrans. Glory tree. A 3–5 ft. tree from China and Japan needing plenty of room. It has roundish-oval, 3–6 in. leaves and densely-clustered 4 in. heads of rose-pink, funnel-shaped flowers, the lobed petals opening flat at the mouth. They open chiefly in late autumn. A minimum temperature of 50°F (10°C) is sufficient.

C. f. pleniflorum. Japanese glory tree. A fine form with very double flowers.

C. speciosissimum. Syn. *C. fallax.* Java glory bean; Glory bush. An erect shrub reaching 5 ft., coming from southeast Asia. It is grown for its superb upright trusses of bright scarlet flowers with long stamens. The 6–10 in., heart-shaped leaves are borne on long, white-hairy stalks.

C. x speciosum. Glory bower. A summer-flowering hybrid between *C. splendens* and *C. thomsoniae.* It is a climbing plant with deep green leaves, and loose clusters of rosy-violet flowers each carried within a pink calyx.

C. splendens. A strong-growing shrub from West Africa with shining, heart-shaped leaves and summer-borne, pendant clusters of bright scarlet flowers.

C. thomsoniae. Bleeding heart vine. A climbing shrub from West Africa which has thin, ovate leaves with a quilted but shiny surface, and clusters of crimson flowers contrasting beautifully with the white calyx which becomes pink as it ages. They are at their best in spring.

C. ugandense. Blue glory bower. A scrambling shrub with bright green, ovate leaves and upright clusters of blue-violet flowers with conspicuous blue stamens which open through winter and spring.

Clianthus

LEGUMINOSAE. A small genus of shrubs, comprising only 3 species. They have long leaves cut into a number of small leaflets and basically, typical pea flowers, but made remarkable by the large size of the upper petals and the elongated keel, like a long beak. They require full sun and a minimum temperature of 50°F (10°C). Water only when the compost feels dry. Propagate by seed or cuttings.

C. formosus. Syn. *C. dampieri.* Glory pea. In Australia where it is found wild, it is a prostrate shrub, but for indoor cultivation is best raised annually from seed and grown in a hanging basket. The stems and leaves are silky, white-hairy, and the brilliant scarlet flowers of 3–4 in., each with a shiny, black bulge, are carried in showy, erect clusters in summer.

C. puniceus. Parrot bill; Kaka beak. A slender, erect, or semi-scrambling shrub from New Zealand with finely dissected, evergreen leaves, and clusters of 4–6 pendant flowers which are brilliant red and 3–4 in. in length.

Clitorea

LEGUMINOSAE.

C. ternatea. A member of a genus of 40 evergreen plants, many of which, like this widespread tropical species, are twining plants. This species can reach 15 ft. in the wild. Its leaves are divided into 3–5 oval leaflets, and the 1 in. solitary flowers are a clear blue with darker markings. They open in succession through the summer. Grow in full sun with a minimum temperature of 61°F (16°C). Water freely. Propagate by seed.

Clivia

AMARYLLIDACEAE. Three South African species make up this genus, and two make fine pot plants. They have broad, strap-shaped, evergreen leaves rising from the base and make strong clumps. The

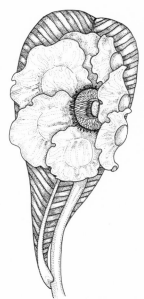

sturdy, flattened, flowering stems arise from these and bear lily-like flowers. Keep in a minimum temperature of 45°F (7°C) in winter. At this time give little water, but keep the compost just moist when the plant is growing and flowering, and at a temperature around 60°F (15°C). Considerable shade is tolerated. Propagate by division or seed.

C. x cyrtanthifolia. This hybrid between *C. miniata* and *C. nobilis* is generally of similar growth form to the former, but has narrow flowers which are borne on pendant stalks.

C. miniata. Syn. *Imantophyllum miniatum.* Kaffir lily. The leaves of this species reach 1½–2 ft., and the 2 in.-long, yellow to red flowers are carried in rounded heads of 12–20 blooms. A number of color forms are grown, and all make very good house plants.

C. m. 'Striata'. A form with variegated leaves.

C. nobilis. Green-tip Kaffir lily. The flower clusters of this species are made up of 30–50 pendant flowers, each 1–2 in. in length. They are a salmon-red with green-tipped petals, and open through summer.

Clusia

GUTTIFERAE. A large genus of 145 species of evergreen trees and shrubs from the Americas. They have handsome, large, leathery leaves and attractive flowers. Grow in light shade with a minimum temperature of 61°F (16°C) and water freely. Propagate by cuttings.

C. grandiflora. An epiphytic shrub with 12 in., dark green, leathery leaves, and small spikes of about 4 wide-open flowers up to 5 in. across. Each has 8 white petals which have a raised central circle and frilled edges. *(illus. left)*

C. rosea. Autograph tree; Fat pork tree. This 7–20 ft. shrub has long, oval, fleshy leaves tapering to the stem, and large, rose-pink flowers which open in summer.

C. r. 'Aureo-variegata'. Monkey-apple tree. In this distinctive form, the leaves are variegated with paler green and yellow streaks.

Clytostoma

BIGNONIACEAE.

C. callistegioides. This South American climber is one of 12 members of the genus. It has evergreen leaves, each having 2 separate leaflets, and a tendril between. The tubular, foxglove-shaped flowers are 2 in. long and pale purple with yellow markings. They are borne in spring and summer in small clusters. Grow in light shade, and maintain a minimum temperature of 45°F (7°C). Water freely. Propagate by cuttings.

Cobaea

COBAEACEAE.

C. scandens. Cup and saucer creeper; Cathedral bells. A rampant climber from South America, belonging to a genus of 18 species. It is perennial, but is best treated as an annual, and is still capable of reaching 20 ft. in one season though can easily be kept smaller. It has ovate, green leaves which are often irregular at the base. In late summer, bell-like flowers emerge sitting in a broad saucer-like calyx. They open pale green, and darken to purple as they mature. Keep a minimum temperature of 45°F (7°C), and water freely. Propagate by seed. *(illus. above)*

59

Coccoloba

POLYGONACEAE.

C. uvifera. Seagrape. One of a genus containing 150 species, of which this 20 ft. tree, commonly found on tropical American shores, makes a decorative plant for a pot or tub. It has glossy, leathery leaves which are rounded and have distinctively marked veins – pink when young, cream when older. The small, white flowers are followed by reddish-purple berries but only appear on mature specimens. Keep in a minimum temperature of 61°F (16°C), and only light shade. Water freely. Propagate by cuttings.

Coccothrinax

PALMAE.

C. argentata. Florida silver palm. One of 50 species in the genus, this American palm, which can reach 20 ft. in the wild, will remain at about 3 ft. in pots, making a very decorative specimen. The fan-shaped leaves have very narrow leaflets, green below and with a silvery sheen above. Maintain a minimum temperature of 45°F (7°C), light shade in summer, and keep the compost just moist at all times. Propagate by seeds in spring.

Cocculus

MENISPERMACEAE.

C. laurifolius. One of a small genus of 11 species. This evergreen Himalayan shrub will reach 15 ft., but can be kept small by pruning. It has long, pointed, shining green leaves, and bears clusters of small, white flowers on larger specimens followed by black berries. Keep in a minimum temperature of 50°F (10°C), in full sun, and water freely. Propagage by cuttings.

Codiaeum

EUPHORBIACEAE.

C. variegatum pictum. Croton. One of a genus of 15 species of evergreen shrubs of which this is the only one commonly cultivated. It makes a showy foliage plant, but is not easy to keep at its best in the home, needing a minimum temperature of at least 61°F (16°C), high humidity, frequent watering, and good light, though not direct midday sun if it is to produce its finest colors. Many cultivars have been raised. Propagate by cuttings if bottom heat can be provided.

C. v. p. 'Aucubaefolium'. Aucuba leaf croton. A form with the long, ovate, firm textured leaves, blotched with yellow.

C. v. p. 'Imperialis'. Apple-leaf croton. A neat plant with broad, ovate leaves which are largely yellow, becoming pinker with age, and having a dark green midrib and margin, which in their turn become purplish.

C. v. p. 'Norwood Beauty'. Oakleaf croton. A long-established form, the leaves lobed like an oak at the base, but with a long, finger-like segment at the tip. It is dark green with coppery-bronze shading and yellow veins.

C. v. p. 'Punctatum Aureum'. Miniature croton. A small plant with long, very narrow, dark green leaves, spotted with yellow.

C. v. p. 'Reidii'. In this form, the long, oval leaves are dark green with yellowish veins becoming pink, then red with age.

Coelogyne

ORCHIDACEAE. A large genus of about 200 species of orchids, some from tropical regions, others from upland forests. The latter species make the best house plants. All are epiphytic and have somewhat angular pseudobulbs bearing spear-shaped leaves and large fragrant flowers. Maintain a minimum temperature of 45°F (7°C), water freely, and keep in shade. Propagate by division.

C. barbata. A Himalayan species with 2 long, narrow leaves up to 18 in. in length rising from each egg-shaped pseudobulb. The large, pure white flowers are 2–3 in. across, with the lip fringed and marked with deep brown. They are borne on long, erect or arching spikes between autumn and spring.

C. corymbosa. From the Himalayas, this summer-to-autumn-flowering species has short, ovate leaves up to 6 in. in length, borne in pairs from oblong pseudobulbs. The erect flower spikes carry 3–5 creamy-white, fragrant blooms, each about 2 in. across, with yellow and brown markings on lip and throat.

C. cristata. Also from the Himalayas, the rounded pseudobulbs each carry 2 narrow leaves up to 12 in. long. The spikes of 3–8 fragrant flowers are pendant, each bloom white with a crystalline texture, the petals slightly wavy, and the lip marked with gold. They are produced from winter to spring.

C. elata. Also from the Himalayas, having longer, angular pseudobulbs and twin leaves which are up to 12 in. in length and narrow. The flower spike is held erect, but curves over when in full bloom. It bears 4–10 waxy, white flowers, each 2 in. across and with yellow markings on the lip.

C. massangeana. A species with a wide range throughout southeast Asia which makes an excellent plant for a hanging basket. The rather pear-shaped pseudobulbs carry pairs of 18 in. leaves, and the pendant flower spikes have up to 20 fragrant flowers, each pale yellow with dark brown and white markings on the lip. They are open mostly in summer, but will also produce blooms at other seasons.

60

C. mooreana. A species from Vietnam, remarkable for its beautifully glossy 10–15 in.-long leaves which are borne in pairs on short, furrowed pseudobulbs. The 3 in., fragrant flowers are snow-white with a golden marking on the lip, and are borne in an erect spike of up to 8 flowers in spring and summer.

Coffea

RUBIACEAE.

C. arabica. Coffee. One of a genus comprising 40 species of shrubs or small trees including the familiar coffee. It has wavy-edged, 3–6 in., oval leaves which are evergreen and shiny, and clusters of pure white flowers followed by red, cherry-like fruit containing the coffee "beans." It makes a decorative plant for a large pot or tub, requiring a minimum temperature of 61°F (16°C), and frequent watering. Propagate by cuttings. *(illus.)*

Coleus

LABIATAE. A genus of 150 tropical species. Of these only a few are in cultivation and are grown either for their multi-colored foliage, or for their spikes of small, but colorful flowers. Grow in sun with a minimum temperature of 61°F (16°C), and water freely. Propagate by cuttings or seed.
C. blumei. Painted nettle. A brilliantly colored foliage plant from Java up to 2 ft. in height, having nettle-like leaves which are patterned and variegated in shades of red, orange, yellow, and white. Many named cultivars have been raised, and seed-strains which come largely true to type are also available. The spikes of small, blue flowers are best pinched out to make the plants more leafy.
C. b. verschaffeltii. A larger-leaved variety with multi-colored leaves, purple in the center, then red, and margined with green.
C. frederici. A tall annual or biennial from central Africa reaching 4 ft., having broadly ovate, toothed leaves and branched spikes of fragrant, blue

flowers which open in winter. Propagate by seed.
C. thyrsoides. An East African perennial species having long, ovate, toothed leaves and large, branched spikes of bright blue flowers, opening in winter. Propagate by cuttings.

Columnea

Goldfish plants. GESNERIACEAE. A large genus of 200 tropical American species which are epiphytes and are superb as hanging basket plants. They have entire, dark green leaves, usually closely hairy, and tubular flowers opening at the mouth to make a long, hood-like upper lip. Grow in a moisture retaining mixture, preferably part sphagnum, maintain a minimum temperature of 61°F (16°C), and keep shaded. Water freely. Propagate by cuttings in summer.
C. allenii. A dainty, trailing plant from Panama. The flexuous stems carry pairs of small, dark green leaves and 3 in., orange-red flowers in summer and autumn.
C. arguta. From Panama, this species produces pendant stems which can reach 5 in. in length. They are densely clothed with ovate, waxy-textured leaves, and in autumn bear along their length a profusion of brilliant, orange-red flowers which are $2\frac{1}{2}$ in. across at the mouth.
C. x banksii. A hybrid between *C. oerstediana* and *C. schiedeana*, it is a showy plant having arching stems and small, ovate leaves, green above and red beneath, and in winter, orange-scarlet flowers with a long, slender tube opening to a yellow-marked mouth.
C. gloriosa. This Costa Rican species is a truly superb sight when in full bloom. The trailing stems have pairs of velvety leaves, the red-brown, hairy surface giving a decorative effect and an excellent foil for the scarlet flowers, 2–3 in. long, and marked yellow in the throat. They are borne most freely through the winter, but some are on the plant almost throughout the year.
C. linearis. A shrubby species from Costa Rica with erect stems, which makes a good pot plant. The glossy leaves are up to $3\frac{1}{2}$ in. long and very narrow, and the long, tubular flowers are rose-pink and open in spring.
C. microphylla. Small-leaved goldfish vine. A handsome trailing plant from Costa Rica with small, rounded leaves which are copper-colored. The $2\frac{1}{2}$–3 in.-long, scarlet flowers have a yellow base and open through winter and spring.
C. oerstediana. A rather similar plant to *C. microphylla*, also from Costa Rica, but with shiny, almost hairless leaves and russet-orange flowers which open in spring.
C. x 'Stavanger'. Norse fire plant. A fine hybrid

between *C. microphylla* and *C. x vedrariensis*. The pendant stems bear pairs of rounded, shiny, almost fleshy leaves, and in late spring 3–4 in., erect flowers, deepening from orange at the base to a brilliant red at the mouth.

C. x 'Vega'. Goldfish bush. A hybrid between *C. x* 'Stavanger' and *C. x vedrariensis*, it has wiry stems, at first erect, then arching over and bearing small, ovate leaves. The flowers which are also erect, are scarlet and open in spring. It should be grown in a pot.

Commelina

COMMELINACEAE.

C. benghalensis. Indian day flower. A tropical Asian plant, belonging to a genus comprising 230 species. It has a creeping form of growth and 2–3 in., gray–green leaves on somewhat succulent stems. The 2-petalled flowers are bright blue, and open from spring to autumn, each lasting only a day. Grow in a minimum temperature of 61°F (16°C), in good light, and water when the compost feels dry. Propagate by seed, cuttings or division.

C. b. 'Variegata'. The form most frequently grown, having white-striped and margined leaves.

Conophyllum

AIZOACEAE.

C. grande. King pins. A succulent plant from South Africa, one of a genus comprising 270 species. The thick, fleshy leaves reach 8 in. and are borne in pairs which open to allow the next leaves or the shining-white flowers to appear. Maintain a minimum temperature of 50°F (10°C), and keep in full sun. Water only when the compost feels dry. Propagate by seed.

Conophytum

Cone plant. AIZOACEAE. A genus of 270 South African succulent plants similar to *Lithops*. They are all very small, the fat plant body formed by two thick leaves which are fused together except for a small opening where the daisy-like flower appears. Grow in full sun with a minimum temperature of 50°F (10°C), water only when the compost feels dry, and give a dry resting period in summer. Propagate by seed or cuttings.

C. bilobum. The pale, green-gray plant body is from 1–1½ in. high, and opens at the top to 2 lobes, from between which yellow flowers, 1 in. across, appear in autumn. Give a dry resting period in spring. *(illus.)*

C. calculus. A tiny species, the oval plant only ½–¾ in. high. The yellow flowers have brown-tipped petals and emerge in autumn.

C. scitulum. The ½–¾ in. plant bodies are gray-green

with a reddish-brown pattern of lines. The autumn-borne flowers are white.

C. simile. The grayish-green plant bodies of this ¾ in. species are dotted with dark green and bear their yellow flowers in winter.

C. truncatum. The rounded, ½–¾ in. plant bodies are bluish-green with darker green markings, and the white or pale yellow flowers open in autumn.

Coprosma

RUBIACEAE.

C. baueri. Mirror plant. A genus of 90 species of which this New Zealand shrub makes an attractive large pot plant. It has roundish, 2–3 in. leaves which are glossy and firm textured. Male and female flowers are on different plants, so a female plant is necessary to get the orange-yellow berries. Keep in light shade with a minimum temperature of 50°F (10°C), and water freely, never allowing the compost to become dry. Propagate by cuttings.

C. b. 'Marginata'. A decorative form, the margins of the leaves creamy-white.

Cordyline

AGAVACEAE. A genus of 15 species of evergreen trees and shrubs often erroneously called dracaenas. When young they make elegant pot plants, somewhat like young palms in appearance. The species have varied requirements in cultivation, but apart from *C. terminalis*, most need a minimum temperature of 50°F (10°C), some shade, and plentiful watering. Propagate by seeds, suckers, or air-layering (mossing).

C. australis. Syn. *Dracaena australis*. Cabbage tree; Grass palm. A New Zealand species which, although often reaching 30 ft. in the wild, remains below 5 ft. for many years when confined to a pot. The single stem carries a dense head of long, narrow, leathery leaves 1 to 2 ft. in length and bronze-green in color. The clusters of white flowers rarely occur on pot plants. A minimum temperature of 45°F (7°C) is sufficient for this species. *(illus.)*

C. stricta. Syn. *Dracaena congesta*. A decorative species from Australia with narrow-arching, sword-shaped leaves which are reddish when young, becoming greener as they age.

C. terminalis. Tree of Kings. Widespread throughout southeast Asia and the islands of Polynesia, this is an elegant species having bronze-red, spear-shaped leaves. It bears clusters of lilac flowers when quite small. It needs a minimum temperature of 60°F (15°C) to thrive well.

C. t. 'Firebrand'. A compact form with reddish-purple leaves which have a satiny sheen.

C. t. 'Red Eagle'. A form with pinkish-red margins to the leaves.

C. t. 'Tricolor'. The green leaves are variegated with streaks of cream, pink, and red.

Correa

RUTACEAE. A genus of 11 evergreen shrubs, all from Australia and Tasmania. They have small, ovate leaves, and long, tubular, showy flowers. Grow in light shade with a minimum temperature of 40°F (5°C), and water freely. Propagate by cuttings.

C. x harrisii. Australian fuchsia. A hybrid of *C. speciosa* and rather similar to that species, but making a neater plant.

C. speciosa. The parent of many hybrids, this spring-flowering plant will reach 6–8 ft. when mature. It is grown for its 1 in. long, scarlet, tubular flowers which have yellow, protruding anthers.

C. s. backhousiana. This shrub has neat, oval leaves which are rusty-haired beneath, and small clusters of long, greenish-yellow, tubular flowers opening in spring. (*illus. right*)

Coryphantha

CACTACEAE. A genus of 64 pincushion cacti, all from North America. They are rounded or cylindrical, with grooved and starry-spined areoles. The flowers open from late summer through autumn. Grow in sunshine with a minimum temperature of 50°F (10°C), and water as soon as the compost feels dry. Keep dry during the winter. Propagate by seed.

C. bumamma. Starry ball. A globular species up to 6 in. in height. The few bluish-green tubercles are woolly when young and bear 5–8 brownish spines. The flowers are large and yellow.

C. clava. Syn. *Mammillaria clava*. A cylindrical species taking many years to reach its full 12 in. The tubercles are cone-shaped and woolly, and each bears about 7 yellowish spines. The large flowers are pale yellow, red-flushed beneath, showing red in bud.

C. desertii. Syn. *Mammillaria desertii*. A most attractive species having pale blue-green, cylindrical bodies, with white spines mixed with red-tipped black ones. The deep pinkish-red flowers open in spring.

C. echinus. A rounded plant, the cone-shaped tubercles bearing white spines. The flowers are yellow.

C. elephantidens. A globular species up to 5 in. in height with blue-green tubercles bearing brownish spines and white wool. The large flowers are 4 in. across and rose-pink.

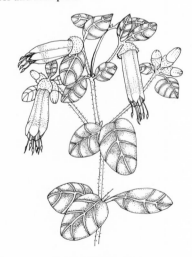

C. erecta. A cylindrical species, the tubercles woolly when young and bearing up to 14 spines. The large flowers are yellow.

C. macromeris. A rounded, gray-green plant up to 8 in. in height, covered with knob-like protuberances, each with a woolly areole bearing both black and white spines. The flowers, which do not open completely flat, are red.

C. radians. The globular stems of this species are green and have conical, woolly tubercles and up to 20 comb-like spines from each areole. The 1½–2 in. flowers are yellow, the petals flushed reddish at the base and tips.

Costus

COSTACEAE. Formally included in *Zingiberaceae*, this genus comprises 150 species of tropical plants, many of which have attractively colored foliage and showy flowers. Grow in a minimum temperature of 61°F (16°C) in light shade, watering freely. Propagate by stem cuttings.

C. igneus. Fiery costus. A beautiful Brazilian species with maroon stems carrying broadly ovate, glossy leaves which are green above and reddish beneath. The orange-scarlet flowers are 2½ in. across, and are borne in a short, erect spike.

C. malortieanus. Syn. *C. zebrinus.* Emerald spiral ginger. A showy plant from Costa Rica which can reach 3 ft. It has ovate to rounded, fleshy leaves banded with 2 shades of green and silky with silvery hairs. The dense, cone-like spikes of yellow flowers are banded with reddish-brown and open in July.

C. speciosus. Spiral ginger. A rather variable species from southeast Asia which can reach 9 ft. in the wild, but kept in a pot it remains much smaller than this. The reed-like stems carry 6–8 in., glossy green, long, ovate leaves, and dense spikes of white or red flowers with an orange-red lip.

Cotyledon

CRASSULACEAE. A genus of 40 species, all from Africa. They have thickened, fleshy stems and leaves, the latter sometimes cylindrical, sometimes flattened. The colorful, tubular flowers are borne in clusters in summer. All need full sun and a minimum temperature of 40°F (5°C) in winter. Water only when the compost feels dry. Propagate by cuttings or seed.

C. barbeyi. Hoary navel-wort. A tall, shrubby species having large, fleshy, spatula-shaped leaves up to 5 in. in length. The 2 ft. flower spike bears nodding, green and orange-red flowers.

C. ladismithensis. Cub's paws. An erect, branching plant with 1–2 in., rounded, fleshy, white-haired leaves, the end of each with a few small, deep red teeth. The small flowers are brownish-red.

C. orbiculata. A tall species, reaching 1½–3 ft., with pairs of pale gray-green, spoon-shaped leaves and bright orange flowers borne in small clusters on a long stalk.

C. o. oophylla. A similar plant with small, egg-shaped leaves.

C. paniculata. Botterboom. A 6 ft. tree in the wild, this curious succulent with a thick, swollen trunk is slow-growing in pots. The few stiff branches bear clusters of gray-green, spoon-shaped leaves at their tips. The red flowers have green stripes.

C. undulata. Silver ruffles. A beautiful species having fan-shaped, silvery-gray leaves, which have a white-frilled edge and are held stiffly upright on a thick, fleshy stem. The orange-red flowers are pendant and borne on 1 ft. stems. *(illus.)*

Crassula

Jade plants. CRASSULACEAE. A genus comprising 300 very varied succulent plants, some of which are small and ground-hugging, others 12 ft. shrubs. They make intriguing house-plants with their decorative shapes, and most are not difficult to grow. Almost all prefer full sun and a minimum temperature of 50°F (10°C). Water only when the compost feels dry. Propagate by seed, cuttings, or with some species, separation of plantlets.

C. arborescens. Silver dollar; Silver jade plant. Although in the wild this can make a 12 ft. tree, it grows very slowly when confined to a pot. The roundly triangular leaves are gray-green with red spots on the upper surface, and a red margin. The summer-borne, pinkish flowers are rarely seen.

C. argentea. See *C. portulacea.*

C. cooperi. A dainty, mat-forming species with crowded tufts of tiny, narrow leaves which are pale green, with reddish, sunken dots above. The pale pink, starry flowers are borne in summer.

C. cornuta. A small, mealy, grayish-white plant, the stems completely covered by the thick, rounded leaves which are packed tightly together and partly joined. The small flowers are white.

C. dubia. The paddle-shaped, gray-green leaves are flat above and rounded beneath, and carried in a

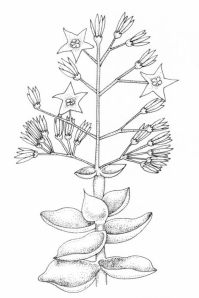

semi-erect position. They have narrow, red margins and the surfaces are white-mealy. Flowers are rarely seen.

C. falcata. Propeller plant. A shrubby species up to 3 ft. in the wild, with thick, 3–4 in., sickle-shaped, gray leaves, which are packed closely above each other. From them rises a long stem bearing flat-topped, branched clusters of scarlet flowers. A very spectacular plant.

C. geopodioides. An 8 in., bushy plant, the stems closely covered with tiny, scale-like leaves. The yellow flowers, which are also very small, are almost hidden among the leaves.

C. hemisphaerica. Arab's turban. A low-growing species, the 1 in., rounded leaves are almost semicircular and are partly joined to give a tight, dome-like mound, the leaves decreasing in size to the top. The flowers are white.

C. lactea. Tailor's patch. A shrubby species with pairs of broadly ovate, green leaves dotted with white. The large clusters of starry-white flowers are borne in late winter. *(illus.)*

C. lycopodioides. Toy cypress. An erect species, with triangular, scaly leaves which overlap each other and are tightly pressed to the stems. The whole effect is remarkably like a club moss. The tiny flowers are white.

C. portulacea. Syn. *C. argentea.* A small shrub with erect stems bearing red-edged, roundish to spoon-shaped leaves and clusters of pinkish, starry flowers in late winter and early spring.

C. rupestris. A small, prostrate plant with pairs of thick, gray-green, ovate to triangular leaves which are rounded beneath and edged with brown. The small flowers are yellow and open in spring.

C. schmidtii. A small, mat-forming plant with flowering stems up to 3 in. in height. It has small, narrow leaves, joined in pairs at the base, and clusters of carmine-red flowers which open throughout winter. They have a light almond fragrance.

C. teres. Rattlesnake tail. A small, erect species forming 2–4 in. columns of tightly overlapping leaves, each with a transparent margin. The yellowish-white flowers are fragrant.

C. tetragona. Miniature pine tree. A small, upright shrub with cylindrical leaves, carried horizontally and joined at the base into pairs. The flowers are small and white.

C. 'Tricolor Jade'. An attractive hybrid between *C. portulacea* and *C. lactea*, this upright plant has green, rounded, ovate leaves, strongly variegated with white and pink. Keep in light shade.

x Crinodonna memoria-corsii

Syn. *Amarcrinum howardii.* AMARYLLIDACEAE. A hybrid between *Amaryllis bella-donna* and *Crinum moorei*, it has the pink, trumpet-shaped flowers of the former species, but rather larger in size, and the large, long-lasting leaves of the latter. Flowering in autumn, it needs a large tub to do well. Keep a minimum temperature of 50°F (10°C), and water freely while growing and flowering. Propagate by offsets.

Crinum

Swamp lily. AMARYLLIDACEAE. A genus of about 100 bulbous plants, most of which have long, strap-shaped leaves and striking, funnel-shaped flowers. Grow in light shade, keeping a minimum temperature of 50°F (10°C) in winter, and watering infrequently. When in growth, water freely. Propagate by offsets or seeds.

C. giganteum. Giant spider lily. The true plant of this name is a West African plant, but in cultivation the name is used for this 3–4 ft. species, which has clusters of funnel-shaped, white flowers up to 6 in. in length, opening at the mouth to 3–4 in., strap-shaped petals giving a spidery effect. They are borne in summer.

C. moorei. Swamp lily. A South African species with 2–3 ft. leaves and rose-pink, lily-like flowers borne in a cluster on the top of a 12–15 in., stiff stem. They open from late summer to autumn.

C. x powellii. A long-established hybrid between *C. bulbispermum*, a South African plant, and *C. moorei*. It has large, 3–4 fts., deep green leaves, and a cluster of up to 10 beautiful, rose-pink, trumpet-shaped flowers, each up to 4 in. long. They are borne on a stiff 2–3 ft. stem and give a succession of bloom in summer.

Crocus

IRIDACEAE. Although mostly hardy in temperate climates, a few spring-flowering members of this genus of some 100 species are grown as pot plants, mostly cultivars of *C. vernus* and *C. chrysanthus*. The familiar cup-shaped flowers and grassy leaves appear in January and February. The corms must be potted in autumn, and need to be kept cool and dark, preferably out of doors, until the shoots are well through. Then bring into a cool room with a temperature around 50°F (10°C). Even when flowering do not keep too warm, 60°F (15°C) being ideal by day, 45–50°F (7–10°C) by night. The corms may be planted in the garden afterwards.

Crossandra

ACANTHACEAE. A genus of 50 shrubby species with showy, tubular flowers and handsome, dark green leaves. Grow in moderate shade with a minimum temperature of 60°F (15°C), and water freely. Propagate by seed or cuttings.

C. nilotica. An erect, 2 ft. plant from East Africa with small, ovate leaves up to 4 in. in length, and dense spikes of brick-red flowers, the spike lengthening as they open through spring and summer.

C. pungens. From Tanzania, this 2 ft. species has distinctive, wavy-edged, oblong leaves which have clear-cream veining. The light orange flowers are borne in dense, leafy clusters in summer.

C. undulata. Syn. *C. infundibuliformis.* Firecracker flower. An Indian species which in the wild can reach 3 ft., though always smaller in pots. It has shiny, 3–5 in., oval leaves and through summer, striking orange-red flowers, opening flat at the mouth with waved petals.

Crotalaria

LEGUMINOSAE.

C. juncea. Sun hemp. An attractive annual from the tropics belonging to a genus of 550 species. It makes an upright plant, with long, narrow leaves the whole covered with silvery, silky hairs. The rich bright yellow, pea-like flowers are borne on a long spike in late summer and autumn. Grow in full sun with a minimum temperature of 45°F (7°C). Propagate by seed.

Cryptanthus

Earthstars. BROMELIACEAE. A genus of 32 species from Brazil, all with very decorative, rippled leaves which are borne in a rosette and spread out into an almost prostrate star. They require a peat compost and a minimum temperature of 60°F (15°C), with light shade. Water only when the compost feels dry. Propagate by offsets.

C. acaulis. Green earth star. A small plant, the rosettes measuring only 4–6 in. across, and the leaves green with wavy margins and gray-flaking on the surface.

C. a. 'Rubra'. Red earth star. A form with red-brown leaves and a fawn meal on the surface.

C. bivittatus. Rose stripe star. This species has strap-shaped leaves in two shades of green, tinted with pinkish-red. They narrow to a point at the tip and arch outwards from the center to form a 6–10 in. rosette.

C. b. minor. Miniature rose stripe star. A very small form, no more than 6 in. across. The striped markings are very sharp and the redness is intensified in strong light.

C. bromelioides. A large species, the rosette 18–24 in. across. The arching leaves are narrow, tapered, and dark green with a coppery sheen.

C. b. 'Tricolor'. The form most commonly seen, with the narrow leaves banded green, ivory-white, and carmine-red.

C. fosterianus. Pheasant leaf. One of the largest species, the rosettes of stiff, strap-shaped leaves up to 30 in. across. Each is crossbanded with stripes of gray scales on a copper-green background.

C. zonatus. Zebra plant. Somewhat similar to *C. forsterianus* having 10–20 in. rosettes of leaves banded with light brown on a copper-green.

C. z. 'Fuscus'. Syn. 'Zebrinus'. A particularly fine form, the crossbanding on the leaves being silvery.

x Cryptbergia rubra

BROMELIACEAE. A hybrid between *Cryptanthus babianus* and *Billbergia nutans* which has a strong, arching rosette of red-tinted, spiny-margined leaves, darker in the center and redder when kept in good light. Cultivate as for *Cryptanthus*.

Ctenanthe

MARANTACEAE. A genus of 15 Brazilian plants, grown for their decorative oblong leaves which are carried on slender, branched stems. Grow in shade with a minimum temperature of 60°F (15°C), and water freely. Propagate by division or cuttings in summer.

C. lubbersiana. The 8 in., oval leaves of this species are variegated with creamy-yellow. They are carried on erect stems, making a low bush about 18 in. in height.

C. oppenheimiana. A strong-growing plant which can eventually reach 4–6 ft., but not in pots. It has firm-textured, long, oval leaves which are dark green with regular, silvery-white markings between the veins. They are red beneath.

C. o. 'Tricolor'. A very colorful smaller form with

narrower leaves haphazardly variegated with green, silver, and white, the red coloration of the reverse side showing through to give a pink tint.

Cunonia

CUNONIACEAE.
C. capensis. African red alder. An attractive South African tree, the only member of its genus, reaching 40 ft. in the wild, but making a decorative shrub when confined to a pot. The leaves are cut into several pairs of leaflets and are glossy green with reddish stalks. The fluffy, white flower spikes are only seen on large plants. Grow in light shade with a minimum temperature of 50°F (10°C), and water only when the compost feels dry. Propagate by seeds in spring or cuttings in summer.

Cuphea

LYTHRACEAE. A large genus comprising 250 species of small shrubs, all from subtropical America. They make pretty pot plants. Grow in sun, keeping a minimum temperature of 50°F (10°C), and water freely. Propagate by seeds in spring or cuttings in summer.
C. hyssopifolia. False heather; Elfin herb. A dainty, little shrub, usually 12–18 in. in height, with slender, wiry branches bearing small, heathery leaves. The starry flowers are purplish-pink, each carried inside a green calyx and abundantly borne through spring and summer.
C. miniata. This 1–2 ft. shrub which can easily be kept smaller, has narrowly ovate white, bristly-hairy leaves and solitary flowers which are pale scarlet and provide a mass of color from early summer to autumn.
C. platycentra. Syn. *C. ignea.* Cigar flower. The long, narrow leaves of this 1 ft. plant show up the colorful tubular flowers. These are made up of a calyx only, the scarlet tube opening to white at the mouth and rimmed with darker red.

Cupressus

CUPRESSACEAE. Of the 15 members of this genus, the following two respond well to pot or tub culture, making very decorative specimen plants when young. Grow in sun with a minimum temperature of 50°F (10°C). Water only when the compost feels dry. Propagate by seeds or cuttings.
C. glabra. Syn. *C. arizonica.* 'Pyramidalis'. A blue-green, erect but compact form of the Arizona cypress which is valuable for effect, the tiny, scale-like leaves, often longer and narrow at first, covering the twigs completely.
C. cashmiriana. A compact species with gray-green,

elegant, fern-like branchlets which are pendant from the erect stem.

Curculigo

HYPOXIDACEAE.
C. capitulata. Syn. *C. recurvata.* Palm grass. One of the 10 species of this genus, formerly part of *Amaryllidaceae.* A native of Java, it makes a decorative foliage plant with 3 ft.-long sword-shaped leaves which arch outwards. The small, yellow flowers are inconspicuous. Grow in light shade with a minimum temperature of 60°F (15°C), and water freely. Propagate by division.

Cussonia

ARALIACEAE.
C. spicata. Spiked cabbage tree. A decorative foliage plant from South Africa, one of 25 species belonging to this genus. It has dark green, leathery leaves which are deeply cut and lobed into an intricate pattern, rather resembling a rather cleverly cut-out green snowflake. Give full sun, a minimum temperature of 50°F (10°C), and water freely. Propagate by seed.

Cyanotis

COMMELINACEAE. A genus containing about 50 species of creeping or climbing plants. The narrow leaves and somewhat fleshy stems are covered with fine, short hair. Grow in full sun with a minimum temperature of 50°F (10°C), water only when the compost feels dry, and propagate by cuttings.
C. kewensis. Teddy-bear vine. An attractive species with stems and leaves covered with short, reddish-brown hair, almost obscuring their deep green coloration and red undersides. The winter- and spring-borne flowers are bright purple with 3 petals.
C. somaliensis. Pussy ears; Fuzzy ears. The sword-shaped leaves of this plant are fleshy and shiny above, but are covered, as are the stems, with long, white hairs. The spring-borne flowers are purplish-blue.

Cyathea

CYATHEACEAE. A genus containing some 600 species of tree fern, all of which are evergreen with fronds at the top of a trunk-like stem. Water is their most vital requirement as the roots must be kept constantly wet. A minimum temperature of 60°F (15°C) should be maintained, and some shade given. Propagate from spores.
C. arborea. A decorative species from Central America and the West Indies with very deeply dissected, finely toothed fronds.

conditions. It grows from a hard, flattened tuber, producing a tufted rosette of heart-shaped leaves which are dark green, and silver-patterned. The solitary flowers are borne on fleshy, reddish stems which uncurl as the shuttlecock-shaped blooms expand. These are purplish-pink in the true species, but are now available in a wide range of colors from white to red-purple. Keep a minimum temperature of 50°F (10°C), and if possible, no more than 65°F (18°C) by day when flowering. *(illus.)*

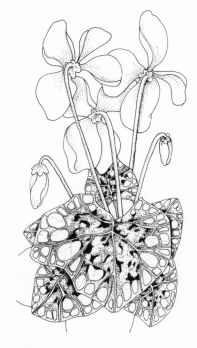

C. dealbata. Coming from New Zealand, the deeply cut fronds are green above and blue-white beneath. *(illus.)*

Cycas

Sago palms. CYCADACEAE. A genus comprising 20 species which are, in appearance, very like the ferns, having when mature, erect, trunk-like stems bearing a crown of stiff, frond-like leaves. When young, the leaves rise almost from soil level, giving a more typically palm-like look. Grow in light shade with a minimum temperature of 50°F (10°C), and water freely in summer, less at other times. Propagate by suckers.

C. circinalis. Fern palm; Crozier cycad. When mature in its native lands around the Indian Ocean, this cycad can reach 40 ft., but when young, the palm-like leaves rise from near ground level, forming a tuft of dark green, arching leaves, cut into narrow leaflets.

C. media. An Australian species, when mature making a tree, but when young a decorative, large, pot or tub plant. The leaves are cut into narrow segments, and arch outwards, producing a feathery effect.

C. revoluta. Sago palm. A slow-growing species from east Asia with tough, rather leathery leaves, having spine-tipped leaflets. Mature specimens produce a thick trunk.

Cyclamen

PRIMULACEAE.

C. persicum. One of a genus containing 15 plants all from the Mediterranean region. Some are hardy, but this species is not, though it prefers cool

C. p. giganteum. Syn. *C. p.* grandiflorum. A robust form with rounder leaves and wider petals.

C. p. g. 'Butterfly'. Syn. *C. p. papilio*. Coming in a wide range of colors, this form has frilled petals.

C. p. g. 'Flore Pleno'. Pink, double flowers distinguish this showy form.

C. p. g. 'Hallo'. Unusual, bright scarlet flowers.

C. p. g. 'White Swan'. A pure white-flowered cultivar.

Cycnoches

Swan orchids. ORCHIDACEAE. A genus containing 12 species of epiphytic orchids, all from tropical America. They have long pseudobulbs which carry 3–4 leaves, and large, long-lasting flowers which are borne on pendant spikes. Male and female flowers are different. Grow in a bark or sphagnum and osmunda compost with a minimum temperature of

60°F (15°C), and shade. Water freely.

C. egertonianum. A very beautiful species having
two distinct sorts of blooms. The male flowers are
2–2½ in. across, green with a purplish flush and
reflexed sepals and petals, the lip sometimes
similarly colored, but often white. Most remarkably
the column is greatly elongated and curved like a
swan's neck. The blooms are borne on 18 in.,
pendulous stems. The female flowers are larger and
fleshy in texture, yellow-green with a creamy-white
lip. The flowers open through autumn and winter.

C. loddigesii. The 4–5 in. flowers of this species are
borne in pendant spikes of up to 9 blooms. They
are fragrant and brownish-green, the fleshy lip
white or pale pink.

C. ventricosum. The fragrant, long-lasting 5 in.
blooms are waxy, with greenish-yellow petals and
sepals, and a white lip. The slender column is
curved over just like the neck of a swan. They are
borne in arching spikes from late summer to early
winter.

Cymbidium

ORCHIDACEAE. A favorite orchid genus containing
about 40 species. From these many thousands of
hybrids have been produced, from which plants
with bigger and better flowers are constantly being
raised. Most members of the genus have flask-
shaped pseudobulbs and strap-shaped leaves. The 3
sepals and 2 petals are similar, the third petal forms
the lip which is patterned in contrasting colors.
Grow in a bark or sphagnum and osmunda
compost. For most species a minimum temperature
of 50°F (10°C) is sufficient. Keep in shade and
water freely.

C. x alexanderi. A fine pink and white hybrid whose
name appears in many cultivars, notably *C. x
alexanderi* 'Westonbirt'. It is a robust plant,
throwing up arching flower sprays which can
exceed 3 ft. in length. Single blooms are 4–4½ in.
across, and the lip has a purple crescent on its
outer edge.

C. 'Balkis'. A strong-growing, white hybrid with a
colorful lip which has again been used in many
modern cultivars, of which the Pearl Balkis group
have a notably good texture.

C. dayanum. A ground-growing, tufted plant from
southeast Asia with slender, almost grassy leaves
and no pseudobulbs. The fragrant flowers, about
8–10 to a spike, are white, the petals and sepals
with a red central line and the lip purple with
yellow and white markings. They open in summer.

C. devonianum. The pseudobulbs of this Himalayan
species are almost hidden by the long, leathery,
blunt-tipped leaves. The 12 in. flower spike carries
from spring into summer, petals and sepals with

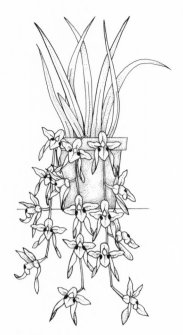

purple markings. The short lip is dark red-purple.
(illus.)

C. eburneum. This Indian and Burmese species, like
C. devonianum has leaves growing almost to the
base of the plant. They can reach 2 ft. in length and
are narrow. The fragrant, spring-borne flowers are
ivory-white, having the lip marked with pink and
purple around a central yellow disc. They are
carried singly or in pairs on 12 in. spikes.

C. ensifolium. This southeast Asian species has no
pseudobulbs and long, slender, almost grass-like
leaves. The fragrant blooms are usually light green
and are sometimes lined with red. The yellow-green
lip also has red markings. They are borne on erect,
12 in. stems in early summer.

C. findlaysonianum. The thick, leathery leaves of
this robust species from southeast Asia are 2–3 ft.
long and carried on short, stout, stem-like
pseudobulbs. The many-flowered spike is pendant,
and can reach 4 ft. in length. The individual blooms
are yellow-green, having the lip white in the center
with purple and yellow markings, and pink at the
sides. They open in spring and summer.

C. grandiflorum. An early winter-flowering species
from the Himalayas with 4–6 in. pseudobulbs
bearing 2 ft., narrow, pointed leaves. The large
flowers are 5 in. across, green with a yellow and
purple marked lip. They are carried on 7–12
flowered spikes which can exceed 2 ft. in length.

C. lowianum. A somewhat similar plant to *C.
grandiflorum* but with the 3 ft., arching, flower

spikes carrying up to 25 blooms from late winter to spring. These are smaller, being 3–4 in. across, and greenish-yellow with red veining. The lip is yellow, red, and white. A striking and fragrant species.

C. pumilum. A small species from China and Japan with 3–6 in. leaves, and the 9–12 in. flowering spikes carrying yellow and white blooms with reddish-brown markings. It is much used in hybridization to create a smaller race of cultivars more suitable for the average home. They open in late summer and early autumn.

C. tigrinum. An early summer-flowering plant from Burma, the leathery leaves up to 6 in. long and carried on small pseudobulbs. The green flowers are 4 in. across and marked with red spots, the lip yellow and brown striped, giving the plant its Latin name.

C. tracyanum. Somewhat similar to *C. grandiflorum*, with the flowering spikes up to 4 ft. in length and carrying 10–20 yellowish-green flowers, the petals and sepals marked with red dots and streaks, as is the yellow lip. They open in late autumn.

Cyperus

Umbrella plants. CYPERACEAE. A genus of about 550 species of grass-like plants, most of which grow in or by water. They have 3-angled stems, and inconspicuous brown, flowering spikelets with a rosette of leafy bracts beneath them, like the ribs of an umbrella, giving them their popular name. Grow in light shade with a minimum temperature of 50°F (10°C), and keep the compost very moist. Propagate by division or seed.

C. alternifolius. Umbrella plant. Coming from the western islands of the Indian Ocean, this tufted plant has long, narrow, arching leaves up to 2 ft. in height, with typical flower spikelets. It is best grown standing in a saucer of water.

C. a. gracilis. A dwarf form, only 12 in. high, coming from Australia.

C. a. 'Variegatus'. A white-striped form. Any all-green shoots should be removed.

C. diffusus elegans. Coming from Mauritius, this species has larger leaves, both basal and bracts, than *C. alternifolius*, all with a more arching habit.

C. d. 'Variegatus'. A variegated form with creamy-yellow striping.

C. esculentus. Chufa; Tiger nut. A grassy plant with a wide distribution in the old world. It produces nut-like, edible tubers. Keep drier than the other species.

Cyrtanthus

AMARYLLIDACEAE. A genus comprising 47 bulbous species from southern Africa. They have long, strap-shaped leaves, and long-stemmed clusters of tubular flowers, opening to 6 small, petal-like lobes at the mouth. Keep relatively cool, with a minimum temperature of 45°F (7°C), and water freely while in growth, allowing to become almost dry when the leaves begin to die down, starting again when new growth appears. Propagate by offsets.

C. mackenii. Bow-lily. A fragrant species, having ivory-white flowers with a 2 in., curving tube, borne in summer in clusters of 4–10, on a 1 ft. stem.

C. o'brienii. 6–8 nodding, pale scarlet flowers are borne on the purplish stems. They open in summer.

C. sanguineus. The 3–4 in. flowers of this distinctive species open in summer to 1 in. across at the throat, and are carried singly or in twos and rarely threes at the top of a 12 in. stem. Dry off completely while dormant.

Cyrtomium

ASPIDIACEAE.

C. falcatum. Syn. *Polystichum falcatum*. Fishtail fern. An attractive fern, one of 20 species belonging to the genus. It is widely distributed in southeast Asia and Hawaii, having ovate, slender-pointed leaflets carried on alternate sides of the central stalk to form the 2 ft.-long frond. The leaflets are dark green and of a firm, glossy texture. Keep in shade with a minimum temperature of 50°F (10°C), and water frequently. Propagate by spores or division.

C. f. 'Rochfordianum'. Holly fern. A very distinctive form, the fronds shorter and carried more densely. The leaflets are toothed and wavy-edged. A very tough plant.

Cytisus

Broom; Genista. LEGUMINOSAE. A genus of 25 shrubs with bright, pea-shaped flowers and small, dark green leaves. Many are hardy, but two make attractive pot plants. To keep them from becoming straggly, shear them over after flowering, and cut back any extra-long growths through the year. Keep in full sun with a winter minimum temperature of 45°F (7°C). Water only when the compost feels dry.

C. canariensis. Canary island broom; Genista. In its native Canary Islands, this broom will reach to 6 ft., and must be kept trimmed when grown in a pot. It has leaves cut into 3 small, silky leaflets and masses of bright yellow flowers borne in long spikes in spring.

C. x racemosus. A similar plant to *C. canariensis*, one of its parents, but neater and equally free-flowering.

D

Dais

THYMELAEACEAE.
D. cotinifolia. An 8–10 ft. shrub, occasionally a
tree in its native South Africa, but smaller in pots.
It is one of only 2 members of the genus and has
oval leaves up to 3 in. long, and erect clusters of
small, pale lilac flowers. Keep a minimum
temperature of 50°F (10°C), and in full sun. Water
only when the compost feels dry.

Dalechampia

EUPHORBIACEAE.
D. roezliana. Of the 110 species that belong to this
genus, this 4 ft. plant makes an attractive specimen.
It has long-oval, dark green leaves up to 6 in. in
length and petal less flowers. These are, however,
made showy by the 2 large, bright pinkish-red
bracts which sit under the flower. They require full
sun and a minimum temperature of 60°F (15°C).
Water only when the compost feels dry.

Daphne

THYMELAEACEAE. A genus of some 70 small
shrubs, most of which are hardy in temperate
climates. They have ovate leaves and clusters of
usually very fragrant flowers. The 2 species which
can be grown indoors are best in light shade with a
minimum temperature of 45°F (7°C). Propagate by
layers or cuttings.
D. bholua. An evergreen shrub from the Himalaya,
it has long, oval leaves, and short-stalked clusters of
purplish-pink, tubular flowers which are very
fragrant. They open in late winter and early spring.
D. odora. This evergreen shrub from China and
Japan has strongly fragrant, pinkish-red flowers,
borne in late winter and early spring in small
clusters.
D. o. 'Marginata'. A form having narrow, creamy
margins to the leaves.

Darlingtonia

SARRACENIACEAE.
D. californica. Syn. *Chrysamphora californica.*
Californian pitcher plant. A most curious
insectivorous plant, the only one of its genus,
coming from the western coast of the USA. It has
long leaves up to 3 ft. in height, but usually much
less in cultivation, pale green below, becoming
mottled with red above. They are joined at the
edges to make a tube and the wide top is arched
over to form a hood. From the front of this hangs
a purplish fang-like appendage, this has nectar-
secreting glands to attract insects in, and a network
of hairs to prevent them from getting out. Yellow
and purple flowers are carried on separate stems in
spring. The plants are best grown in peat or
sphagnum moss within an enclosed glass case. They
do best in a temperature of about 70°F (21°C) or
higher, but will stand short periods of cold.
Propagate by division or seed. *(illus.)*

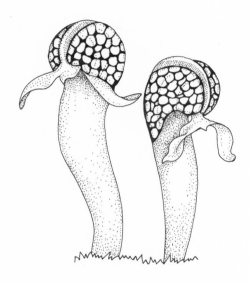

Dasylirion

AGAVACEAE.
D. acrotriche. Bear grass. A Mexican plant, one of a
genus comprising 18 species. In the wild, they carry
their rosettes of 3 ft.-long, narrow, spine-tipped
leaves at the top of a thick trunk, 5 ft. or more in
height. In cultivation the rosettes are usually seen at
ground level, the plants being replaced when they
get too large. The clusters of white flowers on long
stems are rarely, if ever, seen on pot plants. Grow
in full sun with a minimum temperature of 50°F
(10°C), and water only when the compost feels dry.
Propagate by seed.

Datura

Angel's trumpets. SOLANACEAE. A genus of 10
species with a widespread distribution. Many are
large shrubs which make good tub plants with a
long flowering season, but they are somewhat big
for the average home. They have large, ovate leaves
and striking, hanging trumpets which can reach
12 in. in length. They prefer full light and a
minimum temperature of 55°F (13°C), and need
watering freely. Propagate by seed or cuttings.

D. cornigera. Fully grown, this Mexican shrub can reach 10 ft. It has long, pointed leaves and in early autumn, cream or white flowers, the 5 lobes at the mouth ending in long, slightly incurved points. *(illus.)*

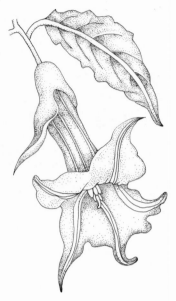

D. c. 'Kingii'. This partly double form is most frequently seen in cultivation.

D. sanguinea. Scarlet trumpets. A 4–8 ft. shrub from Peru with wavy-margined leaves which are softly hairy. The 8 in., pendant flowers are a striking vermilion-red, an unusual color for the genus. They open in late summer.

D. suaveolens. Angel's trumpets. A strong-growing Brazilian species which can eventually reach 15 ft. The large, oval leaves can be 12 in. long, as can the beautiful hanging flowers which are fragrant and open in summer and autumn.

Davallia

DAVALLIACEAE. A genus of 40 small ferns which have the added advantage for home culture of being slow-growing. The fronds are borne on woolly, scaly rhizomes which fancifully resemble animals' feet. In the wild, they are epiphytic, and are best grown in hanging baskets in a peat or sphagnum compost. Maintain a minimum temperature of 60°F (15°C) for most species, keep in shade, and water freely. Propagate by division.

D. bullata mariesii. Syn. *D. mariesii.* Ball fern. A Japanese species which, in that country, is trained on to fanciful shapes covered with the strange, creeping rhizomes. It has dainty, triangular fronds

about 6 in. in length and prefers a cooler atmosphere than the other species, a minimum of 45°F (7°C) being quite acceptable, and a maximum of 65°F (18°C) advisable.

D. canariensis. Syn. *D. trichomanioides.* Carrot fern. An attractive species from the western Mediterranean region and the Canaries. It is of strong growth, the very lacily dissected fronds with a firm texture and up to 12 in. in length.

D. fijiensis. Fiji rabbit's foot fern. As its name suggests, this fern is from the Fiji Islands, but in spite of the widely separated countries of origin, it is very similar in appearance to *D. canariensis.* The fronds are up to 2 ft. long, and rather more decorative, but it is less hardy.

D. f. plumosa. Dainty rabbit's foot fern. An even more dissected form with narrower segments, producing almost feathery fronds.

D. pentaphylla. Dwarf rabbit's foot. From the islands of the Pacific and Java, this dwarf species has small, black-stalked fronds which are made up of 7–11 toothed and wavy, but undivided leaflets.

Dendrobium

ORCHIDACEAE. This genus comprises 1400 species of epiphytic orchids which are widely distributed through the tropical and subtropical areas of Asia, Polynesia, and Australia. As might be expected from such a large genus, the plants are extremely varied in shape and size, and come from a great range of habitats. Their cultivation is not difficult. Grow in pots or pans only just large enough to take the roots, or on bark slabs, in fibrous compost. Most prefer a minimum temperature of 50°F (10°C), and shade in summer. Water freely but allow to almost dry out between waterings. Propagate by division.

D. aggregatum. A low-growing evergreen species from China to Malaya. The pseudobulbs are small, not exceeding 2½ in. and carry short, broad, and leathery leaves. The arching flower spikes are up to 6 in. in length and carry 5–20 rounded, golden-yellow blooms in spring, each with a darker center and a honey-like fragrance. A charming plant.

D. densiflorum. A strong-growing, handsome species with angled, cane-like pseudobulbs up to 15 in. in length. They carry 3–5 leathery leaves, each up to 6 in. long, and dense, pendant clusters sometimes bearing up to 100 fragrant blooms. These are a bright, clear yellow and the lip is orange and softly hairy. They open in spring.

D. devonianum. A magnificent plant from southeast Asia which, when well-grown, can produce pendant, stem-like pseudobulbs up to 5 ft. in length. In the home it will not reach this size. The leaves are small and narrow and the spring- and summer-borne flowers are creamy-white with a pinkish-purple flush and a frilled white lip, marked with yellow and magenta. They are borne in pairs from each joint of the long pseudobulb, producing up to 100 flowers in a spike.

D. falconeri. A pendulous species from southeast Asia producing densely branching, slender, stem-like pseudobulbs up to 3 ft. in length. The narrow leaves fall quickly. The superb $4\frac{1}{2}$ in. flowers are white or bluish-white with deep purple marking and an orange lip, purple-marked in the center. They are borne singly at each joint of the pseudobulbs in spring and early summer.

D. fimbriatum. Another large species from southeast Asia, having semi-erect or arching pseudobulbs which, given ideal conditions, can reach 6 ft. They carry long, narrow, dark green leaves and light to deep yellow, 3 in. flowers with an orange-marked, fringed lip, in spring.

D. f. oculatum. The slightly larger flowers of this form, more often met with in cultivation than the type, have deep brown, velvety blotches on the lips, fancifully resembling two eyes.

D. formosum. The $1\frac{1}{2}$ ft. pseudobulbs of this southeast Asian species are sometimes pendant, sometimes erect, and are covered with blackish leaf-sheaths. The leaves are leathery and oblong, and the 4 in. flowers pure white except for the orange marking within the throat. They are borne in spikes of 2–8, from winter to early spring.

D. infundibulum. Somewhat similar to *D. formosum* with smaller flowers and the lip with a yellow, funnel-shaped throat. The pseudobulbs are up to 2 ft. in length. Coming from Burma and Thailand, the blooms open in spring and early summer.

D. i. jamesianum. Syn. *D. jamesianum.* A form with red markings on the disk, and shorter, more rounded pseudobulbs.

D. johnsoniae. A very distinctive species from New Guinea with cylindrical pseudobulbs up to 10 in. in height, bearing 2–3 leathery leaves and beautiful, 5 in., pure white, fragrant flowers. These have long, narrow sepals and somewhat broader petals with a purple-marked lip. They flower over a long period through autumn and winter.

D. kingianum. An Australian species which is very variable even in the wild. The club-shaped pseudobulbs are up to 12 in. in length and have 4 in., narrow, pointed leaves. The fragrant flowers can be any shade from white, through pink to deep mauve, and are borne in erect spikes in autumn and winter.

D. moschatum. A southeast Asian species with arching pseudobulbs up to 8 ft. in length and long, ovate, leathery leaves. The musk-scented blooms

are $3\frac{1}{2}$ in. across, yellowish-white with a pink flush, while the large, pouch-shaped lip is yellow with black-purple blotches. These flowers are borne in pendant clusters of 5–10, in spring and early summer.

D. nobile. Probably the best known species, coming from the Himalaya ranges. It produces 1–2 ft., stem-like pseudobulbs and oblong, softly leathery leaves. The fragrant flowers are 3 in. across, and white with rose-pink tips usually having a downy pink to cream lip, becoming deep crimson in the throat. The coloration is somewhat variable. They open in spring and summer.

D. pierardii. The slender, stem-like pseudobulbs of this widespread southeast Asian plant are pendant and can reach 6 ft. They carry short-lived 4 in., narrow leaves and 2 in., pale pinkish-white flowers, almost transparent in texture and having a light yellow lip with purplish markings. These are borne in 1–3 flowered clusters at each joint of the long pseudobulb, festooning the stems with bloom in spring and early summer.

D. primulinum. The cane-like, 12 in. pseudobulbs of this species from southeast Asia carry short, leathery leaves and pink-tipped, white flowers with a primrose-yellow lip which is marked with red. They are borne singly at each of the joints of the often pendant pseudobulbs, in late winter and spring.

D. pulchellum. A splendid southeast Asian species, the 8 ft., stem-like pseudobulbs carrying long-lasting, 8 in. leaves and scented 5 in. flowers which are creamy-yellow with a pink flush. The yellow lip has 2 deep red blotches. The flowers are borne in spring in drooping clusters of 6–10.

D. thyrsiflorum. A magnificent species, the stem-like pseudobulbs up to 30 in., and bearing pendant spikes of 2 in., shining white flowers, sometimes flushed with pink, and having a golden-yellow, velvety lip. They open from winter to spring.

Dendrochilum

Syn. *Platyclinis.* Chain orchids. ORCHIDACEAE. A genus comprising about 100 tropical Asian orchids. They produce narrow, hanging spikes of small flowers, like fluffy tails or chains, and evergreen leaves, one to each pseudobulb. They look best in hanging pans or on bark slabs, but can be grown in pots and prefer an equal part sphagnum and osmunda compost. Keep shaded, at a minimum temperature of 50°F (10°C), and water freely. Propagate by division.

D. cobbianum. The leaves of this small growing species are up to 6 in. in length, and the 8 in. chain of fragrant, straw-yellow flowers are carried on wiry, arching 12 in. stems in autumn.

D. glumaceum. This species has chains of white to straw-colored flowers often more than 12 in. in length. They are hay-scented and open in spring. The 10 in., narrow, and somewhat wavy leaves are borne on small, egg-shaped pseudobulbs.

Dendropanax

ARALIACEAE.

D. chevalieri. Tree Aralia. A small tree, one of 75 members of the genus. Comes from Japan and Korea. It makes an attractive foliage plant when young, rarely reaching its maximum of 20 ft. in a pot. The large, 3-lobed leaves are dark green and leathery, becoming smoother in outline with age. Grow in sun and maintain a minimum temperature of 50°F (10°C). Water freely. Propagate by seeds or air layering.

Dermatobotrys

SCROPHULARIACEAE.

D. saundersii. The only species of its genus, coming from southern Africa, it is a small epiphytic shrub which responds well to pot culture, especially if given a peaty compost. It has 2–5 in., toothed, ovate leaves and clusters of long, red, tubular flowers opening to 5 yellow, petal-like lobes at the mouth. Maintain a minimum temperature of 50°F (10°C) and keep in full sun. Water when the compost feels dry. Propagate by cuttings.

Desmodium

LEGUMINOSAE.

D. gyrans. Telegraph plant. One of a large genus, comprising some 450 species, this is a fascinating annual growing to 1–3 ft. in height, with small clusters of violet flowers. Its leaves are cut into three leaflets, the end one large, the other two much smaller. It is these smaller leaflets that provide the interest by visibly revolving during the day, and hanging down at night. To do this they require a day temperature of at least 70°F (21°C), and a minimum of 60°F (15°C). Water freely. Propagate by seed.

Dianella

Flax lilies. LILIACEAE. A genus of 30 species of attractive plants from southeast Asia and Australasia. In spring they have tufts of long, narrow, strap-shaped leaves, and spikes of small, usually bluish flowers, followed by large, attractive, blue-purple, globular berries. Keep in sun, with a minimum temperature of 50°F (10°C), and water freely when in growth, less when dormant. Propagate by seeds or division.

D. caerulea. From Australia, this 2 ft. species has arching, rough-edged leaves, and spikes of small,

light blue flowers. The rounded berries are a purplish-blue.

D. revoluta. From Tasmania and Polynesia, this species has 2–3 ft. stiff leaves with rolled, purple-tinted margins, and small, deep blue-green flowers followed by pale blue berries. These are carried on short stems, giving a looser spike than *D. caerulea*.

D. tasmanica. The largest and most attractive of the flax lilies, this Tasmanian plant can reach 4 ft. with stiffly borne leaves, and tall, open spikes of light blue flowers. The purple-blue berries are oval, and can be up to ¾ in. long.

Dianthus

CARYOPHYLLACEAE.

D. caryophyllus. Of the familiar carnations and pinks of which there are over 300 species known, only the perpetual carnations, derived from this south European species are at all suitable for house plants. Most tend to become too tall and straggly after two or three years, and are then best replaced by young plants. Many color forms are grown, from whites and yellows to pinks and reds, and most are fragrant. Grow in large pots, and maintain a temperature above 50°F (10°C) in winter for good flowering. Pinch out the top of the plant down to about the eighth pair of leaves to promote branching growth. Water when the compost feels dry. Propagate by cuttings or layers. Many cultivars are grown.

D. c. 'Brigadoon'. A good yellow form.

D. c. 'Cardinal Sim'. Brilliant, scarlet blooms.

D. c. 'Fragrant Ann'. A very fragrant, pure white.

D. c. 'Paris'. A fine pink.

Diastema

GESNERIACEAE.

D. quinquevulnerum. One of a genus of 40 species, this dwarf plant comes from Colombia and Venezuela. It makes a 4–6 in. mound of oval, wrinkled, bright green leaves, and carries spikes of small, white, tubular flowers opening to small, rounded lobes, each with a purple spot. Keep in shade with a minimum temperature of 60°F (15°C), and water freely except in winter when it should have a resting period. Propagate by cuttings.

Dichorisandra

COMMELINACEAE. A tropical American genus comprising 35 species of perennial plants, many with decorative foliage. The flowers are 3-petalled, and often brightly colored. Maintain a minimum temperature of 60°F (15°C), and give some shade. Water freely. Propagate by division or cuttings.

D. reginae. Syn. *Tradescantia reginae.* Queen's spiderwort. An attractive, slow-growing plant from

Peru having long, ovate, waxy-textured leaves which are dark green above and reddish-purple below, the upper side banded with silver. The spikes of lavender flowers are borne in summer. *(illus.)*

D. thyrsiflora. Blue ginger. A strong-growing Brazilian plant, the stout stems eventually reaching 4 ft. They carry 6–10 in. leaves, shining green above and purple below, and in summer spikes of showy, brilliant, blue-purple flowers.
D. t. 'Variegata'. This form has shorter leaves, usually less than 6 in. long, which have 2 longitudinal silver bands.

Dicksonia

DICKSONIACEAE. A genus of about 30 species of tree ferns, mostly from Australasia. In the wild, they reach 10–40 ft., but grow slowly, and when young make decorative pot plants with their rosettes of large, deeply cut fronds. They prefer a minimum temperature of about 50°F (10°C), and some shade. Abundant moisture is essential, and they are best standing over a tray of water to provide humidity. They are propagated by spores, but these take many years to reach a usable size.
D. antarctica. Woolly tree fern; Tasmanian tree fern. Coming from Australia and Tasmania, this makes a most attractive tub plant when young, with its arching, dark green fronds which are finely cut, yet leathery in texture. Its trunk is covered with a mat of blackish rootlets as it ages.
D. fibrosa. A New Zealand species, the deeply dissected fronds an attractive light green, and the trunk matted with brownish rootlets.

D. squarrosa. The fronds of this species from New Zealand are rough, and a dark, leathery green. The trunk is black, and covered with rather shaggy leaf bases as it extends upwards. Perhaps the least moisture-demanding of the three.

Didierea

DIDIEREACEAE.
D. madagascariensis. Madagascar cactus. Of the two members of this genus, this one is an extremely thorny succulent, making an interesting pot plant when small with its varying lengths of spines, but eventually becoming tall and cylindrical, reaching more than 15 ft. in the wild. Grow in full sun with a minimum temperature of 60°F (15°C). Water only when the compost feels dry. Propagate by seeds.

Dieffenbachia

Dumb-canes. ARACEAE. 30 species comprise this tropical American genus which contains some very popular foliage plants. They get their common name from the sap which can cause severe swelling especially if it comes into contact with the mouth. Vinegar is a partial antidote. The arum-like flowers are small and only occur on mature plants. Maintain a minimum temperature of 60°F (15°C), and keep out of direct sun. Water when the compost feels dry. Propagate by stem cuttings.
D. amoena. Giant dumb-cane. A strong-growing plant from Colombia, up to 5 ft. in height with 12–18 in. long, oval leaves which are shining, deep green, and marked with featherings of creamy-white along the veins. When plants get too tall or straggly, they are best replaced.
D. 'Exotica'. A fine cultivar, probably derived from the Costa Rican *D. hoffmannii* which is similarly marked. It is a compact plant with ovate, deep green leaves, strongly marked with irregular, cream spotting and feathering.
D. x memoria-corsii. A hybrid of *D. picta* and *D. wallisii*, this plant has long, oval, gray-green leaves with darker veins and lighter areas between. It is also sparingly marked with white spots.
D. oerstedii. From Guatemala and Costa Rica, this species has a more elegant growth form, with long, ovate, very dark green leaves on long stalks.
D. o. variegata. This form has narrower leaves than the species, the midrib of each being picked out in white.
D. picta. Spotted dumb-cane. From Brazil, a robust plant with oval leaves up to 1 ft. in length, mid-green with creamy-white, irregular variegation strongest near the center. Many cultivars with distinctive markings have been raised.
D. p. jenmannii. A form with glossy green leaves

clearly marked with ivory-white feathering.
D. p. 'Rudolph Roehrs'. Syn. *D. roehrsii*. The
margins of the leaves remain green in this very
distinctive cultivar, but the rest of the leaf is
greenish-yellow with white markings.
D. p. 'Superba'. An attractive form, the large area
of creamy-white variegation contrasting with the
glossy, dark green background and mid-rib.

Dimorphotheca

COMPOSITAE.
D. ecklonis. Cape marigold. One of a South
African genus of 20 species. Of these, Cape
marigold makes a bushy mound of narrow,
toothed, dark green leaves, covered in spring with
3 in., daisy-like, black-centered white flowers, the
petals purple on the reverse side. It grows well as an
annual. Keep in sun with a minimum temperature
of 50°F (10°C), and water freely. Propagate by
seeds or division.

Dinteranthus

AIZOACEAE. A genus of remarkable succulents
from South Africa, made up of thick, fleshy leaves
which are joined for more than half their length to
form a rounded plant apparently split open across
the top. They bear large, attractive, daisy-like
flowers. Grow in full sun with a minimum
temperature of 50°F (10°C), and water only in
summer when the compost is dry. Keep quite dry in
winter. Over-watering causes the plants to become
soft and to split. Propagate by seed.
D. inexpectatus. Surprise split rock. This smooth,
whitish species reaches 2 in. in height, the fleshy
leaves opening to release orange, daisy-like flowers
which are 1 in. across and open in summer.

D. microspermus. The fleshy leaves are rounded on
the back, and slightly concave above. When young
they are pure white, becoming gray-green as they
mature. During summer, golden daisy flowers open,
each almost 2 in. across, wider than the whole
plant. *(illus.)*

D. puberulus. In this species the 1–1½ in. wide pairs
of leaves are softly hairy, giving a velvety feel. In
late summer and autumn, the 1 in., golden-yellow
daisy flowers open.

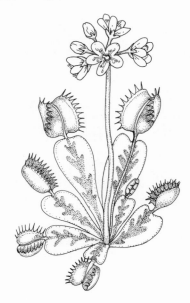

Dionaea

DROSERACEAE.
D. muscipula. Venus fly trap. The only member of
its genus. Coming from the eastern USA, it is a
carnivorous plant adapted to entrap and digest
insects in its leaves. These are up to 4 in. long, and
the yellow-green leaf blade folds along the midrib
allowing the long-toothed margins to spring
together, trapping any insect within. This they do
with surprising speed when the sensitive hairs on
either side are touched. The leaf surface has small
reddish glands which secrete a digestive fluid. The
small, white flowers are borne in summer. They are
best grown in a peaty compost with some form of
glass covering. Keep relatively cool, a minimum
temperature of 40°F (5°C) is quite adequate, but
give good light and abundant moisture. Propagate
by seed, division or bulblets. *(illus.)*

Dioon

ZAMIACEAE.
D. edule. Virgin palm; Chestnut dioon. One of
about 4 species, this Mexican palm-like tree
eventually forms a 6 ft. trunk bearing a dense,
umbrella-like rosette of 3–6 ft., deeply divided,
plume-like leaves, every narrow segment with a
spiny tip. When young they make very decorative
plants for a pot or tub. Keep in full light with a

76

minimum temperature of 60°F (15°C), and water freely. Propagate by seed.

Dioscorea

Yams. DIOSCOREACEAE. Some members of this very large genus of over 600 species are grown as food plants. They are widespread throughout the tropics, as climbing plants in their forest homes. Keep a minimum temperature of 60°F (15°C), and water well while in growth, but gradually dry off as they die down in autumn, and keep dry until growth begins in spring. Propagate by division.
D. discolor. A beautiful foliage plant, the heart-shaped leaves are dark, velvety green above with pale green marbling and silvery veins. Beneath, they are purple. Support in the form of canes or wires is necessary.
D. elephantipes. Syn. *Testudinaria elephantipes.* Elephant's foot. A species remarkable for the large, wrinkled, woody tuber which is mostly above ground, and is fancifully likened to an elephant's foot. From it rise each spring, green, fleshy stems with heart-shaped leaves which soon fall, and clusters of small, greenish-yellow, starry flowers.

Diosma

RUTACEAE.
D. ericoides. Buchu. One of a genus of 15 evergreen shrubs. All are from South Africa, and in appearance are rather like heathers, having tiny, dark green leaves on slender branches. This species is rarely over 2 ft. in height and from spring to autumn is covered with small pink, starry flowers. Keep a minimum temperature of 45°F (7°C), and grow in full sun. Water only when the compost feels dry. Propagate by cuttings.

Dipladenia

ASCLEPIADACEAE. A genus of 30 evergreen climbing plants, all from tropical America. They have pairs of oval, undivided leaves and clusters of showy flowers. Maintain a minimum temperature of 60°F (15°C), and water freely when in growth. If possible, keep in light shade. Propagate by cuttings.
D. x amoena. A hybrid of *D. amabilis* and *D. splendens*, this attractive plant has 4–8 in., wrinkled leaves. It has clusters of very pretty, pink, trumpet-shaped flowers, opening to wide, reflexed lobes at the mouth, which has a deep pink, central ring and is yellow within. These are open in summer and early autumn.
D. boliviensis. A neat species from Bolivia with stems which can reach 6 ft. or more in length. They bear long, shining, oval leaves, and the 2 in., trumpet-shaped flowers are white with slightly recurved petals and a yellow throat. They are at

their best in summer and autumn.
D. splendens. A strong-growing Brazilian species with stems up to 10 ft. or more. The flowers too are large and funnel-shaped, opening to 5 in. across at the mouth. They are white with a pink flush, and are borne in summer and autumn. Once flowering is over, the plant should be cut back almost to soil level.
D. s. profusa. A fine form with rich, rose-pink flowers.
D. s. williamsii. A free-flowering, white form with a deep pink throat.

Dissotis

MELASTOMATACEAE. This African genus contains 140 species of small, shrubby, and herbaceous plants. They have ovate leaves and large, rose to purple flowers which have 5 long, curling stamens and 5 short ones. Grow in light shade with a minimum temperature of 60°F (15°C). Avoid dry heat by standing on a wet gravel tray, and water freely. Propagate by cuttings.
D. plumosa. Syn. *D. rotundifolia.* This is a small, shrubby plant from Sierra Leone, which makes a low mound of deep green leaves. From it in summer are borne rosy-purple, saucer-shaped flowers up to 1½ in. across, and carried singly on short stalks.
D. princeps. This 8 ft. shrub has distinctly veined, short-haired leaves and large, light purple flowers borne in short spikes in summer and autumn.

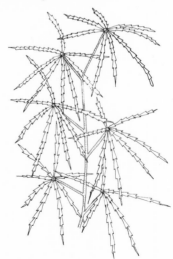

Dizygotheca

ARALIACEAE.
D. elegantissima. Syn. *Aralia elegantissima.* 17 species make up this genus of shrubs and trees. This plant from the New Hebrides is a graceful

species which makes an extremely decorative pot plant, especially when young. Its large leaves comprise a number of ribbon-like, lobed leaflets which are reddish-brown and droop from the stems. As the plant ages, the leaflets become broader and the plant loses much of its appeal. Grow in a minimum temperature of 60°F (15°C) in shade and water freely. Propagate by air layering (mossing) or by seeds. *(illus. prev. page)*

Dolichothele

CACTACEAE.

D. longimamma. Syn. *Mammillaria longimamma*. A curious, clustered cactus from Mexico, one of 3 species often included in *Mammillaria*. It has a rounded body with many finger-shaped knobs, each about 2 in. long and bearing a cluster of soft, yellow spines at the tips. The large, yellow flowers open in summer. Keep in full light with a minimum temperature of 50°F (10°C), and water only when the compost feels dry. Propagate by seed. *(illus.)*

Dombeya

STERCULIACEAE.

D. x cayeauxii. Mexican Rose; Pink Ball. This is a hybrid between *D. mastersii* and *D. wallichii*, two African members of this large genus which comprises 350 species. It makes an attractive winter- and spring-flowering shrub, the round to heart-shaped leaves with deeply incised veins helping to show off the globular, pendant clusters of tightly packed, fragrant, pink flowers. Maintain a minimum temperature of 60°F (15°C), and keep in light shade. Water when the compost feels dry, and propagate by cuttings.

Dorotheanthus

AIZOACEAE.

D. gramineus. Buck Bay daisy. Of the 6 members of this South African genus of succulent plants, this

annual species makes a most attractive pot plant. It has crystalline, textured leaves, each cylindrical in shape and 2–3 in. long, and brightly colored, daisy-like flowers up to 1½ in. across. They are usually a carmine red, but are also grown in shades of pinks, oranges, yellow, and white. All have a dark center, usually almost black but sometimes red or blue. Grow in full sun with a minimum temperature of about 50°F (10°C). Water as soon as the compost looks dry. Propagate by seeds.

Dracaena

Dragon lilies. AGAVACEAE. A genus containing some 150 species of woody-stemmed trees and shrubs. Many have very decorative foliage and make good house plants when young. The long, narrow leaves are borne in tufts on thick stems which elongate as the plant ages. Grow in light shade with a minimum temperature of 60°F (15°C), and water freely. Propagate by cuttings.

D. deremensis. Striped dracaena. The long, narrow, leathery leaves of this African species arch outwards from a single, cane-like stem and are no more than 2 in. in width. They are bright green with a white stripe. A valuable species for air-conditioned homes.

D. d. 'Bausei'. This form has one, broad white stripe along the center of each leaf.

D. d. 'Warneckii'. Three lines of variegation distinguish this cultivar, the inner is greenish-white, the two outer are clear white.

D. fragrans. From Guinea, this species has long leaves which are 2½–4 in. wide, and striped with green and gold.

D. f. 'Massangeana'. This robust form has a broad, golden-yellow band along the center of each leaf. *(illus.)*

D. godseffiana. Gold dust dracaena. Coming from Guinea and the Congo, this is a small species bearing 3–4 in. leaves which are up to 2 in. wide. They are deep green, liberally spotted, and dusted golden-yellow, a color which fades to white as the leaves age.

D. goldieana. Queen of the dracaenas. A most attractive species from Nigeria with broadly ovate leaves which are dark green with bands of lighter color which become whiter with age. Unfortunately, it requires a more humid atmosphere than the other species, and consequently is not so easy to grow.

D. hookerianum. Leather dracaena. This South African species has thick, leathery, sword-shaped leaves which are strongly reflexed, and which are borne on branching stems. This makes a sturdy and decorative species.

D. marginata. Madagascar dragon tree. A narrow-leaved species from Malagasy, the leaves at first held stiffly upright, later arching over. They are a deep, glossy green, and have red-flushed edges. A very good plant for home decoration.

D. sanderiana. A small, neat plant with narrow leaves, 6–8 in. in length, which have broad, white margins and a somewhat translucent green center.

Drimiopsis

LILIACEAE.

D. kirkii. Leopard leaf. An unusual, lily-like plant from Zanzibar, one of a genus of 22 species. It has soft textured, strap-shaped leaves, which are a bluish-green and have darker spots. In summer it has short spikes of white flowers borne on 12 in. stems. Keep a minimum temperature of 60°F (15°C), provide some shade, and water only when the compost feels dry. Keep almost dry during the winter resting period. Propagate by offsets or seed.

Drosera

Sundew. DROSERACEAE. A genus comprising about 100 species of insect-eating plants which are worldwide in distribution. They have glandular, hairy leaves which hold an alighting insect; then the hairs fold inwards to trap it more securely while it is digested. The flowers open in summer. They are best grown in a mixture of sphagnum moss and peat, with the pot standing in a saucer of water. Never allow them to become dry. Maintain a minimum temperature of 45°F (7°C). Propagate by seed or division.

D. binata. Twin-leaved sundew. An unusual species from Australia, the leaves being divided into two, very narrow leaflets, each with red, glandular hairs. The plant reaches 6 in. in height and has small, white flowers on a foot-long stem.

D. capensis. Cape sundew. This South African species has rosettes of narrow, 6 in., oblong leaves. Its flowers are purple.

D. filiformis. Threadleaf sundew. This species from the USA is remarkable for its very narrow leaves

which can reach 15 in. in length. The flowers are white.

D. rotundifolia. This small species is widespread throughout the northern hemisphere, and has rounded, red, spoon-shaped leaves with glandular tentacles along the margins. Each leaf is 1–1½ in. in length. The small, white flowers are carried on 4–6 in. stalks.

Drosophyllum

DROSERACEAE.

D. lusitanicum. The only species of its genus, coming from the western Mediterranean. It has long, thread-like leaves up to 10 in. in length, which have small, stiff, glandular hairs that exude a sweet, sticky substance. This both attracts and captures the plant's insect prey. In summer, clusters of relatively large, bright yellow flowers are borne on long, slender stalks. Grow in better drained conditions than *Drosera*, maintaining a minimum temperature of 50°F (10°C). Propagate by seed.

Dudleya

CRASSULACEAE. A genus of 40 species of succulent plants, many of which can be grown in the home. They are all found in the southwest USA and Mexico. Maintain a minimum temperature of 45°F (7°C), and water only when the compost feels dry. Propagate by seed.

D. greenii. This Mexican plant has a very short stem carrying a small 6 in. rosette of grayish leaves. The yellow flowers are borne in branched clusters. *(illus.)*

D. virens. A rosette-forming plant, the oblong,

3–5 in.-long leaves have a silvery patina. The erect clusters of flowers are white.

Dyckia

BROMELIACEAE. A genus of 80 species of bromeliads from South America. They have rosettes of long, spiny, tapering leaves, the reverse usually silvery. The branched spikes of orange-yellow flowers are borne on long stalks on mature specimens. For the best foliage effect, young plants are most satisfactory. Propagate by suckers or seed.

D. brevifolia. A Brazilian species rather like a small agave, the leaves held erect at the center of the rosette, the outer being recurved. The orange flowers are borne on long stalks.

D. fosteriana. Also from Brazil, this is a very decorative species; the narrow, tapering leaves are deeply toothed and spined on the margins like a fine double-edged saw, and arch outwards from the center of the rosette. The spikes of bright orange flowers are carried high above the leaves.

E

Eccremocarpus

BIGNONIACEAE.

E. scaber. Chilean glory flower. A small genus of climbing plants with leaves divided into small leaflets which bear tendrils. This species from Chile has dark green leaves and tubular flowers which are orange-red. They are borne during summer and autumn. Maintain a minimum temperature of 45°F (7°C), and water freely while in growth. Propagate by seed.

Echeveria

CRASSULACEAE. A genus containing 150 species of succulent plants, most making compact rosettes of thick, fleshy, almost stemless leaves, either oblong or wedge-shaped, wider near the end, and tapering abruptly sometimes to a point. They require full sun and a minimum temperature of 45°F (7°C). Water only when the compost feels dry. Propagate by seed or leaf cuttings. All the species are from Mexico unless otherwise stated.

E. affinis. Black echeveria. The small rosettes of 2 in. waxy leaves which are ovate and pointed, are a very dark green, becoming almost black in strong sunlight. In winter, flat-topped clusters of scarlet-red flowers are borne on 6 in. leafy stems.

E. agavoides. Syn. *Urbina agavoides.* Molded wax. A tough, slow-growing species with close rosettes of very thick, pale green, orange-brown tipped leaves, 1½–3½ in. long, and ovate to triangular in shape.

Small clusters of reddish flowers with yellow-tipped petals are borne in spring on long, pink stems over 1 ft. in height.

E. crenulata. Scallop echeveria. A large species, the 12–15 in. greenish-gray, rounded leaves narrow into a stalk and have decorative, red, wavy margins. They are borne in a loose rosette on a short, stout stem. Stout, 1–3 ft. stems bear the small clusters of yellowish-red flowers in early spring.

E. c. 'Roseo-grandis'. A form in which the leaves have wider, more wavy, purplish-red margins.

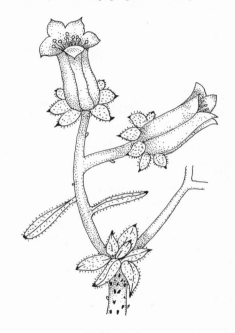

E. derenbergii. Painted lady. A very small species with tight, almost globular rosettes of ovate, fleshy leaves only 1–1½ in. long, and ending abruptly in a red tip. The yellow or reddish-yellow flowers are borne in small clusters on 2–3 in. stems.

E. x 'Doris Taylor'. Woolly rose; Plush rose. An attractive hybrid raised from *E. setosa* and *E. pulvinata.* It deserves its international popularity, making a 5 in., tight rosette of deep green, spoon-shaped leaves which are densely covered with short, white hairs giving a velvety texture. The leaf tips are red, as are the spring-borne flowers, which are also yellow inside and are borne in branched clusters.

E. elegans. Mexican snowball. A very beautiful plant, the rosettes of blunt-ended, ovate leaves, each with a small point, a marbled bluish-white. The almost transparent margins sometimes have a pinkish flush. Through summer, the long, yellow-tipped, pink flowers are borne in clusters on a 4–10 in. stem.

E. gibbiflora. A large species, the rosettes of oval, gray-green leaves 10–15 in. across, and borne on a short stem. The branched, flowering stalk carries a large cluster of reddish flowers which are yellow inside the mouth.

E. g. carunculata. A variety which is more curious than beautiful, the leaves having wart-like growths on their reddish-brown, flushed surfaces.

E. g. metallica. In this variety, the rounded leaves are more bronze colored and have a bluish metallic sheen.

E. glauca. Blue echeveria. The rounded, spoon-shaped leaves are bluish-green with purplish-red margins, and form a 2–4 in. rosette. The bright red flowers are borne in one-sided clusters on an 8–12 in. stem in spring.

E. harmsii. A small, branched, shrubby plant which is softly hairy. The narrow, almost diamond-shaped leaves are 1–1½ in. long, borne in rosettes and along the stems. The red flowers are large, over an inch long, the petals paler at the tips. These are borne in small clusters at the end of 10–12 in. stems in summer. *(illus. left)*

E. multicaulis. Copper rose. A shrubby species with woody stems up to 8 in. in height. They bear rosettes of 1–2½ in., spoon-shaped leaves which are a waxy green, but have brown to coppery margins. The reddish flowers are yellow inside, and are borne on a 12–18 in. stalk.

E. peacockii. Syn. *E. desmetiana.* Forming a 3–5 in. rosette, the long, ovate, fleshy leaves are blue-green with a silvery patina, the tips and margins being dark red. The red flowers are carried on 6–15 in. stems in loose clusters. Withstands cooler conditions than the other species, a minimum of 40°F (5°C) being sufficient.

E. pulvinata. Chenille plant. A beautiful, velvety species, one of the parents of most of the soft-haired hybrids. It has 2½–4 in., silvery, felted leaves, carried in loose rosettes on the short, shrubby stems. The long red flowers are borne on short stalks which are held horizontally, emerging between the lower leaves in spring.

E. x 'Pulv-Oliver'. Plush plant. This hybrid has the fine, velvety texture of *E. pulvinata*, one of its parents, and the narrower, oval leaves of *E. harmsii*, the other parent. (It was named when this plant was known as *Oliveranthus elegans*, hence the curious form of name.) It has orange-red flowers which are freely borne on leafy stems.

E. sedoides. A somewhat shrubby species with the small, but thick, long, ovate leaves carried along the stems, not in a rosette. The clusters of 4–6 bell-shaped, scarlet flowers are borne on short stems.

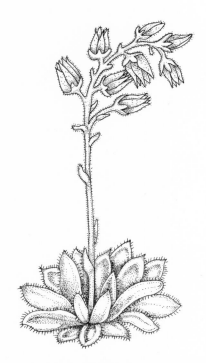

E. x 'Set-Oliver'. Maroon chenille plant. A hybrid between *E. setosa* and *E. harmsii* (as *Oliveranthus elegans*). It has close rosettes of long, ovate leaves which are flushed and margined with maroon. The red and yellow flowers are borne on leafy stems.

E. setosa. A neat, white-haired species with dense, tightly packed rosettes of 3–4 in., oval to spoon-shaped leaves, and long-stalked, nodding clusters of yellow-tipped, red flowers. *(illus.)*

Echinocactus

CACTACEAE. A genus containing 10 species of globular or barrel-shaped cacti, all from Texas, California, and Mexico. The large areoles are woolly and carry many straight spines. The small flowers are mostly yellow, occasionally pink or red. Grow in full light with a minimum temperature of 50°F (10°C), and water only when the compost feels dry. Propagate by seed.

E. grusonii. Golden barrel. A beautiful species which is barrel-shaped and bears glossy yellow spines up to 1½ in. long on mature plants. It grows quickly and will reach 2–3 ft. if given sufficient room. The 1½–2½ in. flowers are yellow, but are only seen on large specimens. A little shade from the hottest summer sun is advisable.

E. horizonthalonius. A globular species reaching 10 in. in height and up to 15 in. across when full grown. It is blue-green in color, and has up to 9

stiff spines radiating from each woolly areole. The 2–2½ in. flowers are brownish-pink. *(illus.)*

E. ingens. Blue barrel. When small, this species makes a blue-green globe with stiff, brown spines on the few ribs. As it grows, it lengthens, becoming barrel-shaped and up to 5 ft. when mature, and having many spiny ribs. The flowers are yellow. A slow-growing species.

Echinocereus

Hedgehogs. CACTACEAE. A genus of 75 North American cacti, most of which are very spiny, earning them their common name. They are column-forming, but most are small and have the advantage of being free-flowering. The flowers are large and colorful, opening in late spring and summer. Keep in full light, watering freely when growing, but allow the compost to become almost dry in winter, and keep cool with a minimum temperature of 45°F (7°C). Propagate by seeds or cuttings.

E. blanckii. A very beautiful, suckering species, upright when young, becoming prostrate as it lengthens to its full 12–15 in. The stems are dark green, and the areoles bear black and white spines. The 2½–3 in.-long funnel-shaped flowers are a rich violet.

E. caespitosus. Syn. *E. reichenbachii*. An erect species, the cylindrical stem up to 8 in. in height with many areoles bearing many dark-tipped yellow or white spines. The 1½–2 in., trumpet-shaped flowers are bright pink.

E. dasyacanthus. A stiffly-held species reaching 8 in. in height. The areoles carry up to 20 starry spines which are reddish at first, becoming gray with age. The bright yellow flowers are large, up to 4 in. long, and funnel-shaped.

E. dubius. A popular species with prostrate, branched, fleshy stems, 6–8 in. in length. The well-spaced areoles carry up to 12 spines, yellowish-gray in color, and some up to 2½ in. in length. The wide,

funnel-shaped, pink flowers are about 2½ in. long.

E. engelmannii. An erect, clump-forming species, the cylindrical stems up to 10 in. in height. They are pale green and covered with a dense network of spines, borne in clusters of 12–16 of varying lengths, from each areole. The spreading, red-purple flowers are 2½–3½ in. across.

E. knippelianus. A small, globular species, only 2½ in. high and deep green. The spines are small, rather like white bristles, and the funnel-shaped flowers, which are 1–1½ in. long, have petals which are dark brown on the backs and deep red-purple on the inside.

E. pentalophus. A prostrate species, the 5 in. stems pale green with woolly, white areoles. They bear 3–5 starry white or gray spines. The 4 in. flowers open widely and are pale purplish-pink. *(illus.)*

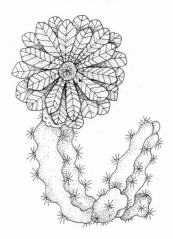

E. scheeri. A slow-growing species with bright, glossy green stems, at first erect, becoming prostrate as they lengthen to their full 10 in. The areoles bear starry and straight spines, and the funnel-shaped flowers are spectacular, being bright pink and up to 5 in. in length.

E. viridiflorus. This species is globular at first, finally lengthening to 8 in. It is dark green, and the many spines are white and brown. The freely-borne flowers are 1 in. long, and an unusual shade of green.

Echinofossulocactus

CACTACEAE.

E. zacatecasensis. Syn. *Stenocactus zacatecasensis*. Brain cactus. A curious species, one of the 32 members of its genus, and grown largely for its remarkable shape. It is globular and up to 3½ in. across, and covered with over 50 ribs which are so tightly packed together that the whole plant appears to have been pleated. The ribs bear both long, hooked, central spines, and smaller, starry ones. The white petals are pink-tipped, and are about 1in. across. Maintain a minimum temperature of 50°F (10°C), grow in sun, and water only when the compost feels dry. Propagate by seed.

Echinomastus

CACTACEAE.

E. macdowellii. One of a genus of 10 species all from Mexico, Texas, and Arizona. This is often considered the most beautiful of the species, making a globular plant eventually up to 6 in. high, pale green, and covered with long, almost transparent, white and straw-colored spines, some straight and starry, others curved. The bright pink flowers are up to 2 in. across. Grow in sun with a minimum temperature of 50°F (10°C), and water only when the compost feels dry. Propagate by seed.

Echinopsis

Sea urchin cacti. CACTACEAE. A genus containing 35 species of free-flowering cacti. They are globular or cylindrical in form, and all are from South America. Grow in sun with a minimum temperature of 50°F (10°C), and water only when the compost feels dry. Propagate by seed.

E. eyriesii. A globular species with gray, woolly areoles, becoming elongated as it matures and eventually reaching 6 in. The spreading spines are brown; the very striking flowers are white and trumpet-shaped, measuring up to 10 in. in length. Plants grown under this name, but having pink or purple-flushed flowers, are mostly of hybrid origin.

E. multiplex. A 6 in. species from Brazil, which is globular at first, becoming barrel-shaped as it matures. It is dark green and brown spined. The 8 in. long, beautiful pink flowers are very fragrant.

E. rhodotricha. A tall species from Argentina and Paraguay forming clumps of oval stems, growing when mature to 30 in. in height. The stems have woolly areoles, at least on the upper part of the stems, and star-like clusters of brown spines around a 1½ in. long central one. The freely-borne white flowers are 6 in. long and up to 3 in. across.

E. silvestrii. An attractive, globular species from Argentina, grayish-green, and up to 6 in. across and high. The spines are white at first, becoming yellow, and finally on mature plants, gray. The freely-borne, white flowers which are seen even on young specimens, are up to 10 in. in length and 6 in. in width.

E. violacea. An Argentinian species, the pale green, globular stems lengthening with age to about 8 in. The spreading spines are yellow, and as the plant matures, straight, brown ones are produced too.

The erect, violet flowers are trumpet-shaped, and up to 3 in. in length. A free-flowering species.

Elettaria

ZINGIBERACEAE.

E. cardamomum. Cardamom. A genus of about 6 tropical species, of which this one from India is grown commercially as a spice plant. It makes clumps of tall stems, up to 10 ft. in the wild, but easily kept below 3 ft. in pots. The evergreen leaves are long, narrow, and a rich green, and make it a useful background plant which is both shade-tolerant and generally tough. The small, white flowers are produced only on large plants. Grow with a minimum temperature of 50°F (10°C), and keep in shade. Water freely. Propagate by division.

Encephalartos

ZAMIACEAE. Among the 30 known species of this genus, two from South Africa make distinctive, if somewhat fearsome, tub or pot plants. They have stout trunks when mature, from which grow rosettes of deeply cut, arching fronds which are spine-tipped. Grow in sun or light shade with a minimum temperature of 50°F (10°C), and propagate by seed.

E. horridus. Ferocious blue cycad. The blue-green, spine-edged fronds of this species are up to 2 ft. long, and well deserve their name. They need plenty of room to grow well, but are most decorative. The long cones which exceed 1 ft. are rarely seen on plants in pots. Water only when the compost feels dry.

E. latifrons. Syn. *E. horridus latifrons.* Spiny Kaffir bread. This makes a very large plant when mature, but while young and still small can be kept in pots or tubs where its sharp-spined, recurving fronds can be given sufficient space. Water freely, especially when in growth.

Epacris

Australian heath. EPACRIDACEAE. 40 species make up this Australasian genus of evergreen heather-like shrubs. They have very small, densely borne leaves, and small, tubular flowers opening flat at the mouth. Keep in good light, and maintain a minimum temperature of 50°F (10°C). Water when the compost feels dry. Propagate by cuttings.

E. impressa' A 3–5 ft. erect shrub with narrow, pointed leaves, and tubular flowers varying in color from red to white and up to ¾ in. in length.

E. longiflora. This shrub can reach 5 ft. and has soft-haired stems which bear tiny, ovate, scale-like leaves. The rose-red flowers open to show white at the lobed mouth, and are up to 1 in. in length. The best flowering is in spring, but a few blooms may be present throughout the year.

Epidendrum

ORCHIDACEAE. The 400 species of this genus all come from the Americas except one which is also found in West Africa. They all have pseudobulbs, but in some species these are long and cane-like, in others they are ovoid and small. The petals and sepals are similar and usually rather narrow, while the lip is variously cut and colored. They grow best in pans or baskets or on bark slabs, with an osmunda and sphagnum compost. Maintain a minimum temperature of 50°F (10°C), keep in light shade, and water freely. Propagate by division.

E. brassavolae. A graceful plant from Central America with narrow, strap-shaped leaves up to 10 in. in length, carried on small, pear-shaped pseudobulbs. The 2–4 in. flowers have extremely narrow, yellow to brown petals and sepals, and a large, uncut, magenta and white lip. They are lightly fragrant, and are borne in spikes of up to 9 blooms, carried on a 15–18 in. stem. They open in summer and autumn.

E. ciliare. Widely spread from Brazil to Mexico, this species has long, oval pseudobulbs which carry rather wide, leathery leaves up to a foot in length. The 12 in.-long, arched, flowering spikes bear widely-spaced, fragrant blooms each up to 7 in. across, with narrow, waxy, yellowish-green sepals and petals, each with a fine thread-like tip. The white lip has a yellow tip and is divided into 3 lobes, the central one sharp and pointed, the outer 2 fringed. They are borne from autumn through winter to spring.

E. cochleatum. Cockleshell orchid. A species found from Brazil to Florida, particularly valuable for its lack of a single flowering season. It has narrowly oval pseudobulbs bearing long, oval leaves which are leathery and shining. The flowers are held upside down, the black-purple, yellow-marked lip which is shaped rather like a cockleshell being above the narrow, pale green sepals and petals. They are borne on 15–18 in. stem.

E. fragrans. Found from Brazil to Peru and northwards to Mexico, this strongly fragrant species has small pseudobulbs which bear 4 in., oval leaves. The 2–8 flowered spikes carry the blooms with the purple-striped, creamy-white lip at the top, above the yellow-green, long, narrow sepals and petals. The flowers appear in winter and spring.

E. ibaguense. Syn. *E. radicans; E. pratense.* Fiery reed orchid. A widely distributed species with long, stem-like pseudobulbs which can reach several feet in height, though fortunately nothing approaching the 30 ft. they can attain in the wild. They bear ovate, yellow-green, fleshy leaves, and dense clusters of small, brilliant orange-scarlet flowers which open throughout the year. Support for the long stems is essential.

E. mariae. A particularly attractive species from Mexico, the 3–6 in. leaves carried on small, pear-shaped pseudobulbs, and the gray-green flowering stems bearing up to 9 blooms. Each has narrow, green, glossy sepals and petals, and a wide, pure white lip, frilled at the edges, and marked in the throat with a yellow-green, feathery spot. They open in summer.

E. polybulbon. A very small species from Central America, the pseudobulbs and leaves together rarely reach more than 5 in. in height. The fragrant flowers are 1¼ in. across, having greenish-yellow sepals and petals with red-brown markings. The wavy-edged lip is creamy-white. They open in winter and spring.

E. prismatocarpum. Rainbow orchid. Coming from Costa Rica and Panama, this very decorative species has ovoid pseudobulbs from which rise long, strap-shaped, leathery leaves up to 15 in. long. The 2 in., waxy flowers open in summer and autumn, and are bright yellow with irregular spots of reddish-brown, and the lip varies in color from cream to rose.

E. stamfordianum. This species is a native of the countries of northern South America to Mexico. It has spindle-shaped pseudobulbs which carry long, tapering, leathery leaves, and the flowering stems from their base. Each of the fragrant blooms has yellow sepals and petals spotted with red, and a 3-lobed, yellow lip. They are borne from winter to spring on 2 ft. stems.

Epiphyllum

Syn. *Phyllocactus.* Orchid cactus. CACTACEAE. A genus of 17 species, all of which have flat, leaf-like branches which are generally toothed or notched. The areoles are sometimes bristly, but spines only occur on young plants, then rarely. The large, colorful flowers are freely borne. Grow in a peaty compost in light shade, maintaining a minimum temperature of 60°F (10°C). Water freely, especially when growing. Propagate by seed or cuttings.

E. anguliger. A Mexican species with the margins of the wide stems deeply notched and toothed, giving the plant great interest even when not in bloom. The white, trumpet-shaped flowers which open in autumn, are 4 in. long, and fragrant.

E. hybrids In Britain often included under the name *E. ackermannii,* which was an early hybrid, and in the USA known as *E. x hybridum,* this group includes many hybrids with related genera as well as within *Epiphyllum.* They are remarkable for

their beautiful, shining, trumpet-shaped flowers, 4–6 in. across, and in a wide range of colors from greenish-blue through purple, red, orange, and yellow to white. They open from spring to autumn. As many as 1000 named cultivars have been raised.
E. oxypetalum. Queen of the night. A beautiful, fragrant, night-flowering species, the white flowers 3–4 in. across, and when closed and showing the reddish backs of the petals, almost a foot in length. They are borne on a 3–4 ft. plant with flat, wavy-margined stems.

Episcia

GESNERIACEAE. A genus comprising 40 species of tropical American plants, most of which are prostrate and creeping. They are evergreen, and many have decorative foliage as well as bright, tubular, or bell-shaped flowers. They require a minimum temperature of 60°F (15°C) and shade. Water freely. Propagate by division or cuttings.
E. cupreata. The best foliage plant of the genus coming from Colombia and Venezuela. It has soft green, netted leaves which have a wide, silver-white area along the central vein. The flowers, which open in spring and early summer, are bright scarlet. Many cultivars are grown and all are attractive.
E. c. 'Acajou'. A very beautiful form having deep red-brown leaves which are overlaid with a feathery network of silvery-green veins merging into the central band. Its flowers are up to 1 in. long, and are a bright vermilion.
E. c. 'Chocolate soldier'. The deep, chocolate-brown leaves of this cultivar are shining and have a wide, white area along the main veins. The flowers are a bright orange-scarlet.
E. c. 'Metallica'. In this form, the rounded leaves have a small area of white along the central vein, while the whole leaf has a shiny, coppery flush, fading almost to pink at the margins. The flowers are orange-scarlet.

E. c. 'Silver Sheen'. A fine form, the bronze-green leaves having a wide, silvery-white, central band, and feathery veining covering a large area of the leaf. The flowers are vermilion.
E. c. viridiflora. A variety in which the leaves are entirely green, and larger than in the species. The wrinkled, netted leaf surface gives it a great attraction.
E. dianthiflora. Lace flower. A pretty Mexican species with small, ovate, short-haired leaves with gently scalloped edges. It is grown however, for its dainty, white flowers which have fringed petals and are 1–1¼ in. long. *(illus. left)*
E. fulgida. Syn. *E. reptans.* Flame violet. Found wild from Brazil to Colombia, the 3–5 in., oval leaves are dark bronze-green and netted with the veins picked out in silvery-green. The deep red, fringed flowers open in summer.
E. punctata. Coming from Guatemala and Mexico, this is a more upright species. The toothed leaves are 2–3 in. long, dark green, and firm in texture, and the 1–1¼ in. flowers are white with daintily fringed petals and an overall freckling of violet-purple dots.

Epithelantha

CACTACEAE.
E. micromeris. Button cactus; Golf balls. The only species of its genus, this strange little cactus comes from Mexico and Texas. The globular stems are pale in color, being almost covered with tufts of about 20 flattened spines. They will reach 2½ in. in height when mature, and are somewhat convex on top as if a thumb has pressed them downwards. They require full sun and a minimum temperature of 50°F (10°C). Water only when the compost feels dry, and allow to become quite dry in winter. Propagate by seed.

Eranthemum

ACANTHACEAE.
E. pulchellum. Syn. *E. nervosum.* Blue sage. Of the 30 species belonging to this genus, this Indian shrub has long, ovate leaves with deeply sunken veins, giving a netted appearance, and spikes of very attractive, bright blue flowers. These are up to 1¼ in. in length and open in late summer and winter. This plant requires a minimum temperature of 60°F (15°C) and some shade. Water freely. It is propagated by cuttings. As it becomes straggly with age, it is best to take cuttings each spring and raise new plants annually.

Eria

ORCHIDACEAE. One of the largest orchid genera, numbering over 500 species. They are widely distributed through tropical Asia and the Pacific islands, most being epiphytic. In form they are extremely variable, but many are very beautiful and not difficult to grow. The species described below are all natives of upland areas, and a minimum winter temperature of 45–50°F (7–10°C) is sufficient. Keep in shade, and water freely when in growth. Propagate by division.

E. coronaria. This southeast Asian species has 6 in., cylindrical pseudobulbs bearing narrow, leathery leaves, and small, arching flower spikes up to 6 in. in length. The waxy blooms are 2 in. across and very fragrant, with white sepals and petals, and a purple-veined lip. These open in late winter and spring.

E. ferruginea. Coming from the Himalayas, this small orchid has 6–8 in. pseudobulbs which carry narrowly oblong, leathery leaves, and arching clusters of flowers, up to 15 to a spike. These are 1½ in. across and have greenish-brown sepals with darker stripes, and white petals with a pink flush. The white lip shades to reddish-purple in the throat. They open in spring.

E. spicata. Widely distributed in southeast Asia from the Himalayas to Vietnam, this species has long, pointed, leathery leaves, borne on 8 in., spindle-shaped pseudobulbs. The densely packed 4–6 in. flower spikes bear many small fragrant flowers, about ½ in. across. The broad, blunt sepals and narrow petals are a pale gold, the lip being darker.

Erica

Heaths and heathers. ERICACEAE. A familiar genus containing almost 500 species. They are wiry, evergreen shrubs which have very narrow, hard leaves, and bell-shaped or tubular flowers which are borne in clusters. Many are not hardy, especially those from South Africa, but they make reasonable house plants as long as they can spend some of the year in the open air. Keep in full light with a minimum temperature of 45°F (7°C), and if possible, not exceeding 70°F (21°C), unless they can also be given plenty of fresh air. Water when the compost feels dry. Propagate by cuttings.

E. canaliculata. A South African species sometimes grown under the name of *E. melanthera* which is quite distinct from it. This plant can make a large shrub, but responds well to pruning. In early spring it is covered with small, white flowers like open bells. *(illus.)*

E. cerinthoides. Red heath. A striking South African species which will make a 2–3 ft. shrub unless kept pruned. Kept small, the dark green leaves make a good background to the dense spikes of bright red flowers, each narrow bell up to 1¼ in. long. A very showy plant with a long flowering season, but at its best in summer.

E. gracilis. Rose heath. A dainty species with pale green leaves, and spikes of abundant, pale rose bells from winter to spring.

E. g. 'Alba'. Syn. *E. nivalis*. A form with snow-white flowers.

E. x hyemalis. African winter heath. The most valuable of the heaths for its flowering season from early autumn through winter. It makes an erect shrub with bright green, narrow leaves, and densely borne white, tubular flowers which are flushed with pink.

E. x 'Wilmorei'. A 1½–2 ft. shrub, the stems densely covered with narrow, green leaves. The pink flowers are tipped with white, and are borne in clusters opening in winter and lasting well into spring.

Ervatamia

APOCYNACEAE.

E. coronaria. Crêpe jasmine. One of a genus comprising about 80 species, this Indian species has long, ovate, glossy evergreen leaves, and makes a 6–8 ft. shrub when grown in the open. In pots it will remain much smaller, and in summer produces white, waxy flowers with a curious crimped surface up to 2 in. across. They are very fragrant, particularly at night. Maintain a minimum temperature of 60°F (15°C), keep in sun, and water freely when the plant is growing. Propagate by cuttings.

Erythrorhipsalis

CACTACEAE.

E. pilocarpa. This Brazilian epiphyte is the only member of its genus. It has gray-green stems up to 15 in. or more which are held erect when short, but soon hang downwards. They are markedly grooved and covered with grayish bristles borne in tufts at the areoles. The 1 in., white flowers open wide in winter, often at Christmas, and are followed by oval, red fruits. Maintain a minimum temperature of 60°F (15°C), keep in shade, and water freely. Propagate by cuttings or seed.

Escobaria
CACTACEAE.
E. tuberculosa. An attractive cactus from Mexico and southern USA. It is one of 20 species and is usually cylindrical, blue-green in color, and eventually reaches 7–8 ft. in height. The areoles are white woolly, and have 20–30 brown-tipped, white spines radiating from them, and 5–9 darker brown, central spines. The 1 in. flowers are purple-pink and are followed by a red berry. A number of varieties are grown, mostly with differing spine characters. Grow in full sun with a minimum temperature of 50°F (10°C), and water only when the compost feels dry. Propagate by seeds or offsets.

Eschontria
CACTACEAE.
E. chiotilla. The only one of its genus, this Mexican cactus is branched and eventually becomes tree-like, reaching 20 ft. When young it makes a good pot plant, the stems bright green, and the strongly ridged ribs bearing down-curving spines. The 1–1½ in., funnel-shaped flowers are yellow, and are followed by edible, reddish-purple fruit. Grow in full sun with a minimum temperature of 50°F (10°C), and water only when the compost feels dry. Propagate by seed or offsets.

Espostoa
CACTACEAE.
E. lanata. Peruvian old man. This columnar cactus from Peru and Ecuador is one of a genus containing 11 species. It grows slowly and takes many years to reach its full 3 ft., even in the wild. The 15–20, rounded ribs bear short, sharp spines, but the plant is remarkable for the silky, white hair in which it becomes completely swathed. The white flowers are followed by red fruits. Grow in full sun with a minimum temperature of 60°F (15°C). Water only when the compost feels dry. Propagate by seed. This cactus is often grown grafted onto *Trichocereus,* but this is not necessary.

Eucalyptus
Gum; Mallee. MYRTACEAE. Most of the members of this large genus which comprises some 500 trees and shrubs, are natives of Australia, and are remarkable for their 2 distinct, foliage forms. When young they bear juvenile leaves which are mostly rounded and often joined together in pairs at the base so that the stem appears to pass through a complete single leaf, rather than between two. It is this form which is grown for decoration. The adult leaves are long, narrow, and willow-like. As pot plants they are best stood outside during summer, and can be cut back to ground level each spring to promote new juvenile foliage. Grow in sun with a minimum temperature of 50°F (10°C), feed regularly, and water freely.
E. cinerea. When juvenile, this attractive species has pairs of stiff, silvery, stalkless leaves, each 1–3 in. across and carried on slender, willowy branches. The more yellow-green, long, ovate leaves of the adult stage have little decorative value.
E. citriodora. Lemon-scented gum. This species has ovate, hairy leaves in its juvenile form. When touched or rubbed these give off a strong scent of lemons.
E. globulus. Blue gum. Familiar as a massive, 300 ft. tree in its native country, this species, when young, has pairs of oval, blue-gray leaves, and is often seen used as a bedding plant. At this stage it is also attractive in pots.
E. gunnii. Cider gum. This species is almost hardy in temperate climates, and its juvenile leaves are rounded and silvery-blue, measuring 2–2½ in. across. As a pot plant, it is best replaced after 2 yrs.
E. polyanthemos. Red box gum; Silver dollar tree. The rounded, silvery-blue, juvenile leaves of this species are neatly outlined in purple.

Eucharis
AMARYLLIDACEAE.
E. grandiflora. Amazon lily. Of the 10 species of its genus, this Colombian plant has long, arching, strap-shaped leaves, the 8 in. leaf blade narrowing

gradually to an equally long stalk. The 2 ft., fleshy, flowering stems carry clusters of clear white, fragrant blooms each up to 4 in. across, and comprising 6 broad petals, open like a star, and a central white corona, like that of a daffodil. Grow in a minimum temperature of 60°F (15°C) in shade, and water freely. Drying off for a month at any time of the year will promote flowering. Propagate by offsets. *(illus. prev. page)*

x Eucodonopsis

Syn. *x Achimenantha*. GESNERIACEAE. A hybrid between *Achimenes* and *Smithiantha* with small, ovate, dark green leaves, and large, creamy-colored, tubular flowers opening to 6 rounded lobes at the mouth. A number of cultivars have been raised. Cultivate as for *Achimenes*.

Eucomis

Pineapple flower. LILIACEAE. This genus of African bulbous plants comprises 14 species. They have long, shining green leaves, and dense spikes of small, greenish-white flowers. These carry at the top a small tuft of green, leaf-like bracts giving a pineapple-like effect, hence the vernacular name. Grow in sun with a minimum temperature of 50°F (10°C), and water freely when growing. Once the leaves have died down, keep almost dry until the following spring. Propagate by offsets.
E. bicolor. The wide, fleshy leaves have slightly wavy margins, while the spike of purple-edged, pale

green flowers is 3–4 in. long and is carried on a 12–15 in. stem. *(illus.)*
E. comosa. Syn. *E. punctata*. The leaves of this species can reach 2 ft. in length. They are grooved and have straight edges. The green flowers have a dark eye and are borne in 3–4 in. spikes on a 15–18 in. purple-spotted stem.
E. zambesiaca. The broad, grooved leaves up to 2 ft. in length, while the small, violet-eyed, green flowers are borne in a very dense, 4–5 in. spike on an unspotted stem. White-flowered plants are also grown under this name.

Eugenia

MYRTACEAE. An extremely large genus, known from all continents except Europe, which is now considered to contain almost 1000 species. It includes evergreen trees and shrubs, some of which are grown as cool greenhouse and patio plants, requiring protection in winter. Grow in sun with a minimum temperature of 50°F (10°C), and water freely, especially when in growth. Propagate by cuttings.
E. myrtifolia. Myrtle-leaf Eugenia. An Australian shrub which has small, ovate leaves, reddish at first, becoming shining green, and dense clusters of small, creamy-white flowers. Unchecked it can reach 20 ft., but responds well to being clipped into a manageable shape and size.
E. m. globulus. A more compact form with smaller, deep green, glossy leaves. Considered a better plant for house culture.

Eulychnia

CACTACEAE.
E. floresii. White fluff-post. One of a small genus of Chilean cacti comprising 5 species, though authorities disagree about their naming. This columnar species has narrow ribs which bear many areoles. Each carries 3–5 long, brown-tipped spines, surrounded by a tuft of dense white hair. When mature, it can exceed 6 ft., but grows slowly. Grow in full sun with a minimum temperature of 60°F (15°C), and water only when the compost feels dry. Propagate by seed.

Euonymus

CELASTRACEAE. 176 species of shrubs and trees make up this genus which is absent only from Africa. Some are hardy in temperate gardens. Grow in light shade with a minimum temperature of 40°F (5°C). Water freely. Propagate by cuttings.
E. japonicus. Japanese spindle tree. In the open ground, this Japanese species can reach 20 ft., but will remain much smaller in pots. It has glossy-

green, oval leaves and is grown chiefly in its many variegated forms.

E. j. 'Albo marginata'. Silver leaf. The narrower leaves are a yellow-green and have a white border.

E. j. 'Argenteo variegatus'. Silver queen. A form with darker green leaves, also white-margined.

E. j. microphyllus. 'Variegata'. A very small, erect plant with leaves less than 1 in. long. They are a dark, shining green with a striking white border. Perhaps the best house plant.

Eupatorium

COMPOSITAE. A genus containing about 1200 species, coming in a variety of forms from small herbaceous plants to large shrubs. It is the shrubby species that make the best pot plants, being particularly valuable for their autumn and winter flowering habit. Maintain a minimum temperature of 50°F (10°C), and grow away from direct sun. Water when the compost feels dry. Propagate by cuttings, pinching out the growing tips twice to promote bushy growth.

E. atrorubens. The large, pointed, oval leaves are toothed and covered with reddish hairs. The small, red-purple flowers are abundantly borne in large clusters at the ends of the branches. In a pot, the plant can be kept to about 2 ft.

E. ianthinum. A 3 ft. shrub, the large leaves being deeply toothed and covered with soft hairs. The deep purple flowers are carried in very large clusters. This species is best with a minimum temperature of 60°F (15°C).

E. micranthum. A taller plant with more erect growth which is best raised annually from cuttings. It has long, ovate leaves, and the fragrant, pink-flushed, white flowers are borne in flat-topped clusters.

Euphorbia

Spurge. EUPHORBIACEAE. A remarkable genus, containing about 2000 very varied species which range from small weedy annuals to spiny, tree-sized succulents, almost all of which have small, inconspicuous flowers. The succulents, of which many species are in cultivation, should be grown in full light with a minimum temperature of 50°F (10°C), and watered only when the compost feels dry. Propagate by seed or cuttings. When taking cuttings, allow the cut ends to dry for one or two weeks before inserting. Other species are best above 60°F (15°C), and should be watered freely when in growth. Propagate by seed or cuttings.

E. bupleurifolia. Tiled spurge. A dwarf, spineless succulent, making a globular to cylindrical stem 4–5 in. tall. It is densely covered with spiral rows of thick scales like a closely tiled roof, and the long,

tapering leaves emerge from the ends of the shoots in summer. The small, green flowers are borne on long stalks. A species needing warmer conditions than most, and some shade. Give a period without watering in winter.

E. caput-medusae. Medusa's head. A most distinctive plant with a short, thick, upright stem from which radiate many ribbed, gray-green, horizontal branches up to 2 ft. in length, with the ends bearing tufts of tiny leaves and curved upwards. It must be propagated from seed as stem cuttings grow lopsided and do not form perfect plants.

E. ceriiformis. A succulent, much branched shrub which can eventually reach 3 ft. in height. The stems are sharply angled and carry small, spiny teeth. It is an easy species to cultivate.

E. clandestina. A striking species with erect, cylindrical stems which can reach 2 ft. in height. They have rows of short tubercles which are arranged in close spirals up the stem, like a tightly twisted stick of barley sugar. The ends of the stems carry the 1–2 in., narrow leaves.

E. coerulescens. An erect, succulent shrub branching at, or below, ground level. The branches are blue-green in color and up to 2 in. thick, and convex between the 4–6 horny and spiny ribs. Valuable for its attractive coloration.

E. flanaganii. Green crown. A very small plant, forming a 2 in., succulent stem which carries layers of spreading branches like a crown. The youngest central branches are held erect, the lower becoming progressively more horizontal, and the oldest at the base, spreading to make a 2½–3 in.-wide mound.

E. fulgens. Scarlet plume. A graceful, shrubby species from Mexico with long, narrow, somewhat gray-green leaves, and tiny flowers borne in clusters and made conspicuous by their bright scarlet, petal-like bracts. It is best grown as an annual, taking cuttings in spring from the previous year's plant before discarding it.

E. globosa. A low shrub with almost globular branches, having furrowed, squared segments and small tubercles. They are irregularly branched and carry narrow, flowering stems.

E. horrida. A very succulent species forming tall, columnar stems which are deeply ribbed, the angles bearing strong spines. A very cactus-like plant.

E. ingens. Candelabra tree. A spiny succulent which makes a tall tree in the wild. In a pot it forms a branched specimen with 5 angled, yellowish-green branches, the angles bearing wavy wings.

E. i. 'Monstrosa'. Totem pole. A curious form with the wings deeply indented and spine-tipped, and the stems contorted and twisted.

E. lophogona. An attractive, leafy succulent from

Madagascar which makes a branching, 2 ft. shrub. The thick stems have 4 or 5 angles, each lined with reddish hair. The dark green leaves have paler veins and are up to 8 in. long, while the small flowers sit between striking, pinkish bracts.

E. mammillaris. Corncob cactus. A small succulent, usually less than 8 in. high, branching and suckering from the base to produce many cylindrical stems. These are closely angled and lined with tubercles, giving a knobby appearance. They also carry scattered ½ in. spines.

E. m. 'Variegata'. Similar in form, the stems are very pale-green with darker markings and a pink tint.

E. marginata. Snow on the mountain. An attractive, variegated annual from the USA, the branched stems bearing ovate, fleshy leaves, 1–3 in. in length, the lower gray-green, the upper margined with white, as are the bracts which form just below the tiny flowers. Propagate by seed.

E. milii milii. Syn. *E. splendens bojeri.* Crown of thorns. A bushy, dwarf shrub with deep green, firm leaves up to 1 in. long, borne at the end of the grayish, spiny stems. The tiny flowers have showy, scarlet bracts, and open in spring.

E. m. splendens. Syn. *E. splendens.* A similar plant, but much larger, having long, sinuous, spiny stems and less brilliant bracts. Water freely when in bloom.

E. obesa. Turkish temple; Baseball plant. A remarkable species, almost completely globular, and always less than 5 in. across. The leaves are marked like lines of reddish stitching, as if the plant has been sewn together from small triangular sections, all meeting at the top. It is extremely decorative. Propagate by seed only. *(illus.)*

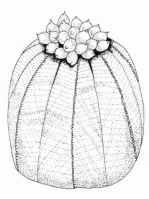

E. polyacantha. Fish bone cactus. An Ethiopian species which can make a branching shrub up to 5 ft. high. Kept in a pot it remains quite small, and the short, grayish stem carries gray-green branches

which have strongly marked angles. These in turn have a horny edge and wide spreading spines.

E. pulcherrima. Poinsettia; Christmas star. A favorite Christmas plant, which in its native Mexico makes a 10 ft. shrub. As a house plant it is best renewed annually unless the necessary time and trouble can be taken to regulate light and temperature as is done by nurserymen. The attraction of the plant is in its brilliant scarlet, starry bracts which surround the tiny yellow flowers. To bring out the full color, good light and a minimum temperature of 60°F (15°C) are necessary. Many named cultivars with bracts of white, pink, and varied shades of red are now available.

E. pulvinata. A small, succulent species, branching from the base to form large mats of 2–3 in. stems, each with 6–8, deep ribs scattered with straight spines.

E. tetragona. In the wild, a 40 ft. tree, but smaller in cultivation. It is freely branched, with 4 or 5 spine-tipped angles, and flat, dark green surfaces between.

E. trigona. Syn. *E. hermentiana.* African milk tree. A West African succulent with a short trunk branching near the base to form slender stems. These have 3–4 angles which are scalloped and carry reddish spines. Between them the stem is bright green with paler markings.

E. valida. At first quite globular, this small succulent becomes cylindrical with age, reaching 12 in. in height. It has up to 8 faces, divided by shallow ribs, and the whole plant is faintly barred with dark green lines.

Eurychone

ORCHIDACEAE.

E. rothschildiana. Syn. *Angraecum rothschildiana.* Belonging to an African genus of only 2 species, this Ugandan plant is sometimes included in *Angraecum.* Its leaves are strap-shaped and up to 8 in. in length. The margins are wavy, and the leaf tip cut into two lobes. The 4–12 fragrant, white flowers are borne in a dense spike, while the inrolled lip is marked with purplish-brown. It is a very attractive plant, requiring shade and a minimum temperature of 60°F (15°C), and a well-drained but moist compost, preferably of equal parts sphagnum and osmunda, or bark chips. Propagate by division of pseudobulbs.

Exacum

GENTIANACEAE. A genus of 40 attractive, small plants from southern Asia. They have pairs of stalkless leaves, and tubular flowers opening to 5 rounded petals. Although those in cultivation are perennials, they are best raised annually from seed. Maintain a minimum temperature of 60°F (15°C), and give some shade. Water freely.

E. affine. A delightful species from the island of Socotra off the Arabian coast. It reaches only 6–8 in. in height, and the ovate leaves are deep green. The fragrant, saucer-shaped, blue-purple flowers have bright yellow stamens, and open from summer to autumn.

E. macranthum. A very similar plant to *E. affine*, but larger, reaching 12–18 in. in height. It comes from Sri Lanka.

F

Fascicularia

BROMELIACEAE.

F. bicolor. One of a genus comprising 6 species of Chilean bromeliads, having rosettes of long, narrow, spiny leaves, and a cluster of almost stemless, blue flowers in the center. This plant has leaves up to 18 in. in length and less than ¾ in.

wide; they are spine-toothed, and near the center of the plant, bright red. The dense cluster of 30–40 pale blue flowers is surrounded by creamy-white, toothed bracts. Grow in shade with a minimum

temperature of 45°F (7°C), and water freely in summer. In winter, especially if kept in a cool place, allow the compost to dry between waterings. Propagate by offsets formed at the base of old rosettes. *(illus.)*

x Fatshedera lizei

Ivy tree. ARALIACEAE. A hybrid between *Hedera helix hibernica*, the Irish ivy, and *Fatsia japonica*, the Japanese aralia, this forms a shrub up to 6 ft. in height, but with rather lax stems which need some support. It is best replaced every two or three years to maintain a smaller, more compact plant. The dark green, glossy leaves are very like a large ivy, and the small clusters of greenish-yellow flowers are long-lived. A very tough plant. Maintain a minimum temperature of 45°F (7°C), and keep in light shade. Water freely. Propagate by cuttings. *(illus.)*

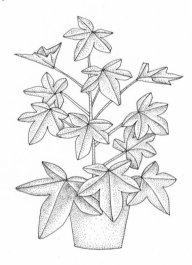

x F.l. 'Variegata'. An attractive form with creamy-white margined leaves.

Fatsia

ARALIACEAE.

F. japonica. Syn. *Aralia sieboldii*. A Japanese plant, one of only two members of the genus which makes a decorative, evergreen specimen for a cool or shady room. It is hardy in most temperate regions. The leaves are deeply cut into 7 or more dark green and glossy, wavy-edged leaflets which can reach 1 ft. across. The clusters of small, white, starry flowers are carried on mature plants. Grow in shade. Minimum temperatures can be as low as 40°F (5°C). Water freely. Propagate by cuttings, air-layering (mossing), or fresh seed.

Faucaria

Tiger jaws. AIZOACEAE. A genus of 36 species of very dwarf succulents, all from the Karoo region of South Africa. They have thick, triangular leaves with spined teeth facing inwards. When young, the teeth meet, but as they become mature, the pairs of leaves separate giving the appearance of an animal's jaws. Grow in full sun with a minimum temperature of 50°F (10°C), and water only when the compost feels dry. Propagate by suckers or seed.

F. felina. Cat's jaws. The 1–1½ in. leaves are bright green with white dots, and the golden-yellow, daisy flowers are carried singly or in pairs in autumn.
F. tigrina. Tiger's jaws. A similar species to F. felina, but a little larger, with gray-green leaves up to 2 in. in length. *(illus.)*

F. tuberculosa. Pebbled tiger jaws. The leaves of this striking plant are dark green with white spots and about 1 in. in length. They also have many white, warty spots, especially just within the thick, spine-toothed edges. The yellow blooms are 1½ in. across.

Felicia

COMPOSITAE.
F. amelloides. Blue daisy. An attractive South African plant, one of 60 in its genus, it makes a bushy plant up to 18 in. in height. The rough, green leaves are broadly ovate, and the daisy flowers are a clear sky-blue, contrasting with the central yellow disc. They first open in autumn and continue through winter. Grow in full light and a minimum temperature of 50°F (10°C). Water freely. Propagate by division, cuttings, or seed.

Fenestraria

Baby toes. AIZOACEAE. There are only two members of this succulent genus from southern Africa, and both are attractive species for indoor cultivation. They produce tufts of cylindrical, club-shaped leaves up to 1½ in. in height, each having a translucent area at the top like a small window. Grow in sun, and maintain a minimum temperature of 60°F (15°C). Water only when the compost feels dry, and keep almost completely dry in winter. Propagate by seed.

F. aurantiaca. The club-shaped leaves of this species from South Africa are blue-gray with a whitish top. The flowers are 2 in. across and golden-yellow in color.
F. rhopalophylla. From South-West Africa, this species is greener in color and has pure white blooms, 1½ in. across.

Ferocactus

CACTACEAE. Most of the 35 species belonging to this genus are in cultivation, and all are remarkable

for their ferocious spines which are hooked or straight, white, red, or yellow. They often completely encircle the globular or cylindrical stems. Full sun is necessary to bring out the color in the spines, and in winter a minimum temperature of 40°F (5°C) is acceptable. At this time of the year they must be kept dry. In summer, water thoroughly when the compost feels dry.

F. acanthodes. Fire barrel; Desert barrel. A very slow-growing, columnar species from the southern USA which can eventually reach 9 ft. in the wild, but in cultivation is usually measured in inches. The gray-green stems bear a network of radiating spines which completely cover the plant. The yellow flowers are borne only on very large specimens.
F. colvillei. Bird cage. At first globular, then elongating to barrel-shaped, this blue-green cactus from Arizona has prominent ribs which bear starry clusters of reflexed spines. The red flowers have yellow-tipped petals.
F. latispinus. Devil's tongue; Fish-hook barrel. A globular species from Mexico with a somewhat concave top, it is slow-growing and takes many years to reach its full 12–16 in. The ribs carry white, woolly areoles from which grow many spines, of

92

which the central one in each group is broad and red, hence one of its popular names. The pink-flushed, white flowers are seldom seen.

F. melocactiformis. This rounded species from Mexico becomes oval with age, and has many woolly areoles bearing yellow spines. The outer radiate like a star, the central one which can be $2\frac{1}{2}$ in. long is straight and yellow. The pale yellow flowers have red-backed petals. *(illus. left)*

F. wislizenii. Another globular species which lengthens with age, having dark green stems, eventually reaching 6 ft. The ribs bear small, oval areoles, each with a tuft of woolly hairs and hooked central spines, surrounded by straight radial ones. The reddish-yellow flowers are small.

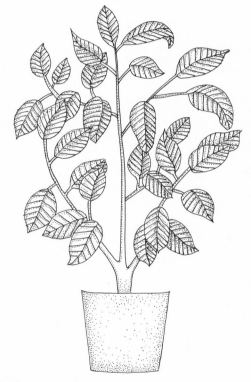

Ficus

MORACEAE. A very large genus comprising some 800 species of tropical and subtropical evergreens. Many have proved to be excellent house plants and are widely grown for the decorative value of their dark green, glossy foliage. Grow in good light, though some shade from summer sun is advisable. Maintain a minimum temperature of 60°F (15°C), and water when the compost feels dry. Propagate by cuttings or air-layering (mossing).

F. benjamina. Weeping fig. An attractive, small tree in a pot, though capable of reaching 30 ft. or more in its native India and Malaya. It has 3–4 in., slender, deep green leaves tapering to a point and borne on weeping branches. Valuable for its tolerance of air-conditioning. *(illus.)*

F. cyathistipula. From tropical Africa, this plant makes a sturdy, small tree, with stiff branches bearing 6–10 in. leathery, long, ovate leaves, widest at the rounded ends which terminate in a fine point. The $1\frac{1}{2}$ in., green fruit is borne on young plants.

F. diversifolia. Syn. *F. lutescens*. Mistletoe fig. A most elegant plant, the slender, woody stems reaching 3 ft. and carrying well-spaced, 2 in. leaves, which are almost round in outline. They are freckled with brown on their upper surfaces, and a light green beneath. The yellow fruit is freely produced on young plants.

F. elastica. Rubber plant. Perhaps the most commonly grown of all house plants, replacing the *Aspidistra* of earlier years. In the wild it can reach a magnificent 100 ft., but in a small pot or tub rarely exceeds 6 ft. It has broadly ovate, glossy green leaves which have a leathery texture. To grow this plant and its cultivars well, an even warmth is necessary, and it is therefore ideal for centrally-heated homes.

F. e. 'Decora'. This cultivar has wider leaves and a marked ivory, central vein. It grows best in good light, but not direct sunlight.

F. e. 'Doescheri'. A variegated plant, the central area of the leaves colored in shades of green and white; the irregular marginal band and the midrib are yellow.

F. e. 'Variegata'. This form is also variegated with yellow, but the marginal band is narrower, and the shades of green less strongly contrasting.

F. glomerata. Syn. *F. racemosa*. Cluster fig. This tree from southeast Asia and Australia has the curious habit of producing clusters of flowers and fruits directly from the trunk. As a house plant however, it is unlikely to reach flowering size and is grown for its long, ovate leaves which have a luminous metallic sheen. Keep the compost always just moist.

F. jacquinifolia. West Indian laurel fig. In the West Indies this makes a 30 ft. tree, but produces a decorative small shrub for pot growth. The dark, glossy green leaves are bluntly oval and only 2–3 in. in length.

F. lyrata. Syn. *F. pandurata*. Fiddle leaf fig. This West African species, which reaches 40 ft. in the wild, makes a most decorative pot plant. The erect stems are hidden by the 1–2 ft., broadly oval leaves which are leathery in texture yet have a wavy surface. In shape they resemble a violin, hence their

popular name. Allow the compost to become just dry between waterings. *(illus.)*

F. macrophylla. Moreton Bay fig; Australian banyan. An erect plant from Australia, a tree in the wild, but a shrub in pots. The dark green, glossy leaves are broadly oblong and up to 10 in. in length, having ivory-white veining.

F. microcarpa. Syn. *F. nitida; F. retusa nitida.* Indian laurel. A popular tub plant from southeast Asia and Australia which is grown under a number of incorrect names, mostly applied through an original misidentification. It has thick, waxy, ovate leaves up to 4 in. in length, and is amenable to being trimmed into shape. Give a position in full sun.

F. pumila. Syn. *F. repens.* Climbing, or Creeping fig. A neat climbing or trailing plant from China and Japan which climbs like ivy and will spread across an area of wall. It has small, dark green leaves which are broadly oval and somewhat heart-shaped at the base. Given root room, it will produce fruiting branches which have longer, narrower leaves, and brownish-purple figs. In pots however, it rarely becomes large enough for this. Requires shade.

F. quercifolia. Oakleaf fig. A trailing southeast Asian plant with deeply lobed, oak-like leaves up to 8 in. in length. When young it makes an interesting pot plant.

F. radicans. Rooting fig. A trailing species from the East Indies which is very popular for hanging baskets. The narrow leaves reach 2 in. in length,

longer on older plants, and are dark green and shiny on the upper surface.

F. r. 'Variegata'. A decorative cultivar, the leaves variegated with irregular, creamy-white, marginal bands.

F. religiosa. Peepul; Sacred Bo tree. A decorative, foliage plant from India and Ceylon, in the wild making a 100 ft. tree. Its chief attraction as a pot plant lies in the thin, heart-shaped, somewhat blue-green leaves which end in a fine point almost like a tail.

F. rubiginosa. Syn. *F. australis.* Rusty fig. A slow-growing, shrubby species from Australia which makes an attractive, bushy specimen in a pot. The 3–6 in., oval leaves are a shining green above and have rusty hairs beneath when young.

F. sycomorus. Sycamore fig. An African species having long, ovate leaves, heart-shaped at the base, with a somewhat wrinkled surface and conspicuous veins. Water freely.

Fittonia

ACANTHACEAE. Two species of dwarf, evergreen plants make up this Peruvian genus, and both make extremely decorative plants. The leaves are oval and dark green, with conspicuous veins, while the inconspicuous flowers are borne in small spikes which are best removed. Grow in light shade with a minimum temperature of 60°F (15°C), and keep the compost moist at all times. A humid atmosphere is necessary to bring out the best in these plants, and they can be grown well under a glass cover, or standing over a tray of wet pebbles. Propagate by division.

F. gigantea. This makes an upright, semi-shrubby plant up to 18 in. in height. It is grown for its dark green, ovate leaves which have bright red veins. The spikes of small, pale red flowers and bracts are not very decorative.

F. verschaffeltii. Mosaic plant. The dark green leaves are patterned with deep red veining.

F. v. argyroneura. Syn. *F. argyroneura.* Nerve plant. A form with brighter green leaves with white veining.

F. v. pearcei. Snake skin plant. This variety has light green leaves and the veining is pinkish-red.

Fortunella

RUTACEAE. A genus containing 6 species which is very close to *Citrus,* the orange family. They come from southeast Asia, and make attractive small trees for pot or tub culture. Grow in full light with a minimum temperature of 50°F (10°C), and water freely. Propagate from cuttings.

F. hindsii. Dwarf or Hongkong Kumquat. A small spiny tree from Hong Kong which has shining

green, long, oval leaves and small white flowers
which do not open fully. The fruits are small, only
$\frac{1}{2}-\frac{3}{4}$ in. across and are a bright orange-scarlet.

F. margarita. This ornamental species from China
makes a shrub or small tree up to 10 ft. in height.
The dark green, glossy leaves are long ovate and
the small, fragrant, white flowers are followed by
the $1\frac{1}{2}$ in., golden oranges. These have a good
flavor, and ripen through late autumn and winter.

Fralia

CACTACEAE.

F. pumila. One of a genus of 12 species of South
American cacti, this small, globular species has
brown, woolly areoles bearing soft, radiating spines,
and long, central ones which are stiffer. The
flowers, which only open in full sun, are brownish-
green with a yellow center. Maintain a minimum
temperature of 50°F (10°C), and water only when
the compost feels dry. Propagate by offsets or seed.

Francoa

FRANCOACEAE.

F. appendiculata. Formerly included in
Saxifragaceae, this single variable species of the
Chilean genus is sometimes given several names. It
is a tufted plant with long, oval, lobed leaves
tapering from a narrow base, and spikes of small,
pale red, starry flowers marked with darker red
dots. They open in summer and make good plants
for a cool room, needing some shade and a
minimum temperature of 45°F (7°C). Propagate by
division or seed.

F. a. sonchifolia. Syn. *F. sonchifolia*. This form has
lighter pink flowers, borne on a more open spike.

Freesia x hybrida

Syn. *F. x kewensis*. IRIDACEAE. A genus of 20
bulbous plants from South Africa. They have long,
slender leaves carried in flat, fan-like tufts, and
arching spikes of very fragrant, tubular flowers.
Grow in sun, potting the corms in autumn, and
keeping cool at night through the winter with a
minimum temperature of 45°F (7°C), though day
temperatures can rise to 70°F (21°C). Provide
some support as the shoots grow, and water
regularly until flowering has finished in late spring.
When the leaves turn yellow in summer, dry off.
Propagate by offsets or seeds, which take about
9 months to flower. Almost all the popular cultivars
grown belong to a group of hybrid origin.

F. x h. 'Blue Banner'. A cultivar with deep blue
flowers on long stems, very useful for cut flowers.

F. x h. 'Gold Coast'. A good, Indian yellow form.

F. x h. 'Irene'. A pure white cultivar.

F. x h. 'Orange Favorite'. A large-flowered form,
with deep orange-yellow blooms.

F. x h. 'Helsinki'. An unusual reddish-purple
colored form.

Fuchsia

ONAGRACEAE. A genus of about 100 shrubby
species, many of which are extremely popular as
pot plants, they are however, not ideal as full-time
house plants, requiring plenty of light and air, and
temperatures in the 50°F–65°F (10°C–18°C) range.
They can be kept in the open while temperatures
are above about 45°F (7°C) and brought indoors
for flowering and over wintering. Many can be
grown as annuals, the old plants being cut back in
the spring, providing cuttings for the next season.
Water freely. The best pot plants are hybrids
derived basically from *F. fulgens* and *F. magellanica*,
but other species are also involved.

F. x hybrida. 'Arabella'. A single form with narrow,
white, flared sepals and cherry-red petals.

F. x h. 'Cascade'. A trailing form, excellent for
hanging baskets. The wide-spread sepals are white,
and the hanging, bell-like corolla, deep red.

F. x h. 'Citation'. An erect, single-flowered species,
the sepals pale pink, and the wide-spread, saucer-
shaped corolla, white.

F. x h. 'Golden Marinka'. Of weeping habit, this
single cultivar has the leaves variegated with golden-
yellow, and the sepals and corolla red.

F. x h. 'Lena'. A very old, semi-double cultivar
which is still popular. It has flesh-pink sepals and a
purple-rose corolla.

F. x h. 'Madame Cornelissen'. A vigorous cultivar,
easy to grow, and now over 100 years old. It has
bright scarlet petals and a pure white corolla.

F. x h. 'Mission Bells'. A good, upright species
having bright red sepals and rich purple petals.

F. x h. 'Pacific Queen'. A double-flowered cultivar,
the white-tipped sepals are pink, and the corolla
rose-red. A free-flowering plant.

F. x h. 'Rufus'. Syn. 'Rufus the Red'. A single form
which is all deep red.

F. x h. 'Swingtime'. A fine plant with showy
double flowers, the sepals a rich red, and the large
corolla pure white.

F. x h. 'Tingaling'. A very free-flowering, pure
white, single cultivar.

F. x h. 'Warpaint'. A double form, the wide-spread
sepals white, and the corolla purple with pink
markings.

F. x h. 'Winston Churchill'. A well-shaped plant
with double blooms, the sepals pink, and the
corolla a pale silvery-blue.

F. fulgens. An extremely attractive, Mexican species
which makes a fleshy shrub with broadly oval

leaves, heart-shaped at the base, and pendant clusters of 3 in., bright scarlet, trumpet-shaped blooms, the sepals tipped with green. *(illus.)*

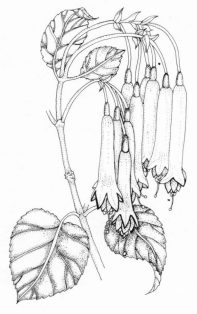

F. procumbens. A remarkably pretty, trailing species from New Zealand, making a delightful plant for a hanging basket. The small, roundish leaves are heart-shaped at the base and borne on long, slender stalks. The flowers have an orange-yellow tube and purple-tipped, green, reflexed sepals. They are followed by large, red berries.
F. serratifolia. A Peruvian species which, in the wild, can make a 6 ft. bush. It carries whorls of 3–4 narrow leaves on red, fleshy stems, and pinkish-red, tubular flowers with bright scarlet petals.
F. triphylla. This West Indian species makes a short, 1–2 ft. shrub, its leaves in whorls of 3. The nodding clusters of flowers are scarlet and $1\frac{1}{2}$ in. long.

Furcraea

False agave. AGAVACEAE. The 20 species of this genus make very large rosettes of sword-shaped leaves, sometimes up to 20 ft. across, and eventually bearing a long, flowering stem, in some plants over 20 ft. tall, with a cluster of white flowers. When small, they make decorative indoor plants, and if kept in small pots will remain of manageable size for many years. Grow in sun with a minimum temperature of 60°F (15°C), and water only when the compost feels dry, then soak thoroughly. Propagate by bulbils borne on the flowering stems, or by offsets.

96

F. gigantea. Mauritius hemp; Giant false agave. The leaves of this Brazilian plant have very small spines and are a shining green.
F. selloa. 'Marginata'. A variegated form from Colombia with cream margins to the very spiny shining green leaves. Protect from strong sunlight.

G

Galeandra

ORCHIDACEAE.
G. devoniana. Belonging to a genus of 20 species this handsome, epiphytic orchid from Venezuela and Colombia has 2 ft., upright, stem-like pseudobulbs which carry dark green, strap-shaped leaves. At the ends of the stems are clusters of very fragrant flowers which have narrow, brownish-purple petals, and sepals which are held stiffly above the large, white, inrolled lip. This has a frilled margin, and is marked with heavy purple lines. Grow in shade in a minimum temperature of 60°F (15°C). Water freely. Propagate by division.

Gardenia

RUBIACEAE.
G. jasminoides. Cape jasmine. One of the 250 species belonging to the genus, this evergreen shrub is the one familiar to most people. The wild form from China is single-flowered, with a rich fragrance, the shining whiteness of the flowers beautifully backed by the dark, glossy green leaves. They

require full sun and a minimum temperature of 60°F (15°C), as well as a moist atmosphere, so are not among the easiest house plants. Normally they flower from spring onwards, but if kept sufficiently warm in winter, will flower earlier. Propagate by cuttings in spring. *(illus.)*

G. j. 'Fortuniana'. This is the form most frequently grown, its double, waxy flowers reaching 4 in. across; pure white at first, they become ivory as they age.

G. j. radicans flore pleno. Miniature gardenia. An attractive 8–12 in. shrub with a creeping habit. The 2–3 in. leaves are narrow and pointed, and the very fragrant but somewhat irregular flowers are 1–2 in. across and open in summer.

Gasteria

LILIACEAE. 70 species make up this genus of succulent plants from South Africa. They have their variously shaped and patterned leaves in pairs, each pair set alternately on opposite sides of a very short stem, creating tufts or rosettes. When mature they produce spikes of red flowers. Grow in sun or light shade with a minimum temperature of 50°F (10°C), and water only when the compost feels dry. Propagate by division or by seed.

G. brevifolia. The stemless, thick leaves of this species are held erect at first, later spreading as a new pair grows. They are 3–6 in. in length and are dark green and rather rough, with bands of white spots.

G. candicans. A rosette-forming species with many, long, sword-shaped leaves at first erect, later becoming spreading and up to 12 in. in length. They are glossy green with indistinct bands of white dots.

G. x hybrida. Ox tongue; Bowtie plant. This name covers the many hybrids raised within this genus. They all have the basic form of pairs of long, tongue-like leaves, and most have white spots. Propagation must be by offsets if the same form is wanted, as no plant will come true from seed. However, interesting plants can be raised this way.

G. lilliputana. An attractive little plant, the narrow leaves up to 2 in. long and carried flat, each rosette like a small, white-patterned, green starfish.

G. maculata. The long leaves of this plant can reach 8 in. in length. They are boat-shaped and curve upwards at the end, and the dark green surface is marked with irregular bands of white dots.

G. verrucosa. One of the most popular species, the pairs of 6 in. leaves tapering gradually from the central stem, and ranged above each other, making the plant straight rather than starry in form. The leaf surfaces are covered with white, tubercular spots.

Gastrochilus

ORCHIDACEAE. A genus of about 20 southeast Asian orchids which are mostly epiphytic and have a few small, but leathery leaves, and small spikes of large, showy flowers. They grow best in a sphagnum-osmunda compost, and need shade and a minimum temperature of 60°F (15°C). Water freely. Propagate by division.

G. bigibbus. The short stems carry 5 in. leaves which are lobed at the ends. The pendant flower spikes open in autumn and carry up to 20 blooms, each with a waxy texture and about 1 in. across. They are golden-yellow with a white, yellow-marked, fringed lip and a short spur. They are very fragrant. A rewarding plant which will tolerate a minimum temperature of 50°F (10°C).

G. calceolaris. The leathery leaves of this species are up to 7 in. long and notched at the apex. The autumn-borne flowers are carried in a short spike, and are ¾ in. across, the greenish-yellow petals and sepals being marked with purplish spots. The showy lip is fringed with a purple central zone, marked with yellow, and white at the sides.

Geogenanthus

COMMELINACEAE

G. undatus. Of the 4 members of this small, South American genus, this species comes from Peru. It makes a decorative foliage plant, forming low-growing clumps of broadly oval leaves which are thick and fleshy. The dark green, quilted upper surface is marked lengthwise with wavy, gray bands, and the leaf is red-purple beneath. Shade, a minimum temperature of 60°F (15°C), and high humidity are needed for the best results. Propagate by division or cuttings. *(illus.)*

Gerbera

COMPOSITAE.

G. jamesonii. Transvaal daisy. Of this South African genus comprising 70 species of perennial plants, the Transvaal daisy makes an attractive house plant, and is especially valued for cut flowers. The narrow, 8–10 in., lobed leaves are hairy beneath, and the 4 in., daisy-like flowers are carried on long, leafless stalks which reach 15–18 in. In the wild they are flame-colored, but many cultivars of hybrid origin are now available, giving single and double flowers in shades of yellow, orange, red, pink, and white. Grow in sun with a minimum temperature of 45°F (7°C), and keep below about 75°F (24°C) if possible. Water when the compost feels dry and propagate by seed or division. *(illus.)*

Gladiolus

IRIDACEAE. A genus of some 300 species, all from warm temperate and subtropical areas of the old world. They have stiff, sword-shaped leaves, held in flat, fan-like clusters, and spikes of very attractive flowers which are held so that all the blooms face in the same direction. Many of the species make good pot plants for a cool position, and the garden hybrids and cultivars can be brought in for flowering. Grow in full sun with a minimum temperature of 45°F (7°C), and water freely when in growth. Once the foliage starts to yellow after flowering, dry off, and store the corms in a cool but frost-free place. Pot *carneus*, *x colvillei*, and other South African species in late autumn, the *primulinus* and large-flowered garden cultivars in early spring. Propagate by offsets, cormlets, or seeds.

G. carneus. Painted lady. A graceful, South African species; the red, pink, or white flowers have somewhat pointed petals, giving a starry effect, the lowest petal having a deeper red, semi-circular marking. They open in spring and summer.

G. x colvillei. A hybrid between *G. cardinalis* and *G. tristis*, merging the colors of the two, the flowers being red with yellow markings. They are borne in late spring and early summer.

G. x c. 'The Bride'. A very attractive pure white form.

G. primulinus. The original species comes from East Africa, but in cultivation it is largely replaced by a

98

group of hybrids raised from it. It has yellow blooms which have the upper petal hooded over, a characteristic shown by all its hybrids.

Globba

ZINGIBERACEAE. There are 50 members of this Asian genus. All are erect, perennial plants bearing long, narrow, usually stalkless leaves, and spikes of curious white, pink, or yellow flowers borne above colorful bracts. They require some shade and a minimum temperature of 60°F (15°C). Water freely. Propagate by division.

G. schomburgkii. This species makes an 18 in. plant with leaves up to 6 in. in length and pendant spikes made up of many separate spikelets of yellow flowers spotted with red. Below each spikelet are wide, pale green bracts. They flower in late summer.

G. winitii. An arresting plant from Thailand reaching 3 ft. in height. They have 8 in., pointed, ovate leaves, and the strange flowers are yellow with a long, curving tube. They are borne on short stalks, each with a rose-purple bract at its base, and grouped together into a long, arching spike.

Gloriosa

Glory lily. LILIACEAE. A genus of 5 tuberous plants which have long, soft stems and leaves tipped with tendrils. They make beautiful climbers where they can be given good sunlight and a minimum temperature of 45°F (7°C). Water freely when in growth. Plant the tubers in early spring, providing some means of support for the young stems. Dry off when the stems die back in autumn after flowering. Propagate by seed or offsets.

G. rothschildiana. A beautiful plant from East Africa, the leaves narrow and bright green, and the petals up to 4 in. long, strongly reflexed to show the gradation in color from yellow at the center to brilliant scarlet-red at the tips. The margins are yellow and wavy.

G. simplex. This small climber comes from Mozambique. It has deep orange flowers shading to yellow, and softly waved margins.

G. superba. From India and Ceylon, this species is very similar to *G. rothschildiana*, but has slightly smaller, more markedly waved petals which are more orange in color.

Glottiphyllum

AIZOACEAE. A genus of 50 perennial, succulent plants, all from South Africa. They have pairs of very fleshy leaves which are long and somewhat cylindrical in section, curving upwards at their blunt tips. In autumn and winter the colorful, daisy-like flowers open. They are easy to grow, requiring a sunny position and a temperature near 50°F (10°C), if possible, in winter. Water only when the compost feels dry. Propagate by cuttings or seed.

G. fragrans. The tongue-shaped leaves of this species are densely packed and up to 3 in. in length. The bright yellow, fragrant flowers are 4 in. across.

G. linguiforme. Green tongue. The most familiar name in cultivation, but most of the species grown are in fact hybrids. The leaves are up to 3 in. in length and are concave. The 2–3 in. flowers are golden-yellow.

G. marlothii. A particularly free-flowering species with 3 in. wide, golden-yellow blooms. The leaves are borne in pairs of unequal length and are concave on the upper surfaces.

Gomesa

Little man orchids. ORCHIDACEAE. A small, Brazilian genus containing about 10 epiphytic orchids. They have flattened pseudobulbs which carry long, strap-shaped leaves and arching spikes of long-lasting, fragrant flowers. They are easy to grow on bark slabs in a fiber compost in light shade. Maintain a minimum temperature of 50°F (10°C), and water freely.

G. crispa. The 4 in. pseudobulbs of this species bear pairs of soft, 8 in. leaves. The fragrant, yellow-green blooms which have wavy petals and sepals, are carried in many-flowered, pendant spikes.

G. planifolia. A similar species to *G. crispa*, with longer, more erect leaves and 8–10 in., laxer, pendant spikes of greenish-yellow flowers.

Graptopetalum

CRASSULACEAE.

G. paraguayense. Mother-of-pearl plant. One of a genus of 10 succulent plants all from Mexico and Arizona. This rewarding plant has basal rosettes of thick, pearly, pinkish-gray, fleshy leaves 2–3 in. long, and widely-spaced clusters of white, starry flowers. Grow in full sun with a minimum temperature of 50°F (10°C), and water only when the compost feels dry. Propagate by offsets or seed.

Graptophyllum

ACANTHACEAE.

G. pictum. Caricature plant. Among 10 species making up this tropical genus of small shrubs, this species has decorative, oval leaves which are bright green with yellow or white irregular markings, sometimes fancifully like faces, hence its popular name. When mature, the plants bear tubular, dull red flowers throughout summer. Grow in light shade with a minimum temperature of 60°F (15°C), and water freely. For best results a humid atmosphere is necessary. Propagate by cuttings.

G. p. albo marginatum. A variety with white, cream, and gray variegation and an all-white margin.

Grevillea

PROTEACEAE. An Australian genus containing 190 species of evergreen trees and shrubs of very varied appearance. Grow in pots or tubs if large specimens are required. Keep in full sun, and maintain a temperature above 50°F (10°C). Water when the compost feels dry. Propagate *G. robusta* from seed, and *G. rosmarinifolia* from cuttings with a heel.

G. robusta. Silk oak. In Australia, this is a 100 ft. tree, but confined to a pot, makes a most decorative specimen plant only a few feet high. Its leaves are so deeply dissected as to resemble fern fronds, and arch gracefully from the single erect stem. Flowers are not formed while the plant is this size.

G. rosmarinifolia. A bushy shrub having narrow, pointed leaves, rather like those of rosemary, carried on branched wiry stems. The red flowers which are curled and tubular are borne from spring to summer.

Griselinia

GRISELINIACEAE.

G. lucida. Shining broadleaf; Puka. Formerly included in *Cornaceae*, this evergreen shrub from New Zealand is one of a genus of 6 species. It makes a most decorative tub or pot plant, with broadly ovate, glossy green leaves up to 8 in. in length. In the wild it is often an epiphytic shrub; in the soil it can form a 30 ft. tree. Although remaining small when confined to a pot, it will still produce aerial roots. Grow in good light with a minimum temperature of 50°F (10°C), and water freely when growing. Propagate by cuttings.

Guzmannia

BROMELIACEAE. A large genus comprising 110 species of mostly epiphytic plants from the forests of Central and South America. They have long, strap-shaped leaves borne in a rosette and joined at the center to form a well-like waterholder. When the plant is in flower, the leaves become brightly colored at the center. Grow in shade with a minimum temperature of 60°F (15°C), and water freely, topping up the central well when necessary. Propagate by offsets and seed.

G. berteroniana. Flaming torch. A Puerto Rican plant with green leaves which deepen to red in good light. The small, yellow flowers are enclosed in bright scarlet bracts which overlap to form a solid, flame-like spike.

G. lingulata. Scarlet star. This species, which is found from the West Indies to Brazil, has $1\frac{1}{2}$ ft. leaves and brilliant scarlet flowers formed by the long, reflexed bracts which surround the tubular, yellow flowers. They are carried erect on a foot-long stem.

G. l. 'Major'. A fine cultivar with shining green leaves and a larger, more brightly colored flower spike, the bracts close to the small, white flowers having yellow margins.

G. l. 'Minor'. Orange star. A smaller plant with yellowish-green leaves marked with narrow, purplish lines. The flower bracts are a bright reddish-orange.

G. sanguinea. The narrow leaves of this Colombian species can reach 1 ft. in length. The center ones become red at flowering time. The cluster of yellow-white flowers are borne in the center of the leaf rosettes.

G. zahnii. An attractive species with soft-textured, green leaves which are almost translucent at the center and are finely striped with deep red. The tiny, white flowers are borne within pinkish-yellow bracts on a branching spike. This species needs rather more humidity than the others described.

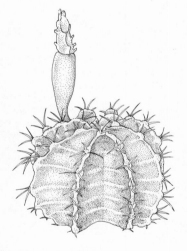

Gymnocalycium

Chin cacti. CACTACEAE. A South American genus containing about 60 species of mostly globular cacti. They are easy to grow and flower, and have marked ridges, or chins beneath each spiny areole. The large, daisy-like flowers open from spring to autumn. Grow in good light with a minimum temperature of 45°F (7°C), and water only when the compost feels dry. Propagate by seed.

G. baldianum. Native to Argentina, this 2–3 in. plant has a blue-gray stem with white radiating spines. The funnel-shaped flowers are reddish-purple.

G. gibbosum. Globular at first, later lengthening to 6–8 in. in height, the blue-green stems have brownish, radiating spines and $2\frac{1}{2}$ in. flowers, which are white with a pink flush.

G. mihanovichii. A $2\frac{1}{2}$ in. globular species with pale yellow spines. The abundant blooms have deep red outer petals and whitish inner ones. *(illus.)*

G. 'Blondie', 'Hibotan', 'Red Head'. These are the result of the occurrence of plants of *Gymnocalycium* which are without green coloring and so appear red or yellow. Without the green chlorophyll, they cannot grow properly, so are grafted onto green species, usually of *Hylocereus*, to produce the curious forms grown under these and similar cultivar names. The first is yellow, the other two red.

Gynura

COMPOSITAE. About 100 species make up this Asian genus of shrubby or herbaceous plants which are grown chiefly for their decorative foliage. Grow in sun or light shade, in a minimum temperature of 50°F (10°C), and water freely. Propagate by cuttings.

G. aurantiaca. Velvet plant. Coming from Java, this decorative species is covered in soft, purplish hairs. It is inclined to become tall and straggly if the leading growths are not pinched out when it is young. The leaves are broadly ovate and finely toothed, the green coloration showing through the velvety pile. The yellow flowers, like those of a daisy without the white petals, are borne in late winter and spring.

G. bicolor. Oak-leaved velvet plant. The fleshy leaves of this species are very deeply lobed like those of an oak, and are deep green with a purplish, metallic sheen. Beneath they are a rich violet-purple. The orange flowers open in spring.

G. sarmentosa. Syn. *G. scandens; G. aurantiaca sarmentosa.* Although at first rather similar to *G. aurantiaca*, this plant later develops a twining stem, and the leaves on it become lobed, rather than toothed as they were at first. Given a light support, it makes an attractive twining plant.

H

Habranthus

AMARYLLIDACEAE. A genus of 20 small, bulbous plants mostly from South America, only one reaching as far north as Texas. They have long, narrow, strap-shaped leaves, and funnel or trumpet-like flowers on long stems. Grow in full light with a minimum temperature of 45°F (7°C). Water when the compost feels dry, and keep barely moist through the winter. Propagate by offsets or seeds.

H. andersonii. A small, slender species from Argentina and Uruguay, the 1 in. wide flowers being gold or copper with a bronzy flush on the outside. They are borne from summer to autumn. **H. a. texanus.** A form from Texas with yellow flowers similarly marked on the outside, but also having purple streaks. They are borne on reddish stalks.

H. robustus. This species from Argentina and Paraguay has grayish-green leaves, and in summer and autumn, bright pink, trumpet-shaped flowers 2½–3 in. long.

Haemanthus

Blood lilies. AMARYLLIDACEAE. An African genus which contains 50 varied but always attractive species of bulbous plants. Grow in sun with a minimum temperature of 45°F (7°C), and water freely while in growth, drying off the deciduous species when the leaves begin to yellow, resuming watering when the young leaves appear in autumn. Propagate by offsets or seeds.

H. albiflos. White paintbrush. Reaching 1 ft. in height, this South African species has broadly ovate to oblong, fleshy, dark, evergreen leaves and curious flower heads made up of many small, greenish-white flowers held within a cup of creamy-white bracts. From the flowers protrude a mass of white, orange-tipped stamens like the bristles of a shaving brush. They open in summer and autumn. **(illus.)**

H. coccineus. Ox-tongue lily. This South African, deciduous species has large, 1–2 ft., oval leaves which die down before the flowers open in late summer and autumn. These are small with red, protruding stamens, all enclosed in a large cup of bright red, petal-like bracts.

H. katherinae. Blood lily. A very attractive, deciduous species from South Africa, which does best with a minimum temperature of 55°F (13°C). The long, sword-shaped leaves have wavy margins and are produced at the same time as the 6 in. clusters of tiny, pinky-red blooms which are held on a 1–1½ ft. stem. Flowering time is late summer and the leaves remain evergreen through winter. It is, however, still necessary to give the plants a rest, and they should be dried off gradually in the same way as the other species.

H. multiflorus. Salmon blood lily. A very striking plant with 1 ft. long, broad leaves, and globular, 6 in. heads of salmon-pink flowers with protruding, red stamens. They are borne on 2–3 ft. stems in early summer, before the new leaves expand. Needs a minimum temperature of 55°F (13°C).

Hamatocactus

CACTACEAE.

H. setispinus. A genus of only 2 or 3 species from Mexico and the southern USA. They are globular at first, but elongate as they age, eventually reaching 1–2 ft. in height. This species is bright green, with the areoles each bearing 12–18 fine brown or white spines. The freely produced, funnel-shaped flowers are yellow with a red throat and open in summer. Grow in sun with a minimum temperature of 45°F (7°C), and water only when the compost feels dry. Propagate by offsets or seed.

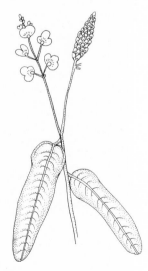

Hardenbergia

LEGUMINOSAE. Both species belonging to this genus are from Australia, and both are evergreen climbers. They have crowded spikes of violet or purple, pea-like flowers. Occasionally, white or pink forms occur. They are very effective trained on trellises or on wires formed into loops over the pot. Grow in sun with a minimum temperature of 45°F (7°C). Propagate by cuttings.

H. comptoniana. The 2–5 in. leaves are divided into 3 or 5 leaflets, and the clusters of violet-blue, white-marked flowers open in late winter.

H. violacea. The leaves of this species are narrowly oval and undivided, reaching 5 in. in length. The long clusters of violet-purple flowers are borne in spring. *(illus. prev. page)*

Hariota

CACTACEAE.

H. salicornioides. Syn. *Hatiora salicornioides.* Drunkard's dream. Of the 4 species in this genus, this strange Brazilian plant is upright with slender, greenish-purple stems divided into short sections with bottle-shaped joints, hence its popular name. The areoles are without spines, and the small, bright yellow flowers are red-flushed outside. The fruit are a translucent white, tipped with red. Grow in shade with a minimum temperature of 60°F (15°C), and keep the compost just moist. Propagate by cuttings.

Harrisia

CACTACEAE. A genus of 13 species, all narrowly cylindrical in growth, the stems erect at first, but becoming arching and then prostrate as they lengthen. The large, freely-borne flowers open at night. Many are tropical in origin and need full sun with a minimum temperature of 60°F (15°C). Water only when the compost feels dry, and propagate by seeds.

H. gracilis. Slender dog's tail. A graceful plant from Jamaica; the dark green stems up to 1½ in. thick have 1 in., black-tipped, white spines growing in clusters of 10–16 from the areoles. The flowers, which can reach 8 in. in length, are white inside with a brown flush outside. They are followed by round, 1½ in., yellow fruit.

H. tortuosa. Red-tipped dog's tail. An Argentinian species with dark, purplish-green stems and rather blunt, short, red-brown spines. The funnel-shaped flowers are up to 6 in. long and white with greenish-brown markings outside. The large, round fruit are red and spiny.

Haworthia

LILIACEAE. A genus containing about 150 species of small, succulent plants from South Africa. They have stiff, fleshy leaves and most form tight rosettes, though some have erect stems. The small, tubular flowers are green to pink. Grow preferably

in full sun, though a little shade is tolerated, and keep a minimum temperature of 40°F (7°C). Water only when the compost feels dry. Propagate by division, offsets, or seed.

H. attenuata. The dark green leaves of this plant are up to 3 in. in length, tapering to a point, and banded and spotted with white tubercles. *(illus.)*

H. batesiana. The 1 in. leaves of this tiny species are oblong, tapering to an incurved, bristly tip. They are mid-green and patterned with darker lines.

H. coarctata. Cowhorn haworthia. An erect plant, growing 6–8 in. in height, with spiralled, 1½–2½ in. long, triangular leaves tapering to the tip. They are dark green and covered with rows of pale green tubercles.

H. cuspidata. A flat, rosette-forming plant, the ½–¾ in. leaves pale green and broadly triangular, narrowing suddenly to a point. Near the tip they have transparent lines which let sunlight into the plant, which in the wild, grows largely buried in the sand.

H. cymbiformis. A similar species in habit to *H. cuspidata,* but with concave, boat-shaped leaves which are gray-green and transparent at the tips.

H. fasciata. Zebra haworthia. A small rosette with 1–1½ in. leaves which are curved upwards from the base to a tapering tip. They are dark green, and the white tubercles are borne close together in bands across the leaves. A distinctive plant.

H. limifolia. The dark green, thickly wedge-shaped leaves of this plant are held almost horizontally, with only the uppermost at a more erect angle. They are dark green, and the lines of tubercles are thin and less distinct than in *H. fasciata*.

H. margaritifera. Pearl plant. The leaves of this tightly clustered plant are horizontal at the base, but then arch erect. They are very dark green, 3–4 in. long, and taper to a fine tip. They have scattered, large, creamy-white tubercles.

H. papillosa. Pearly dots. Rather similar in form to *H. fasciata* but longer, the leaves up to 3 in. long and erect, incurved at the tips. The white tubercles are evenly scattered over the surface.

H. reinwardtii. Wart plant. A tall, stem-forming species, reaching 6 in., the small, triangular leaves overlapping and incurved. They are covered with irregular lines of white tubercles.

H. retusa. A low-growing plant, the very thick, wedge-shaped triangular leaves up to 2 in. long; the upper part, with a transparent area near the tip, is held almost horizontally.

H. truncata. Clipped window plant. A curious plant, the leaves looking as if they should be oval in outline, but have been accidentally sliced in half. In the wild, flat ends of the leaves have transparent areas held up to the light, the rest of the plant being buried.

Hechtia

BROMELIACEAE.

H. argentea. One of a genus of 35 species of spiny perennials, this rosette-forming plant from Mexico makes an impressive house plant. It has very narrow, silvery-gray, 12 in. leaves which have strongly recurved spines along the margins. The spikes of whitish flowers are borne on strong, erect stems, but rarely on pot specimens. Grow in moderate shade with a minimum temperature of 50°F (10°C). Keep the compost just moist at all times. Propagate by offsets.

Hedera

ARALIACEAE. A genus containing 15 species of evergreen, self-clinging climbers or trailers. They make splendid ground cover for large plantings, or can be grown climbing on small supports in pots, or as trailers from hanging baskets. As a house plant, it does need a cool night temperature, though it thrives in temperatures up to 75°F (24°C) by day. It will withstand minimum temperatures down to 35°F (2°C). Grow in shade, and keep the compost just moist. Propagate by cuttings.

H. canariensis. Canary Island ivy. A very handsome ivy found wild in Madeira and West Africa as well as the Canary Islands. It has glossy, bright green leaves which are broadly ovate and sometimes also lobed.

H. c. 'Variegata'. Syn. 'Gloire de Marengo'. A colorful form, the broad leaves shading from dark green at the center to a silvery-gray, and with a broad, white margin.

H. helix. Common ivy. Native to western and southern Europe and into Asia as far as Persia, this is a most adaptable and variable species. A large number of cultivars with variations upon the normal 3–5 lobed leaves are available, and many make good indoor plants.

H. h. baltica. Baltic ivy. A particularly hardy form from northern Europe having smaller, less deeply cut leaves which have clearly marked, pale veins.

H. h. 'Buttercup'. Gold ivy. One of the best yellow forms, the leaves a rich buttercup-yellow when young, fading to a paler yellowish-green as they age.

H. h. 'Chicago'. Emerald ivy. This form has small, 5-lobed leaves which are usually a clear green, but can have a purplish flush.

H. h. 'Conglomerata'. Japanese ivy. A slow-growing, bushy, non-climbing form, the stems crowded together and bearing overlapping, dark green leaves which are not lobed.

H. h. 'Curlilocks'. The congested leaves of this decorative form are crisped and curled, making a tight, bushy plant.

H. h. 'Digitata'. The broad, very dark green leaves of this form are deeply cut into 5 finger-like lobes.

H. h. 'Glacier'. A variegated form with small, almost triangular leaves which are silvery-gray with a white edging.

H. h. 'Glymii'. A form with oval leaves which are slightly curled up at the edges and sometimes twisted.

H. h. 'Gold Heart'. A neat growing form, the dark green leaves with a large golden area in the center. It is often grown under the incorrect name of 'Jubilee' which is quite a distinct form.

H. h. 'Green Ripple'. A form grown for its deeply lobed and cut leaves which are often crimped or rippled at the margins.

H. h. hibernica. Irish ivy. A variety with large leaves up to 5 in. across, which make a dense mat.

H. h. 'Manda's Crested'. An unusual form, the leaves deeply lobed, each lobe fluted along the margins, which are sometimes deep pink on the edge.

H. h. 'Marginata'. Syn. 'Argentea Elegans'. Silver garland ivy. The somewhat triangular leaves of this form are dark, glossy green with silvery-white margins.

H. h. 'Marmorata'. An attractive, small-leaved plant, the leaves marbled with cream and silver.

H. h. 'Megheri'. Syn. 'Meagheri'; 'Green Feather'. A form with very deeply cut, leathery leaves.

H. h. 'Pedata'. An attractive form with deeply and

narrowly lobed light green leaves, strongly marked with a whitish vein pattern. *(illus.)*
H. h. 'Pittsburgh'. A small-leaved form with long, pointed, mid-green leaves.
H. h. 'Sagittifolia'. A compact plant with 5-lobed leaves, the center lobe larger than the others.
H. h. 'Shamrock'. The tiny, 3-lobed leaves of this form have the side lobes folded up like those of the shamrock. They are bright green.
H. h. 'Walthamensis'. Baby ivy. A very small form, the leaves deep green and leathery.

Hedychium

ZINGIBERACEAE.
H. flavescens. One of a genus of 50 species, this Indian plant can reach 6 ft. in a large pot or tub. It has 10–15 in. leaves which are narrow and pointed, and spikes of beautiful, pale yellow flowers with a long slender tube opening in summer to wide-spreading, greenish petals, the lowest flushed with red at the base. Grow in light shade with a minimum temperature of 60°F (15°C) and water freely. Propagate by division. *(illus.)*

x Heliaporus

Syn. *Aporocactus mallisonii.* CACTACEAE. A hybrid between *Aporocactus flagelliformis* and *Heliocereus speciosus.* It is most like the former, with long stems which can reach 2 ft. in length. The flowers, which are less freely borne, are larger and a more brilliant red. They are open in March and April. Grow in full light with a minimum temperature of 45°F (7°C) and water only when the compost feels dry. Propagate by cuttings.

Heliocereus

Sun cactus. CACTACEAE. A genus of 3 or 4 species of epiphytic cacti with branched stems which are arching or prostrate, and large, colorful flowers. Grow in sun or light shade with a minimum temperature of 50°F (10°C). Propagate by cuttings.
H. amecamensis. A Mexican plant which is very like *H. speciosus*, but has white flowers.
H. cinnabarinus. A native of Guatemala, this species has long, dark green stems which have fine spines on the 3 angles. The trumpet-shaped flowers are cinnabar-red, and open in summer.
H. speciosus. This species comes from Mexico and has 3 ft. long stems which have small, yellowish-white spines on the four angles. The summer-borne, funnel-shaped flowers are 6 in. long and carmine, with a metallic, blue sheen. *(illus. fol. page)*

Heliotropium

BORAGINACEAE.
H. x hybridum. Cherry pie. Of the 250 species making up this large genus, the plant generally seen in cultivation, sometimes listed as *H.*

peruvianum or *H. arborescens,* is a hybrid between the former species and *H. corymbosum.* Both are natives of Peru. They form shrubs which will reach 6 ft in height. As pot plants, they are best freshly raised either annually or every 2–3 yrs. The long, ovate leaves are dull green and wrinkled, and the clusters of small, blue-purple flowers are very fragrant. They open from summer to winter. Grow with a minimum temperature of 45°F (7°C) and water freely. Propagate by seeds or cuttings.
H. x h. 'Marina'. An attractive, deep blue-violet form with darker green foliage than the type.

Helxine

Syn. *Soleirolia soleirolii.* URTICACEAE.
H. soleirolii. Baby's tears; Mind your own business. The only species of its genus, coming from the Mediterranean islands of Sardinia and Corsica. It forms dense, prostrate mats with rounded, $\frac{1}{4}$ in. leaves borne on fine, rooting stems. It is excellent ground cover under a planting of large species. The greenish-white flowers are minute and inconspicuous. Grow in shade with a minimum temperature of 45°F (5°C), and water freely. Propagate by division.

Hesperaloe

LILIACEAE.
H. parviflora. Western aloe; Red yucca. Of the 2 species in this genus, this Texan plant makes

stemless rosettes of narrow, deep green leaves which can eventually reach 4 ft. in length but are only 1 in. wide. They have fibrous margins and are strongly grooved. The 3–4 ft. flower stems bear spikes of small, pinkish-red, bell-shaped blooms in summer. Grow in full sun with a minimum temperature of 50°F (10°C), and water only when the compost feels dry. Propagate by division or offsets.

Heterocentron

MELASTOMATACEAE.
H. roseum. A Mexican plant belonging to a genus comprising 12 species. It is erect and bushy, with pairs of long, narrow, thin-textured leaves. The clusters of pink flowers, each opening flat and 1 in. across are borne in autumn and winter on the ends of the stems. Grow with a minimum temperature of 50°F (10°C), and water freely. Cut back plants in spring, and use the resulting shoots as cuttings. The best plants are those raised annually in this way.

Hibbertia

DILLENIACEAE. A genus comprising about 100 species of evergreen shrubs, both those described being climbers. They need some form of support. Grow in sun or light shade with a minimum temperature of 45°F (7°C), and water when the compost feels dry. Propagate by cuttings.
H. dentata. An Australian twining shrub, the ovate, dark green, glossy leaves reaching 3 in. in length. The bright yellow flowers are $1\frac{1}{2}$ in. across, and open from spring to late summer.
H. volubilis. This Australian species is stronger growing than *H. dentata*, and has longer, narrower leaves and 2 in. wide, fragrant, yellow flowers borne in summer.

Hibiscus

Rose mallow. MALVACEAE. A genus of some 300 species containing a number of showy flowering shrubs which grow well in pots. Keep in light shade with a minimum temperature of 55°F (13°C), and water freely. Propagate by cuttings.
H. rosa-sinensis. Rose of China. A very popular species found wild in China. It has large, oval leaves which are a shining green, and in summer and autumn pinkish-red blooms which open flat and measure up to 5 in. across. Many cultivars are grown.
H. r-s. 'Cooperi'. A form having narrow leaves which are bright green with creamy-white variegation, and red and pink marbling. The flowers are small and scarlet.
H. r-s. 'Hubba'. This pretty form has waved margins on its rose-pink petals.
H. r-s. 'Miss Betty'. The flowers of this form are

pale yellow and reach 5–6 in. across.

H. r-s. 'The President'. A rich crimson-red form with wavy-edged petals.

H. r-s. 'Veronica'. A most striking plant, the yellow flowers shot with purple, veined with white, and having a purple eye.

H. r-s. 'White Wings'. The white flowers of this unusual form have narrow petals which do not overlap and a deep red eye in the center.

H. schizopetalus. Chinese lantern. A most decorative plant from tropical Africa, having arching branches with ovate, toothed leaves, and remarkable orange-red flowers which are borne on long, pendant stalks. The petals are deeply cut and recurved, and from them a tuft of stamens and stigmas hangs on a long slender tube. (*illus.*)

H. waimae. This beautiful species from the Hawaiian Islands has bright green, ovate leaves up to 6 in. long. The large, white blooms, open flat to show the boss of red stamens and stigmas which is borne in the center.

Hippeastrum

Amaryllis. AMARYLLIDACEAE. A genus containing about 75 species, all from South America. In cultivation they are much confused with the true *Amaryllis* which is a South African genus. They are bulbous plants with tufts of strap-shaped leaves, and striking clusters of trumpet-shaped flowers which are carried on tall, strong stems, often before the leaves. Grow in sun, giving some light shade in summer, with a minimum temperature of 45°F (7°C). Water freely during the period of growth, then dry off once the foliage has become yellow. Repot every third year, keeping the top of the bulb above soil level. Propagate by seeds or offsets.

H. equestre. Syn. *H. puniceum.* A handsome species with 1½ ft., leathery, arching strap-shaped leaves, and 12–18 in. flowering stems which appear before the leaves. In winter and early spring they bear two to four 4–5 in., trumpet-shaped, red flowers streaked with green or white.

H. hybrids. Most of the plants now in cultivation are of hybrid origin, and have flowers up to 8 in. across. Many named cultivars are grown and unnamed color forms of this group are listed as Dutch hybrids.

H. 'Claret'. The very large trumpets are very deep red, streaked with even darker, almost blackish lines.

H. 'King of the Striped'. The large, white flowers have red-striped petals.

H. 'Queen of the Whites'. A superb, pure white form.

H. 'Scarlet Leader'. The brightest and largest flowered of the red cultivars.

Hoffmannia

Taffeta plants. RUBIACEAE. A genus of about 100 Central and South American plants grown for their decorative foliage. Although perennials, they produce the most showy leaves when replaced every year, or every other year. Grow in shade from cuttings taken in spring, and maintain a minimum temperature of 55°F (13°C). Water freely. The tips of the stems should be pinched out when young to make the plant more bushy and leafy.

H. ghiesbreghtii. The long, ovate leaves of this ornamental plant are deep, velvety green above, with a glossy surface and deep veins giving a quilted effect. The underside is purplish. The small flowers are yellow with red spots.

H. x roezlii. A similar plant to *H. ghiesbreghtii*, but smaller with paler leaves and dark red flowers.

Hohenbergia

BROMELIACEAE.

H. stellata. One of a genus of about 30 epiphytic plants, this species has basal rosettes of 2–3 ft., narrow, toothed leaves, and small clusters of purple flowers held within red bracts. Grow in full sun with a minimum temperature of 60°F (15°C), and water freely. Propagate by offsets.

Homalomena

ARACEAE.

H. rubescens. One of a genus containing about 140 species of herbaceous and shrubby plants, many of which have decorative foliage. The leaves of this species are heart-shaped and rather fleshy, being dark green with a reddish stem, veins and margin. The arum-like flowering spathe is small and purplish-red. Grow in shade with a minimum temperature of 60°F (15°C), and water freely when in growth. Propagate by offsets.

Homeria

Cape tulips. IRIDACEAE. Of the 37 species included in this genus, some make attractive late spring- to summer-flowering plants. They are all natives of South Africa, and have long, narrow leaves which over top the flowers. These are cup-shaped at first, later opening flat. Grow in sun with a minimum temperature of 45°F (7°C) and water sparingly in summer, drying off when the foliage yellows in autumn, starting into growth in early spring. Propagate by seed or offsets.

H. breyniana. Syn. *H. collina.* Cape tulip. This slender species reaches 18 in. in height and has long, slender leaves, borne both basally and along the flowering stem. This carries orange-red flowers, 2–3 in. across, which are yellow in the center.

H. b. ochroleuca. A variety with all pale yellow flowers.

H. lilacina. Lilac shower. The basal leaves of this species are long and narrow, and the purple-veined and flecked lilac flowers are borne on 8–9 in. stems in summer.

Hoodia

ASCLEPIADACEAE.

H. rosea. African hat plant. One of a genus of 10 species, this plant from southern Africa makes an erect, branching succulent, the stems up to 12 in. in height with close, spiny ribs. The saucer-shaped flowers have broad, bronzy-red petals, each ending in a fine point and up to 1½ in. long. Grow in sun with a minimum temperature of 55°F (13°C), and water only when the compost feels dry. Give a dry period in winter. Propagate by seed.

Howeia

Syn. *Howea; Kentia.* PALMAE. A genus which contains 2 species of very decorative palms which can reach 40–50 ft. in their native home, Lord Howe Island in the Pacific. Both make excellent pot plants having very elegant foliage when young, and taking many years to become too large for indoor growth. Grow in light shade with a minimum temperature of 50°F (10°C) or lower if away from any drafts. Do not allow the compost to become dry, though good drainage is also essential. Propagate by seeds.

H. belmoreana. Curly or Sentry palm. This species has its arching, pendant-tipped fronds, cut into many slender segments, and its habit is generally rather spreading.

H. forsteriana. Thatch leaf; Paradise or Forster's sentry palm. The fronds of this species are more erect at first on longer leaf stalks, then arch gracefully outwards, spreading to make an excellent specimen plant.

Hoya

ASCLEPIADACEAE. A large genus containing some 200 species of climbing and trailing plants, having somewhat woody stems and fleshy leaves. The flowers are carried in domed clusters and are waxy in texture and long-lasting. Support is necessary. Grow in light shade with a minimum temperature of 50°F (10°C), watering when the compost feels just dry. Propagate by cuttings or by layering.

H. australis. Porcelain flower. Coming from Australia, this is a strong-growing climber with pairs of shining green, ovate leaves, 3–5 in. in length, and clusters of small, white, waxy flowers which are red at the center.

H. bella. Miniature wax plant. A shrubby plant from India with branched, arching, or trailing stems carrying the thick, dark green leaves which are 1 in. long and have white freckling. The small, starry flowers are white with a red-purple center, and are carried in pendant clusters. Best grown as a hanging plant so that the stems can trail downwards.

H. carnosa. Wax plant. Found wild in both Australia and China this climber can reach 10 ft. if given room. It has waxy green, ovate leaves, 3–4 in. in length, and rounded, hanging clusters of pinkish-white, waxy flowers which have a red center and open from late spring through summer and autumn. Can withstand minimum temperatures to 45°F (7°C). *(illus. prev. page)*

H. c. 'Variegata'. A similar plant to *H. carnosa* but is somewhat smaller, and the leathery leaves have a creamy-white border, sometimes also red-flushed.

H. imperialis. Honey plant. This beautiful climbing species has leathery, ovate leaves, borne on felty stems, and pendant clusters of reddish-brown flowers with a white eye.

Huernia

ASCLEPIADACEAE. A genus containing 30 succulent plants with cactus-like stems, usually less than 4 in. high, and sharply toothed along the 4–7 angles. The 1–1½ in. flowers are borne at the base of the stems in summer and have an unpleasant carrion smell. Grow in good light with a minimum temperature of 50°F (10°C), and water only when the compost feels dry, and in winter very sparingly. Propagate by division, cuttings of whole stems, and seed.

H. aspera. A prostrate species from central Africa, with branching stems up to 6 in. in length. They are reddish-green in color and carry bell-shaped flowers with triangular lobes which open almost flat, the outside being reddish-brown and the inside purplish-brown, both surfaces being covered with small white dots.

H. pillansii. A South African plant with very narrow, purplish-green stems up to 2 in. high and set with spirals of bristly spines. The flowers are borne in twos or threes, and have a creamy-pink tube opening to pale yellow, tapering, triangular lobes which are covered in soft red bristles and spots.

Humea

COMPOSITAE.

H. elegans. One of a genus of 7 species, this elegant biennial plant from Australia makes a fine pot plant. The long, narrow leaves are aromatic and covered in sticky hairs. The many small, red or pink flowers are borne in loose, pendulous clusters which cover the plant in summer and autumn. Grow in light shade with a minimum temperature of 50°F (10°C), and water when the compost feels dry. Propagate by seed.

Hyacinthus

LILIACEAE. Of the 30 species belonging to this genus, *H. orientalis* is the plant which has given rise to most of those in cultivation. These are erect plants with sturdy 6–9 in. stems, and long, narrow, hood-tipped leaves. The long, closely packed flower spike comprises many waxy, very fragrant, bell-shaped flowers, spreading at the mouth. Many named cultivars are now available in shades of red, blue, yellow, and white. Those specially treated for Christmas flowering should be potted in September, and kept cool until November when they can be brought indoors to flower in December. For later flowering, keep cool until the flower spikes show, then bring into the room. After flowering, they can be grown outdoors, but are best replaced for indoor culture. Keep the compost moist, and propagate by offsets.

H. 'Delft Blue'. Very strongly fragrant, medium blue flowers in a very heavy spike.

H. 'L'Innocence'. A fine white sort with a good fragrance and stiff, waxy flowers.

H. 'Pink Pearl'. An excellent pink form with wider spaced florets making a looser spike. Very fragrant.

Hydrangea

HYDRANGEACEAE.

H. macrophylla. One of a genus containing 80 species of shrubby plants. *H. macrophylla* and its forms make good pot plants if they can be kept in the open for part of the year. The Hortensia group, which have rounded heads with florets all the same size are the best for indoor growing. They have ovate, toothed leaves, 4–8 in. long, and flowers in close packed clusters. Most are naturally pink flowering, but if grown in an acid compost will turn blue. An alkaline (chalky) compost will keep them pink. They are best raised from cuttings taken from cut-back, old plants in spring. Keep in light shade with a minimum temperature of 45°F (7°C), and water freely when growing. Propagate by cuttings. Many cultivars are available.

H. m. 'Altona'. A good rose-pink which turns a clear blue when treated.

H. m. 'Goliath'. This large flowered, deep pink form becomes purplish-blue with treatment.

H. m. 'Soeur Therese'. A very fine, white cultivar with compact growth and dark green foliage.

H. m. 'Strafford'. A very good, rose-red form.

Hylocereus

CACTACEAE. 23 species make up this genus of climbing cacti which have long, slender stems, and large, funnel-shaped flowers when mature. Grow in light shade with a minimum temperature of 45°F (7°C), and water freely, particularly when in growth. Propagate by cuttings, using stem sections.

H. triangularis. This Jamaican species has long stems which are triangular in section, and in summer, white flowers which open to their full 8 in. in length only in the evening and night.

H. undatus. Honolulu queen. This strong-growing climber from the West Indies has conspicuous wings along its triangular-sectioned stems, which can reach 10 ft. in length if given sufficient root and head room. The remarkable creamy-white flowers open in summer at dusk, and are 10–12 in. long. *(illus.)*

Basket flower. The leaves of this plant from Peru and Bolivia are carried in two rows along the stem. The large flowers have a fringed cup and 3–4 in. spreading, strap-like segments. They are borne in clusters of 2–6 blooms, on a 2–2½ ft. flowering stem in spring and summer.

H. littoralis. A small species from South America with 12 in. long, broad leaves and pure white flowers 3–4 in. long having a wavy corona. They open in late spring and summer. *(illus.)*

Hymenocallis

Spider lily. AMARYLLIDACEAE. A genus comprising 50 lily-like plants, all but one of which come from South America, the exception being West African. They have basal rosettes of strap-shaped leaves, and very decorative flowers with a small central cup or corona, and long, slender, spidery segments. Grow in light shade with a minimum temperature of 50°F (10°C), and water freely during summer. When the foliage yellows, reduce the water, and keep barely moist through winter. Propagate by offsets.

H. americana. Crown beauty. The basal leaves of this splendid species from tropical America can reach 2½ ft. in length. They are strongly reflexed and form a dense rosette from which rise stiffly erect stems, bearing clusters of spidery, white flowers in summer.

H. caribaea. Caribbean spider lily. The broader leaves of this West Indian species are 2–3 ft. long, and show off the small cluster of pure white, fragrant flowers. The central cup is toothed, and the long segments are white inside and green on the reverse.

H. calathina. Syn. *H. narcissiflora; Ismene calathina.*

H. speciosa. A beautiful West Indian plant having wide, 1½–2 ft. long, dark green leaves, and very fragrant, pure white flowers with 2 in., white segments. They open in autumn.

H. 'Daphne'. A hybrid between *H. speciosa* and *H. calathina.* A vigorous plant with large flowers, and wide, strap-shaped leaves.

Hypocyrta

GESNERIACEAE. The 17 members of this genus are all tropical plants from South America. They are somewhat fleshy, and have undivided leaves and pouched flowers. Grow in shade in a minimum temperature of 60°F (15°C); water freely. Propagate by cuttings.

H. glabra. An erect plant with a single, purplish stem, and glossy, yet closely downy, long, oval leaves. The bright scarlet flowers, borne in summer, are made up of a large, inflated, pouch-like tube, with five, small, reflexed petals at its mouth.

H. nummularia. A creeping species, epiphytic in the wild, which has fine, red stems that carry small, oval, velvety leaves. The scarlet, pouched, flower tube opens to five yellow, lobe-like petals. Summer and autumn is the usual flowering period, sometimes later.

H. teuscheri. An attractive foliage plant, the 6 in. long, hairy leaves being olive-green with silvery veins, and purplish-red beneath. The flowers are yellow with bright red, lobe-like petals. They open in spring and summer.

Hypoestes

ACANTHACEAE. A large genus of about 150 shrubs and perennials from Africa, with undivided, toothed leaves, and tubular flowers. Grow in shade with a minimum temperature of 50°F (10°C), and water freely. Although perennials, they are best raised annually, taking cuttings in spring from plants cut back in late winter.

H. aristata. Ribbon bush. An erect plant from South Africa, 2–3 ft. tall, with pairs of downy, ovate leaves about 3 in. long, and tubular, rose-purple flowers, striped and spotted with a darker purple, or sometimes with white.

H. sanguinolenta. Coming from Malagasy, this attractive foliage plant needs warmer conditions, with a minimum temperature of 55–60°F (13–15°C). It is grown for its dark green leaves which are splashed and spotted with cerise, except for the green central vein and margins. The small, tubular flowers are lilac and white.

H. taeniata. A bushy species from Malagasy, grown for its attractive flowers which are purplish-pink and carried within bright pink bracts. They are borne in large clusters. The mid-green leaves provide a pleasant background.

I

Impatiens

BALSAMINACEAE. A genus of 500–600 species, native to every continent except Australasia. They are generally fleshy, and have undivided, but toothed leaves, and spurred flowers. These are followed by a capsule which springs open when touched, flinging the seeds out. Grow in sun or slight shade, with a minimum temperature of 45°F (7°C), and water freely. Propagate by cuttings.

I. balsamina. An annual plant from southeast Asia, with fleshy stems carrying long, oval, toothed leaves, and rose-pink, single flowers. The true species is now seldom seen in cultivation being replaced by double forms known variously as Camelliaeflora, Camellia or Rose flowered. They have blooms in a wide range of shades of red, pink, lilac, and white.

I. hawkeri. An erect, bushy plant from southeast Asia which grows to about 2 ft. The shiny, ovate leaves are dark green and toothed, and the 3 in., spurred, brick-red flowers open in summer and autumn.

I. h. 'Exotica'. A fine form, the bronzy-green leaves having a broad, creamy-gold line along the center, and redder flowers, white in the throat.

I. marianae. Silvery patience plant. A good foliage plant from India, the dark green, oval leaves having silvery markings between the sunken veins, and long-spurred, lilac flowers. It makes a trailing plant which quickly becomes straggly, and is best propagated annually from cuttings.

I. oliveri. A very large, shrubby plant needing a large pot and plenty of room. It has 6–8 in., fleshy, dull green leaves and large, lilac-pink blooms with long spurs.

I. wallerana. Busy Lizzie; Patient Lucy; Sultana. A familiar house plant, native to tropical Africa. It has succulent, reddish stems, and long, ovate, shining green or bronze leaves. The bright carmine-to-scarlet flowers open flat to $1\frac{1}{2}$–2 in. across, and have a 1–$1\frac{1}{2}$ in. spur. They are very freely borne, even on young plants. Two varieties of this plant are in cultivation, *I. w. holstii* and *I. w. sultanii*, and the hybrids between them give a great range of color from purples and reds through pinks and orange to white, as well as bicolors, and also dwarf forms such as 'Elfin' and 'Imp'.

I. w. sultanii. 'Variegata'. This form from Zanzibar has its pale green leaves margined with white. Like most variegated plants, it needs protection from strong sunlight.

I. w. petersiana. This is a decorative form which has a bronze-red flush, and narrowly ovate leaves.

Iochroma

SOLANACEAE. A genus comprising 25 species of shrubs and trees from Central and South America. They have undivided leaves, and colorful, tubular flowers. Grow in sun or light shade with a minimum temperature of 50°F (10°C), and water only when the compost feels dry. Propagate by cuttings.

I. coccinea. Although 4–6 ft. in the wilds, this plant can easily be kept smaller by pruning. It has 3–5 in., ovate leaves which are downy beneath, and pendant clusters of bright scarlet blooms, each up to 2 in. long, and pale yellow in the throat. They open from summer to autumn.

I. tubulosum. Violet bush. This 4–6 ft. shrub can be kept below this height in pots. It has 2–5 in., long, ovate, soft-haired leaves, and pendant clusters of 15–20 blue-purple flowers opening in summer to early autumn.

Ipomoea

CONVOLVULACEAE. A large genus containing over 300 annual and perennial plants which are widely distributed throughout the world. They make attractive plants for a wall trellis or for training around a window. Where space is limited they can be grown around a looped wire support in a pot. Keep a minimum temperature of 45°F (7°C), and the compost moist, but not wet, at all times. Propagate by seed or cuttings.

I. batatas. Sweet potato. A valuable food crop in many tropical countries, this decorative plant comes from southeast Asia. It has 5-lobed leaves, the middle lobe the longest and each tapering to a fine point. The summer-borne flowers are funnel-shaped, and purplish-red and white.

I. b. 'Blackie'. A fine form having a very dark, almost blackish-red coloration over the whole plant. Keep warmer than the ordinary species, with a minimum temperature of 55°F (13°C).

I. purpurea. Morning glory. An annual species from South America with thin, light green, heart-shaped leaves tapering to a point, and rich purple, trumpet-shaped flowers opening flat at the mouth to 3–4 in. across. A number of cultivars and varied colored forms are grown – from white to pink and bright scarlet. Needs a sunny window to flower well.

Iresine

AMARANTACEAE. 80 species of perennial plants make up this tropical American genus. A number are grown for their decorative foliage. The flowers are inconspicuous. Grow in sun with a minimum temperature of 45–50°F (7–10°C), and water freely. Propagate by cuttings.

I. herbstii. Beefsteak plant. The rounded leaves of this 1½–2 ft. Brazilian plant are notched at the tip, and have a shiny, maroon surface picked out with paler veins. Full sun is needed to bring out the best color.

I. h. 'Acuminata'. Painted bloodleaf. A form with more pointed, ovate leaves, which are deep red with paler veins.

I. h. 'Aureo-reticulata'. The small, rounded leaves of this form are more deeply notched and are green with yellow veining.

I. lindenii. Bloodleaf. Coming from Ecuador this plant has long, narrow, pointed, deep red leaves. Keep in full sun for the best color.

I. l. formosa. Yellow bloodleaf. A yellow-leaved form with green markings on the leaves, which are borne on red stems.

Ixia

IRIDACEAE.
I. viridiflora. Corn lily. One of a genus containing 45 species of bulbous plants, all but one from South Africa, with long, slender leaves, and in spring and early summer, wide-open, star-shaped flowers in short spikes borne on a long, slender stem. In this species, they are jade-green with a darker center. They need a minimum temperature of 45°F (7°C) and full sun. Water only when the compost feels dry, and dry off completely in early summer when the leaves begin to yellow. Propagate by offsets removed in autumn when potting, or by seed. *(illus.)*

I. hybrids. Many hybrids are grown with varying flower colors.

I. 'Afterglow'. An attractively colored form, the flowers a golden-fawn inside with a red eye, and pink on the reverse.

I. 'Artemis'. A striking form, the pink-flushed, white flowers have a black center.

I. 'Conqueror'. A form with unusual contrasting colors, being yellow inside, red on the reverse, and with a red eye.

I. 'Rose Queen'. A delicate, soft pink form.

Ixora

RUBIACEAE. A genus of about 400 species of evergreen shrubs, grown both for their foliage and their flowers, the clustered blooms having a long tube which opens flat at the mouth. Those described flower in summer. Grow in sun or light shade with a minimum temperature of 55°F (13°C) and water freely. Propagate by cuttings.

I. borbonica. A most handsome foliage plant from Reunion in the Indian Ocean, which has narrow, pointed, leathery leaves up to 9 in. in length, the dark, glossy upper surface with light green mottling between the bright red veins. The flowers are small and white.

I. chinensis. A 2–3 ft. shrub from India, not China as might be expected. It has long, slender, pointed leaves which are dark green and glossy, and the long clusters of flowers are orange-yellow.

I. c. rosea. A rather tall form with flowers in a pretty shade of pink.

I. coccinea. Flame of the woods. A dense shrub, 6 ft. or more in its native India and the East Indies, but only 2–3 ft. in pots. The stalkless, leathery leaves are oval with a heart-shaped base, and against them are borne clusters of brilliant red flowers.

I. javanica. Jungle geranium. This 3–4 ft. Javanese shrub has pairs of long, slender, pointed leaves, borne on erect, branching stems. The orange-red blooms are borne in large clusters.

J

Jacaranda

BIGNONIACEAE.

J. mimosifolia. Syn. *J. acutifolia; J. ovalifolia.* One of a genus of 50 shrubs and trees with deeply dissected leaves, and trumpet-shaped flowers. This species makes a very elegant pot plant when young, with lacy, frond-like leaves divided into many tiny, oval leaflets. They will not flower at this size. Grow in sun with a minimum temperature of 50°F (10°C), and water when the compost feels dry. To keep a good shaped plant it is best to replace it every few years. Propagate by seeds.

Jacobinia

Brazilian plume. ACANTHACEAE. 50 evergreen semi-shrubby plants make up this tropical American genus. They have long, undivided leaves, and very decorative heads of long, tubular flowers which seem to erupt from the tops of the leafy stems. Grow in light with a minimum temperature of 50°F (10°C). Water freely. They are best propagated annually by cuttings taken in spring from cut-back plants.

J. carnea. Syn. *Justicia carnea.* A very attractive, large pot plant from Brazil, reaching 4–6 ft. in

height. It has dark green, long, ovate leaves, and large, massed, pink flower heads opening in autumn.

J. coccinea. Syn. *Pachystachys coccinea.* This Brazilian species can reach 5 ft. in height. It has long, oval leaves, and large spikes of bright scarlet flowers which open in late winter. Maintain a minimum temperature of 55°F (13°C) while flowering.

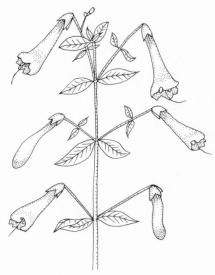

J. pauciflora. Syn. *Libonia floribunda.* This a 1–2 ft., twiggy shrub from Brazil with small oval leaves. The scarlet-tipped, yellow flowers are solitary or in twos or threes. They are borne from autumn to Spring. *(illus.)*

J. suberecta. A low, gray-green shrub from Uruguay, with small, oval leaves having a velvety texture, and small clusters of 1–1¼ in., bright scarlet flowers from spring to autumn.

J. velutina. A shrubby species from Brazil, having long, soft-haired leaves, and a dense cluster of bright pink flowers at the end of the stems; they open in early summer.

Jasminum

Jasmine. OLEACEAE. A widespread genus containing some 300 species. All are shrubby, some making erect bushes, others climbing. They prefer sun, and require a minimum temperature of 45°F (7°C). Water freely. Propagate by cuttings or layering.

J. grandiflorum. Spanish or Poet's jasmine. A straggling bush from the Himalayas, with dark green leaves made up of 5 or 7 small leaflets. The fragrant white flowers are 1½ in. across and reddish on the reverse. They are borne in clusters, and open from summer to autumn.

J. mesnyi. Syn. *J. primulinum.* Primrose jasmine. Coming from China, this is an evergreen rambling shrub, which needs some form of support. Its leaves are made up of 3, long, oval leaflets; the bright yellow flowers have up to 10 lobes, giving it a semi-double, primrose-like appearance. They open in spring.

J. polyanthum. Pink jasmine. A tall climbing plant from China, with its leaves cut into 5 to 7 leaflets. The abundantly borne, white blooms are flushed with pink, and are very fragrant. They open from autumn to spring.

J. rex. A winter flowering evergreen, climbing species from Thailand. The 4–8 in. oblong leaves taper to a point and are dark and glossy above. The white flowers open to 2 in. across and are borne in small, pendant clusters. *(illus.)*

J. sambac. Arabian jasmine. An evergreen clambering species from Arabia and India, the source of blooms for jasmine tea. It has broad, oval leaves, and very fragrant, white flowers which open from spring to autumn.

J. simplicifolium. Star jasmine. A climbing shrub from the South Sea Islands and Australia, which has 2 in., oval, undivided evergreen leaves and small, white-starry flowers.

Jovellana

SCROPHULARIACEAE. Seven species make up this small genus of plants which are rather similar to *Calceolaria.* The leaves are undivided but toothed, and the flowers have 2 unequal lips. Grow in light shade with a minimum temperature of 45°F (7°C). Water freely. Propagate by cuttings from cut-back plants in spring. They are best replaced every 2–3 years, when they become straggly.

J. sinclairii. An erect species from New Zealand, having 3 in., oval, toothed leaves which are hairy above, and borne in opposite pairs on short stalks. The small flowers are white to pale purple, scattered with red dots, and borne in loose clusters in summer.

J. violacea. An evergreen, Chilean plant, with ovate, toothed leaves, flattened at the base and thinly hairy above. The clusters of yellowish-white blooms are dotted with purple, and open in late summer.

Juanulloa

SOLANACEAE.

J. aurantiaca. Among 12 members of this genus of leathery-leaved shrubs, this epiphytic species makes a 3 ft. plant, with long, slender-pointed leaves, and loose, pendant clusters of tubular, orange flowers. Grow in shade with a minimum temperature of 50°F (10°C). Water freely and propagate by cuttings.

K

Kalanchoe

CRASSULACEAE. A genus comprising some 200 tropical and subtropical species. All are succulent, and many are shrubby. They have fleshy leaves which, in many species, produce tiny plantlets, usually along the margins. Grow in sun with a minimum temperature of 45°F (7°C), and water only when the compost feels dry. Propagate by cuttings, seeds, or by detaching the small plantlets.

K. beharensis. Velvet leaf; Elephant ear. A woody shrub from Malagasy, eventually reaching 3–5 ft. in height. It has large, triangular leaves up to 8 in. long, which are strongly waved, and are densely covered with short hair, white on young leaves, becoming brown when older. The pretty purple and yellow flowers are borne in long-stalked clusters at the top of 3–4 ft. stems on mature plants. A minimum temperature of 55°F (13°C) is necessary for this species to thrive satisfactorily.

K. blossfeldiana. A popular species originating from Malagasy. It reaches only 6–12 in. in height, and has rounded, shining green leaves which are often red along the edge. The large spikes of bright red flowers are carried on an erect stem. They open in winter, making the plant particularly valuable. Many cultivars and hybrids are now grown, some having yellow or white flowers.

K. crenata. Syn. *Bryophyllum crenatum.* Coming from tropical Africa, this shrubby species can reach 3 ft., if given sufficient root room, otherwise it will stay much smaller. It has long, narrow leaves, with large and small teeth along its red margins. These also produce small plantlets. The yellow, bell-shaped flowers emerge from red calyces during winter and spring, being borne in clusters at the top of the upright stems.

K. daigremontianum. Syn. *Bryophyllum daigremontianum.* A strong-growing plant from Malagasy, usually reaching 1½ ft. though it can be taller. The deeply toothed leaves are long-triangular, tapering to a point, with red edges and markings and light green flecking. They produce many small plantlets. The gray-violet, bell-shaped flowers are pendant, and borne on short stalks at the top of the plant from winter to spring.

K. fedtschenkoi. Purple scallops. A densely branched plant from Malagasy, with wiry stems reaching 1 ft. and carrying 2 in. oval, gray-green leaves with rounded, purple-edged teeth. In winter they produce large clusters of pinkish buff flowers.
K. f. 'Marginata'. Aurora borealis; Rainbow Kalanchoe. A most attractive form with broad, white margins to the blue-green leaves.

K. flammea. The erect stems of this plant from Somalia reach 12–15 in. in height, and have oval leaves, tapering to the base, with a slightly wavy, toothed margin. The loose cluster of bright orange flowers is borne throughout winter.

K. x kewensis. Spindle kalanchoe. A distinctive plant, a hybrid between *K. teretifolia* and *K. flammea*, it has spindle-shaped leaves up to 5½ in. in length and bronzy-green. The pink flowers open wide at the mouth, and are carried in small clusters at the end of erect, slender stems.

K. manginii. This small species from Malagasy has short, erect, sterile stems, and flowering branches up to 12 in. long, arching downwards at the tips. The oval leaves are small and fleshy, and the bright red flowers are tubular and pendant.

K. marmorata. Pen-wiper plant. An Ethiopian species with much branched, erect or prostrate stems, closely covered with oval, crenulate-margined leaves, which are greenish-gray, marked with brown blotches, and up to 4 in. in length. The long, tubular, white flowers open in spring, and

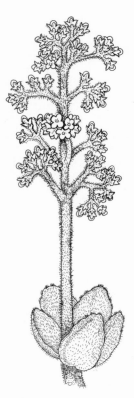

have a 2–3 in. tube opening to 5 small, starry lobes at the mouth.

K. millotii. Kola ears. A low-growing, shrubby plant from Malagasy, covered with short, soft hairs. The ovate leaves are toothed, and about 1 in. long. A plant grown for its foliage, as it rarely flowers.

K. pinnata. Syn. *Bryophyllum pinnatum.* Miracle leaf; Floppers; Curtain plant. A species now found in all the tropical regions of the world, but originally from Africa. It has strong, erect stems, which can reach 3 ft. in height, and fleshy leaves up to 8 in. long, and divided into 3–5 toothed leaflets, each margined with red. These leaflets produce abundant plantlets. The tubular, pinkish-green flowers open from summer to autumn.

K. pumila. A dwarf species, native to Malagasy, and only 6 in. tall. It is bushy in growth, with spreading stems which carry many 1 in., oval leaves, tapering to the stem; these leaves are blunt and notched at the tip. They are purplish-green with a waxy film. The winter-borne flowers are red-purple, the petals reflexed. A good basket plant.
K. x 'Red Glow'. Syn. 'Grob's Rotglut'. A Swiss-raised hybrid, with compact branches carrying deep green, crenate leaves, and clusters of bright scarlet

flowers borne well above the leaves on erect, branched stems.

K. x 'Roseleaf'. A hybrid between *K. beharensis* and *K. tomentosa*, making a decorative plant with diamond-shaped, toothed leaves, having strongly felted surfaces, rusty-brown above and silver beneath. It will not flower at pot size.

K. tomentosa. Syn. *K. pilosa*. Panda plant. This densely short-haired plant is native to Malagasy, and has most decorative, oval, thick leaves, white woolly in color, with deep brown markings on the marginal teeth. It rarely flowers in cultivation. *(illus. left)*

K. tubiflora. Good luck plant. The plant in cultivation under this name may be of hybrid origin. The erect stems, sometimes up to 3 ft., carry fleshy, pinkish-brown leaves with darker spots and up to 2 in. in length. The long, tubular flowers are purplish-red and open in winter.

K. uniflora. Syn. *Bryophyllum uniflorum; Kitchingia uniflora*. Another species from Malagasy, and one which makes a very attractive hanging plant. It is epiphytic in the wild, and has pendant or trailing stems up to 2 ft. long, bearing rounded, fleshy leaves, which are notched along the purplish margins. The delicate, urn-shaped flowers are a coral-pink, and profusely borne on short, pendant stems, almost covering the plant from winter to spring.

Kennedya

LEGUMINOSAE.
K. rubicunda. Coral pea. An Australian genus containing 15 climbers and trailers of which this species can reach 6 ft. if grown in a large pot or tub. Support is essential. It has softly brown-hairy stems bearing dark green, oval leaflets, mostly in threes and beautiful coral-red pea flowers with long petals, the upper bent upwards to show its lighter yellow center. Grow in sun with a minimum temperature of 50°F (10°C) and give plenty of light and ventilation. Water when the compost feels dry. Propagate by cuttings or seed. *(illus.)*

Kochia

CHENOPODIACEAE.
K. scoparia tricophylla. Summer cypress; Fire bush. One of a genus which contains 90 species, this ornamental annual has an erect shape rather like a cypress, reaching 3 ft. in the best specimens, but usually smaller. The very narrow leaves are 2 in. long and bright green, covering the whole plant with a dense mass of foliage. In autumn if kept cool, it turns red. Grow in sun with a minimum temperature of 45°F (7°C), water freely, and propagate by seed.

Kohleria

Tree gloxinias. GESNERIACEAE. A genus comprising about 50 species of herbaceous plants from tropical America. The pairs of undivided leaves are decorative, and the tubular flowers open to showy, often spotted, petals in some species. Grow in shade with a minimum temperature of 55°F (13°C). Water freely. Propagate by division of the rhizomes, cuttings of young basal shoots, or by seed.

K. bogotensis. Syn. *Isoloma bogotensis*. An erect, 2 ft. plant from Colombia, with toothed and velvety, oval leaves up to 4 in. long. The summer-borne, orange-yellow flowers are profusely red-spotted, and up to 1½ in. in length.

K. digitaliflora. Foxglove kohleria. A strong-growing, compact, hairy plant from Colombia reaching 1½ ft. in height. It has very large, oval leaves which can reach 8 in., and tubular pinkish-purple flowers, widening at the mouth rather like a foxglove. They are borne in summer and autumn.

K. eriantha. A Colombian species, which when well-grown can reach 4 ft., but will flower freely when smaller, and is best grown from cuttings every few years. It has oval, hairy leaves, with red marginal hairs, and red flowers which are spotted with yellow. They open through summer and autumn.

K. lanata. Woolly kohleria. The upright stems of this Mexican species can reach 18–20 in., and the whole plant is covered with whitish hairs. The 2½ in. oval leaves are bright green and softly downy, while the bright orange-red flowers have a yellow throat. A very attractive species.

K. tubiflora. Painted kohleria. A 1½–2 ft. plant from Costa Rica and Colombia. The dark green, ovate leaves have a beautiful sheen and are reddish beneath, while the orange flowers are long, tubular, and yellow within, with very small, red lobes at the mouth.

L

Lachenalia

Cape cowslip. A genus of 65 bulbous plants from southern Africa, having strap-shaped leaves, and long-lasting, waxy, bell-shaped or tubular flowers. These are carried on a leafless, fleshy stem. Grow in sun with a minimum temperature of 45°F (7°C). Water freely from autumn to spring when the plants are growing and flowering, then dry off when the foliage turns yellow, and keep dry until next autumn. Propagate by seed or offsets.

L. aloides. Tricolor cape cowslip. A very variable species with dark green, purple-spotted leaves, and pendant, bell-shaped flowers borne in a spike of 10–20 at the top of a stiffly erect stem. The blooms have 6 narrow, petal-like segments, the outer 3 half the length of the inner ones. They are red, yellow, or green, and many varieties are known. **(illus.)**
L. a. nelsonii. Yellow cape cowslip. This form has bright yellow flowers.
L. bulbifera. Syn. *L. pendula.* A strong-growing plant, up to 10 in. in height, having nodding blooms which are in shades of red, purple, or yellow. The 6 segments are the same size.

L. glaucina. Opal lachenalia. A small plant, usually below 6 in., with blue-purple, almost erect buds which open to produce bright green, tubular flowers, changing to brownish-green as they mature.
L. lilacina. Lilac bells. A 4–6 in. plant, with brown and green mottled stems, bearing an erect cluster of up to 20 lilac, tubular flowers.
L. purpureo-caerulea. Purple cape cowslip. A slender, 1 ft. plant, having a long spike which carries up to 100 very small, purplish-blue, bell-shaped flowers.

Laelia

ORCHIDACEAE. A genus comprising about 30 species of epiphytic orchids. They grow from pseudobulbs, most carrying a single leaf and erect or arching clusters of very beautiful flowers with similarly colored sepals and petals, and a 3-lobed lip, the side lobes rolled inwards to form a tube. They are carried on stiff, wiry stems. Grow in good light with a minimum temperature of 50°F (10°C). Water freely, and maintain a humid atmosphere with gravel trays beneath the plants. After flowering, give less water for about 6 weeks. Propagate by division. All the species described are Brazilian unless stated otherwise.

L. anceps. A very attractive species from Mexico and Honduras, with egg-shaped pseudobulbs each bearing a single long, oval leaf, and in winter, clusters of 2–5 flowers on long, erect or arching stems. The blooms have white, pink, or purple sepals and petals, and a brightly colored lip with markings of red, purple, and yellow.
L. crispa. This plant has long, club-shaped pseudobulbs each carrying an oblong, dark green leaf. The white flowers are 4–5 in. across, with a purple and white, waved lip, yellow in the throat. They open in spring.
L. harpophylla. This species has very long, stem-like pseudobulbs which bear long, narrow leaves, and the flower clusters are borne on a short stalk. The 2–3 in. flowers are a striking brick-red, and open in late winter.
L. perrinii. A very attractive plant with club-shaped pseudobulbs, each carrying a single, ft.-long, dark green leaf. The short flowering spike has blooms up to 5½ in. across, lilac-pink with the edge of the lip a deep red-purple. They open in autumn and winter.
L. pumila. A smaller plant with egg-shaped pseudobulbs and solitary, dark green, fleshy leaves usually less than 5 in. in length. The fragrant flowers are 2–4 in. across, and a delicate pinkish-purple. The lip has strong purple markings and yellow lines in the throat. They open in autumn.
L. purpurata. Queen of the orchids. This splendid plant is the national flower of Brazil. It has club-

shaped pseudobulbs carrying solitary, dark green leaves up to 15 in. in length, and in summer, very large blooms which can reach 8 in. in diameter. The sepals and petals are white, sometimes with a pink or purplish flush, and the lip is a deep crimson-purple with a yellow throat.

L. xanthina. The 8 in., club-shaped pseudobulbs carry stiff, dark green leaves, and 2½–3 in. flowers with yellow petals and sepals remaining partly furled, and a white lip marked with reddish-purple. They are produced in summer.

x Laeliocattleya

ORCHIDACEAE. A hybrid between two orchid genera, *Laelia* and *Cattleya*, which has been bred to try and produce a flower which combines the superb shape of the *Cattleya* blooms with the variety of color found in *Laelia*. Many fine cultivars will be found listed in orchid raisers' catalogs. Cultivate as for *Laelia*.

Lampranthus

AIZOACEAE. A South African genus containing 100 species of small, succulent plants, most with spreading stems and very narrow, almost cylindrical leaves. They are grown for their freely produced, colorful, daisy-like flowers which open in summer, and make excellent basket or pot plants. Grow in good light with cool conditions in winter, preferably a temperature below 50°F (10°C). Water sparingly but do not allow to become completely dry. Propagate by seed or cuttings.

L. aureus. Golden ice plant. A creeping plant with short, erect, flowering stems carrying many golden-yellow flowers, opening to 2 in. across in good light.

L. coccineus. An erect species with gray-green leaves with darker spots, and bright scarlet flowers, 1–1½ in. across.

L. emarginatus. The short, erect branches carry many white-dotted, gray-green leaves, and a profusion of 1–1½ in., violet-pink flowers.

L. roseus. Pink ice plant. The original species is an erect, but low-growing plant, spreading to form cushions of color when the 2 in., pale pink flowers are open. Many hybrid forms have been raised and are grown under this name. Propagate these from cuttings only.

L. spectabilis. Red ice plant. A prostrate species with gray-green leaves, and bright purple flowers. The comments made under *L. roseus* also apply to this plant.

Lantana

VERBENACEAE. 150 species of evergreen shrubs and herbs make up this genus. They have undivided, wrinkled leaves, and clustered heads of tubular flowers. Grow in sun with a minimum temperature of 45°F (7°C), and water only when the compost feels dry. Propagate by cuttings or seed.

L. camara. Shrub verbena; Yellow sage. This West Indian species makes a colorful pot plant, usually less than 4 ft. tall, with somewhat prickly stems bearing ovate, wrinkled leaves which are bright green, and many 2 in. wide, flat clusters of flowers. Most darken as they age, giving a varied range of shades on the plant. White, yellow, and pink forms are in cultivation. They open from spring through summer.

L. selloviana. A low-growing species which makes an excellent plant for a hanging basket. It has slender stems carrying ovate, rich green, downy leaves, and bright pink flowers which are yellow-centered and borne in small, rounded clusters in summer.

Lapageria

PHILESIACEAE.
L. rosea. Copihue; Chilean bell flower. One of a genus containing just this one, very beautiful species, the national flower of Chile. It is evergreen and climbs by means of its twining stems which can reach 10 ft. in length. The slender pointed leaves are ovate and a shining green, and the superb, waxy, bell-shaped blooms which are deep rose-pink and 3–4 in. long are borne throughout the summer. hanging on short stalks. Grow in lime-free compost, in light shade, with some form of support. Maintain a minimum temperature of 50°F (10°C), and water freely. Propagate by seed or by layering.

L. r. 'Alba'. A distinctive white flowering form.

Laurus

LAURACEAE.
L. nobilis. Bay tree; Grecian laurel. Of the two species which comprise this genus, this evergreen tree responds happily both to pot culture and to regular clipping and shearing to keep it a small, ornamental shape. The leathery, ovate leaves are 3–4 in. long, and are used for flavoring in cooking. The plants tolerate sun and partial shade, and need a minimum temperature of 40°F (5°C). They are best in a cool place. Propagate by cuttings.

Lemairocereus

CACTACEAE. A genus of 25 cacti, most of which reach 9 ft. or more in the wild. In cultivation they grow slowly if grown in small pots, making interestingly shaped and spined columns. Grow in sun with a minimum temperature of 50°F (10°C), and water only when the compost feels dry. Propagate by seed.

L. stellatus. A Mexican species, the stems blue-green, with the white woolly areoles bearing long spines. The small flowers are pink, and are followed by edible red fruit.

L. thurberi. From Arizona and Mexico, this species has many ribs and close set areoles bearing brownish-black spines. The reddish-pink flowers reach 3 in., and are followed by dull green fruit.

Leptospermum

MYRTACEAE. About 50 species make up this largely Australasian genus of evergreen shrubs. They have small, undivided leaves and pretty pink or white, 5-petalled flowers. Grow in sun with a minimum temperature of 45°F (7°C), and water only when the compost feels dry. Propagate by cuttings.

L. cunninghamii. An Australian species, rather similar to *L. scoparium*, but with silvery-gray hairs on the leaves, and white flowers in summer.

L. scoparium. Manuka; Tea tree. A small shrub of bushy growth from New Zealand with small, oblong leaves which are a dark green and slightly fragrant. Flowers are not produced until the plants are several years old. They are white with ¼ in., widely spreading petals, wreathing the stems in summer.

L. s. 'Keatleyi'. Has larger pink flowers which are ¾ in. across.

L. s. 'Nichollsii'. A single crimson form.

L. s. 'Ruby Glow'. This early flowering form has deep red, double flowers, and a bronze flush to the foliage.

Leuchtenbergia

CACTACEAE.

L. principis. Prism cactus; Agave cactus. The only species of its genus, this Mexican cactus has a very short stem which carries long tubercles, looking like fleshy, elongated leaves, but recognizable for what they are by the areoles and thin, starry spines borne at their tips. The yellow flowers are fragrant. Grow in sun or light shade with a minimum temperature of 50°F (10°C), and water only when the compost feels dry. Propagate by seed or by using the tubercles as cuttings.

Licuala

PALMAE.

L. grandis. Ruffled fan palm. Of the 100 members of this genus, this graceful palm will reach 8 ft. if given root and head room, but will remain smaller in a pot. It has an almost circular fan of light green leaves, borne on slender, erect stems. Grow in shade in a temperature of 50°F (10°C) or more, increasing humidity by standing the pot in a wet gravel tray. Water freely. Propagate by seed.

Ligularia

COMPOSITAE.

L. tussilaginea. Of the 150 plants included in this genus, this Japanese species makes a 1–2 ft. plant. The upright, woolly stems bear rounded, toothed leaves, and pale yellow daisy flowers, 1½–2 in. across, in spring. The forms with variegated foliage are those usually seen. Grow in shade with a minimum temperature of 50°F (10°C), and water freely. Propagate by division.

L. t. 'Argentea'. The rounded leaves are grayish-green with white marginal variegation.

L. t. 'Aureo-maculata'. Leopard plant. The leaves are irregularly blotched with creamy-yellow.

Ligustrum

OLEACEAE. Some 40 to 50 species comprise this genus of evergreen shrubs. They have oval, undivided leaves carried in opposite pairs, and spikes of small, white, funnel-shaped flowers. They require cool conditions with a minimum temperature of 40°F (5°C). Water as soon as the compost feels dry. Propagate by cuttings.

L. japonicum. Japanese privet. Coming from Japan and Korea, this makes an erect bush which responds well to pruning. The spikes of flowers are followed by small, glossy black berries, but rarely on clipped specimens.

L. lucidum. Glossy privet; White wax tree. Native to the mainland of southeast Asia, this evergreen shrub can be kept in a compact shape by clipping, and will produce a dense covering of 3–6 in., glossy, oval leaves. The white flowers are followed by black berries. It is very tolerant of drafts and poor light, though thriving best in a cool, sunny position.

Lilium

LILIACEAE. Of the 80 members of this genus of bulbous plants, a number make very showy subjects for pot culture with their trumpet-shaped or reflexed blooms, and long, strap-shaped leaves. Many superb hybrids have been raised, and most of these are excellent in the home. Pot the bulbs in autumn and keep cool until the young shoots are well through; then bring into warmer conditions and keep the compost moist through flowering time until the leaves begin to yellow; then keep just moist with a minimum temperature of 45°F (7°C) until autumn. Repot each year. Propagate by offsets or seed.

L. auratum. Gold-rayed lily. A magnificent species from Japan, the strong, erect stems in late summer carrying clusters of dazzling white blooms, each petal marked with a central gold band and a scattering of reddish spots. Cultivars with red rays and of more dwarf growth are available.

L. formosanum. A slender plant, native to Taiwan, it has long, deep green, very narrow leaves, and a short cluster of pure white, trumpet-shaped flowers which are firm-textured and open in summer and autumn. The petals are flushed red on the reverse.

L. longiflorum. Easter lily. This Japanese species has been much improved in cultivation by hybridization and selection. The true species has white flowers and waxy, slightly reflexed petals which are very strongly fragrant and 6–7 in. in length. They are borne on stems up to 3 ft. tall, in late spring and early summer. Plants belonging to the Croft hybrids from Oregon are those most frequently sold under this name.

L. Mid-Century hybrids. A group of splendidly colorful lilies of complex hybrid origin. They have clusters of up to 20, trumpet-shaped flowers, in shades of yellow, orange, and red, often speckled and streaked with deep red or purple. Individual blooms are up to 6 in. across. They all make superb pot lilies, and many named cultivars are available.

L. nepalense. An unusual colored lily from Nepal, the flowers being greenish-yellow and funnel-shaped with a purplish-red throat. They hang down from the top of 2–3 ft. stems, and open in summer.

L. speciosum. The pure white flowers of this Chinese plant are flushed and spotted with red. They are very fragrant and are borne on stiffly erect stems, 2–4 ft. high. They open in late summer and early autumn.

Limonium

PLUMBAGINACEAE.

L. suworowii. Sea lavender. This annual species from central Asia belongs to a genus of about 300 species. It has narrow leaves which broaden towards the tips and have wavy edges. The crowded spikes of small, pink flowers are branched and borne on erect, wiry stems from summer onwards. Grow in sun, sowing the seeds in spring for late summer flowering, or in late summer to flower early in the following year. Overwinter with a minimum temperature of 45°F (7°C).

Liparis

ORCHIDACEAE.

L. longipes. This southeast Asian plant belongs to a genus of some 250 species with a worldwide distribution. It is compact, the clusters of pseudobulbs carrying erect, long, ovate leaves up to 8 in. in length, and tiny, creamy flowers, in dense spikes, just longer than the leaves. They open in

winter. Grow in shade with a minimum temperature of 50°F (10°C), and keep the compost just moist. Propagate by division.

Lippia

VERBENACEAE.

L. citriodora. Syn. *Aloysia citriodora.* Of the 220 members of this genus, this Chilean shrub can reach 5 ft. if given enough root room, and has strongly lemon-scented leaves which are narrow and tapering, rather like those of a willow. The branched spikes of small, mauve flowers appear in summer on large plants. Grow in light shade with a minimum temperature of 45°F (7°C), and water freely. Propagate by cuttings.

Lithops

Living stones. AIZOACEAE. A genus comprising 50 succulent plants from southern Africa. They bear 2 thick, fleshy leaves which are joined together at the sides to give the impression of a stone, cracked at the center. Each year, a new pair of leaves emerges from this crack, forcing apart the old leaves which wither and then decay. The single, daisy-like flowers cover the top of the plant in autumn. Grow in sun with a minimum temperature of 45°F (7°C), and keep just moist while growing, drying off when the old leaves are full size, until the new leaves appear. Propagate by seed or division of those which form clumps.

L. bella. The 1 in.-wide plant body forms clumps and is yellowish-fawn with darker marbling, and the 1¼ in. flowers are pure white.

L. erniana. A gray-green plant with red-brown markings. It is 1 in. across and has white flowers.

L. lesliei. This taller species reaches 2 in., and is reddish-brown with duller brown marblings. The 1 in. flowers are yellow. *(illus.)*

L. marmorata. The pale gray-green plant body has a brown mottling and slightly fragrant, white flowers.

L. olivacea. This small plant, only ¾ in. in height, is olive-green with paler marbling. The flowers are yellow.

L. pseudotruncatella. This plant is of variable color

from a yellowish-fawn to dull brown, with darker brown lines. The yellow blooms are up to 1¼ in. across.

L. salicola. An olive-green species, 1 in. in height, with beautifully contrasting white flowers.

L. turbiniformis. The flat top of this plant is wrinkled and grayish-brown with a network of darker lines, and the sides are gray. The yellow flowers are up to 1½ in. across.

Littonia

LILIACEAE.

L. modesta. One of a small genus of 8 climbing plants, this species can reach 5 ft. in height, though it is usually smaller in pots. It has long, slender leaves which end in a tendril, and bright golden-yellow, bell-shaped blooms. Grow in light shade with a minimum temperature of 45°F (7°C). Water freely when in growth, and dry off when the leaves yellow after flowering. Pot in spring and provide support for the slender stems. Propagate by division or seed.

Livistona

PALMAE. A genus of 30 species of palms which have fan-shaped leaves divided into fine segments, and borne on tall trunks when mature. When young they make excellent decorative pot plants and remain small for several years. Grow in light shade with a minimum temperature of 50°F (10°C), and water freely. Propagate by seeds.

L. australis. Australian fountain palm. The leaves of this attractive Australian species are cut to the base into long, slender, dark green leaflets.

L. chinensis. Syn. *Latania borbonica.* Chinese fan palm. A very handsome species from China, the leaves cut to halfway only, giving a less light appearance than the other two species.

L. rotundifolia. This southeast Asian species has deeply cut leaves which are almost circular in outline and carried on reddish stems. It prefers warmer conditions with a minimum temperature of 55°F (13°C).

Lobivia

CACTACEAE. A South American genus containing 75 species of globular or cylindrical cacti which have beautiful, funnel-shaped flowers. They require full sun and a minimum temperature of 40°F (5°C). If kept at this temperature for about 6 weeks in late autumn, without water, they will flower more profusely, otherwise water sparingly. Propagate by offsets or seed.

L. allegraiana. A small, cylindrical species from Peru, reaching 6 in. in height. The green stem has slender, sharp spines on the ribs, and the pink or

red flowers are 2 in. across at the mouth. They open in summer.

L. aurea. Golden lily cactus. An Argentinian species, globular at first, then lengthening to 4 in. in height. The dark green stems are closely ribbed and have light brown spines, while the golden yellow, shining flowers open to 2 in. across in summer.

L. jajoiana. This 6 in. plant is from Argentina. The green stems produce many offsets and all are covered with reddish spines. Those at the center of each cluster are black and hooked. The summer-borne, bright orange-red flowers are 2 in. across and darker in the throat.

Lophophora

CACTACEAE.

L. williamsii. Peyote; Mescal. Of the two cacti belonging to this North American genus, this is a slow-growing, blue-gray, globular species which reaches 6 in. after many years. It has areoles but no spines. The funnel-shaped flowers which open during spring and summer are white, usually with a pink flush. They open to 1 in. across at the mouth. Grow in sun with a minimum temperature of 40°F (5°C), and water only when the compost feels dry. Propagate by seed. *(illus.)*

Lotus

LEGUMINOSAE.

L. bertholetii. Coral gem; Winged pea. This small shrub from the Canary Islands belongs to a genus made up of about 100 species. It has silvery hairy leaves, divided into slender leaflets, and the orange-scarlet pea flowers, each 1 in. in length, are borne at the end of long, arching, leafy stems in spring. Very good for a hanging basket. Grow in sun with a minimum temperature of 45°F (7°C), and water sparingly, but do not allow the compost to become completely dry. Propagate by seed.

Luculia

RUBIACEAE. Five deciduous shrubs make up this Asian genus. They make tall bushes in the wild, but are very amenable to pot culture and can be kept the desired size by pruning after flowering. They have ovate leaves, carried in pairs, and large clusters of tubular flowers opening flat at the mouth. Grow in light shade with a minimum temperature of 45°F (7°C), and water freely. Propagate by seed or cuttings.

L. grandifolia. This shrub has large, oval leaves, reaching up to 1 ft. in length on large specimens. The large, fragrant flowers which are 2½ in. in length are white, and are borne in spring in large clusters.

L. gratissima. The ovate leaves of this shrub reach only 4–8 in., and are carried on red, downy stems. The large clusters of very fragrant flowers are rosy-pink, and open in winter.

L. pinceana. Flowering from spring to autumn, this is a smaller shrub with long, narrow leaves, and very fragrant, creamy white blooms which are flushed with pink. *(illus.)*

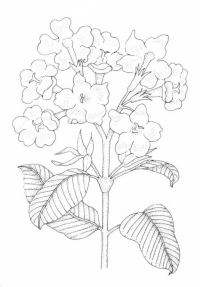

Luffa

CUCURBITACEAE.

L. cylindrica. Vegetable sponge, loofah. This genus of 6 annual climbing or scrambling plants contains the source of the original bath sponge, the loofah. It was made from the fibrous skeleton of the fruits of this species. It has roundish, lobed leaves, and small, yellow flowers similar to those of the marrow or pumpkin, which open in summer. To obtain the fruits, which are edible when young, it is best to pollinate by hand. Grow in sun with a minimum temperature of 55°F (13°C), and water freely. Propagate by seed.

Lycaste

ORCHIDACEAE. A genus containing 45 species of epiphytic orchids from tropical America. They have egg-shaped pseudobulbs which produce strap-shaped, pleated leaves, usually about 18 in. long, and large flowers which are usually borne singly on erect stems. Each has large, oval sepals and small petals forming a hooded collar in the center of the bloom. Grow in shade with a minimum temperature of 55°F (13°C), and water freely while in growth, but keep just moist when the leaves die down. Propagate by division.

L. aromatica. A low-growing species with a cluster of 4–6 in. flower stalks each carrying a fragrant, yellow bloom, 2–3 in. across, and of a waxy texture. It is very free flowering, and is at its best in late winter and early spring.

L. cruenta. The 2–4 in., long-lasting blossoms of this species have yellow-green sepals and golden petals with a deep red throat. They are very fragrant and open in spring.

L. deppei. A somewhat variable species which has waxy blooms up to 4½ in. across. The sepals are a pale green, or yellowish-green with red spotting, and the small petals are white, also with red markings. Their main flowering seasons are autumn and spring, but some blooms can be produced at almost any time of the year.

L. macrophylla. A most attractive species bearing clusters of fragrant, 4–5 in. flowers through summer and autumn. They have olive-green sepals, sometimes flushed with red, and white petals which are spotted with red.

L. virginalis. Syn. *L. skinneri.* Better known in cultivation as *L. skinneri*, this is an ideal orchid for the beginner, with fragrant flowers which can reach 6 in. across. The sepals vary in color from pure white to a pale lilac-pink, while the petals are a reddish purple. They open most freely through autumn and winter, but flowers can be produced at any time of the year.

Lycoris

Spider lilies. AMARYLLIDACEAE. There are 10 species in this genus of sturdy bulbous plants which have somewhat spidery flowers, opening before the leaves appear. Grow in sun with a minimum temperature of 45°F (7°C), and water freely while the plant is growing, drying off as the leaves die off, and keeping the compost only just moist, even when the flowers appear. Propagate by offsets or seed.

L. aurea. Golden spider lily. This golden-yellow flowered species is native to China. It has narrow petals and long stamens, and the blossoms are clustered at the top of a 1 ft. stem in late summer and autumn. While growing, this plant responds best to a temperature of 60–65°F (15–18°C). It is said to flower earlier and more freely if grown as an evergreen and kept moist throughout the year.

L. cinnabarina. Coming from eastern Asia, this species has 3 in. blooms of a striking terracotta. They are borne in a cluster at the top of an 18 in. stem in late summer and autumn.

L. sanguinea. The dark red flowers of this Japanese plant are more lily-like than those typical of the genus. They are 2–3 in. wide, and the clusters are borne on a slender, 12–18 in. stem in late summer.

L. squamigera. This Japanese species has charming pink flowers which are lightly fragrant. They open in summer at the top of a sturdy, 2 ft. stem.

Lygodium

SCHIZAEACEAE.

L. japonicum. Climbing fern. 40 species belong to this widespread genus of twining ferns. This chiefly southeast Asian species has thin, wiry stems which bear the delicate green fronds. Some form of support is necessary, thin wires or string being most appropriate. Grow in partial shade with a minimum temperature of 50°F (10°C), and water freely, especially when growing. Propagate by spores.

M

Malpighia

MALPIGHIACEAE. A genus comprising 35 evergreen trees or shrubs, mostly from tropical America. They have dark green, glossy leaves, borne in pairs along the branching stems, and small flowers. Grow in sun with a minimum temperature of 50°F (10°C). Water when the compost feels dry. Propagate by cuttings.

M. coccigera. Miniature holly. The leaves of this 2 ft., West Indian shrub are remarkably like those of the holly in shape, but are no more than ¾ in. long. In summer, small, pale pink flowers star the bush.

M. glabra. Barbados cherry. Found wild throughout tropical America, this will eventually make a small tree with smooth-edged, glossy leaves, and bright pinkish-purple flowers which are present from spring to autumn. They are followed by small, red, cherry-like fruit, edible but less flavorsome than a true cherry.

Malvaviscus

MALVACEAE. This genus contains about 12 species of trees, shrubs, and herbaceous plants, though some members are considered to be nearer *Hibiscus*. Grow in sun with a minimum temperature of 50° F (10°C), and water when the compost feels dry. Propagate by cuttings.

M. arboreus. This Mexican shrub can reach 10–12 ft. in the wild, but if cut back by at least a half each spring, can be kept much smaller. It has ovate, lobed leaves which are softly hairy beneath, and toothed. The rich red petals remain furled, giving cigar-shaped blooms opening in summer and autumn.

M. penduliflorus. Turks cap; Sleepy mallow. This colorful shrub from Mexico and Guatemala has long, ovate, toothed leaves, and brilliant red, pendant flowers, the petals opening to give a bell-shaped bloom. They open in summer and autumn.

Mammillaria

Pincushion cacti. CACTACEAE. There are up to 300 members of this genus of cacti, and almost all respond well to cultivation. Most are small and globular in shape, a few cylindrical, with small, wart-like tubercles. Their colorful flowers are freely produced in spring and summer, even on young plants. Grow in sun with a minimum temperature of 40°F (7°C). In summer, water only when the compost feels dry, and in winter only if the plant shows signs of shrivelling. Propagate by seed, or offsets where these are produced. The species described are from Mexico unless otherwise stated.

M. aurihamata. Yellow hook cushion. A globular plant 2½ in. high, the green tubercles carrying yellow-brown, straight spines surrounded by silky white hairs. The ring of yellow flowers is borne near the top of the plant.

M. bocasana. Powder puff. The blue-green, globular stem of this species is completely covered by the white spines which end in a silky-haired tip. The pale yellow petals are red on the reverse, showing this color in bud.

M. candida. Snowball pincushion. A delightful plant, the blue-green stem smothered with white wool and armed with starry clusters of white spines. The small flowers are white, with each petal striped pink on the reverse.

M. celsiana. Snowy pincushion. The deep green, globular stems are covered with white wool, through which protrude the very long, yellowish spines. The deep pink flowers form a ring around the top of the plant which forms clumps as it ages.

M. compressa. Syn. *M. angularis*. Mother of hundreds. The white woolliness of this plant is confined to the top, the rest of the stem bearing only long, hooked spines from its areoles. It can eventually reach 8 in. in height, and will form large clumps. The pinkish flowers are rarely produced.

M. densispina. Prickly tufts. At first globular, this species becomes cylindrical as it ages, eventually reaching 6–8 in. The central spines are red and held erect, and are surrounded by a spreading ring of yellowish-white ones. The flowers are bright yellow, with purplish-pink backs to the petals.

M. elegans. Blue puffs. A very elegant species, the globular stems elongating with age, eventually to 6 in. in height and tufted. The blue-green stems carry many, long, bristle-like spines which spread out like stars. The flowers are purplish-red.

M. elongata. Golden lace; Golden stars. An attractive cylindrical species which is easy to grow and forms dense clusters of stems. They get their popular names from the network of yellow spines, set like stars on the tubercles. The flowers are very pale yellow. This plant must be kept dry in the winter.

M. erythrosperma. A small species forming dark green hummocks only 2 in. high. The areoles bear up to 20 fine, white, bristle-like spines, surrounding the few, longer, hooked, central ones. The flowers are a deep carmine.

M. gemispina. Whitey. A very beautiful species which is easy to grow. It makes a distinctive blue-green, club-shaped stem, which elongates with age and is covered with white spines, the long central ones with a very deep brown tip. The flowers are deep red.

M. gracilis. Syn. *M. fragilis*. Thimble cactus. This unusual plant has a branching stem giving the effect of a number of white, spiny thimbles. The pale yellow flowers are pink on the reverse.

M. hahniana. Old lady cactus. This species forms rich green globes, which are densely covered with long, somewhat curling, white hairs giving it a slightly dishevelled appearance. The flowers are a deep rich purple.

M. hidalgensis. A tall, cylindrical species which can reach 12 in. in height. It is dark green and covered at first with soft white hairs. The spines are few, but long, and the flowers an attractive dark pink. An easy plant to grow.

M. magnimamma. Syn. *M. centricirrha*. Mexican pincushion. This plant has conspicuous, dark green, conical tubercles which carry a few, long, curved spines. The creamy flowers have a red central line.

M. microhelia. Little suns. A cylindrical species, the whole stem covered with radiating, yellowish-white spines, like the rays of the sun in a child's drawing. The 1–2 long central spines are very deep red, and are borne only near the top of the plant. The flowers are yellow-white.

M. plumosa. Feather cactus. Found wild in Cuba, Haiti, and Texas, as well as Mexico, this most decorative globular species has whorls of such fine white spines, that the effect is feathery, hence its name. It has white flowers but these are rarely produced.

M. rhodantha. Rainbow pincushion. This plant is most attractive when it is young, forming a green globe with white radiating spines around a cluster of reddish-brown ones. As it ages it elongates, eventually reaching 1 ft. The flowers are pinky-red, and are borne like a circlet around the top.

M. sempervivi. A free-flowering species, the reddish-green blooms borne near the top of the globular to shortly cylindrical stem, which is woolly when young and carries only a few spines. *(illus.)*

M. vaupelii. This blue-green, globular species is densely covered with long, shiny, needle-like spines which rise from the center of a yellow bristly star. The white flowers are pink on the reverse.

M. zeilmanniana. Starting globular, this species lengthens with age and eventually forms a clump of 2–2½ in. stems. The radiating spines are white, and the erect ones a dull brick-red. The purple or white flowers are freely produced even on very young plants.

Mandevilla

APOCYNACEAE. A large genus comprising 114 climbing species which have very fragrant, jasmine-shaped flowers, but of far larger size. They need plenty of space and can be used around a window. Grow in light shade with a minimum temperature of 45°F (7°C), and water freely. Propagate by cuttings.

M. splendens. This Brazilian plant has dark green, glossy leaves which narrow suddenly to a sharp tip, and are heart-shaped at the base. In summer, the trumpet-shaped flowers open flat at the mouth to 5 wavy-edged, bright carmine petals.

M. suaveolens. Chilean jasmine. This species has narrow, bright green, slender-pointed leaves, and clusters of very fragrant, 2 in., creamy-white flowers, opening in summer.

Manettia

RUBIACEAE. There are 130 members of this genus of evergreen plants, a few of which make twining plants suitable for training around a window or on a trellis. Some form of support is essential. Grow in light shade with a minimum temperature of 50°F (10°C), and water freely. Propagate by cuttings.

M. bicolor. Firecracker plant. This Brazilian twiner can be kept below its full 6 ft. if the tips are pinched out regularly. It has narrow, shining leaves, and showy, bright scarlet, tubular flowers which are tipped with yellow. They open in late spring through summer to autumn. *(illus.)*

M. inflata. A very similar species to *M. bicolor*, but the blooms are somewhat inflated and have a smaller yellow area. They are borne within leafy, green calyces.

Maranta

MARANTACEAE. 23 species belong to this tropical American genus which includes some most attractively patterned foliage plants. To keep them in the best condition, maintain a minimum temperature of 55°F (13°C), and water freely. If possible, keep a humid atmosphere around them, as the leaves will curl up if they become too dry. Propagate by division or cuttings.

M. bicolor. Prayer plant. A neat, tufted species from Brazil; the long, ovate leaves are a pale olive-green with darker edges either side of the central vein, shading away to the margins. The underside is flushed with purple. During the day these leaves are held horizontally, displaying their patterning, but at night they fold upwards, parallel to the main stem, a habit which has given them their common name.

M. leuconeura. Prayer plant. A Brazilian species which has been divided into three varieties, each

with a distinctive leaf pattern. The leaves fold up at night in the same way as *M. bicolor*.

M. l. erythrophylla. Red-veined prayer plant; Red herringbone. The light green leaves of this variety, sometimes sold as *M. tricolor*, shade to a darker tone towards the middle, and are overlain by a fluted, silvery, central stripe and fine red veining.

M. l. kerchoveana. Rabbit tracks. This variety has light green leaves with a row of chocolate blotches on each side of the main vein.

M. l. massangeana. Rabbit's foot; Rabbit tracks. This form has the basic pattern of *M. l. erythrophylla*, a dark green center shading to a paler margin, but the central stripe and the veins are ivory-white.

Martynia

MARTYNIACEAE.

M. louisiana. Unicorn plant. This rather sticky, hairy 2–3 ft. tall annual from central USA, is the only one of its genus. It has rounded, wavy-edged leaves. The tubular white flowers are spotted with red, green, and yellow, and are followed by curious 6 in., beaked seedpods. Propagate by seeds in spring, and keep in a temperature above 55°F (13°C). Water freely.

Masdevilla

ORCHIDACEAE. A remarkable genus containing 275 species of orchids from South America, all those described below being Colombian. They have no pseudobulbs, which is unusual for epiphytes, but have large, fleshy leaves. The flowers are usually borne singly, and have 3 large sepals, which are often joined together for part of their length, and which end in fine, tail-like points. The petals and lip are small. Grow in shade with a minimum temperature of 50°F (10°C), and keep always moist. Propagate by division.

M. bella. The flowers of this species are almost triangular, each sepal ending in a 4 in. long, tapering point. They are light yellow, spotted with red brown, the tails entirely of this color, and open in winter and spring. The 5–7 in. long, narrow leaves are leathery in texture.

M. carderi. This plant has creamy-white blooms, the sepals joined to form a bell-shape with dull purple markings near the base, and light yellow tails. They open in summer. The 3–5 shining leaves are erect and clustered.

M. caudata. Syn. *M. shuttleworthii.* The 8 in. long flowers of this species are lightly fragrant. One sepal is erect and pale yellow with red markings, the other two are reddish purple with white markings. All have yellowish tails and are borne in winter and early spring. The leaves are short, only

2–3 in. in length, and are carried on short, slender stalks.

M. chimaera. A somewhat variable plant with bizarre flowers. They have slender-tailed sepals which are joined for half their length, and are very pale yellow with red, purple, or black spots. There is a small white lip. They are borne in winter on pendant stems varying from 8 to 24 in. in length, in clusters of 3–8. The strap-shaped leaves are up to 9 in. in length, and leathery.

M. coccinea. This spring- to early summer-flowering species has two ovate, pendant sepals, and a very narrow, erect tail-like one. In color they can vary from yellow through orange and red to purple. They are carried on slender, erect stems. The glossy, strap-shaped leaves are 6–9 in. long.

2 in., pink to purple flowers are borne in summer and autumn.

M. erubescens. This Mexican plant has very triangular leaves and 3 in. blooms, produced in summer and autumn. They are white with pink spotting on the tube, the 5 petal-like lobes are also pink. *(illus.)*

M. scandens. A slender plant also from Mexico with narrower, arrow-shaped leaves. The 1½ in. flowers are lilac to purplish-red, and open in summer and autumn.

Maxillaria

ORCHIDACEAE. Of the 300 members of this evergreen, epiphytic genus of orchids, a number make very good indoor plants. The triangular flowers are not large, compared with those of some other orchid genera, but they are freely borne, even on young plants. They should be grown in shade in pans or baskets, or on pieces of bark. Maintain a temperature above 50°F (10°C), and water freely when growing. Propagate by division.

Maurandia

Syn. *Asarina*. SCROPHULARIACEAE. This is a genus of 10 species of climbers which need some form of support for their twining stems. They have large, foxglove-like flowers, opening to 5 small lobes at the mouth. Grow in light shade with a minimum temperature of 45°F (7°C), and water freely when growing, but keep only just moist in winter. Propagate by seed or cuttings. Smaller plants are obtained by raising them annually.

M. barclaiana. The dark green leaves of this Mexican species are almost triangular, while the

M. lepidota. The 9–12 in., glossy leaves of this species from Colombia and Ecuador, are carried on small pseudobulbs. The spidery blooms are very narrow and yellow and brown in color, as is the pointed lip. They open in summer.

M. luteo-alba. This attractive species from the forests of South America from Costa Rica and Panama south to Ecuador, has long, 8–18 in., strap-shaped leaves and freely produced flowers on short stalks, borne near their bases. They are up to 4 in. across. The slender petals and sepals are yellow in the center, fading to white at the tips,

125

while the lip is a deeper yellow. They open in spring and early summer. *(illus. prev. page)*

M. picta. This attractive plant from Brazil has 9–15 in., narrow, glossy leaves, and pale yellowish blooms which are spotted with purple. The white lip has purple markings. They are borne in late winter and early spring on 8 in. stems.

M. sanderiana. A splendid species from Ecuador with long, narrow leaves, up to 12 in. in length. The large flowers, 5–6 in. across and ivory-white, are variously spotted and marked with crimson. They are carried on slender 5–6 in. stems in late summer and autumn.

M. tenuifolia. A summer and autumn flowerer from Central America, with 12–15 in., dark green leaves, and small, but abundantly borne, dark red flowers which are marked with yellow. They have a strong fragrance rather like coconut.

Medinilla

MELASTOMATACEAE.

M. magnifica. Rose grape. Belonging to a genus of 400 species, this plant from the Philippines and Java is considered one of the most beautiful tropical plants in cultivation. It is slow growing, reaching about 3 ft. in a pot, and has large, deeply veined, oval leaves up to 1 ft. in length, and pendant clusters of small, light red flowers hanging from large, pink bracts. Grow in light shade with a minimum temperature of 60°F (15°C), water freely, and keep a moderate humidity by standing on a gravel tray. Propagate by cuttings or air layering (mossing).

Melianthus

MELIANTHACEAE.

M. major. Honeybush. This handsome, evergreen shrub is one of a genus of only 6 species. All are from South Africa, though this plant is also native to India. It has large, bluish-green leaves up to 1½ ft. long, divided into 9–11 leaflets, and is a very attractive pot plant when small. As it ages it becomes more straggly, and is best then cut to ground level, when it will shoot again. The reddish-brown flower spikes are only borne on mature plants. Grow in light shade with a minimum temperature of 45°F (7°C), and water freely. Propagate by cuttings or by removing rooted suckers.

Melocactus

CACTACEAE.

M. bahiensis. Turkscap. This intriguing, globular cactus from Brazil is one of a genus containing 30 species. It can reach 6 in. across, and is dark green and strongly ribbed. The areoles bear about 6 radiating spines and one straight one, and the top of the plant is covered with a white woolly cap. Grow in sun with a minimum temperature of 55°F (13°C). Water only when the compost feels dry. Propagate by seed.

Mesembryanthemum

AIZOACEAE.

M. cristallinum. Of the 350 members of this genus, this South African succulent plant is now widely naturalized in suitable climates. It has soft fleshy leaves up to 2 in. in length, the surface covered in crystalline spots. The light mauve-tinted flowers open flat like colorful daisies in summer. Grow in sun with a minimum temperature of 45°F (7°C). Water only when the compost feels dry. Propagate by seed.

Mikania

COMPOSITAE.

M. ternata. Plush vine. Of the 250 species of climbers or trailers belonging to this genus, this fast-growing plant from Brazil has long, velvety, brown stems, and 1½ in., dark, bronzy-green leaves which are divided hand-like into 5 wavy-edged leaflets. These are purple on the reverse, and the whole leaf is covered with fine, whitish hairs. Grow in shade with a minimum temperature of 60°F (15°C), and water freely. Propagate by cuttings.

Miltonia

Pansy orchids. ORCHIDACEAE. There are 25 members of this genus, distinctive in their broad, flat petals which look remarkably pansy-like. They require shade, a minimum temperature of 50°F (10°C), and a plentiful supply of water when growing, and are best in hanging baskets or on bark slabs. Keep cooler and drier in winter. Propagate by division.

M. clowesii. An epiphytic species from Brazil with flattened pseudobulbs and sword-shaped leaves up to 2 ft. in length. The deep brown flowers are striped with yellow and have a large white lip with purple markings. They can reach 2½ in. across, and are borne in clusters on arching, wiry stems in autumn.

M. cuneata. This Brazilian species is, like *M. clowesii*, epiphytic with long, strap-shaped leaves, rising from small, flattened pseudobulbs. Its brown-and yellow-striped flowers are larger, up to 3 in. across, and are borne on 2 ft.-long, arching stems in late winter and early spring.

M. flavescens. From Brazil and Paraguay, this plant has 4–5 in., flattened pseudobulbs which carry 9–12 in., yellow-green, strap-shaped leaves.

The flowers are light yellow and up to 3 in. across, with rather narrow petals and sepals. They open in late summer and autumn.

M. regnelii. This Brazilian species has egg-shaped, yellowish pseudobulbs, and 12 in. long, yellow-green leaves. The white flowers have a faint pink tinge, and the red-purple lip is edged with white. They are borne on a slender, 2 ft. stem in late summer.

M. roezlii. From Panama and Colombia, this species has 1 ft., blue-green leaves borne on small, flattened pseudobulbs, and pansy-faced blooms which are 3–4 in. long, and white with purplish markings. They are carried on 1 ft. stems in autumn.

M. spectabilis. Both pseudobulbs and leaves of this Brazilian species are yellowish-green. The flat blooms are creamy-white with a pinkish flush, while the lip is maroon-purple with a white edge. They open in late summer.

M. vexillaria. This large-flowered plant from Ecuador has blue-green leaves borne on small pseudobulbs, and pinkish-red flowers, sometimes very pale, carried on 12–20 in. stems in summer.

Mimosa

LEGUMINOSAE. A very large genus, comprising almost 500 species and including small herbaceous plants, shrubs, and trees, though not the 'mimosa' grown as a cut flower – this belongs to the genus *Acacia* q.v. The two species mentioned are among a group having leaves which close up and droop when touched. Grow in shade with a minimum temperature of 60°F (15°C), and water freely. Propagate by seeds.

M. pudica. Humble plant; Sensitive plant. This species from tropical America is best raised annually as it is fast growing and soon becomes straggly. Its leaves are divided into 4 feathered leaflets, and are borne on prickly stems. The tiny, pompon flower clusters are pinkish-purple, and are borne in summer.

M. sensitiva. Sensitive plant. Also from tropical America, this plant is less sensitive than *M. pudica*, and makes a taller, shrubbier plant.

Mimulus

SCROPHULARIACEAE.
M. aurantiacus. Syn. *Diplacus glutinosus*. California monkey flower. This attractive shrub from the western USA is one of a genus containing over 200 varied plants from America and Africa. It has slender branches which carry narrow, rich green, glossy leaves, and 2-lipped, orange-pink flowers which are up to 3 in. across and are thought fancifully to resemble a monkey's face. They open

in summer. Grow in sun with a minimum temperature of 45°F (7°C), and water when the compost feels dry. Prune to keep in shape, and propagate by cuttings.

Mitraria

GESNERIACEAE.
M. coccinea. This climbing or trailing plant from Chile is the only one of its genus. It can be kept as a more bushy shrub by pinching out the leading shoots. It has deep green, ovate leaves with a shiny surface, and bright scarlet, tubular, pendant flowers up to 1½ in. long, which open through summer. Grow in light shade with a minimum temperature of 45°F (7°C), and water freely. Propagate by cuttings.

Monstera

ARACEAE. This tropical genus contains 50 species of evergreen climbers, two of which make extremely popular foliage plants. They rarely flower in pots. Grow in shade, with a minimum temperature of 60°F (15°C), use a lime-free compost, and provide some form of support. Water freely. Propagate by cuttings, but these are not easy without heat; or by seed.

M. deliciosa. Mexican bread fruit; Swiss cheese plant. This popular pot plant is, in its native Mexico, a very large climber. Even in cultivation it will soon outgrow a normal room and is best as a decorator for a large area. The very glossy, oval leaves are deep green and deeply slit, more so in young plants.

M. pertusa. A very similar plant to *M. deliciosa* when young. It comes from Panama and Guyana, and has deeper cut, slightly smaller leaves. **(illus.)**

Moraea

IRIDACEAE. A genus of about 100 species of iris-like plants, most of which are from South Africa. They have narrow, slender leaves, and brightly colored, fragrant flowers, having 3 broad, spreading outer petals, and 3 very narrow inner ones. They require sun and a free circulation of air, preferably with a temperature not exceeding 65–70°F (18–21°C). Water freely while in growth; then after flowering, once the foliage has begun to die down, dry off and keep dry until late winter. Propagate by offsets or division.

M. iridioides. The very iris-like flowers of this species have large, pure white outer petals with yellow and brown central markings, and a blue style. They grow from 1–2 ft. in height.

M. villosa. Syn. *M. pavonia.* Peacock flower. A most beautiful flower, the segments bright purple with a golden center, between them a half circle of iridescent blue. They grow to 18 in. in height.

Moschosma

LABIATAE.

M. riparium. Now correctly called *Basilicum riparium*, this strong-growing South African sub-shrub is one of three members of the genus. It has pairs of broadly oval, light green leaves which are toothed, and branched flower clusters, made up of many small, creamy-white or pale lilac blooms. Grow in sun or light shade with a minimum temperature of 45°F (7°C), and water freely. It is best raised annually from cuttings. Keep the growing tips pinched out when small, to encourage bushy growth.

Muehlenbeckia

POLYGONACEAE.

M. platycladum. Syn. *Homalocladium.* Ribbon bush; Tapeworm plant. This curious plant is one of 15 species belonging to its genus. It is native to the Solomon Islands and is remarkable for its stems which are flat, yet up to 1 in. in width, looking like green leathery ribbons. Its flowers are small and insignificant. Grow in sun with a minimum temperature of 45°F (7°C). Water freely. Propagate by cuttings.

Murraya

RUTACEAE.

M. exotica. Orange jessamine. Of the 12 species belonging to the genus, this is a most decorative shrub. It comes from southeast Asia and Northern Australia, and has dark, glossy green, evergreen leaves divided into 5–9 leaflets, and white, bell-shaped, jasmine-scented flowers. They open at any time of the year and are followed by scarlet berries.

Grow in shade with a minimum temperature of 55°F (13°C), and water freely. Propagate by seed or cuttings.

Musa

MUSACEAE. The 35 species of this genus include the banana and its allies, as well as a number of more ornamental plants. They are mostly very large with trunk-like stems and long, broad leaves, but a few are suitable for indoor growth. Grow in light shade with a minimum temperature of 60°F (15°C), and water freely. Propagate by division or from suckers.

M. acuminata. 'Dwarf Cavendish'. Syn. *M. cavendishii; M. nana.* Dwarf banana. As a tub plant this southeast Asian species reaches 4–6 ft. in height, and has a similar spread. It has 2–3 ft. leaves which arch outwards from a short stem made of the bases of the leaves. The relatively small flowers are carried within large, red, leathery bracts in long, pendant spikes. As the bracts fall, the young fruit turn upwards to produce a small version of the familiar hand of bananas.

M. coccinea. Scarlet banana. This Vietnamese plant is 3–4 ft. tall, and has long, strap-shaped leaves. The flowering spikes are held erect, each cluster of yellow blooms held within bright scarlet bracts.

M. velutina. A slender species from India, having 3 ft., shining green leaves with a red midrib and erect spikes of pale yellow flowers with pinky-red bracts. The oval fruits have a velvety skin and are bright red.

Myoporum

MYOPORACEAE.

M. laetum. One of a genus containing 32 species of evergreen trees and shrubs, this New Zealander makes a decorative specimen plant for a large pot or tub. It has long, narrow, rather fleshy leaves which are a bright, shining green with translucent dots, and are borne on slender, willowy stems. It has clusters of white, purple-spotted flowers which are bell-shaped and open in summer. Grow in sun with a minimum temperature of 45°F (7°C), and water freely. Propagate by cuttings or seed.

Myrsine

MYRSINACEAE.

M. africana. African boxwood. One of a small genus containing only 7 species, this neat, 2–3 ft. evergreen plant has decorative foliage. The small, oval leaves are a deep glossy green with a prominent mid-vein and a notched tip, while the tiny flowers are followed by round, purple-blue fruits. As male and female flowers occur on separate plants, it is necessary to have both if fruits are to form. Grow in light shade with a minimum temperature of 45°F (7°C), and water freely. Propagate by cuttings. *(illus.)*

Myrtus

MYRTACEAE. A genus of about 100 shrubs with evergreen, aromatic leaves. They make good foliage plants in pots, and are best if they can be kept outside for part of the year. Grow in sun with a minimum temperature of 45°F (7°C), and water when the compost feels dry. Propagate by cuttings.
M. bullata. Syn. *Lophomyrtus bullata.* Ramarama. A shrub from New Zealand which will make a 3–4 ft. pot plant, though larger in the wild. It has oval, bronzy-green leaves which are puckered between the veins, and small, white flowers in early summer. These are followed by very dark red berries.
M. communis. Classic or Common myrtle. This species from the Mediterranean region as far east as western Asia makes a dense shrub, to 10 ft. in the wild, but much smaller in pots. The 1–2 in., ovate leaves are shining green, and the fragrant flowers are borne in July before the purplish-black fruits. A number of varieties are recognized.
M. c. 'Microphylla'. Dwarf myrtle. This small-scale replica of the common myrtle is often kept sheared into neat shapes.
M. c. tarentina. A very similar form to *M. c.* 'Microphylla', but with creamy-white berries.
M. c. 'Variegata'. The leaves of this form are up to 2 in. in length, and are edged and variegated with creamy-white. Keep in light shade.

N

Nananthus

AIZOACEAE.
N. malherbei. Syn. *Aloinopsis malherbei.* A delightful small, succulent plant from South Africa, one of 30 in its genus, with rather flat, spoon-shaped leaves with a bluish bloom. The leaf margins

have a row of glistening white tubercles, and the buff-colored flowers are an inch across. Grow in sun with a minimum temperature of 45°F (7°C), and water only when the compost feels dry. Propagate by seeds and division.

Nandina

BERBERIDACEAE.
N. domestica. Heavenly bamboo. The only member of its genus, this evergreen shrub from China and Japan makes a decorative specimen plant. It has 1–1½ ft. leaves which are 2–3 times divided, like the fronds of a fern, into narrow, bronzy, slender-pointed leaflets. In summer, loose clusters of small, white flowers are borne, though only on large plants. The red berries rarely form. Grow in light shade with a minimum temperature of 45°F (7°C), and water freely. Propagate by cuttings. *(illus.)*

Narcissus

AMARYLLIDACEAE. Of the 60 species included in this genus, a number make good winter- and spring-flowering pot plants, as long as they can be kept cool for as much of the time as possible. They should be potted in October and kept in a cool, dark place until the shoots are about 2 in. high. Bring them into a cool room where they should be kept well watered and in good light until the buds begin to open. If put in a warm room for flowering, return to a cool place at night, or the flowers will quickly fade. After the leaves have begun to die down, plant outside as they will not flower so successfully a second year. Many cultivars suitable for indoors use are available: those with a long trumpet often listed as daffodils, those with a short crown as narcissus.
N. 'Fortune'. A cultivar with large, golden petals and a central crown of rich orange-red.
N. 'Geranium'. A very beautiful plant with white petals and an orange-red crown.
N. 'Golden Harvest'. This golden-colored form has striking flowers up to 6 in. across the petals, and a long, broad trumpet.
N. 'Irene Copeland'. A double, camellia-like flower,

the petals white and the yellow crown split into segments.

N. 'King Alfred'. A favorite, with rich golden-yellow trumpet and petals.

N. 'La Riante'. The snow-white blooms are centered with a bright orange crown.

N. 'Mount Hood'. A snow-white trumpet daffodil with large blooms.

N. 'Orange Wonder'. An excellent cultivar, carrying its white flowers with an orange crown to great advantage.

N. 'Paper White'. A most popular white narcissus with many flowers to each stem.

N. 'Queen of the Bicolors'. A fine, two-colored cultivar with white petals and a yellow trumpet. *(illus.)*

N. 'Texas'. A very large, double flowered cultivar with white petals and a yellow trumpet.

N. 'Trousseau'. A most attractive plant, the petals pure white, and the trumpet pale yellow with a pale pink flush.

Nautilocalyx

GESNERIACEAE. This South American genus contains 14 species of herbaceous plants, all making attractive foliage plants with small, creamy-yellow flowers. They have ovate leaves which taper to a point, and are borne in pairs on the stout, erect stems. Grow in shade with a minimum temperature of 55°F (13°C), and water freely. Although quite long lived, they tend to get straggly as they age, and are best replaced every few years from cuttings.

N. bullatus. Syn. *Episcia tesselata.* This Peruvian species is grown for its glossy, bronze-green leaves which are covered with a network of sunken veins giving a wrinkled, yet shiny appearance. The undersides are purplish-red. Dense clusters of golden-yellow flowers are borne in summer.

N. forgetii. Peruvian foliage plant. The shining, fleshy leaves of this species from Peru are bright green, flushed with red along the main veins, the same coloring being repeated beneath. The light yellow flowers are borne in clusters in summer.

N. lynchii. Syn. *Alloplectus lynchii.* Black alloplectus. This Colombian species has very colorful bronze leaves which become almost black as they age. They are long ovate, tapering from the brownish-purple, succulent stems. The small, cream flowers are borne in dense clusters in summer.

Neomarica

IRIDACEAE. A genus comprising 15 species of iris-like plants from Mexico, south to Brazil. They have fans of stiff, sword-shaped leaves, and showy, iris-like flowers, the outer 3 petals large, the inner small and recurved. They open in late spring and summer. Grow in light shade with a minimum temperature of 45°F (7°C), and water freely when growing. Allow to become almost dry when the leaves die down. Propagate by division or seeds.

N. caerulea. A very attractive plant, sometimes exceeding 3 ft. in height. The outer petals are sky-blue, and the inner striped yellow and brown.

N. gracilis. Apostle plant. The leaves of this species are up to 15 in. in length, and a bright green. The flowers are 2 in. across, having white outer petals and small, bluish recurved ones, marked brown at the center.

N. northiana. Walking iris; Twelve apostles. This plant can reach 2 ft., and is grown for its 3–4 in., fragrant blooms with white outer petals, streaked with brown at the base, and yellow-brown striped inner ones, recurved to show a purple tip. The flowering stems arch over to the ground as the blooms die and root, forming new plants. A curious and attractive species.

Neoporteria

CACTACEAE.

N. subgibbosa. This coastal Chilean species is one of 30 members of the genus, all coming from the same country. Many forms of it are grown, often with separate names, including *N. nigrihorrida* and *N. heteracantha.* It is globular at first, lengthening with age to about 5 in., and the dark green body is closely ribbed and covered with woolly areoles. The short, radial spines are straw-colored, and those in the center, longer and darker. The flowers are a rich reddish-pink. Grow in sun with a minimum temperature of 45°F (7°C), and water only when the compost feels dry.

Neoregelia

BROMELIACEAE. A South American genus comprising about 40 species of epiphytes, all of which except one come from Brazil. They make rosettes of long, spreading leaves, those in the center often colorful and surrounding the short, erect, flower spike. This is frequently hidden in the water-filled cup formed by the joined leaf bases. Maintain a temperature above 50°F (10°C), and grow in light shade. Water freely. Propagate by offsets.

N. ampullacea. The glossy, gray-green leaves of this plant are banded with brownish zones and are short-toothed. They can reach 1½ ft. in length, and the heads of tiny, lavender flowers are borne deep within the central cup.

N. carolinae. Perhaps the most frequently seen plant of its genus, it has strap-shaped, bright, glossy green leaves up to 1 ft. in length. They have shallow teeth along the margins, and at flowering time, the central leaves become a rich red-purple. The violet and white flowers are borne deep in the center.

N. c. 'Marechaieii'. A fine form, the central leaves a rich crimson, the color lasting for many months.

N. c. 'Tricolor'. A very decorative cultivar, the long leaves having white stripes along their length, which become pinkish in good light.

N. marmorata. The 18 in. leaves of this species are green with reddish marbling; the faintly spiny margins have a red tinge. The flower spikes are lavender.

N. spectabilis. Fingernail plant. The strap-shaped, olive-green leaves have indistinctly spiny margins and gray bands beneath. Their most distinctive feature is, however, the scarlet tip, like a well-painted fingernail. The light blue flowers are surrounded by brilliant red leaves.

N. tristis. Miniature marble plant. A small plant, the 5–7 in. leaves olive-green with purplish-brown marbling, and toothed margins. The flowers are lilac.

Nepenthes

Pitcher plants. NEPENTHACEAE. A remarkable genus from the tropical forests of southeast Asia, which contains 67 species of insect-catching plants. The strap-shaped leaves end in a tendril which usually enlarges and curves upwards to form a hollow tube, topped with a small, leaf-like lid. Inside the tube are honey glands which attract insects in. They are then unable to escape up the slippery sides and drown in the liquid at the bottom of the pitcher. Their decayed bodies give the plant an extra food supply. They should be grown in a minimum temperature of 60°F (15°C). Very high temperatures are not essential as long as humidity is high, and these plants are best grown with a glass or plastic covering. Propagate by cuttings.

N. ampullaria. A Malayan species having broad leaves, and 2–4 in., pale green pitchers, it is a strong grower and capable of reaching 6 ft., if given sufficient root room and support.

N. maxima. This good climbing species comes from the islands of southeast Asia. It has long, leathery leaves ending in 8 in. long, green pitchers, marbled all over with reddish-purple.

N. rafflesiana. Coming from Malaya this climbing plant has 3–7 in., greenish-yellow pitchers with reddish-brown markings. *(illus.)*

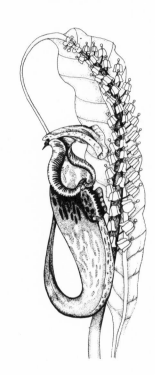

Nephrolepis

Sword ferns. OLEANDRACEAE. Some of the 40 species which make up this genus of most attractive ferns are found native in every continent except Europe. They are very good for hanging baskets and grow from creeping runners, throwing up arching, deeply dissected fronds. Grow in shade and keep a minimum temperature of 50–55°F (10–13°C). Water freely. Propagate by division.

N. cordifolia. The 2 ft. fronds are cut into narrow,

slender segments. A number of forms are known.

N. c. 'Plumosa'. The fronds of this decorative cultivar are wider, and are cut into small segments, each deeply lobed and overlapping to give a feathery effect.

N. exaltata. Perhaps the most valuable of all indoor ferns and one which has been grown in almost a hundred varieties and cultivars. Its fronds are usually about 2 ft. in length and divided into long, pointed segments.

N. e. 'Elegantissima'. A compact cultivar with more deeply divided segments giving a very light, elegant effect.

N. e. 'Fluffy Ruffles'. A dwarf form, the fronds usually less than 1 ft. in length, and cut into crisped and lobed segments which are crowded together giving a frothy look.

N. e. 'Hillii'. The crisped and curled segments of this cultivar are borne on 2–3 ft. fronds. A handsome plant.

N. e. 'Whitmanii'. The arching, feathery fronds are cut into segments which are themselves again divided.

Nerine

AMARYLLIDACEAE. 30 species of bulbous plants make up this most attractive South African genus. The strap-shaped leaves appear after the clusters of flowers, which are borne on erect stems in autumn. Each bloom has 6 narrow petals which are mostly recurved. Grow in full sun with the top of the bulb above the compost in a minimum temperature of 45°F (7°C), and water freely only when the plant is growing. As soon as the leaves die down, dry off, and do not water again until leaves or flower spikes appear the following autumn. Propagate by seeds or offsets.

N. filifolia. The narrow, grassy leaves are up to 12 in. long, and the cluster of slender, rose-pink flowers borne on 1½ ft. stems.

N. flexuosa. A strong-growing plant with strap-shaped leaves over 1½ ft. long, followed by sturdy, 2 ft. flowering stems bearing narrow petalled, pink blooms, often marked with white.

N. f. 'Alba'. Has pure white flowers.

N. masonorum. A slender species with narrow, grass-like leaves about 12 in. long, and a cluster of very fine petalled, pink flowers on a short stem.

N. sarniensis. Syn. *N. curvifolia.* Guernsey lily. A robust plant with thick, blue-green, strap-shaped leaves, and 2–2½ in. orange-pink flowers in large clusters on a 1½ ft. stem.

N. s. corusca. A shorter plant with brighter colored flowers.

N. s. c. major. Somewhat larger than the species, this form has deep red blooms.

Nerium

APOCYNACEAE.

N. oleander. Oleander. This evergreen shrub from the Mediterranean region is one of only three members of its genus. In the open it can reach 6 ft., but can be kept smaller by removing the stem tips while it is young. It has pairs of narrow, sword-shaped leaves tapering at the tips, and clusters of funnel-shaped blooms opening to 5 flat lobes at the mouth. They are usually pink, but red and white cultivars are also known, as is a double-flowered form. The flowers open through summer to autumn. Grow in sun with a minimum temperature of 45°F (7°C), and water freely, especially in summer. Propagate by cuttings. *(illus.)*

Nertera

RUBIACEAE.

N. granadensis. Syn. *N. depressa.* Coral bead plant. A small, mat-forming plant from the cooler areas of the Southern Hemisphere, and one of 12 species which make up the genus. It has tiny, ovate leaves, covering the surface, and abundant inconspicuous flowers which are followed by bright orange, pea-sized berries. It requires shade and abundant moisture. A minimum temperature of 45°F (7°C) is desirable, and in general the warmer it is kept, the more humidity should be provided. Ideally it prefers coolness. Propagate by division or seed.

Nicodemia

LOGANIACEAE.

N. diversifolia. Indoor oak. One of a genus of 6 species, this small shrub from Malagasy has oak-shaped leaves which have sunken veins and a shiny, quilted, blue-green surface. Flowers are not produced on pot plants. Keep in shade in a minimum temperature of 55°F (13°C), and water freely. Propagate by cuttings.

Nidularium

BROMELIACEAE. 22 species of these splendid epiphytes from Brazil are known. Of these, 2 species are widely grown, and a number of forms have been raised from them. They have strap-shaped leaves joined at the base into the flask or cup, typical of many bromeliads, and clusters of flowers borne on a short, erect stem. Grow in shade with a minimum temperature of 60°F (15°C), and water freely. Propagate by seed or suckers.

N. fulgens. Syn. *N. picta; Guzmannia picta.* Blushing cup. The light green leaves form a 2 ft. rosette, and those in the center turn a magnificent bright red at flowering time. The small blooms are purple and white.

N. innocentii. The strap-shaped, toothed leaves of this species have a deep purplish-brown overlay, and those around the white flowers turn orange-red when the head of blooms develops.

N. i. 'Lineatum'. Striped birdsnest. In this variety, the green leaves have bands of white running along the leaves.

N. i. 'Nana'. A very dwarf form, the gray-green leaves purplish beneath.

N. i. 'Striatum'. The light green leaves of this cultivar have creamy-white longitudinal stripes and a deep red center.

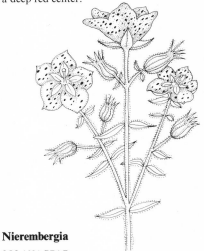

Nierembergia

SOLANACEAE.

N. caerulea. Cup flower; Purple robe. This charming plant comes from Argentina and is one of a genus of 35 species. It is a low-growing perennial which forms a dense mound of narrow leaves which are studded through summer with wide-open, lavender-blue flowers, the petals streaked with purple and centered with yellow. It makes an attractive, short-term house plant for a cool, sunny room, and is best raised annually from cuttings or seed for this purpose. If kept over winter, it needs a minimum temperature of 40°F (5°C) and cool conditions. Water freely when growing and flowering. *(illus.)*

Nopalxochia

CACTACEAE.

N. phyllanthoides. The only species of this cactus genus, native to Mexico. It is epiphytic, and has long, pendant branches which have flattened wings along either side. They bear beautiful, rose-red flowers up to 4 in. in length, which open wide by day. It is best grown as a basket plant and requires light shade. Keep a minimum temperature of 50°F (10°C), and water when the compost feels dry. Propagate by cuttings. Many hybrids have been raised between this genus and *Epiphyllum*, and they are included under that name.

Notocactus

Ball cacti. CACTACEAE. A genus of 15 species of free-flowering cacti, all from South America. They make small, globular, spiny plants, a few of which elongate to form narrow columns as they age. The large, colorful flowers open in summer. Grow in sun or light shade, and maintain a minimum temperature of 45°F (7°C). Keep the compost just moist in summer and drier in winter. Propagate by seed.

N. apricus. From Uruguay, this small cactus forms a 2 in. globe, covered with clusters of yellowish, bristly spines, each centered with a few longer ones. The 3–3½ in. flowers are yellow with a red flush on the backs of the petals.

N. concinnus. This rather flattened species from Brazil and Uruguay forms globes 2 in. in height and up to 4 in. across. The shortly woolly areoles bear yellow, bristle-like spines. The funnel-shaped flowers have yellow inner petals shading to red outer ones. A cristate form is grown.

N. haselbergii. This Brazilian species eventually forms an elongate globe up to 5 in. high and 4 in. across, but grows only slowly. The areoles bear slender, yellowish spines which fade to white. The orange-red flowers darken to a true red in the center.

N. leninghausii. Golden ball. This cylindrical Brazilian species can reach 3 ft. in height. The soft, yellowish, bristly spines cover the plant, and the yellow flowers have a greenish tint on the outside.

N. ottonis. A very popular plant from the drier areas of eastern South America, this forms a 4–5 in. globe which frequently sprouts around the base. The slender, spreading spines are yellow, and the straight, central ones, brownish-red. The flowers are yellow and the petals shining.

133

N. scopa. Silver ball. A globular species from Brazil, lengthening as it ages to reach 1½ ft. in height. It is covered with spreading, white spines, and also has long, sharp, brown central ones. The flowers are a glossy yellow.

O

Ochna

Mickey Mouse plants. OCHNACEAE. A genus of 85 trees and shrubs with glossy leaves and bright yellow flowers, which are followed by the curious but very ornamental fruits. Grow in light shade with a minimum temperature of 55°F (13°C), and water when the compost feels dry. Propagate by cuttings.

O. atropurpurea. A 4 ft. shrub from South Africa, with ovate leaves and pretty yellow flowers set within a purple calyx. The shiny, black fruits are borne on the enlarged base of the flower. *(illus.)*

O. serrulata. This South African shrub can reach 5 ft. when full grown. It has narrowly ovate leaves and bright yellow flowers carried within a red calyx in summer. The swollen disk is red and bears up to 5 round, black fruits. Often there are only 3, giving the effect of 2 eyes and a nose, fancifully like Mickey Mouse.

x Odontioda

ORCHIDACEAE. A group of hybrids between species of *Odontoglossum* and *Cochlioda*, which have been bred to mix the colors of the latter genus with the attractive flower form of *Odontoglossum*. Many named cultivars are available. Grow in shade with a minimum temperature of 55°F (13°C), and water freely. Propagate by division.

Odontoglossum

ORCHIDACEAE. A genus comprising 200 species of epiphytic orchids from tropical America. They have short, leathery leaves, and long, usually erect spikes of very showy flowers. Many make good house plants. Grow in light shade with a minimum

temperature of 55°F (13°C). Water freely, especially when young. Propagate by division.

O. bictoniense. Coming from Central America, this species has 6–7 in. pseudobulbs which bear long, strap-shaped, rather yellowish-green leaves, and erect spikes of 1½ in. flowers in winter and spring. These have narrow petals and sepals, banded with green and brown, and the large, flat, heart-shaped lip is pinky-white to lavender.

O. b. 'Alba'. An attractive form which has a pure white lip.

O. cervantesii. The 2½ in., egg-shaped pseudobulbs of this small species from Mexico and Guatemala carry 6–7 in. leaves, and erect or arching spikes of fragrant flowers. These are white, banded with brown, and open from autumn to spring.

O. crispum. Lace orchid. A variable and most attractive species from Colombia which has small, ridged pseudobulbs bearing 15 in., slender, pointed leaves, and arching spikes of up to 20 decorative blooms. Each has pink or white, waved and crisped petals, sometimes spotted with reddish-brown, and a notched, oval, striped and spotted lip. The flowers open in autumn and winter.

O. grande. Tiger or Clown orchid. This is one of the easiest members of the genus and is native to Mexico and Guatemala. The oval pseudobulbs bear firm, strap-shaped leaves up to 15 in. in length, and erect spikes of large flowers which can be 6 in. across. The sepals and petals are striped with yellow and brown, but the outer half of the petals is clear yellow. The broad, rounded lip is creamy-white with brown spotting. The blooms open from autumn to spring.

O. egertonii. Often grown as *O. pulchellum*, this is a pretty Central American orchid, with small pseudobulbs bearing erect leaves up to 1½ ft. in length, and small, fragrant, white flowers, the lip spotted with red. They open in autumn and winter.

O. rossii. This Central American species has small, egg-shaped pseudobulbs which carry 6-7 in. leaves and small, but erect spikes of relatively large blooms, up to 3 in. across. They are pale yellow or pink, with reddish-brown spotting, and flower in spring.

Oncidium

Butterfly orchids. ORCHIDACEAE. A large genus from Central and South America, containing over 350 species of epiphytic orchids, best grown in hanging pans and baskets, or on bark slabs. Their chief attraction is in their arching sprays of small, but abundantly borne flowers. Keep a minimum temperature of 55°F (13°C) and light shade, and water freely when in growth, giving a 6 weeks resting period when growth finishes. This promotes good flowers. Propagate by division.

O. crispum. The small, purplish-brown pseudobulbs of this Brazilian species carry 6–8 in., broad, pointed leaves, and 2½ ft. flowering stems which carry abundant 2–3 in., yellow and brown crisped flowers, sometimes as many as 80 to one spray. They open in autumn and early winter.

O. ornithorhynchum. From Central America, this most attractive species has blue-green leaves carried on oval pseudobulbs, and arching, dense sprays of lilac-pink flowers. These are very fragrant and open in autumn and winter.

O. papilio. A largely South American species, this orchid has erect, purplish leaves up to 9 in. high, and carried on small, clustered pseudobulbs. Its flowers are however most remarkable, somewhat like *O. kramerianum* in form, the upper 2 sepals and petals are greenish-red, up to 4 in. long, but very narrow and erect, while the lower 2 petals are yellow and rich brown, curving downwards around the golden-yellow lip. The blooms are formed on the same stem for much of the year.

O. sarcodes. A Brazilian species with leathery, pointed leaves, 1 ft. long, carried on 4–6 in. pseudobulbs. The long, flowering spike bears glossy blooms up to 2 in. across, with chestnut-brown sepals and petals, marked with yellow, and a large, wavy, yellow lip. They open in spring.

O. sphacelatum. Golden shower orchid. This showy plant is native to a wide area of tropical America. It has 2 ft. long, strap-shaped, stiff leaves borne on 6 in. oblong pseudobulbs. The abundant 1 in., rich brown blooms, marked with yellow and with a golden-yellow lip are borne from late autumn through to early summer on long, arching stems.

O. splendidum. A handsome species from Honduras and Guatemala, the small, egg-shaped pseudobulbs, and long, thick leaves a dull greenish-purple. The brown and yellow petals and sepals are narrow, while the large, bright yellow lip can be up to 3 in. in length. They open in spring and early summer.

Ophiopogon

LILIACEAE. 20 species belong to this genus of evergreen plants, with long, narrow, grassy foliage. They will grow in shade, though this is not essential, with a minimum temperature of 40°F (5°C). Water freely. Propagate by division.

O. jaburan. White lily turf. A Japanese species which forms clumps of dark green leaves up to 1½ ft. in length. In summer, some of them bear white, starry flowers in small clusters, followed by small, purplish-blue berries.

O. j. 'Vittata'. Syn. 'Variegata'. A form with the leaves striped with white and paler green.

O. japonicus. Dwarf lily turf; Mondo grass. Rather similar to *O. jaburan* in form, this species from Japan and Korea is much smaller, the leaves rarely

reaching 1 ft. in length. The flowers are pale lilac, and are followed by blue berries.

O. planiscapus. A slow-growing Japanese species with 6–10 in., broader leaves, and lilac flowers.

O. p. 'Nigrescens'. Black lily turf. This is the form usually seen, and is popular for its very deep purple foliage. It is sometimes grown as *O. arabicus.*

Oplismenus

GRAMINEAE.

O. hirtellus. Basket grass. A decorative grass, one of 15 species of its genus and widespread through the tropics. It is of creeping growth, and is best confined to a hanging basket. The long stems bear many 3–4 in., broadly strap-shaped leaves. Grow in shade with a minimum temperature of 55°F (13°C), and propagate by stem sections or cuttings.

O. h. 'Variegatus'. Sometimes called *Panicum variegatum*, this form has the short leaves striped with pink and white.

Opuntia

CACTACEAE. A genus comprising over 250 species of cactus, all from South America. They are easily recognizable by their curiously flattened stems which form oval or pear-shaped sections, and are called pads. The genus includes large, tree-like plants, and some which are small and creeping. Grow in full sun with a minimum temperature of 40°F (5°C), and water only when the compost feels dry. Propagate by cuttings, allowing the cut surface to dry before insertion.

O. bigelowii. Cholla cactus; Teddy bear. In its native southwest USA, a 3 ft. shrub having rounded joints on erect and very branched stems. The entire plant is covered in glossy, creamy spines, and the 1½–2 in., purple flowers are followed by yellow fruit.

O. brasiliensis. Tropical tree opuntia. This South American species makes a 12 ft. tree in the wild, but when young is quite happy in a pot, and quickly develops its tree-like form on a small scale. It has pale green pads, and scattered areoles with small spines. The flowers and fruit are yellow. Keep somewhat warmer than other species of *Opuntia*.

O. clavaroides. Sea coral; Fairy castles. An unusual plant from Chile making a low, spreading bush. It is most frequently seen in a densely cristose form, the stems growing together to form curled fans. It rarely flowers.

O. erinacea. An upright, branched plant from southwest USA. When young it makes a small plant with oval, dark green pads covered with many small, slender spines and bristles. The deep pink or yellow flowers are more than 2 in. across.

O. e. ursina. Grizzly bear. This Californian variety is smaller with longer and more slender brown or white spines, often over 5 in. in length.

O. kleiniae. This bushy species from Mexico and Texas has long, slender joints bearing tubercles. The white areoles bear yellow-brown bristles and single spines up to 2 in. long, occasionally more. The pink flowers are flushed with fawn on the reverse.

O. linguiformis. A Texan cactus, in the wild a 3 ft. bush with pale green pads carrying yellow, curved and straight spines. The yellow flowers are 3 in. across and followed by red-purple fruits.

O. l. 'Maverick'. A curious form, the pads covered with small, rounded and cylindrical growths tipped with bristles.

O. macrorhiza. This prostrate shrub from the USA has oval pads with large areoles. The upper carry long, yellow to white spines, as well as the brown bristles which cover the entire plant. The flowers are large and red. *(illus.)*

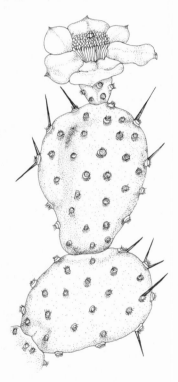

O. microdasys. Bunny ears. A decorative plant from Mexico, eventually reaching 3 ft. It has yellow-green pads set with many tufts of deep golden-brown bristles. The flowers are pale yellow, but only seen on large plants.

O. m. albispina. Polka dots. A form with pure white hairs and bristles from each areole.

O. monacantha. Irish mittens. Often grown under the name *O. vulgaris*, this plant from South America has glossy green pads which are almost spineless. The deep yellow flowers are followed by red fruit, though these are rarely seen on small plants. Although capable of reaching 7 ft., it is easily propagated so is best renewed every few years.

O. m. 'Variegata'. Joseph's coat. A variegated form, the pads marbled with cream and pale pink.

O. rufida. Cinnamon cactus. This bushy, spineless species from Mexico and Texas has dark gray-green pads with deep brown bristles arising from the areoles. The flowers are bright yellow and contrast well with the dark plant.

O. salmiana. A much branched, bushy plant from South America, with deep, blue-green pads carrying a few spines and bristles from the small areoles. The yellow flowers are freely borne and are flushed with red. They are followed by red fruits.

O. scheerii. A Mexican cactus with rounded, gray or blue-green pads, set with fine, pale gold spines, and long, somewhat curly hairs forming a tangle over the surface. The large flowers are bright yellow, shading to red, and can reach 4 in. in length, but are not freely borne.

O. strobiliformis. Spruce cones. An unusual species from Argentina, with erect branched stems. These have spiralled ribs bearing tubercles and without spines, giving a remarkable resemblance to a spruce cone. The 1–1½ in. flowers are creamy-white.

O. subulata. Eve's pin cactus. A distinctive spineless cactus from Chile and Argentina, eventually reaching 12 ft. in the wild, but most intriguing when small. The smooth, bright green stems bear cylindrical leaves which are carried at first horizontally, then turning upwards like bent spindles. The flowers are yellow.

O. tunicata. Syn. *O. furiosa.* Coming from Mexico, Chile, and Ecuador, this bushy species reaches 1½ ft., and has whorls of branches. In keeping with its former name, the whole plant is covered with long, yellow spines, each up to 2 in. long and barbed at the tip. The 2 in., yellow-green flowers are followed by fruits of a similar color.

O. turpinii. Syn. *O. glomerata.* Paper-spine cactus. This Argentinian species forms low clumps, made up of small, rounded or egg-shaped pads. These carry 1–3 broad, papery spines from the areoles, each up to 2 in. in length. The flowers are creamy-white.

O. verschaffeltii. The cluster of cylindrical stems are dull green in this Bolivian species, and bear 1–1¼ in. leaves, rounded in section and reddish-green in color. The areoles carry yellow bristles and sometimes very fine, white spines. The 1½ in. wide flowers are a deep orange-red.

Oreocereus

CACTACEAE.

O. celsianus. Old man of the Andes. From the mountains of Chile, Peru, and Bolivia, this erect, branching cactus is slow-growing and most attractive while young, making a ribbed, cylindrical stem, with the areoles at the top bearing long, silky hairs which almost cover the slender, yellow-brown spines. The 3–4 in. flowers are pink inside, deepening to a dark red on the outside. Grow in sun with a minimum temperature of 40°F (5°C), and water only when the compost feels dry. Propagate by cuttings and seed.

Oreopanax

ARALIACEAE. 120 species make up this genus of trees and shrubs from the mountains of tropical America. They have deeply lobed leaves and make good decorating plants. Grow in shade with a minimum temperature of 55°F (13°C), and water freely. Propagate by cuttings.

O. andreanus. A decorative plant from Ecuador, with variable leaves, roundish in outline, and cut into a number of long, ovate lobes. They are covered with red hairs, as are the stems. The white flowers are borne in close heads on an erect spike.

O. peltatus. Mountain Aralia. This Mexican species has its round- to heart-shaped, light green leaves cut into lobes like the fingers of a hand, each lobe being itself cut or toothed.

O. xalapensis. Also from Mexico, the evergreen leaves are cut into 5–7 long, narrow leaflets. The roundish heads of green flowers are borne in loosely branched spikes.

Ornithogalum

LILIACEAE.

O. thyrsoides. Chincherinchee. One of a genus of 150 bulbous plants, this South African species has green, strap-shaped, rather fleshy leaves, and spikes of white, starry flowers, each bloom up to 2 in. across and borne on a 1½–2½ ft. stem. The cut flowers bought in the winter are imported from South Africa, as in the northern hemisphere they flower in summer. They are very long-lasting in water. Plant in early winter and keep just moist until the flower spike is visible, then water freely. When the leaves yellow, dry off. Propagate by offsets.

Othonna

COMPOSITAE.

O. capensis. Ragwort vine. One of a genus of about 150 plants, this trailer comes from South Africa. It has slender stems up to 3 ft. in length which root as they go, and which have curious

rounded, fleshy leaves scattered along them. The yellow, daisy flowers are borne in summer. Grow in full sun, preferably in a hanging pan or basket, and keep a minimum temperature of 45°F (7°C). Water only when the compost feels dry. Propagate by rooted stem sections.

Oxalis

OXALIDACEAE. A genus with worldwide distribution which contains about 800 very variable species. Some grow from small tubers, others have fibrous roots. They have clover-like leaves which fold up in the dark, and brightly colored flowers, opening in sun. Grow in sun with a minimum temperature of 45°F (7°C), and water when the compost feels dry. Propagate by cuttings.

O. brasiliensis. A bulbous species from Brazil up to 6 in. high, with shiny leaves and beautiful rose-pink blooms, 1 in. across, flowering in winter and spring.

O. bupleurifolia. A small, twiggy shrub from Brazil growing to 1 ft. in height. The clover-like leaves are borne at the ends of the flattened, leaf-like stalks, giving a curious effect. The small flowers open from spring to autumn.

O. carnosa. From Chile and Peru, this species has a thick, erect stem carrying branched clusters of small, bright green leaves, like a miniature tree. The bright yellow flowers open in spring.

O. deppei. Good luck plant. This species gets its popular name from its 4 leaflets, looking like a 4-leaved clover. Each leaflet appears to have been snipped off at the end, and has a brown central patch. The pinky-red flowers open in winter or spring.

O. dispar. A sub-shrub from Guyana, which has large soft-haired leaves, and small, yellow flowers. It is best replaced every 2–3 years, as it tends to get straggly in a pot.

O. herrerae. A small, bushy, succulent plant from Peru, the swollen leaf stalks carrying small leaves. The yellow flowers are held above the leaves on long stalks in summer and autumn. Often sold as *O. henrei* or *O. succulenta.*

O. martiana. From tropical America this species has 1–1½ in. long leaflets, and deep pink flowers, lined with red and carried on long stalks in summer. *O. m.* 'Aureo-reticulata'. A cultivar with the veins lacking green color, giving it a network of pale gold on the green leaves.

O. ortgiesii. Tree oxalis. An erect, shrubby species from Peru, this plant has each 2 in. leaflet notched deeply at the tip and red-purple underneath. It is grown largely for its foliage, but has pretty yellow flowers which open spasmodically throughout the year. *(illus. fol. page)*

O. siliquosa. Coming from Costa Rica, this low-growing plant has stems and leaves flushed with red. The bright yellow flowers are marked with maroon lines radiating from the center of the petals.

P

Pachyphytum

CRASSULACEAE. A genus of 12 species of succulent plants from Mexico, closely related to *Echeveria*. They have rosettes of thick, cylindrical, gray-green leaves, several inches tall, both stems and leaves being rather sticky, and red, bell-shaped flowers carried in clusters on long stalks in spring and summer. Grow in sun with a minimum temperature of 45°F (7°C), and water when the compost feels dry. Propagate by leaf cuttings.
P. brevifolium. Sticky moonstones. A slow-growing, branched plant, eventually reaching 10 in. The stems are sticky, as are the blunt, fleshy leaves when young. The flowers are deep red.
P. compactum. Thick plant. A small plant with cylindrical leaves, 1 in. long and pointed, borne in a dense rosette only a few inches high. The whole plant is blue-green with a dull red flush and the red blooms are borne on a 12–15 in. stalk.
P. oviferum. Pearly moonstones. This plant gets its popular name from the silvery, opalescent sheen on its egg-shaped leaves. These are borne on a low, spreading plant. The deep red flowers bloom in spring.

Pachystachys

ACANTHACEAE.
P. lutea. Lollipop plant. One of a small genus containing only 5 species, all sub-shrubs from

South America. It has many erect stems which bear pairs of long, ovate leaves with conspicuous green veining, and which end in a long spike of orange-yellow, overlapping bracts which protect white, tubular flowers. Although a good perennial, it is best grown annually from cuttings taken in spring. Grow in light shade with a minimum temperature of 50–55°F (10–13°C), and water freely.

Palisota

COMMELINACEAE.
P. barteri. An interesting East African member of a genus of 25 species, having a rosette of broadly oval, shiny leaves, up to 3 ft. across in really large specimens, but usually smaller. The purplish flowers open in early summer, and are followed by brilliant, orange-scarlet berries. Grow in light shade with a minimum temperature of 60°F (15°C), and water freely. Propagate by division or seed.

Pamianthe

AMARYLLIDACEAE.
P. peruviana. Peruvian daffodil. There are only 3 members of this genus of bulbous plants, this one coming from Peru. It has 1 ft., strap-shaped leaves, and sweet scented blooms opening in late winter and early spring. They have a green tube, opening to 6 broad white petals, each ending in an abrupt point, and a central, daffodil-like, white corona marked with fine green lines. Grow in light shade with a minimum temperature of 50°F (10°C), and water freely when growing. Propagate by offsets or seed. *(illus.)*

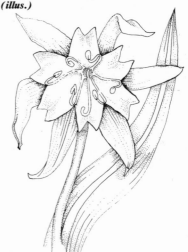

Pancratium

AMARYLLIDACEAE. A genus of 15 species of bulbous plants with strap-shaped leaves and large, white flowers, with a long tube opening to 6 spreading lobes, and a lobed central corona. Grow in full sun and light to promote good flowering, in a minimum temperature of 40°F (5°C), and water freely while growing, otherwise keep just moist. Propagate by offsets or seed.

P. maritimum. Sea daffodil. A 2 ft. plant from the Mediterranean region with very fragrant flowers in clusters at the top of short stems. They open in late summer. *(illus.)*

P. zeylanicum. A small species reaching only 1 ft. in height. It is a native of Ceylon and needs a minimum temperature of 50°F (10°C). The white flowers have slender petals recurved at the tips, and open in summer.

Pandanus

Screw pine. PANDANACEAE. A genus of 600 species which make shrubs or small trees, the leaves arranged spirally like the thread of a screw. A few make attractive foliage plants when young. Grow in light shade with a minimum temperature of 55°F (13°C), and water freely. Propagate by offsets or suckers.

P. baptisii. Blue screw pine. Coming from near New Guinea, this decorative species has stiff blue-green leaves which taper to a fine point and are striped with white. The margins are spineless.

P. sanderi. This species has spiny margins to its long, narrow leaves, and lines of yellow variegation. It comes from New Guinea.

P. veitchii. Coming from Polynesia, this plant has long, pointed, 3 in. wide leaves, which are deep

glossy green and banded with silvery-white, especially along the margins.

Pandorea

BIGNONIACEAE. An Australian genus comprising 8 species of evergreen climbers. They have opposite pairs of divided leaves, and large clusters of pink or white, largely funnel-shaped flowers. Grow in sun with a minimum temperature of 45°F (7°C), and water freely when growing. Propagate by cuttings or seed.

P. jasminoides. Bower plant. The leaves of this attractive species are divided into 5–9 slender pointed, oval leaflets, and the large, pink-flushed, white flowers open to a widely expanded bell-shape. It makes a feature growing around the edge of a large window.

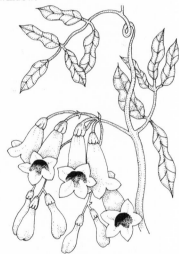

P. pandorana. Wonga-wonga vine. When young, this plant has finely divided leaves, but as it matures, the divisions decrease, leaving only 3 leaflets. The small flowers are pink or yellowish with violet spotting in the mouth. *(illus.)*

Paphiopedilum

Syn. *Cypripedium.* Slipper orchids. ORCHIDACEAE. A genus of 50 species of largely ground-growing orchids from southeast Asia, to which has been added many hybrid groups. They have tufts of narrow, strap-shaped leaves and are without pseudobulbs. The lip is shaped to form the toe of a slipper, hence the plant's popular name. The largest sepal is erect at the back of the flower with narrower petals at each side. They grow in light shade with a minimum temperature of 50°F (10°C). Water freely, keeping the compost just moist throughout the year. Propagate by division.

139

P. barbatum. The short, rather wide, mottled leaves of this species are 4–6 in. long, while the solitary blooms are borne on 10 in. stems. Each has an almost round, white erect sepal, shaded with green at the base and streaked with brown. The side petals are purplish-green, and the lip purplish-brown. They open from spring to autumn.

P. callosum. The leaves of this species are a light bluish-green, having darker shading. The solitary flowers are about 4 in. across and carried on 15 in. stems. They have a large, purple-streaked, white erect sepal, dull purplish-green, deflexed petals, and a large, purplish lip. The blooms are borne in spring and summer.

P. fairrieanum. A small, neat plant, the 6 in. leaves, narrow and light green, and the 2½ in. flowers borne on a slender, 10 in. stem. The erect sepal is white with purple streaks, and the petals which curve up at the ends like a fancy moustache are a similar color. The greenish lip has a purplish flush and lines.

P. insigne. The large, arching leaves can reach a ft. in length, as can the flowering stem which carries a normally solitary, large bloom, usually about 4 in. across. The erect sepal is pale green, marked with purple, while the petals and lip are greenish-brown. They are borne from autumn to spring. A good house plant, and one recommended for beginners.

P. x maudiae. A hybrid between *P. callosum* and *P. lawrenceanum*, raised in cultivation. The broad, 8–10 in. leaves are light green and marbled, while the erect flowering stem carries 3–4 in., white blooms with green shading and striping. They open from late spring through summer.

P. rothschildianum. This species has 2 ft.-long leaves, and a tall, flowering stem carrying up to 5 blooms from summer to autumn. These are very distinctive in form, having a diamond-shaped, erect sepal, and long, tapering petals, both light green with violet-purple markings, the sepal streaked, the petals spotted. The inflated lip is red-brown.

P. venustum. This low-growing plant has 4–6 in., broad leaves, strongly marbled, and 1–2 flowers on a 6–8 in. stem. They are 3 in. across with a green-striped, white sepal, purplish-green side petals, and a pink-flushed, green lip. They open from winter to spring.

Parodia

Tom Thumb cacti. CACTACEAE. A genus of 35 species of small, mostly globular cacti which thrive in cultivation. The areoles bear white woolly hairs, especially near the top of the plants, and many curved and straight spines. Grow in sun with a minimum temperature of 40°F (5°C), and water only when the compost feels dry. Propagate by seeds or offsets where available.

P. chrysacanthion. This small Argentinian species elongates with age, but never exceeds 2½ in. in height. The pale green stem is strongly spirally ribbed, and has areoles which bear yellowish, bristly spines. The funnel-shaped flowers are yellow.

P. nivosa. An attractive, largely globular plant from Argentina, the green stem closely ribbed and with areoles tufted with long, white wool, especially near the top of the plant. The straight spines are also white. The bright scarlet flowers are up to 1 in. across.

P. sanguiniflora. This pale green species is white woolly at the top, and has bristly, white spines from each areole, around a brown central one. The deep red flowers are freely borne.

P. s. violacea. This variety has red-violet flowers.

Parthenocissus

VITIDACEAE.

P. henryi. One of a genus containing 15 species of climbers. This Chinese plant has four-angled stems, and tendrils which adhere closely to any rough surface. The leaves are divided from the center into 5 leaflets, each olive-green, marked with silver veining. Grow in light shade with a minimum temperature of 45°F (5°C), and water freely. Cut back in spring to keep a small plant. Propagate by cuttings.

Passiflora

Passion flower. PASSIFLORACEAE. A genus containing about 500 species, most of which are evergreen climbers with tendrils. They have beautiful flowers with 6 petals and sepals similar, with a central corona. They are mostly large and are suitable for growing on a support or around a window in a large room. Grow in light shade with a minimum temperature of 45–55°F (7–13°C). Water freely. Propagate by cuttings.

P. x alata-caerulea. A hybrid between *P. alata* and *P. caerulea*, this plant has fragrant flowers 4 in. across. The petals and sepals are pink with a purple and white fringed corona. The leaves are 5-lobed.

P. x allardii. This hybrid is between *P. caerulea* and *P. quadrangularis*. It has 5-lobed leaves, and white sepals and petals, flushed with pinkish-purple. The corona is blue. A minimum temperature of 45°F (7°C) is sufficient for this plant.

P. caerulea. This Brazilian species has narrowly lobed leaves up to 7 in. across, and pink-flushed, white petals centered with a white, blue, and purple banded corona. They open in summer and early autumn. A minimum temperature of 45°F (7°C) is adequate.

P. x caponii. This hybrid between *P. quadrangularis* and *P. racemosa* is a particularly fine plant. Its leaves are basically 3-lobed, while the 4–5 in.

blooms have red-purple petals and sepals, centered with a deep red, white, and purple corona, bearing 2 in. filaments. It flowers throughout the year, and is best in a minimum temperature of 55°F (13°C).

P. coriacea. Bat leaf. Coming from Mexico, south to Peru, this species is grown chiefly for its foliage, the curious, broadly oblong leaves like bats' wings, and blue-green with silvery patches. The small, green flowers have a purple and yellow center.

P. edulis. Purple granadilla. This Brazilian species has wavy-edged, lobed leaves up to 6 in. across, and pure white flowers with a purple and white banded corona. They are followed by purple, edible fruits up to 3 in. in length.

P. mixta. This South American climber has 3-lobed leaves, and $3\frac{1}{2}$ in., pink flowers which open out from a narrow tube.

P. quadrangularis. Granadilla. A strong grower from tropical America, with long, ovate leaves. It has $4\frac{1}{2}$ in. flowers, with red and white petals and sepals, and a purple and white corona with long rays. The flowers are followed by yellow-green fruit with purple juices. These rarely set without hand pollination. *(illus.)*

P. racemosa. This Brazilian species has 3-lobed or oval leaves, and pendant clusters of 4 in. flowers, the petals deep red and the corona purple and white. A most attractive pot plant.

Pavonia

MALVACEAE.

P. multiflora. Belonging to a genus of over 200 species of evergreen plants, this makes a usually single-stemmed shrub, with dark green, long, ovate leaves, 6 in. in length and tapering to a point. The clusters of purple flowers are carried within showy, thread-like, bright pink bracts. Grow in shade with a minimum temperature of 55–60°F (13–15°C), and water freely. Propagate by cuttings.

Pedilanthes

EUPHORBIACEAE.

P. tithymaloides. Redbird cactus. This is one of a genus containing 14 species of shrubby plants, this one being succulent. It has zig-zag stems which carry waxy green, ovate leaves and clusters of small, red flowers, fancifully looking like a bird. Grow in light shade with a minimum temperature of 55°F (13°C), and water freely. Propagate by cuttings.

P. t. 'Variegata'. A form with red-tinged, white-edged leaves.

Pelargonium

GERANIACEAE. A genus of 250 herbs and shrubs coming from southern Africa, and including many of the most popular house plants. Many have soft, almost fleshy stems and rounded leaves, the 5-petalled flowers in shades of red, white, and purple. These are held in small to large, rounded clusters. Grow in sun or light shade with a minimum temperature of 45°F (7°C), and water freely when in full growth. Propagate from cuttings.

P. acetosum. A shrubby species up to 18 in. in height with bluntly oval, wavy-margined leaves and long, slender, pale pink petals having darker veins on the two upper, erect ones. *(illus.)*

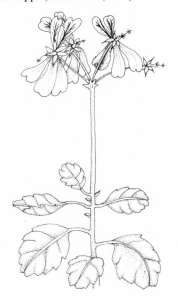

P. crispum. This species makes an erect, 2 ft. shrub with slender stems carrying small, 1 in., aromatic leaves, and 1 in. blooms in pink or lilac-pink with unequal sized petals, the 2 upper larger than the others. They are borne in small clusters from late spring to autumn.

P. denticulatum. To keep this 3 ft. shrub smaller and neater, pinch out the growing tips in spring. The erect stems have deeply cut leaves, dissected in the center into toothed and lobed segments. The small flowers are pinkish-lilac with red-purple veining, and the upper petals are notched. They open from late spring to autumn.

P. x domesticum. Show geraniums; Regal pelargoniums. A popular range of hybrids raised from *P. cucullatum*, *P. fulgidum* and *P. grandiflorum*. They make bushy plants which can reach 2 ft. in height, and many cultivars are now available from nurserymen, with double and single flowers, waved petals, and single-colored or bicolor. They open from spring to autumn.

P. x d. 'Applause'. A pale pink form with waved petals which are marked with light red.

P. x d. 'Chicago Market'. The blooms of this low-growing plant are lavender-pink with red markings only on the upper petals.

P. x d. 'Earliana'. A very free-flowering cultivar with light purple, pansy-like blooms, the upper petals strongly marked with red.

P. x d. 'Grand Slam'. A bushy plant having large, bright scarlet flowers in bold clusters.

P. x d. 'Jessie Jarrett'. A very dark form with purple-red petals, shading to near black at the center.

P. x d. 'Mrs. Mary Bard'. A very attractive cultivar having white blooms with purple striping at the base of each petal.

P. x fragrans. Nutmeg geranium. Possibly of wild origin, though usually thought of as a hybrid, this 2 ft. plant has small, hairy, heart-shaped leaves, lobed and toothed around the margins and smelling strongly of nutmeg. The small, white flowers are veined with red and held in neat clusters, opening through summer.

P. x f. 'Variegatum. The small leaves of this form are variegated with white.

P. graveolens. Rose geranium. This bushy plant, which can reach 3 ft. in height, has 5-lobed, gray-green leaves with a strong rose fragrance. The pink blooms are borne in small heads and have purple markings on the 2 upper petals. The flowers open from summer to autumn.

P. g. 'Lady Plymouth'. A strong-growing cultivar with a narrow white margin to the softly hairy leaves.

P. x hortorum. Zonal, Bedding, or Fancy-leaf geraniums. This hybrid group is derived largely from *P. zonale*. They make bushy plants with rounded leaves, often marked with an almost circular, purple-brown zone. The blooms range in color from pink to purple and white, and both double- and single-flowered cultivars are available among the hundreds which have been raised.

P. x h. 'Alpha'. A small form with a reddish-brown marking on the yellow-green leaves, and single, scarlet blooms.

P. x h. 'Black Vesuvius'. A dwarf form having very dark brown markings on the dull green leaves, and single vermilion flowers.

P. x h. 'Bronze Beauty'. This cultivar has golden-green, bronze-marked leaves, and single, salmon-pink flowers.

P. x h. 'Brownie'. A very small form, usually less than 6 in. tall, with deep purple marking on the green leaves, and single, scarlet blooms.

P. x h. 'Glacier Queen'. This is one of a race of compact plants known as Irene geraniums. It has dark green, rounded leaves and palest pink to white flowers.

P. x h. 'Happy Thought'. A charming cultivar, the green leaves marked with a creamy-white central area. The single flowers are a soft pinky-red.

P. x h. 'Maxime Kovaleski'. An unusual color form having rich orange blooms.

P. x h. 'Miss Burdett Coutts'. A cultivar with tricolor leaves which has been grown for over a hundred years. The round leaves are white-margined with a red circular zoning and a gray-green center, all overlain with a silvery patina. It is compact in growth, and has single scarlet flowers.

P. x h. 'Mrs Henry Cox'. A very fancy-leaved cultivar, each with a pale yellow margin and a red ring marking which is partly covered by the central green area giving a bronze effect. The single flowers are clear pink.

P. x h. 'Mrs. Parker'. A charming form with white margins to the green, quilted leaves, and pale pink, double flowers.

P. x h. 'Rosy Dawn'. A miniature form, less than 6 in. high, with dark leaves and double, orange-pink flowers.

P. x h. 'Rusty'. A bronze-leaved form with a darker ring marking, and double, bright red blooms.

P. x h. 'Tiny Tim Pink'. One of the smallest pelargoniums, making a mound of purplish, brown-zoned, green foliage, with single pink flowers.

P. odoratissimum. Apple geranium. A dwarf plant with apple-colored and -scented leaves which are softly hairy and kidney-shaped. The white flowers have the upper 2 petals with red markings. They open in summer.

P. peltatum. Ivy-leaved geranium. This is a low-

142

growing, trailing plant which looks best in a hanging basket. It has fleshy, bright green, ivy-like leaves, and a wide range of color forms, and double or single blooms opening in summer and autumn.

P. p. 'Cesar Franck'. A dark pink, single form.

P. p. 'Carlos Uhden'. A form with double, bright red flowers having a white eye.

P. p. 'Gay Baby'. A pretty miniature cultivar with pure white flowers.

P. p. 'L'élégante'. A most decorative form having white-margined, gray-green leaves with a pink flush, and white flowers flushed and striped with purple.

P. quercifolium. Oakleaf geranium. Making a 2–3 ft. shrub, this species has deeply lobed, oak-like leaves with darker markings. The bright pink flowers have purple markings, and are borne in small clusters from spring to autumn.

P. tetragonum. A succulent plant with bright green, fleshy stems, and small, dull green, lobed leaves with a dark ring. The pink flowers are distinctive in that the 2 upper petals, which are veined with purple, are much longer than the rest. They open in summer.

P. tomentosum. Peppermint geranium. A strong-growing species which needs pinching to keep shapely. It has large, bright green leaves which are lobed and toothed, and are covered with soft white hairs. It has small, rather insignificant white flowers.

Pellaea

SINOPTERIDACEAE. A genus of 80 species of fern with soft, evergreen fronds. They prefer light shade and a minimum temperature of 45–55°F (7–13°C), depending upon the plant's country of origin. Water freely. Propagate by division or spores.

P. rotundifolia. Button fern. Coming from New Zealand and Norfolk Island, this species is happy in cool conditions. It has low-growing, narrow fronds, bearing almost circular leaflets alternately along the stalk, as the plant matures they lengthen to oblong. A very decorative plant. *(illus.)*

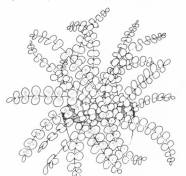

P. viridis. Syn. *P. hastata.* Cliff brake. This more typically fern-like species comes from southeast Africa and adjacent islands, needing warmer and moister conditions than *P. rotundifolia.* The fronds are twice-dissected and dark green, up to 2 ft. in length.

P. v. macrophylla. Often grown as *Pteris adiantoides*, this fern has somewhat triangular-shaped fronds, the lower leaflets divided again, and all ovate in outline, tapering from a wider base to a point.

Pellionia

URTICACEAE. A genus of about 50 evergreen perennials from southeast Asia and the Pacific Islands. A few are cultivated for their decorative foliage and are good for growing in hanging baskets. The flowers are insignificant. Grow in shade with a minimum temperature of 55°F (13°C), and water freely. Propagate by cuttings.

P. daveauana. Syn. *P. repens.* Coming from the mainland of southeast Asia, this creeping plant has ovate, ½–2 in. leaves, rounded at the base. They are dull green with a purplish overlay, and have a bright green, irregular central stripe.

P. pulchra. This plant from Vietnam has oval leaves which are pale green above, purplish below, the upper surface patterned with a network of deep violet veins.

Pentas

RUBIACEAE.

P. lanceolata. Egyptian star cluster. This shrubby plant is one of a genus of about 50 species. It makes an effective pot plant reaching 2 ft. or more in height, and having long, ovate, bright green leaves with a finely quilted surface. The pinkish-purple, starry flowers are borne in rounded clusters at the ends of the stems from late summer to early autumn. 'Kermesina' is a bright red form, and 'Quartiniana' has clear pink blooms. Grow in sun with a minimum temperature of 50°F (10C°); water freely. To keep the plants bushy, they must be kept pinched when in growth, and are best raised annually from cuttings.

Peperomia

PEPEROMIACEAE. One of a large genus containing over 1000 species of tropical, evergreen plants, most of which are creeping or spreading in form. They have undivided, often attractively surfaced or patterned leaves, and many make excellent foliage plants. Grow in light shade with a minimum temperature of 55–60°F (13–15°C). Water only when the compost feels dry. Propagate by cuttings of stems or leaves.

P. argyreia. Syn. *P. sandersii.* Watermelon peperomia. A very decorative tufted species from Brazil, about 6 in. in height, having fleshy, broadly ovate leaves, 2–4 in. in length, basically dark green with glistening, silvery-gray zones between the veins. The leaf blade is held on the reddish stalk from behind, in the same way as a shield.

P. caperata. Emerald ripple. Perhaps the most familiar species, this Brazilian plant makes a neat mound of dark green, shiny leaves which are heart-shaped and strongly quilted. The flowers are borne in long, white, tail-like spikes.

P. c. 'Tricolor'. This form has light green leaves with wide, creamy margins, and a red flush around the main vein and base of the leaf. It must be kept in shade at all times.

P. clusiaefolia. This West Indian species has 4 in. long, fleshy, spoon-shaped leaves. They are a shining silvery-green, and are outlined with a deep red margin; beneath they are pale green with a red-purple midrib.

P. fosteri. A red-stemmed climbing or trailing plant from Brazil, the thick, deep green, ovate leaves are borne in twos or threes, arising from the same point, and are marked with paler green veins.

P. glabella. Wax privet. A waxy-leaved trailing plant from Central America, the 1½ in. privet-like, ovate, green leaves borne on pretty, pinkish-red stems.

P. g. 'Variegata'. In this attractive form, the leaves have broad, white margins.

P. hederifolia. Syn. *P. griseo-argentea.* Ivy peperomia. This Brazilian plant has heart-shaped leaves with sunken veins, a dull green surface, overlain with a metallic sheen on the raised areas. It has erect, greenish-white, tail-like catkins.

P. incana. Almost succulent, this little plant is native to Brazil, and has round to heart-shaped leaves which are very firm in texture and are covered with short, white hairs. Keep in full sun.

P. maculosa. Radiator plant. This Brazilian plant is larger than most peperomias, and has ovate pointed leaves up to 7 in. in length, the waxy, gray-green surface lined with white veins. They are held almost erect at first, later becoming pendant, on purplish-red spotted stems.

P. magnoliifolia. Desert privet. A rather fleshy plant from the West Indies, with 4–5 in., ovate, glossy leaves, borne on red-purple stems, and making a low, compact bush. 'Variegata' is a form with whitish variegation.

P. marmorata. Silver heart. This Brazilian species has heart-shaped leaves which taper to a fine point, and has sunken green veins, separated by raised silvery areas. The leaves are also silvery on the reverse and are borne on reddish stems.

P. nivalis. A semi-erect succulent species from Peru, the 4 in. stems clothed with stalkless, boat-shaped leaves filled with translucent tissue. *(illus.)*

P. obtusifolia. Baby rubber plant. The waxy leaves of this plant from the West Indies and Florida, are almost round in outline, tapering into the short, erect stem. They are dark green and are slightly notched at the tip.

P. o. 'Variegata'. This cultivar has more ovate, light green leaves, with a broad area of creamy-white variegation spreading in from the margins.

P. orba. Princess Astrid peperomia. A most decorative small plant not known in the wild. It has light green, spoon-shaped leaves with a waxy patina, and borne on red-spotted stems which are short haired.

P. ornata. A most attractive plant from Venezuela, having a cluster of stiff-stemmed, oval leaves which taper to the base. They are held almost erect, and are a soft green with clearly marked main veins which show purplish beneath.

P. pulchella. Whorled peperomia. Coming from Cuba and Jamaica, this erect plant has a different appearance from the typical peperomia. It has small, roundly oval, rather waxy leaves which are borne in groups of 4 around the reddish stems. The whole plant is finely hairy.

P. resediflora. Syn. *P. fraseri.* Mignonette peperomia. Although this species from Ecuador and Columbia has attractive heart-shaped leaves which are white-haired and with sunken veins giving a quilted look, it is grown chiefly for its flower spikes. These form erect tails of small, fluffy blooms with an overall appearance of mignonette, hence its popular name.

P. rotundifolia. Syn. *P. nummularia.* A prostrate plant from the West Indies and Central America, this species has round, thick leaves, less than ½ in. long, which are carried on very fine trailing stems and form a dense mat of foliage.

P. rubella. Yerba Linda. A small-leaved species from Mexico, with whorls of small, ovate, dull

144

green leaves showing red beneath. They are borne on erect, red stems making a low, bushy plant.

P. scandens. Syn. *P. serpens*. A Peruvian species which has pointed, heart-shaped, fleshy leaves, spaced well apart on the reddish stems. It is best grown as a basket plant where its stems can trail.

P. s. 'Variegata'. Of similar growth, this cultivar has creamy-white margins to the leaves, which are paler green than the type.

P. tithymaloides. A strong-growing species from Central America, which has deep, glossy green, oval leaves and spikes of greenish flowers.

P. velutina. Velvet peperomia. A most decorative species from Ecuador, which is ideal for a bottle garden or growing under a glass cover. It has ovate, velvety, hairy leaves, the bronze-green surface marked with pale green, longitudinal veins, and red beneath.

P. verschaffeltii. Sweetheart peperomia. A most attractive plant with a rosette of blue-green, heart-shaped leaves with rounded ends. The veins are sunken and yellow-green, while the crests of the raised areas are silvery.

Pereskia

CACTACEAE.

P. aculeata. Barbados gooseberry. This plant belongs to a genus containing 20 species of leafy cacti. At first appearance, they are very unlike other members of the family, but they are recognizable by the fact that they do have areoles. This West Indian species is a climber which can be trained around a window. It has pale pink or yellow fragrant flowers followed by edible green fruits. Grow in sun with a minimum temperature of 45°F (7°C), and water when the compost feels dry. Propagate by cuttings. *(illus.)*

Peristrophe

ACANTHACEAE. About 30 species make up this genus of tropical plants. Many are shrubby and have entire leaves, and pretty, colorful, tubular flowers. Grow in light shade with a minimum temperature of 55°F (13°C), and water freely. Propagate by cuttings.

P. angustifolia. A small, spreading plant from Java, having 3 in.-long, narrow leaves, and freely-borne, terminal clusters of rose-pink flowers. It is a good hanging plant.

P. a. 'Aureo-variegata'. This is the form most frequently seen. It has dark green leaves with broad, yellow bands along the main veins.

P. speciosa. Native to India, this winter-flowering, sub-shrubby plant can reach 4 ft., but is best raised annually from cuttings when it will make a compact, 2 ft. plant. It has bright green, oval leaves, and deep purple flowers, the 2 in.-long tube curving back to form 2 lobes at the mouth.

Persea

LAURACEAE.

P. americana. Avocado; Alligator pear. One of 150 members of this genus, the avocado cannot be called a good house plant, but the seeds germinate so easily that it is often kept for amusement or curiosity. It develops into an interesting seedling which will grow happily. When too large, it must be discarded, unless the climate allows it to be planted outside. Keep in sun with a minimum temperature of 50°F (10°C), and once established, water only when the compost feels dry.

Phaedranassa

AMARYLLIDACEAE.

P. carmioli. Queen lily. This showy flowered, bulbous plant is one of 6 species, and is native to Costa Rica. It has 2 ft., strap-shaped leaves, and a cluster of nodding, deep red flowers, each tipped with green and about 2 in. long. They are carried on an erect, 2 ft. stem. Grow in sun or very light shade with a minimum temperature of 55°F (13°C), and water freely when in growth, keeping drier while resting. Propagate by offsets.

Phalaenopsis

Moth orchids. ORCHIDACEAE. A genus which comprises 35 species of particularly beautiful epiphytic orchids. They have no pseudobulbs, the broad, leathery leaves growing from a short, thick stem. The large petals and usually smaller sepals spread widely, while the short, lobed lip is almost central to the flower. Grow in light shade with a minimum temperature of 60°F (15°C), and keep the compost just moist at all times. Propagate

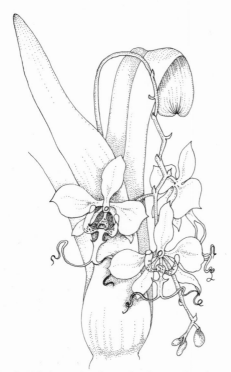

Water freely, propagate by stem sections, top, or leaf bud cuttings.

P. andreanum. Syn. *P. melanochryson*. Velour philodendron. This Colombian species makes an impressive decorator plant with its long, spear-shaped, velvety-surfaced leaves which have a metallic sheen and finely drawn, white veins. *(illus.)*

preferably by seed or from plantlets produced on flowering stems. Division is not generally advised as the plants resent disturbance. Many hybrids have now been raised, combining the best features of the species.

P. amabilis. This orchid from southeast Asia has 1 ft.-long, light green, drooping leaves, and pure white blooms, 3–4 in. across, with yellow and red markings on the lip. They are held on arching stems, and open from autumn to spring. *(illus.)*

P. lueddemanniana. From the Philippines, this orchid has yellow-green, broad, 6–8 in.-long leaves, and very fragrant, waxy, long-lasting blooms which are striped with chestnut-red and white, overlain with light purple barring. They open mainly in spring and summer, and are carried on short stems.

P. schilleriana. Rosy moth orchid. This species from the Philippines has broad, fleshy leaves up to 1 ft. long, which are dark green with silvery markings. The reverse is purplish-red. The winter- and spring-borne, fragrant flowers are light pink, and borne on short, arching stalks.

Philodendron

ARACEAE. Many of the 275 members of this tropical American genus make good house plants, especially when they are young. In the wild, most are climbing shrubs. They have decorative, dark green, leathery leaves, and many are best trained around a moss stick. Keep in shade with a minimum temperature of 55–60°F (13–15°C).

P. bipinnatifidum. Tree philodendron. Originating from Brazil, this erect species has heart-shaped leaves when small, but they become divided as the plant ages, being cut into a number of wavy lobes and eventually reaching well over a ft. across. At this stage it is suitable only for a large room or foyer.

P. cannifolium. Flask philodendron. The long, ovate leaves of this species from Guyana taper down to the widened, channelled leaf stalk, creating a most distinctive effect.

P. elegans. Elegant philodendron. This vigorous species, widely distributed through tropical South America, has large leaves which are deeply dissected into narrow segments. It is a most decorative plant, and grows best on a moss stick.

P. erubescens. Blushing philodendron. This Colombian plant has 9 in. long, heart-shaped leaves tapering to a point, and dark green surface flushed with pink when young, and deep red on the reverse. They are borne on purplish stalks.

P. e. 'Burgundy', a very similar plant though sometimes considered to be a hybrid, it has coppery-colored leaves when young.

P. gloriosum. Satin-leaf. The heart-shaped leaves of this Colombian creeping plant have a silvery-green, satiny surface, lined with fine, creamy-white veins, broadening to the stem.

P. hastatum. Syn. *P. domesticum*. Elephant's ear. A climbing species from Brazil, having shining leaves shaped like a spearhead, and held almost vertically.

P. imbe. A Brazilian species having long, arrow-shaped leaves, with a thin, stiff, shiny texture. The veins are paler above and reddish beneath as are the leaf stalks.

P. lacerum. A West Indian plant with two different foliage forms. When young, the leaves are ovate with a wavy edge, but as they mature, the waviness deepens until when full grown they are deeply cut. Only suitable for the home when young.

P. laciniatum. An attractive climber from Peru with deeply and variously lobed, leathery leaves, the veins somewhat sunken. *(illus.)*

P. x mandaianum. Red-leaf philodendron. This hybrid between *P. hastatum* and *P. erubescens* has long, arrow-shaped leaves which are a metallic wine-red, as are the leaf stalks.

P. micans. Velvet-leaf vine. A climbing plant from the West Indies which has small, tapering, heart-shaped leaves, with a velvety surface which has a bronze sheen above and red beneath.

P. oxycardium. Syn. *P. scandens; P. cordatum.* Parlor ivy; Heart-leaf. A climbing plant, widespread in Central America and the West Indies, with glossy, heart-shaped leaves which taper to a point. In cultivation, they are rarely longer than 6 in. A popular plant, especially for hanging baskets or pans; if grown in a pot, support is necessary.

P. panduriforme. Horsehead; Fiddle-leaf. A Brazilian climber with curiously shaped leaves, considered by some to resemble a horse's head, others a fiddle. They are leathery and mid-green in color.

P. pinnatilobum. Fern-leaf philodendron. A climbing species from Brazil, with the tough leaves cut into very fine segments which are held almost

rigid, and well-spaced along the center rib.

P. sagittifolium. A Mexican plant which has long, arrow-shaped leaves, of a shining, dark green, and with a leathery texture.

P. selloum. Lacy-tree philodendron. A large tree in its native Brazil, this plant grows slowly and makes a superb accent plant for a large area. The leaves are a glossy green and cut into long segments which are themselves lobed. They are borne in a rosette when young, which gradually develops a trunk as it matures.

P. sellowianum. A Brazilian species with leaves deeply cut into lobed segments and rather similar to *P. bipinnatifidum.*

P. squamiferum. Red-bristle philodendron. A twining climber from Guyana which has long, lobed leaves rather like those of *P. laciniatum,* but which are borne on dull green, bristly stalks.

P. verrucosum. Syn. *P. lindenii.* Velvet-leaf. Coming from Costa Rica, this species has the most attractive foliage of all the philodendrons. The leaves are heart-shaped, with a deep green, glossy, velvety texture. The veins are paler and spread out to the wavy margins. The underside of the leaf is a light pinkish-purple.

P. wendlandii. Birds' nest philodendron. A rosette-forming species from Costa Rica and Panama, which has long, ovate leaves of a stiff, waxy texture, held erect and arching over at the ends to make a bird's nest shape.

Phoenix

PALMAE. There are 17 species in this genus which contains the familiar date palm. Although most make tall trees when mature, they are attractive decorator plants when small, with their elegant, deeply dissected fronds borne in arching tufts. Grow in light shade with a minimum temperature 45–50°F (7–10°C), and water freely. Propagate by seed, or from suckers when produced.

P. canariensis. Canary Islands date palm. When young, the stiff fronds of this palm from the Canary Islands are borne in erect, arching tufts. The long leaflets are folded along the midrib and are bright green. It is very good for large rooms which do not become too hot.

P. dactylifera. Date palm. This is the palm which produces the dates of commerce, and comes from North Africa and Arabia. It has arching fronds with widely spaced leaflets, and is seen frequently rather because of the ease with which it can be grown from date stones, than for its own attractions.

P. reclinata. Senegal date palm. The stiff, arching fronds of this African species are borne in dense tufts, giving a rather congested appearance.

147

P. roebelinii. Pigmy date palm. Native of southeast Asia, this is the best species for indoor growth, its graceful, arching fronds regularly spaced and finely divided into soft, grooved leaflets. It is slow growing and when mature reaches only 12 ft.

Phyllanthus

EUPHORBIACEAE.

P. speciosus. Woody-leaf flower. A member of a very large genus containing about 600 species, this remarkable evergreen shrub has strangely widened and flattened branches which have the appearance of deeply dissected leaves. The small white flowers are borne on the margins of these "leaves." Grow in light shade with a minimum temperature of 60°F (15°C), and keep the compost just moist at all times. Propagate by cuttings.

Phyllostachys

GRAMINEAE. A genus of 40 bamboos, some of which can, in their native homes, reach 80 ft. in height. Some make attractive container plants while young, forming a dense clump of slender stems with narrow leaves. Grow in sun in a minimum temperature of 32°F (0°C), and water freely. Propagate by division.

P. aurea. Golden, or Fish-pole bamboo. A tall plant from China which has yellowish, hollow stems and 2–4 in., pointed, pale green leaves.

P. nigra. Black bamboo. This bamboo, native to China, has slender, erect canes, spotted with black when young, later becoming black all over. The 3 in. leaves are light green.

P. sulphurea. Moss bamboo. From China and Japan, this species has arching, yellow canes and narrow leaves up to 5 in. long, and carried on purplish stalks.

Pilea

URTICACEAE. There are 400 members of this widespread tropical genus, some of which make good foliage plants for indoor growth. They have pairs of undivided leaves and small, insignificant flowers. Grow in shade with a minimum temperature of 50–55°F (10–13°C), and water freely, though do not let the compost stay wet. Propagate by cuttings.

P. cadieri. Aluminum plant. This somewhat fleshy species from southeast Asia will make a 9–12 in., bushy plant. The 3 in., ovate leaves are dark green with a silvery-white overlay between the sunken veins.

P. c. 'Nana' or 'Minima'. Names for a dwarf and more compact form.

P. involucrata. Syn. *P. spruceana*. Friendship plant. This most decorative species comes from Peru. It has dark green leaves with a bronzy sheen and deeply sunken veins which are maroon-red on the reverse.

P. microphylla. Syn. *P. muscosa*. Artillery or Pistol plant. This bushy plant from Central America has fleshy stems and leaves, these being only ¼ in. in length, giving the plant a mossy look. It is, however, grown for its tiny flowers which discharge their pollen in explosive puffs, thus giving rise to its popular names.

P. 'Moon Valley'. An attractive cultivar of unknown origin which makes a compact mound of bronze-green leaves with deeply sunken veins and light green margins.

P. nummularifolia. Creeping Charlie. Coming from the West Indies, south to Peru, this creeping plant has ¾ in., rounded, light green leaves borne on fine red stems which root as they spread.

P. repens. Black-leaf panamiga. This decorative plant from Mexico has dark, glossy, rounded leaves which are deeply notched along their margins and have sunken veins. The tiny, whitish flowers are borne in clustered heads.

Pinguicula

Butterworts. LENTIBULARIACEAE. 46 species with a wide distribution outside the tropics comprise this genus of specialized plants. They are insect-catchers, making use of a sticky fluid produced from shining glands on the upper leaf surface. This fluid digests insects' bodies, providing the plant with minerals it was lacking. The flowers are violet-shaped with a spur. Grow in sun or light shade with a minimum temperature of 45°F (7°C), and keep permanently moist by standing in a saucer of water. Propagate by division or seed.

P. caudata. Syn. *P. bakeriana*. Tailed butterwort. A Mexican species with long-spurred, red flowers which open in autumn.

P. grandiflora. Large flowered butterwort. This species has deep purple flowers with a white throat and a short spur. They open in late spring and summer. Keep cool in winter when the plant has died off.

P. gypsicola. An unusual species from Mexico, having 2 leaf forms. In winter it has tiny, rounded leaves only ⅓ in. long, while in summer it produces narrow leaves up to 2½ in. long. The red-purple flowers open in summer.

Piper

PIPERACEAE. An extremely large genus with 2000 species of climbing plants, widely distributed throughout the tropics. Amongst them is the true pepper, as well as a number of plants which are grown for their decorative foliage. Grow in light shade with a minimum temperature of 60°F (15°C), and water freely. Apart from *P. ornatum*, they need extra humidity if possible and a constantly warm temperature. Propagate by cuttings.

P. magnificum. Lacquered pepper tree. An erect shrub from Peru, having large, roundly oval leaves which can reach 8 in. in length and have a brilliant gloss. The veins are slightly sunken and whitish, and the leaves are maroon on the reverse.

P. nigrum. Black pepper. This climbing species from southeast Asia has ovate leaves up to 6 in. long and a deep glossy green. The small flowers are followed by clusters of berries which ripen from green to red, then black.

P. ornatum. Coming from southeast Asia, this decorative species makes an excellent house plant. It has heart-shaped, waxy leaves, deep green in color with a silvery-pink network over the surface which becomes whiter with age.

P. porphyrophyllum. Velvet cissus. Sometimes confused with *P. ornatum*, this Indonesian plant has heart-shaped, green leaves with silvery-pink markings largely confined to the veins.

Pitcairnea

BROMELIACEAE. There are 250 members of this genus of bromeliads, all of those frequently seen in cultivation being ground-growing species with rosettes of leaves and spikes of colorful flowers. Grow in light shade with a minimum temperature of 45°F (7°C), and water freely. Propagate by offsets.

P. andreana. This Colombian species has narrow, soft, leaves, up to 1½ ft. long, which arch outwards. The upper surface is covered with silver freckling, and the lower is white scaly. The 2½ in., orange, tubular flowers are tipped with green, and borne in summer on short stalks.

P. corallina. Palm bromeliad. A large species from Colombia which can reach 3 ft. in height. The strap-shaped leaves are dark green and deeply furrowed along the parallel veins. Their undersurfaces are white. The flower stems are almost prostrate and carry heads of coral-red blooms in spring.

P. heterophylla. A small, Mexican species with a rosette of short, triangular leaves enclosing the base of the plant. From it rise the slender arching stems up to 9 in. in length, and the clusters of bright red flowers which open in spring.

P. xanthocalyx. Syn. *P. flavescens.* This attractive species from Mexico and the West Indies has slender, arching leaves, up to 3 ft. in length, and borne in a close rosette. They are light green above, scaly white beneath. The loose spikes of yellow flowers open in summer.

Pittosporum

PITTOSPORACEAE. A genus of 200 species found throughout the "Old World," except Europe, most of which are evergreen shrubs. Some make good container plants grown for their glossy foliage. Keep in sun and fresh air when possible, with a minimum temperature of 45°F (7°C), and water when the compost begins to feel dry. Propagate by seed or cuttings.

P. tenuifolium. Kohuhu. A very decorative plant from New Zealand which has 1–2 in.-long, pale green leaves with a smooth, wavy margin and deep purplish stems, which when young are almost black. The brown-purple flowers are borne on large plants only.

P. t. 'Purpureum'. A form with a purplish-bronze flush to the leaves.

P. t. 'Variegatum'. This cultivar has a creamy-white band around the edge of the leaves.

P. tobira. Japanese pittosporum. An attractive shrub from China and Japan with whorls of bright green leaves, and clusters of creamy-white flowers with a strong scent of orange.

P. t. 'Variegatum'. A form with an irregular, creamy-white margin to the leaves.

Platycerium

Stag's horn fern. POLYPODIACEAE. Of the 17 species of epiphytic fern which make up the genus, a number make interesting house plants. They have two forms of fronds, those which are sterile are broad and flat, growing at the base of the plant, while the fertile ones which carry the spores are long and antler-like. Grow in shade with a minimum temperature of 55–60°F (13–15°C), and keep the compost just moist at all times. Propagate by offsets.

P. bifurcatum. Syn. *P. alcicorne.* Stag's horn fern. This Australasian fern has gray-green, kidney-shaped, sterile fronds, and somewhat pendant, leathery, fertile fronds which are deeply forked and can reach 2–3 ft. in length. It is a very variable species and a number of forms are grown.

P. b. 'Majus'. This form from Polynesia is stronger growing with larger fronds.

P. b. 'Netherlands'. A Dutch cultivar with slightly hairy, shorter fronds.

P. grande. Elk-horn fern. Coming from Australia and southeast Asia, this fern, at first suitable for the home, later becomes too large for all but the largest rooms, the fronds being capable of reaching 4–6 ft. in length. The sterile fronds are of two forms, some rounded and some fan-shaped, while the fertile fronds are partly erect and deeply lobed. *(illus. fol. page)*

P. hillii. An Australian fern with flat basal fronds,

149

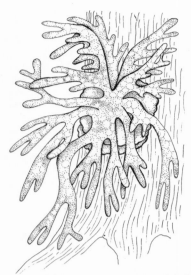

and the fertile ones erect, broadening before being cut into many lobes.

P. x lemoinei. A hybrid having rounded, basal fronds and slender, forked, fertile ones arching downwards. The surfaces are covered with short, white hair.

P. madagascariense. A distinctive species from Malagasy with the surface of the prostrate, sterile fronds deeply honeycombed, and small, erect, fertile fronds widening to about 10 in. long and wide.

P. wallichii. This small species from southeast Asia has rounded, wavy, basal fronds, and deeply forked, 1–2 ft., fertile fronds.

Plectranthus

LABIATAE. A genus of 250 species of perennial plants, some of which have attractive flowers as well as decorative foliage. Grow in light shade with a minimum temperature of 50°F (10°C), and water freely. Propagate by cuttings.

P. coleoides. Candle plant. Coming from India, this is a bushy plant, 1 ft. tall with green, crenate leaves.

P. c. 'Marginata'. This is the form most frequently grown, having 2–3 in., dark green leaves fading to paler green towards the edges, the margins themselves being white. The tubular flowers are purple and white.

P. oertendahlii. Prostrate coleus. This Brazilian plant makes a prostrate mat of colorful foliage, the trailing stems being particularly effective in a hanging basket. It has rounded, green leaves with silvery-white veins and a purple surface beneath.

P. purpuratus. Moth king. A South African species

with small, softly hairy, deep green leaves, purplish beneath. They are borne on slender, wiry stems, along with small, lilac flowers.

P. tomentosus. This small, fleshy, almost shrubby species has brown-red spots on its white hairy stems, and similarly covered crenate leaves, green above with silvery beneath. The small, purple flowers are borne in spikes.

Pleione

ORCHIDACEAE. This genus contains about 10 species of small, mostly terrestrial orchids, many of which make very good house plants. They have small, flask-shaped pseudobulbs carrying the handsome flowers which usually open just before the new leaves unfold. Grow in good light, shading from direct sun only when in leaf, and keep a minimum temperature of 45°F (7°C). Water when in growth and when flowering, but keep almost dry when resting. Propagate by offsets or bulbils which appear on the pseudobulbs of most species.

P. bulbocodioides. Syn. *P. formosana*. This charming plant from China and Taiwan has 3–4 in. blooms with narrow lilac to pale purple petals and sepals which curve gently forward, and a fringed, trumpet-shaped lip spotted with red and yellow. They open in spring.

P. b. 'Alba'. A beautiful, pure white form.

P. b. limprichtii. Syn. *P. limprichtii*. A deep red-purple variety.

P. b. 'Oriental Splendour'. Syn. *P. pricei*. A cultivar with pinkish-purple blooms, and a purple tint to the pseudobulbs.

P. forrestii. The blooms of this Chinese plant are a bright orange-yellow with brown spotting on the trumpet-shaped lip. They are borne on 6 in., erect stems, and open in spring and early summer. The leaves, which appear after the flowers, are narrowly strap-shaped.

P. humilis. This species from India to Nepal has 1–2 in. flowers with pale lavender to purple petals, with red or brown striping inside the trumpet-shaped lip. They are lightly fragrant and are borne in autumn on 2–3 in. stems. The leaves are narrow and ribbed.

P. praecox. Coming from China and Nepal, this autumn-flowering plant has 3 in., deep rose-pink flowers with a narrowly trumpet-shaped, fringed lip which is marked with yellow inside. The leaves are ovate and strongly ribbed.

Pleiospilos

AIZOACEAE. A genus of 38 succulent species from South Africa, the plants basically with pairs of very swollen leaves looking remarkably like chips of stone. They should be grown in sun with a minimum temperature of 45°F (7°C), and watered only during their summer growing season. At the end of this they will flower, and they should then be kept dry until the following spring. Propagate by seed.

P. bolusii. Living rock cactus. This species forms pairs of leaves looking remarkably like a 4–5 in.-long, egg-shaped boulder which has been cut in two. The upper surface is gray-green and forms the flat, inward-facing portion of the leaf. The brownish-green lower surface is curved over to form the rest. Many of the plants now in cultivation under this name are hybrids and have the "cut" upper leaf surface forming the greater part of the top of the plant. In shade, the leaves can become elongated and tongue-like. The 2–3 in., golden-yellow flowers with a pink center open in summer.

P. nelii. This species is almost globular in shape with a vertical "cut" face. In color it is a dark grayish-green, spotted with red-brown. The 2–3 in. flowers open in spring, and are a soft orange-pink.

P. purpusii. A species with flatter leaves, with the "cut" surface yellowish-green and facing upwards. The curved, lower side is darker green. In summer the plants can be almost completely obscured by the 3½ in., yellow flowers.

Pleomele

LILIACEAE.

P. reflexa. Syn. *Dracaena*. One of a genus of 100 tropical plants, often considered part of *Dracaena*. This species from countries around the Indian Ocean eventually forms a lax shrub of 4 ft. or more, with narrowly strap-shaped, glossy green leaves which are reflexed at the tips. Grow in light shade with a minimum temperature of 55°F (13°C), and water freely. Propagate by cuttings.

P. r. 'Variegata'. Song of India. This form has broad, white margins to the leaves.

Plumbago

PLUMBAGINACEAE. Of the 700 species which make up this widespread genus, 2 make very decorative house plants. Grow in light shade with a minimum temperature of 45–50°F (7–10°C), and water freely. Propagate by cuttings.

P. capensis. Cape plumbago. A strong-growing, scrambling shrub which is most effective trained around a window where it can get good light and will produce abundant clusters of saucer-shaped, light blue blooms covering the 3 in., ovate leaves. It can also be grown in small pots where it will flower from summer to late autumn, even when young. If grown as a climber the stems must be tied to a support.

P. rosea. Syn. *P. indica*. Scarlet leadwort. A 2 ft., semi-shrubby plant with 4 in., oblong leaves. In summer it bears spikes of bright scarlet, saucer-shaped flowers. It makes a more shapely plant if cut back annually in spring.

Plumeria

APOCYNACEAE.

P. rubra. Frangipani; Temple tree. One of a small genus of only 7 species, this strong-growing shrub has long, narrow leaves up to 1 ft. in length, and superb trusses of 2 in., waxy flowers which are very fragrant. Unfortunately it is suitable only for a large room as it does not flower when small. Grow in sun with a minimum temperature of 45°F (7°C), and water freely in summer, but keep almost dry once the leaves have fallen.

Podocarpus

PODOCARPACEAE. A genus containing about 100 species of evergreen trees and shrubs with broader leaves than most conifers and small, catkin-like flowers. These are not, however, produced on small plants. Grow in sun or light shade with a minimum temperature of 45°F (7°C), and keep the compost just moist. Propagate by cuttings.

P. elongatus. African yellow wood. A very decorative tree from Africa having pendant branches and long, very narrow, tapering leaves reminiscent of a weeping willow.

P. gracilior. African fern pine. A graceful African tree which is very similar to *P. elongatus*, with pendant branches, and slender, almost grassy leaves.

P. macrophyllus. Buddhist pine. Coming from China and Japan, this species is more erect, with slender, deep glossy green leaves.

P. m. 'Maki'. This is the form most frequently seen, having denser, brighter green leaves.

Polianthes

AGAVACEAE.

P. tuberosa. Tuberose. This very fragrant plant from Mexico is one of 13 members of its genus. It is tuberous rooted and has strap-shaped leaves, and clusters of white, tubular flowers, borne at the top of a 3 ft. stem. They are waxy in texture and open to 6 petal-like lobes at the mouth.

P. t. 'The Pearl'. A form with double flowers, the one most frequently seen. Grow in sun with a minimum temperature of 45°F (7°C), and water freely when the leaves are growing, drying off as they yellow. Propagate by offsets. *(illus. prev. page)*

Polygala

POLYGALACEAE.

P. myrtifolia grandiflora. Milkwort. This shrubby plant from South Africa is one of 800 species in the genus. It has light, grayish-green leaves, and pea-like flowers which are a bright rose-purple and fringed. They are borne in clusters from late spring to late summer. To keep a shapely 2 ft. or less, cut back hard in spring. Grow in sun with a minimum temperature of 45°F (7°C), and water when the compost feels dry. Propagate by cuttings.

Polypodium

POLYPODIACEAE.

P. aureum. Hare's foot fern. One of a genus containing 75 species which have a worldwide distribution, many growing on the ground, others epiphytic on trees or rocks. This species has arching fronds divided into many narrow lobes. Each frond is usually 2–3 ft. long, but can reach 4 ft. The creeping rhizomes are covered with rust-colored, furry scales.

P. a. 'Glaucum'. A cultivar with decorative blue-green foliage. Grow in shade with a minimum temperature of 50–55°F (10–13°C), and water freely, maintaining extra humidity if possible. Propagate by division or spores.

Polyscias

ARALIACEAE. There are 80 species in this genus of trees and shrubs from southeast Asia and the Pacific Islands. All have deeply dissected and often variegated leaves. Grow in light shade with a minimum temperature of 55°F (13°C), and water freely. Propagate by cuttings.

P. balfouriana. Dinner plate aralia. A small shrub with 4 in., rounded leaves when young, later producing 3 similar shaped leaflets. They are shining green and toothed.

P. b. 'Marginata'. A form with duller green leaflets which are irregularly bordered with white.

P. filicifolia. Fern-like aralia; Angelica. An erect shrub, the slender stems carrying deeply dissected, bright green leaves which have a purplish midrib. As the plant ages, the leaflets become larger and coarser.

P. fruticosa. Ming aralia. A most decorative small shrub with well placed, very deeply dissected, almost fern-like leaves, the tiny leaflets borne on slender purplish stalks.

P. f. 'Elegans'. This cultivar has shorter leaves cut into slightly larger segments than the species. Perhaps also lacking some of its grace.

P. guilfoylei. Wild coffee. An erect shrub with the leaves divided into lobed, toothed segments, sometimes margined with white. Many forms are grown and are seen more frequently than the species.

P. g. 'Victoriae'. Lace aralia. This delightful form is much smaller than the species and has deeply cut leaflets borne on slender, wand-like stems. The segments have narrow, white borders.

Polystichum

ASPIDIACEAE. A genus comprising 135 species of worldwide distribution. They have firm, leathery fronds usually divided into smaller leaflets. Grow in light shade with a minimum temperature of 40–50°F (5–10°C), and keep the compost moist. Propagate by division or spores.

P. acrostichoides. Christmas fern. A North American species with 1–2 ft., glossy green fronds, divided into finely toothed leaflets and borne in arching tufts. This species is very hardy and prefers a cool place. It is not suitable for a warm, dry atmosphere.

P. aristatum. East Indian holly fern. This decorative fern is native to southeast Asia and northern Australia, and has broadly triangular fronds, 1–2 ft. in length, and divided into well-spaced leaflets which are themselves again divided. This species prefers warmer conditions.

P. a. 'Variegatum'. This form has a central, yellow-green band along each leaflet.

Portulaca

PORTULACACEAE.

P. grandiflora. Rose moss; Sun plant. One of a chiefly American genus of about 200 species of fleshy plants, including both annuals and perennials, this decorative plant makes a 6 in., succulent plant, the narrow, 1 in. leaves almost cylindrical and scattered along the stems. In summer the flat flowers open, each 1–1½ in. across like single roses. They are normally a pinkish-purple, but are now available in a wide variety of cultivars and seed strains, in shades of pink, red, orange, and yellow, and also in white, with single or double flowers, opening in spring. Raise annually from seed or cuttings, and keep in sun with a minimum temperature of 50°F (10°C). Water when the compost feels dry.

152

Portulacaria

PORTULACACEAE.

P. afra. Rainbow bush; Elephant bush. One of only two members of this South African genus, this shrubby succulent makes a small tree in the wild, but in a pot will remain small and neat. It has pairs of ½–¾ in., rounded leaves, and rose-pink blooms.
P. a. 'Variegata'. This form with paler green leaves, margined with cream, is most attractive. Grow in sun with a minimum temperature of 45°F (7°C), and water only when the compost feels dry. Propagate by cuttings.

Primula

PRIMULACEAE. A genus containing 500 species, mostly native to the cooler regions of the world. They have undivided basal leaves, and single or clustered flowers borne on erect stems. A few tender species are grown as pot plants. Keep in light shade with a minimum temperature of 45–50°F (7–10°C), and water freely. Propagate by seed.
P. x kewensis. A decorative hybrid between *P. floribunda* and *P. verticillata*, with long, ovate leaves narrowing to the base, and a long flowering stem, both with a fine white meal. The bright yellow, fragrant blooms are borne in up to 5 separate whorls along the stem in winter and spring.
P. malacoides. Fairy primrose. A Chinese species with wavy-edged, roundish leaves, and whorls of rose-purple flowers on 1 ft. tall stems in winter and spring. Many cultivars and seed strains are available, all in shades of pink, lavender, and white.
P. obconica. A very attractive pot plant from China, this species has the disadvantage that the broad, almost rounded leaves have glandular hairs to which some people are allergic, causing a rash. The flowers can reach 2 in. across, and are borne in shades of purple, red, pink, and white in winter and spring.
P. sinensis. Chinese primrose. This species from China has soft-haired, toothed leaves which are ovate and 3–4 in. long. The pink, red, purple, or white flowers are borne in whorls on the 1 ft. stems in winter and spring.

Prostanthera

Australian mint bush. LABIATAE. 50 species make up this decorative genus of evergreen shrubs with aromatic foliage. All come from Australia. Grow in sun with a minimum temperature of 45°F (7°C), and water only when the compost feels dry. Keep in a well-ventilated position when possible. Propagate by cuttings or seed.
P. lasianthus. A tall shrub, the long, pointed leaves are toothed and light green. The white flowers are

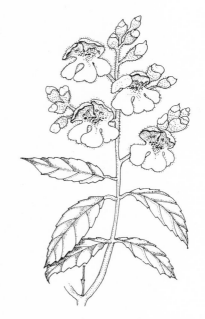

flushed with purple and make dense clusters in summer. *(illus.)*
P. melissifolia. Balm mint bush. This erect shrub has pairs of fragrant, toothed, ovate leaves, up to 2 in. long and a dark, shining green. The dainty, 2-lipped flowers open at the mouth to 5 lobes, and are borne in small clusters in summer.
P. nivea. Snowy mint bush. A strong-growing species which can exceed 6 ft. It has narrow leaves, to 1½ in. long, and solitary white flowers, sometimes with a blue flush, and the lower lobes large and wavy. They open in late spring.
P. rotundifolia. Mint bush. This erect shrub can reach 12 ft. in the open, but considerably less in pots. Its oval leaves are toothed and carried on soft-haired stems. The lilac flowers are borne in clusters in spring.

Pseuderanthemum

ACANTHACEAE. Of the 120 species in this genus, a number are grown for their decorative flowers and foliage. Grow in shade with a minimum temperature of 55–60°F (13–15°C), and water freely. Propagate by cuttings, preferably growing new stock every other year to avoid straggly plants.
P. alatum. Chocolate plant. A low-growing plant from Mexico which has thin textured, brownish leaves, marked with a central row of silvery-white blotches. The small, flat, purple flowers are borne in long clusters in spring.
P. kewense. Syn. *P. atropurpureum.* A small, shrubby plant from the Pacific Islands with oblong,

dark purple leaves, and 2-lipped white blooms, dotted with red. These appear in summer.

P. k. 'Tricolor'. This form has patches of variegation showing pale green, white, and pink.

P. reticulatum. A decorative species from the western Pacific islands with long, bright green leaves, overlain by golden veins. The white flowers have purplish spotting, and open in spring and summer.

Pseudopanax

ARALIACEAE.

P. lessonii. False panax. The 6 species of this genus are all evergreen trees and shrubs from New Zealand. Of them, this small tree, which can reach 20 ft. in the wild, makes a good tub plant for a cool room. It develops its divided leaves when small. They have 3–5 segments divided from one central point, and are glossy green.

P. l. 'Purpureum'. A form with purple-tinted foliage, perhaps a hybrid. Grow in sun with a minimum temperature of 45°F (7°C), and water freely. Propagate by seed and cuttings.

Psidium

MYRTACEAE. 140 species make up this American genus of trees and shrubs. They have undivided leaves and bell-shaped flowers, opening wide to 4 or 5 lobes, which are followed by large berries. Grow in sun with a minimum temperature of 50°F (10°C), and water freely. Propagate by seed or layers.

P. cattleianum. Purple or Strawberry guava. A densely branched shrub from Brazil with ovate, glossy leaves, 2–3 in. long, and short-stalked, white flowers centered with a large boss of stamens. The fruit are rounded and deep red with a strawberry-like flavor.

P. guajava. Guava. This small tree from South America has oblong to oval, pale green leaves with long hairs beneath, and white flowers borne on short stalks in summer and followed by the yellow, pear-shaped fruit.

Pteris

PTERIDACEAE. A genus comprising 250 species of mostly tropical ferns. They are strong growers and many make excellent house plants not needing too much attention. Grow in shade with a minimum temperature of 50°F (10°C), and water freely. Propagate from spores or by division.

P. cretica. A very widespread species, the 6–12 in. fronds cut into up to 6 pairs of slender leaflets, the lowest often themselves cut into smaller segments.

P. c. 'Albo-lineata'. A form with a wide, central white line, covering half the width of each leaflet.

P. c. 'Cristata'. A crested form with a narrow, lighter stripe along each leaflet.

P. ensiformis. A very attractive fern from tropical Asia and Australia with fronds up to 12 in. long, cut into 3 or 4 pairs of leaflets with deeply lobed segments.

P. e. 'Cristata'. A form with crested fronds.

P. e. 'Victoriae'. This most decorative cultivar has broadly variegated fronds.

P. multifida. Chinese brake. Coming from China and Japan, this dainty fern is cut into long, slender, widely spaced leaflets. The fertile fronds are erect, the barren, prostrate.

P. quadriaurita. Syn. *P. biaurita quadriaurita.* A very decorative tropical species, the 1½–2½ ft. fronds cut into long, narrow leaflets, edged with rounded teeth. A number of forms are grown.

P. q. 'Argyraea'. Silver bracken. This is a strong-growing fern, each leaflet marked with a central, silvery-white stripe.

P. q. 'Tricolor'. This form has a dark red midrib, the color flushing the leaves when young and later replaced by a silvery zone.

P. tremula. Trembling or Australian brake. A large fern from Australia and New Zealand, with deeply dissected fronds, 2–4 ft. long when mature.

P. t. 'Variegata'. This variegated form has a central silvery stripe on each leaflet.

Punica

PUNICACEAE.

P. granatum. Pomegranate. Only two plants make up this genus and this one, the pomegranate, is not itself suitable as a house plant, but its dwarf cultivar, 'Nana' is. It rarely exceeds 3 ft. in height, with narrow, shining green leaves, and large, bell-shaped, scarlet flowers which are borne in summer. They are followed by the small, deep yellow fruits. Grow in sun with a minimum temperature of 45°F (7°C), and water when the compost feels dry. Propagate by cuttings.

Puya

BROMELIACEAE.

P. alpestris. Of the 120 species which form this South American genus, this makes the most decorative house plant. Coming from Chile, it has tufted rosettes of spiny-edged leaves, and in summer, a tall, branched cluster of 2 in., greenish-blue flowers carried on a 2–3 ft. stem.

P. a. 'Marginata'. This is a form with pale yellow margins to the gray-green leaves. Grow in sun with a minimum temperature of 45°F (7°C), and water when the compost feels dry. Propagate by seed or suckers. *(illus.)*

154

Q

Quesnelia

BROMELIACEAE. A genus of 12 South American plants, containing both ground-growing and epiphytic species. They have rosettes of long, narrow, spiny leaves, and red or blue flower heads. Grow in shade with a minimum temperature of 50–55°F (10–13°C), and water freely. Propagate by offsets.

Q. liboniana. The leathery, dark green leaves form a narrow, tubular base to the rosette, and have gray scales on the reverse. The salmon-pink bracts hold small, blue flowers.

Q. marmorata. Grecian vase. The long, bluish-green leaves have dark red marbling, and are held stiffly, the bases forming a vase shape. The blue flowers and pink bracts are borne on arching spikes.

Pycnostachys

LABIATAE. This genus from central and southern Africa comprises 37 species of annual and perennial plants. Those suitable as house plants are perennials, having long, narrow leaves, and dense spikes of blue flowers, opening upwards from the base in summer. Grow in light shade with a minimum temperature of 50°F (10°C), and water freely. Propagate by cuttings.

P. dawei. This strong-growing plant can reach 4–6 ft. Keep the leading growths pinched out to promote bushy growth, and ideally, propagate annually unless large plants are wanted. The bright blue flower spikes are tightly packed and pyramidal in outline.

P. urticifolia. This species reaches only 3 ft., and has deeply toothed, ovate leaves, and an oval spike of blue flowers. Cultivate as for *P. dawei*.

Pyrrosia

POLYPODIACEAE.

P. lingua. Tongue fern. This east Asian fern is one of a genus of about 100 species. It has 9 in., strap-shaped, wavy fronds, leathery in texture and dark green in color. They are carried on short stalks and arch outwards as they grow. Keep in shade with a minimum temperature of 50°F (10°C), and water freely. Propagate by division.

Quisqualis

COMBRETACEAE.

Q. indica. Rangoon creeper. This climbing plant belongs to a genus of 17 species of evergreen shrubs which can, in the wild, reach 20 ft. In a pot it will remain smaller than this and is effective trained around a window. It has pointed, oval leaves, and bright orange-red, fragrant, funnel-shaped flowers borne in late spring and summer. Grow in light shade with a minimum temperature of 55–60°F (13–15°C), and water freely. Propagate by cuttings. *(illus.)*

R

Rebutia

CACTACEAE. A genus of 35 species of small cacti
from South America. They are mostly globular and
have rows of tubercles bearing small, branching
spines. The freely borne flowers open by day and
are followed by a small berry. Grow in sun with a
minimum temperature of 40°F (5°C). Water only
when the compost feels dry. Propagate by seed.
R. deminuta. An Argentinian plant forming clumps
of 2–4 in. stems. The white-tipped, brown spines
are short and borne in clusters from each tubercle.
The flowers are a deep scarlet.
R. marsoneri. A delightful small plant from
Argentina, only 2 in. high, and bearing tiny spines
on the tubercles. The 1½ in.-wide, golden-yellow
blooms open in spring.
R. minuscula. This Argentinian species is pale green
and broadly globular, usually reaching 1 in. in
height and 1½ in. in width. The tubercles bear many
small, yellowish-white spines, and the freely borne
flowers are red with yellow at the base and about
1½ in. across. They open in summer.
R. senilis. This pale green species is Argentinian and
can reach almost 3 in. in height. The clear, white,
bristle-like spines are borne in clusters of up to 40,
and the summer-borne flowers are 2 in. across and
bright red.
R. spegezziniana. This species from Argentina
forms clumps of 2½ in., globular stems, the
tubercles bearing white spines. The red-flushed,
yellow flowers open in late spring and summer.

Rechsteineria

GESNERIACEAE. A number of the 75 members of
this tropical American genus make very good house
plants. They are tuberous rooted and have large
undivided leaves and very showy flowers. Grow in
shade with a minimum temperature of 55–60°F
(13–15°C), and water freely while growing. When
the leaves yellow in autumn, dry off, and keep
until the following spring. Propagate by division,
seed, or cuttings.
R. cardinalis. Cardinal flower. This very attractive
Brazilian plant has velvet textured, ovate leaves,
covered with fine purplish hairs and 1½–2 in. long,
brilliant scarlet, tubular flowers. These are borne in
arching clusters on white hairy stems. Normal
flowering time is summer and early autumn, but
they can be brought into flower earlier by keeping
the plants actively growing over winter.
R. leucotricha. The large, ovate leaves of this
Brazilian plant are covered with silky, silvery hairs
giving it a bright sheen. The pendant, bright

orange-scarlet flowers are up to 2 in. long in small
clusters at the top of 10–15 in. stems.
R. macropoda. This Brazilian plant has almost
round, wrinkled leaves with a velvety surface. The
bright scarlet flowers are narrowly tubular up to
1¼ in. long, and open in spring.

Rehmannia

GESNERIACEAE or SCROPHULARIACEAE.
R. angulata. Foxglove gloxinia. A delightful
flowering plant from China, one of 10 members of
its genus. It reaches 2–3 ft. in height, and has
oblong, lobed leaves borne on sticky, glandular,
hairy leaf stalks. The large, deep pinky-red,
foxglove-like flowers are up to 3 in. long and are
purple-spotted inside. Grow in sun with a minimum
temperature of 45°F (7°C), and keep in a cool and
airy position. Propagate by seed.

Reineckia

LILIACEAE.
R. carnea. Fangrass. Of the 2 species making up
this genus, this grass-like plant from China and
Japan has 12–18 in. leaves, erect from their
overlapping bases, then recurved. The pale pink,
fragrant flowers are borne in a loose spike in spring.
R. c. 'Variegata'. Has creamy-white striped leaves.
Grow in light shade with a minimum temperature
of 45°F (7°C), and water freely. Propagate by
division.

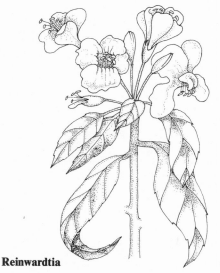

Reinwardtia

LINACEAE.
R. trigyna. Syn. *R. indica*. Yellow flax. One of only
two species in this genus, it makes a 2 ft. shrub
with pointed, ovate leaves, and clusters of funnel-

shaped, yellow flowers, blooming from autumn, through winter to spring. Grow in light shade with a minimum temperature of 45–50°F (7–10°C), and water freely. Propagate by cuttings. *(illus.)*

Renanthera

ORCHIDACEAE.
R. coccinea. One of 13 species making up this genus of epiphytic orchids from tropical Asia. This is a most beautiful plant with 4–5 in., leathery, strap-shaped leaves, and long, branching sprays of 3–4 in., bright red blooms, the narrow, twisted petals and sepals spotted with yellow. At their best, each branched, flowering stem can carry up to 150 flowers. Give light shade in summer only, and grow in osmunda or bark and sphagnum mix, with a minimum temperature of 55–60°F (13–15°C). Water freely. Propagate by rooted stem sections.

Rhapis

Lady palms. PALMAE. A genus of 15 species of palm from China and Japan, of which 2 make attractive foliage plants for a large room. They have almost semi-circular leaves cut into long segments like a fan. Grow in light shade with a minimum temperature of 45–50°F (7–10°C), and water freely. Propagate by suckers and seeds.
R. excelsa. Lady palm. A clump-forming species, the long, cane-like stems bearing shining, dark green, leathery leaves divided into pleated segments.
R. e. 'Variegata'. A most decorative form with ivory-white variegation, which must be kept in shade.
R. humilis. Slender lady palm. A very graceful plant, the finely divided leaves carried on slender stems. It is very slow growing, and an excellent palm for indoor culture.

Rhektophyllum

ARACEAE.
R. mirabile. The only species of its genus, this west African climber can reach 30 ft. in the wild. It makes a decorative pot plant when small; the arrow-shaped leaves are dark green and glossy with paler variegation which disappears as the plant ages. Grow in shade with a minimum temperature of 55°F (13°C), and water freely. Propagate by cuttings of stem sections.

Rhipsalidopsis

CACTACEAE. This genus contains only 2 species, both from Brazil. Their stems are divided into flat, oval sections, joined at the ends rather like the links of a chain. They are naturally epiphytic and do well in hanging baskets. Their colorful blooms are abundantly borne in spring. Grow in shade with

a minimum temperature of 50–55°F (10–13°C), and keep just moist.
R. gaertneri. Syn. *Schlumbergera gaertneri.* Easter cactus. This species has stiffly ascending stems which arch over as they lengthen, and have red-edged, notched margins. The 2 in., scarlet flowers are trumpet-shaped, opening wide at the mouth to reveal the pointed tips to the many petals.
R. x graeseri. This hybrid between *R. gaertneri* and *R. rosea* is a more compact plant than the former, having the fuller, pinky-red flowers of the latter.
R. rosea. Dwarf Easter cactus. This low growing, compact species has narrowly oval stem sections and wide, rose pink blooms in spring.

Rhipsalis

CACTACEAE. A remarkable genus of 60 species of epiphytic cacti which make hanging masses of slender, branched stems. They are grown for their curious appearance, and are best in hanging baskets or fastened to pieces of bark. Grow in shade with a minimum temperature of 50–55°F (10–13°C), and water freely. Propagate by cuttings.
R. capilliformis. Old man's head. The very narrow stems of this Brazilian species are densely branched and pale green in color. They have tiny, white flowers near the ends and these are followed by white, pea-sized fruits.
R. cassutha. Syn. *R. baccifera.* Mistletoe cactus. This Central and South American species is widely naturalized through the tropics. It has long, light green stems, and creamy-white flowers which are followed by mistletoe-like fruits, sometimes with a pink flush.
R. cereuscula. Coral cactus. This Brazilian and Argentinian plant is erect and somewhat bushy, the lower stems, long and cylindrical, branching at the top and made up of smaller sections which are minutely bristly. The white or pink flowers are followed by white fruit.
R. paradoxa. Chain cactus. A strange species from Brazil, the stems, triangular and winged, narrowing at uneven intervals and sometimes also twisted. They are pendant, and have small, greenish-white flowers followed by reddish fruits.
R. rhombea. Copperbranch. Coming from Brazil, this is a bushy plant with irregularly winged, leaf-like branch sections which are erect at first but which become pendant as the stems grow longer. They are notched along the margins. The creamy-white flowers are followed by red fruit.

Rhododendron

ERICACEAE. This genus contains 550 species of evergreen and deciduous trees and shrubs, amongst them a smaller group long known by the botanical name *Azalea.* Although often still given this name, the azaleas are all correctly classified under *Rhododendron* as there is no consistent difference between the two groups. Those suitable as house plants are small-leaved, evergreen shrubs with colorful, funnel-shaped flowers. Grow in light shade, using a peat-based compost, and keep just moist at all times. Maintain a minimum temperature of 45°F (7°C), and keep cool at night and over winter, in a temperature below 60°F (15°C) if possible. Propagate by heel cuttings.

R. bullatum. This evergreen bush from China grows to about 4 ft. in pots. It has dark green, ovate, wrinkled leaves, and pink-tinged, white, fragrant flowers, 3–4 in. long, and opening in spring and early summer. *(illus.)*

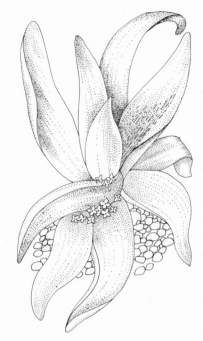

R. kaempferi. A most attractive shrub from Japan with oval, largely deciduous, dark green leaves, and bright vermilion, funnel-shaped flowers up to 2 in. across, opening in late spring.

R. simsii. Indian azalea. This plant is the origin of most of the florists' azaleas, being hybrids raised from it and similar species, or selected forms. Many cultivars are available in shades of red, white, and pink, and the 2–3 in. flowers are single or double. They open in late spring.

R. s. 'Alaska'. This large-flowered plant has clusters of 2½ in., semi-double, pure white flowers which open in winter.

R. s. 'Hexe'. A beautiful single, crimson form with a neat, compact habit and very free flowering.

R. s. 'Sweetheart Supreme'. A cultivar with deep pink buds opening flat to 2 in. across, with double pink blooms.

Rhoeo

COMMELINACEAE.

R. spathacea. Syn. *R. discolor.* Moses in the cradle.

The only member of its genus, this plant forms rosettes of sword-shaped leaves up to 1 ft. in length, and dark green above, purple beneath. The small, 3-petalled, white flowers are carried within purple, boat-shaped bracts. *(illus.)*

R. s. 'Vittatum'. Has creamy-yellow stripes running the length of the leaves. Grow in shade in a minimum temperature of 50°F (10°C) (55–60°F (13–15°C) for the variegated form). Water freely. Propagate by cuttings or seeds.

Rhoicissus

VITIDACEAE.

R. capensis. Cape grape. Of the 12 species

belonging to this genus of evergreen climbers, the cape grape is a good foliage plant for the home. It has large, broadly lobed, shining green, leathery leaves with a heart-shaped base, borne on strong-growing, brownish stems. Grow in sun or light shade with a minimum temperature of 45–50°F (7–10°C), and water only when the compost feels dry. Propagate by cuttings. *(illus.)*

Ricinus

EUPHORBIACEAE.
R. communis. Castor oil plant. A genus containing only this one species, originally from tropical Africa. It is widely cultivated for the oil from its seeds. It makes a small shrub up to 5 ft. in pots, with large leaves divided hand-like into up to 10 rather pointed lobes. They are green to bronze in color. The flower spikes are followed by prickly fruits.
R. c. 'Coccineus'. This cultivar has red to coppery leaves.
R. c. 'Gibsonii'. A form with the leaves suffused with a purplish sheen. This plant soon becomes straggly, and is best raised annually. Grow in sun with a minimum temperature of 45°F (7°C), and water freely. Propagate by seed.

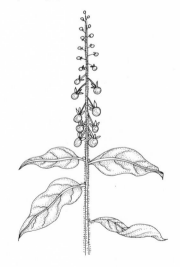

Rivina

PHYTOLACCACEAE.
R. humilis. Rouge plant; Bloodberry. 3 species make up this tropical American genus. This is a bushy plant up to 2 ft. in height with thin textured, ovate, tapering leaves, and erect spikes of tiny, pinkish-white flowers blooming from summer to late autumn. These are followed by shining red, ¼ in. berries. *(illus.)*

R. h. 'Aurantiaca'. A form with orange-yellow berries. Grow in sun or light shade with a minimum temperature of 50°F (10°C), and keep the compost just moist. Propagate by seed or cuttings.

Rochea

CRASSULACEAE.
R. coccinea. Of 4 species in this South African genus, the one described is an excellent pot plant. It makes an erect plant, 12–15 in. in height, and has crowded pairs of opposite, leathery, ovate leaves, and 4-petalled, scarlet flowers. They are borne in flat clusters at the ends of the stems. Grow in sun with a minimum temperature of 45°F (7°C), and water only when the compost feels dry. Propagate by seeds or cuttings.

Rohdea

LILIACEAE.
R. japonica. Sacred lily of Japan. Of the 3 species in this genus, this lily-like plant from Japan is grown largely as a foliage plant. It has 2–3 in. wide, leathery, folded leaves which are up to 12 in. in length and borne in arching tufts. The tiny, white flowers are clustered onto the end of a long stalk and are followed by a red berry.
R. j. 'Marginata'. A form with darker leaves than the true species, and narrow, white margins. Grow in sun with a minimum temperature of 45–50°F (7–10°C), the warmer temperature for the variegated plant, and water freely when in growth. Propagate by division.

Rondeletia

RUBIACEAE. A genus of 120 species of evergreen shrubs from tropical America. They have undivided, rather leathery leaves, and clusters of attractive flowers. Grow in light shade with a minimum temperature of 50–55°F (10–13°C). Water freely and propagate by cuttings.
R. amoena. This eventually makes a 4 ft. shrub bearing 3–4 in., ovate leaves, and in summer, clusters of pink flowers with a golden-bearded throat.
R. roezlii. This shrub, reaching 4 ft., has thin, ovate leaves and summer-borne clusters of reddish-purple, golden-bearded flowers.

Ruellia

ACANTHACEAE. A genus containing 200 species, distributed in every continent except Europe, but most frequent in America. A number are grown as pot plants, most for their pretty tubular flowers, but a few also for their foliage. Keep in light shade with a minimum temperature of 55°F (13°C), and water freely. Propagate by cuttings.

159

R. amoena. Red spray; Red Christmas pride. This South American plant makes a 1–2 ft. shrub with undivided, hairless leaves, 4–6 in. long, and large clusters of bright red, trumpet-shaped flowers, each up to 2 in. long. They open in winter.

R. devosiana. A sub-shrub from Brazil with attractive foliage. The leaves are long, ovate, and dark green, with white veining above and purple-flushed beneath. The white flowers are tinted with pink, and open in spring.

R. macrantha. Christmas pride. A strong-growing Brazilian shrub with pairs of narrow, oval leaves. The large, trumpet-shaped flowers are 2–3½ in. long, and are bright pink with reddish veins in the throat. They open throughout winter. To keep this plant compact, it is best raised annually from cuttings taken in spring.

R. portellae. A low-growing Brazilian species having deep green, ovate, tapering leaves with white veins above and red-purple beneath. The rose-pink flowers are 1½ in. long, opening to rounded lobes at the mouth.

R. strepens. This North American spreading plant has oval, 3 in. leaves, and purplish-pink flowers up to 2 in. long. It is hardier than the other species described and will withstand temperatures to 40°F (5°C).

Rumohra

DAVALLIACEAE.

R. adiantiformis. Leather fern; Leather leaf. Sometimes grown under the names *Polystichum coriaceum* or *Aspidium capense*, this fern from the southern hemisphere is the only one of its genus. It forms dense clusters of deeply divided, arching fronds, 1–3 ft. long, the small segments conspicuously toothed. Grow in light shade with a minimum temperature of 50°F (10°C). Water freely. Propagate by division or spores.

Ruscus

LILIACEAE. 7 species belong to this Mediterranean genus, all being low, evergreen shrubs. They have curiously winged and flattened branches which look like leaves yet carry the tiny flowers and berries. Grow in light shade with a minimum temperature of 40°F (5°C), and water when the compost feels dry. Propagate by division.

R. aculeatus. Butcher's broom. An erect, stiff, spiny evergreen shrub from Europe and western Asia. It has shiny, 1–1½ in., dark green branches, and tiny, greenish flowers which are followed by red berries if the flowers are female. Flowers of both sexes occur, but usually separately on each plant.

R. hypoglossum. Mouse thorn. This Mediterranean species has firm, bright green, glossy branches

without spines, and makes a soft-stemmed shrub, 12–18 in. high. The tiny flowers are yellow, and the berries red.

Russelia

SCROPHULARIACEAE.

R. juncea. Syn. *R. equisetiformis*. Coral plant. One of 40 plants making up this genus of evergreen shrubs from Mexico and Central America. This Mexican species is most effective in a pot or hanging basket having long, pendant branches bearing tiny, scale-like leaves giving it an almost leafless appearance. The 1 in. long, scarlet flowers are borne abundantly in clusters along the bare, rush-like stems. Grow in sun with a minimum temperature of 50°F (10°C), and water only when the compost feels dry. Propagate by cuttings. *(illus.)*

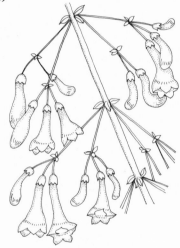

S

Saintpaulia

GESNERIACEAE.

S. ionantha. African violet. All the 12 species belonging to this genus make good house plants, and all are from Africa. They are very similar in appearance, and almost all those seen in cultivation are hybrids and cultivars raised from *S. ionantha*. The species has single, violet-blue flowers, opening flat and centered with golden stamens. They have soft, dark green leaves which are red below and form a dense mound of foliage. They grow best in light shade with a minimum temperature of 55°F (13°C). Water freely. Propagate by leaf cuttings or by division.

S. i. 'Azure Beauty'. This form has double white flowers, 1 in. across, and with violet markings around the eye.

S. *i.* 'Blue Fandango'. A light blue form with fully double flowers.

S. *i.* 'Butterfly White'. A form with snow-white double blooms.

S. *i.* 'Calypso'. A pretty, single purple form with the wavy margins to the petals, pure white.

S. *i.* 'Diana'. One of the closest cultivars to the original species with wide, single violet flowers. It is one of a strain known under the name Harmonie.

S. *i.* 'Elfriede'. A large, blue-flowered single form, one of the Rhapsodie strain.

S. *i.* 'Gisela'. This single pink form is a Rhapsodie, a strain which has the advantage of holding its flowers well. Many other cultivars are liable to drop their petals quickly.

S. *i.* 'My Flame'. A colorful, double pink form with violet-edged petals.

S. *i.* 'Ophelia'. An unusual plum-colored form with single blooms. A Rhapsodie violet.

S. *i.* 'Pink Amour'. A pretty, single pink cultivar having frilled petals.

S. *i.* 'Red Spark'. A good red form with semi-double blooms.

S. *i.* 'Triple Threat'. A very bright pink, double form.

Salpiglossis

SOLANACEAE.

S. sinuata. Painted tongue. One of 18 members of this genus, all of which come from South America. It has lobed leaves, with sticky hairs, and large, 2 in., funnel-shaped blooms, which are purplish, pink, or even straw-colored, with darker veins. They are borne in summer in spikes at the ends of the 1–2 ft. stems.

S. *s.* 'Superbissima'. This fine form has golden spots on the blooms. Grow in sun with a minimum temperature of 45°F (7°C), and water when the compost feels dry. Propagate by seed.

Salvia

LABIATAE. A large genus comprising over 700 species found throughout the world. They have long, tubular flowers with 2 lips, the upper usually hooded, which are carried in a 2-lipped, green calyx. Grow in sun with a minimum temperature of 45°F (7°C), and keep just moist. The plants described are best grown as annuals, raised each spring from cuttings.

S. ambigens. Syn. *S. caerulea*. This South American plant makes a 3 ft. bush when grown in a pot. It has pairs of 2–5 in., bright green, ovate leaves, and spikes of 1½–2 in., purplish-blue flowers in autumn. *(illus.)*

S. greggii. Autumn sage. A 2–3 ft. shrub from Mexico, with pale green, long, oval leaves, and

small, red flowers which form 2 in. spikes in autumn.

S. rutilans. Pineapple-scented sage. This 2–3 ft. shrub from South America has ovate leaves with a heart-shaped base and a pineapple scent. The bright scarlet flowers are borne in erect, leafy clusters from summer to late autumn and early winter.

Sanchezia

ACANTHACEAE.

S. nobilis. Of the 30 species of this tropical American genus, this makes a decorative foliage plant, with narrowly oblong, deep green leaves up to 9 in. in length, and yellow flowers borne in clusters within the red bracts in summer.

S. *n.* 'Glaucophylla'. A form with creamy-white veins forming stripes across the leaves. Grow in light shade with a minimum temperature of 55–60°F (13–15°C). Propagate by cuttings.

Sandersonia

LILIACEAE.

S. aurantiaca. Chinese lanterns. This most attractive plant has slender stems to 18 in., which carry long, narrow leaves along their length. The nodding, lantern-shaped flowers are orange and are carried singly on fine stalks in summer. Some form of support is necessary. Grow in sun with a minimum temperature of 45°F (7°C), and water freely while in growth. When the leaves yellow, dry off, and re-pot again in spring. Propagate by seed or offsets.

Sansevieria

LILIACEAE. This genus of perennial plants from Africa and the East Indies contains 60 species,

161

many of which make good house plants. They have rosettes of erect, almost flat, tough, evergreen leaves which are frequently striped or mottled. The narrow spikes of small, fragrant, white flowers are occasionally borne. Grow in shade with a minimum temperature of 60°F (15°C), and water when the compost feels dry. Propagate by leaf sections or division.

S. cylindrica. Spear sansevieria. The dark green leaves of this central African plant are rounded and stiffly erect, tapering at the end and slightly arching. They are dark green with pale gray bands when young.

S. grandis. Grand Somali hemp. This succulent species from tropical Africa has broadly oblong leaves banded with 2 shades of green and reaching 6–12 in. in length.

S. hahnii. Syn. *S. trifasciata hahnii.* A low, rosette-forming plant from West Africa which has ovate leaves, 4–6 in. long, and banded with light and dark green.

S. h. 'Golden'. Syn. *S. trifasciata* 'Golden Hahnii'. The leaves of this form are dark green with wide, golden-yellow bands at each edge.

S. h. 'Marginata'. Syn. *S. trifasciata* 'Silver Hahnii Marginata'. A very attractive form having pearly-gray and green-banded leaves with a narrow creamy-yellow edge.

S. intermedia. Pygmy bowstring. A tropical African plant with 10–12 in., narrow, stiffly arching leaves. They are striped with shades of gray-green and have horny margins.

S. trifasciata. Mother-in-law's tongue; Snake plant. The erect leaves of this West African species are narrow and rigid, usually up to 2 ft. in length, though they can double this. They have dark green and gray bands.

S. t. 'Laurentii'. This cultivar is more frequently seen than the species, having wide, yellow margins to the leaves. *(illus.)*

S. zeylanica. Bowstring hemp. The 1–2 ft. leaves of this East Indian species arch outwards from the base. They are banded with dark and gray-green.

Sarmienta

GESNERIACEAE. This creeping, epiphytic shrub from Chile, is the only member of its genus. It has small, oval leaves borne on wiry stems and long-tubular red flowers which open to five lobes at the mouth in late winter to early summer. It is best in a moisture-retentive compost of sphagnum and peat in a hanging pan. Grow in light shade with a minimum temperature of 45°F (7°C) and water freely. Propagate by cuttings.

Sarracenia

Pitcher plant. SARRACENIACEAE. A genus of 10 species of carnivorous plants from North America, with rosettes of basal leaves which are erect and tubular, forming a hidden pitcher-shaped trap into which flies and small insects are attracted by a sugar-secreting gland near the top. Once inside they are unable to escape because of the downward pointing hairs, and fall into the digestive fluid below. The flowers have large, colored sepals. Grow in light shade in a permanently moist compost. The plants are hardy and most will withstand many

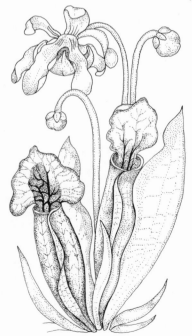

degrees of frost. Propagate by seeds or division.

S. drummondii. Lace trumpets. The long, tubular leaves are pale green with purplish veining and a white-patterned lip. The greenish-purple flowers are 3 in. across.

S. flava. Yellow pitcher plant. The light green pitchers have reddish markings, while the lid is marked with yellow-green. The 2–3 in. flowers are yellow and nodding.

S. purpurea. Northern pitcher plant. The small pitchers are reddish-green and mostly sit on the surface of the ground. The purple flowers are nodding and borne on long stems. *(illus.)*

Sauromatum

ARACEAE.

S. guttatum. Monarch of the East. One of a genus containing 6 species, this Asian plant responds well to pot culture. It grows from tubers, each producing a strong, 2 ft. stalk bearing a deeply lobed, dark green leaf up to 1 ft. across. The arum-like flowers can be up to 1½ ft. long, the spathe is pale green with purplish markings. Grow in shade with a minimum temperature of 60°F (15°C). Water freely while growing, and dry off when the leaves yellow. Propagate by offsets.

Saxifraga

SAXIFRAGACEAE.

S. stolonifera. Syn. *S. sarmentosa.* Mother of thousands; Strawberry geranium. The only member of this 370 strong genus suitable as a house plant. It has rosettes of rounded leaves, hairy above with faint white markings, and purplish beneath. The light sprays of tiny, white flowers, each with 2 large petals and 3 small, are borne in summer on slender 9–12 in. stems. Grow in sun or light shade with a minimum temperature of 45°F (7°C), keeping as cool as possible. Water freely. Propagate by removing the strawberry-like runners which produce abundant small plantlets.

S. s. 'Tricolor'. This smaller form has white-variegated leaves, the pinkish-purple sometimes showing through from the reverse side.

Schefflera

ARALIACEAE. There are 200 species in this genus of evergreen trees and shrubs. Those described make excellent decorator plants for large rooms. Grow in shade with a minimum temperature of 50–55°F (10–13°C), and water freely. Propagate by seeds.

S. actinophylla. Syn. *Brassaia actinophylla.* Umbrella tree. Coming from Australasia, this species makes a tree in the wild, but in pots will remain under 6 ft. It is grown for its glossy, dark green leaves which are divided into 3 to 16 long leaflets, each with its short stalk arising from the same point.

S. arboricola. Syn. *Heptapleurum arboricolum.* Green rays. This southeast Asian species is rather similar in form to *S. actinophylla*, but has up to 10 bright, shining green leaflets.

Schinus

ANARCARDIACEAE.

S. terebinthifolius. Brazilian pepper tree. One of a genus of 30 species, this is an evergreen tree reaching 30 ft. in the wild, but attractive when small and making a good container plant. It has stiffly spreading branches and 4–8 in., deep green leaves cut into up to 9 glossy leaflets. It has small, white flowers, the sexes on separate trees, followed by red berries on female plants. These, however, will only appear on large specimens. Grow in sun with a minimum temperature of 45°F (7°C), and water freely. Propagate by seeds or cuttings.

Schizanthus

SOLANACEAE.

S. pinnatus. Poor man's orchid. There are 15 annual and perennial members of this genus, all from Chile. Those commonly grown as annual pot plants reach about 1½ ft. and are mostly hybrids derived largely from this species and known as *S. x wisetonensis.* Its widely divided leaves provide a ferny background to the colorful flowers which carry remarkably decorative patterning. Cultivars in shades of pink, purple, mauve, and yellow are grown.

S. p. 'Dwarf Bouquet'. This is a small form which makes a neat, bushy plant.

S. p. 'Pansy Flowered'. This group has large, flat flowers with pansy-like markings. Grow in sun with a minimum temperature of 45°F (7°C), and try to keep below 65°F (18°C), unless in well-ventilated position. Water when the compost feels dry. Propagate by seed, sowing in late summer.

Schizocentron

MELASTOMATACEAE.

S. elegans. Syn. *Heterocentron elegans; Heeria*

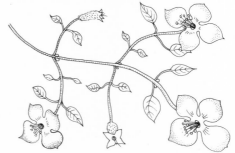

elegans. This Mexican plant is the only one of its genus. It has creeping stems covered with almost heart-shaped, bright green, evergreen leaves which are decoratively pendant grown in a hanging basket. The 4-petalled flowers are pinkish-purple and open wide to 1 in. across in summer. Grow in sun with a minimum temperature of 45°F (7°C), and water freely. Propagate by division or cuttings. *(illus.)*

Schlumbergera

CACTACEAE. 245 species make up this genus of epiphytic cacti from South America. The bright green stems are flattened at the joints like rather oval leaves, while the colorful flowers open in winter when days are short. Grow in light shade with a minimum temperature of 50°F (10°C), and water when the compost feels dry. Propagate by cuttings.

S. x buckleyi. Christmas cactus. One of the most popular of all cacti, partly from its habit of producing its 2–3 in. long, bright rose-purple, trumpet-shaped flowers in winter, and partly from its general tolerance of neglect. It has notched "leaves" and grows from 6–12 in. tall.

S. russelliana. Shrimp cactus. This 1–1½ ft. plant comes from Brazil and has long, pink, trumpet-shaped flowers with a purplish sheen, opening in winter and spring. The leaf-like joints are 1½ in. long.

S. truncata. Syn. *Zygocactus truncatus*. Crab cactus. A number of cultivars of this colorful cactus are grown. They have 2–3 in., trumpet-shaped flowers in shades of pink, red, mauve, and purple, and long, leaf-like, bright green stem joints often flushed with red.

Scilla

Squill. LILIACEAE. A genus of 80 bulbous plants from Europe, southwest Asia and Africa. They have undivided, oval to strap-shaped leaves and small, starry or bell-shaped flowers. The tender species make good pot plants, though some of the hardy ones, notably *S. sibirica* and *S. tubergeniana* can be brought indoors for early spring flowering in the same way as crocuses. Grow the tender species in sun with a minimum temperature of 45°F (7°C), and when growing, water when the compost feels dry. Propagate by offsets or seed.

S. adlamii. The plant grown under this name is from South Africa and has decorative 6–9 in. leaves, each bulb producing one only. They are pleated and a bronze-green. The clusters of small, deep mauve, bell flowers are produced in spring.

S. sibirica. From southeast Russia and eastern Europe, this hardy bulb has long, narrow, deep green leaves and small, bright blue, starry flowers borne in small clusters.

S. s. 'Spring Beauty'. This pretty cultivar has a darker stripe along the center of each petal.

S. tubergeniana. This hardy species from Iran has 1 in., light blue flowers with a darker central line. They are borne in loose clusters and open in spring before the wide, bright green leaves.

S. violacea. Syn. *Ledebouria socialis*. A most attractive foliage plant from South Africa having 3–5 in., oval to strap-shaped, green leaves which have purple spots above and an all-over suffusion below. The small, purple and green flowers open in winter.

Scindapsus

Ivy arum. ARACEAE. Of the 40 climbing species in this largely southeast Asian genus, a few are grown for their decorative foliage. Grow in shade with a minimum temperature of 55°F (13°C), and water when the compost feels dry. Propagate by cuttings.

S. aureus. Syn. *Rhaphidophora aurea*. Devils ivy; Golden pothos. Although this climber can reach 40 ft. in its native Solomon Islands, it can easily be kept to a few feet in pots, and is most effective if allowed to climb up a moss stick. It has ovate, deep green leaves with irregular yellow areas.

S. a. 'Marble Queen'. A cultivar with the leaves basically white with only small, green splashes.

S. a. 'Tricolor'. This form has varying degrees of variegation from yellow, through cream and pale green to the normal mid-green.

S. pictus. The dark green, ovate leaves have the tips curved to one side, and silvery marbling on the surface.

S. p. argyraeus. Syn. *Pothos argyreus*. An extremely decorative form with a blue-green sheen to the leaves and silvery markings and margins.

Scirpus

CYPERACEAE.

S. cernuus. Syn. *Isolepis gracilis*. Miniature bulrush. 300 species make up this genus which is found throughout the world. This southeast Asian rush makes a tufted plant with 8 in., grassy leaves which arch over at the tips. The tiny, white flower heads are borne at the end of the stems. Grow in light shade with a minimum temperature of 55°F (13°C), and keep always moist, preferably standing the pot in a saucer of water. Propagate by division.

Sedum

Stonecrops. CRASSULACEAE. 600 species make up this almost worldwide genus, being absent only from Australasia. They are succulent plants having thick, fleshy leaves, sometimes cylindrical, sometimes flat. The small, 4–5 petalled flowers are borne in small clusters. Grow in sun with a minimum temperature of 45°F (7°C), and water only when the compost feels dry. Propagate by cuttings.

S. adolphii. Golden sedum; Butter plant. The stout, erect stems of this Mexican species have 1–1½ in., fleshy, almost cylindrical leaves which are a yellowish-green and edged with red. The flowers are white.

S. bellum. This Mexican species has flattened leaves, tapering from a narrow base to a rounded end. They are pale green and covered with a fine white, waxy powder. The clusters of white flowers are borne on long stems in winter.

S. lineare. A low, tufted plant from China and Japan having narrow, pale green leaves which are clustered together, especially at the tips of the stems. The yellow flowers open flat like stars and are borne in spring and summer.

S. l. 'Variegatum'. This form which has white margins and sometimes other white markings on the light green leaves, is the one most frequently cultivated.

S. morganianum. Burro tail. A Mexican species producing long, prostrate branches which are pendant when grown in a hanging basket and can reach several feet in length. They are densely covered with thick, fleshy, overlapping leaves which are pale green with a bluish, waxy bloom. The small clusters of red flowers are borne at the end of the stems in summer and autumn. It is best shaded from the hottest summer sun. *(illus.)*

S. multiceps. A small, shrubby plant from Algeria with the branched stems becoming bare as they age and terminating in clusters of densely borne, tiny, narrow leaves, giving the appearance of tiny trees. It can reach 8 in. in height.

S. pachyphyllum. A Mexican species forming a small, somewhat shrubby plant with closely clustered, cylindrical, light green leaves, each tipped with red. The pale yellow flowers open in April.

S. platyphyllum. Jade plant. This small, shrubby species from Mexico has light green, flattened leaves, tapering from the broadly rounded tip which has a fine point, to the stem. They have a bluish, waxy texture. The small, whitish flowers are spotted with red.

S. praealtum. A Mexican shrub which can reach 5 ft. in height, and has long, spoon-shaped, pale green leaves, and yellow flowers in summer.

S. p. 'Cristatum'. This is the form usually grown, the stem widening and bearing a crest-like fan of partly joined leaves. A plant grown for its curiosity value rather than for its beauty.

S. rubrotinctum. Jelly beans; Christmas cheer. This 6–9 in. shrub from Mexico has bright green, cylindrical leaves, tipped and flushed with red.

S. r. 'Aurora'. A cultivar with lighter green leaves which are flushed with salmon-pink.

S. sieboldii. October plant. A most attractive Japanese species which is excellent in a hanging basket. It has arching, red stems up to 10 in. long, which bear whorls of rounded, fleshy leaves, the blue-gray coloration becoming flushed with bronze as it ages. The clusters of pink flowers are borne at the end of the stems in autumn.

S. s. 'Medio-variegatum'. A frequently grown form having a cream band at the center of each leaf.

S. treleasei. Coming from Mexico, this erect stemmed plant has thick, fleshy, blue-green leaves with a grayish bloom. The yellow flowers open in spring.

Selaginella

SELAGINELLACEAE. A worldwide genus containing 700 species of slender, fern-like plants with finely dissected, almost mossy fronds. Those that are dwarf are ideal for growing beneath a glass or plastic cover as in a terrarium. They need shade and a minimum temperature of 55–60°F (13–15°C). A high humidity is needed, and the compost must not be allowed to become dry. Propagate by layering or division.

S. apus. Syn. *S. apoda*. Parsley moss. A low, hummock-forming plant from North America, up to 4 in. in height. It has delicate, bright green foliage and is excellent for a bottle garden, revelling in the extra humidity.

S. emmeliana. Moss fern. The lacy fronds of this 3–6 in. South American species are held stiffly erect or horizontal. They must have constant moisture.

S. kraussiana. Irish moss. This African species is hardier than the others described, and if kept in a temperature of 60–65°F (15–18°C) can be grown successfully without any extra humidity. It forms mats of tiny, bright green leaves and is most

165

effective with its mossy stems trailing from a hanging basket. It can also be used as ground cover in terraria.

S. k. brownii. Cushion moss. This is a prostrate, mat-forming variety which makes 1 in. high cushions.

S. lepidophylla. Resurrection plant; Rose of Jericho. A Central American species which has the ability to curl up tightly when dry, allowing it to survive droughts, and open out again into a rosette of bright green fronds when put in water. An interesting novelty.

S. martensii. Coming from Mexico, this spreading plant has deeply cut, erect fronds up to 6 in. long, which are a bright green.

S. m. 'Watsoniana'. This is a variegated form with light green and silvery markings at the ends of the fronds.

S. uncinata. Rainbow fern. A creeping plant from China with an almost metallic sheen to its delicate blue-green fronds. Most attractive as ground cover in a terrarium, but ultimately getting too large.

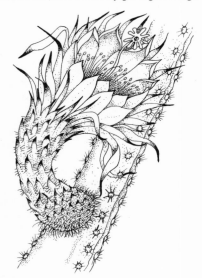

Selenicereus

CACTACEAE. A genus of 25 species of night-flowering cacti from Central America. They have climbing or trailing stems, and very large, fragrant flowers which open at nightfall. Grow in sun with a minimum temperature of 55°F (13°C), and water freely except when dormant in winter. They require some form of support. Propagate by cuttings.

S. grandiflorus. Queen of the night. This epiphytic species from the West Indies has very large flowers, pale orange-pink in bud, but opening to reveal pure white petals inside. *(illus.)*

S. hamatus. Big hook cactus. This strong-growing Mexican epiphyte has white flowers which are green on the reverse.

S. urbanianus. Moon cereus. The flowers of this Central American plant open white from light golden-brown buds.

Semele

LILIACEAE.

S. androgyna. Climbing butcher's broom. This evergreen twiner is one of a genus of only 5 species. It comes from the Canary Islands and has the leaves represented by tiny scales, and 4 in., ovate, leaf-like branches. It is an intriguing plant which needs support. The tiny flowers are yellow-green with a purple center. Grow in sun in a minimum temperature of 45–50°F (7–10°C), and water when the compost feels dry. Propagate by division or seed.

Senecio

COMPOSITAE. A very large genus comprising over 2000 species with a worldwide distribution. They vary in character from small, prostrate succulents to shrubs and tree-like herbaceous plants. It is the succulents which make the most suitable house plants and these grow best in sun with a minimum temperature of 45°F (7°C). Water when the compost feels dry. Propagate by cuttings.

S. articulatus. Syn. *Kleinia articulata*. Candle plant. A curious plant from South Africa having swollen, succulent stems which are often jointed. At first they carry deeply lobed leaves, but as they age these drop off leaving only a small group of leaves at the top. In summer, small, yellow-tufted flowers open.

S. cruentus. Syn. *Cineraria cruenta*. This Canary Island species is familiar to most people as cineraria. It makes a compact plant with broadly ovate leaves and brightly colored daisy flowers. It is available in shades of mauve, red, pink, and white. Although a perennial, it is best raised annually, if possible raising the plants outside and bringing them in in early autumn for winter and spring flowering.

S. grandiflorus. A large shrub from Mexico which can reach 10 ft. in the wild. In pots it is best raised annually, still growing to about 3 ft. in the season. The large leaves are ovate and up to 18 in. long, and the yellow, daisy-like flowers appear in dense clusters in winter.

S. haworthii. Syn. *Kleinia tomentosa*. Cocoon plant. A small, shrubby, succulent species from South Africa which has cylindrical, white woolly leaves which narrow at both ends like a cocoon. The orange-yellow flowers open in summer. Avoid handling more than necessary, and give a dry period in winter.

S. herreianus. A creeping species from South-West Africa which produces green, round to ovoid leaves rather like small berries and ending in a short point. They have translucent stripes running along their length. The small flower heads are borne largely on 2–3 in. stems.

S. jacobsenii. Syn. *Notonia petraeus.* An east African creeping species having 3 in. long, bright green, fleshy, spoon-shaped leaves, and small orange flowers. It is very effective in a hanging basket.

S. macroglossus. Wax ivy. An attractive small creeper from southern Africa, the thin fleshy leaves remarkably like those of an ivy in shape. The flowers are daisy-like with white petals. It grows well with support, or it can be allowed to trail from a hanging basket.

S. m. 'Variegatus'. A form with cream and lighter green markings.

S. mikanioides. German ivy. This South African herbaceous plant has soft, fleshy, lobed leaves held on slender but stiff stems. It can be kept bushy by pinching, or it can be allowed to produce climbing shoots.

S. radicans. Syn. *Kleinia radicans.* A South African creeping plant which looks well in a hanging basket. It has light green, cylindrical leaves about 1 in. long with a darker band along one side. The small, tufted flower heads are white.

S. rowleyanus. String of beads. Coming from South-West Africa, this trailing plant has almost perfectly globular leaves just like light green beads. Each has a single transparent line and ends in a fine point. The $\frac{1}{2}$ in., white flowers, enlivened by dark red stigmas, open in winter. It is ideal for a hanging basket, the stems being capable of reaching 2–3 ft. in length.

S. scaposus. Silver coral. A remarkable succulent plant from South Africa having rosettes of long, silvery gray-green leaves, thinly hairy at first, later becoming smooth.

S. serpens. Syn. *Kleinia repens.* Blue chalk sticks. A succulent shrub from South Africa rarely above 1 ft. in a pot, but up to 3 ft. in the wild. It has thickened, fleshy stems and long, semi-cylindrical leaves, all a pale gray-green with a blue-white, powdery surface. The small, white flowers are borne on long stalks.

S. stapeliaeformis. Syn. *Kleinia stapeliaeformis.* Candy stick. An erect plant from South Africa which grows to 1 ft., with long, stiff, 5–7 angled stems set with tiny, dark green, spiny leaves. The red, tufted flowers are borne on long stalks. Water very sparingly at all times and keep dry in summer.

S. tamoides. A showy, Central African climber with bright green, ivy-like leaves. In late autumn it is covered with bright yellow, $1-1\frac{1}{2}$ in. daisies.

Serissa

RUBIACEAE.

S. foetida. One of three species belonging to the genus, this 2 ft. shrub from China and Japan has small, dark green, leathery leaves and neat white, starry flowers.

S. f. 'Variegata'. This form has white-lined and -edged leaves.

S. f. 'Plena'. A very attractive double flowered cultivar. Grow in light shade with a minimum temperature of 50°F (10°C), and water freely. Propagate by cuttings.

Serjania

SAPINDACEAE.

S. glabrata. There are 215 species in this genus of South American climbers. This plant from Peru has slender, light green leaves which are deeply divided into small, toothed, ovate leaflets. The clusters of yellow flowers are borne only on large specimens. To keep the plant small, pinch out the growing point regularly. Grow in shade with a minimum temperature of 55°F (13°C). Water freely. Propagate by cuttings.

Setcreasea

Purple heart. COMMELINACEAE.

S. purpurea. This good foliage plant from Mexico is one of a small genus of 9 species. It will reach $1-1\frac{1}{2}$ ft. in height, and has long, pointed leaves which are a rich purple in color if kept in a good light. When shaded they become more green. The pretty, 3-petaled, rose-purple flowers are held between 2 large, purple, leafy bracts. Grow in full sun with a minimum temperature of 45°F (7°C), and water when the compost feels dry. Propagate by cuttings.

Sibthorpia

SCROPHULARIACEAE.

S. europaea. Cornish moneywort. This small, trailing plant comes from western Europe and belongs to a genus comprising only 5 species. It has very slender stems which bear small, rounded, light green, lobed leaves, and tiny, 5-petaled flowers. It is particularly useful as ground cover under a larger planting.

S. e. 'Variegata'. This form has creamy-white markings on the leaves. Grow in light shade with a minimum temperature of 40°F (5°C). Water freely. Propagate by division.

167

Siderasis

COMMELINACEAE.

S. fuscata. This is the only member of the genus and comes from Brazil. It forms rosettes of broadly oblong, dull green leaves, brightened by a central, silver stripe. The undersides are purple, and both are covered by a fine brown hair. The 3-petalled flowers are blue-mauve. Grow in shade with a minimum temperature of 60°F (15°C), and water freely, providing increased humidity where possible. Propagate by cuttings and division.

Sinningia

Syn. *Gloxinia.* GESNERIACEAE. A genus comprising 20 species of perennials from Brazil, often incorrectly described as *Gloxinia.* Most are tuberous rooted and have large, velvety leaves, showing off the richly colored, widely tubular flowers. Grow in shade with a minimum temperature of 55°F (13°C), and water freely. Propagate by seeds, cuttings, or division of tubers.

S. barbata. This species is unusual in that it is not tuberous rooted. It is erect, and the stems carry long, narrow, deep green leaves which are red beneath and taper to a point. The white flowers which are marked with red are hairy within the throat. They open chiefly in summer but can produce blooms through the year. *(illus.)*

S. pusilla. Miniature slipper plant. A tiny plant reaching only 1–2 in. in height with dull green, wrinkled leaves, and pinkish-purple and white flowers. It is ideal for growing in a covered container as it requires extra humidity.

S. regina. An attractive dwarf species with 6 in. mounds of dark, velvety, green leaves which are marked with clear, silvery-white veins. The undersides are purple. The 2 in., blue-purple flowers are borne on erect stems from late spring through summer.

S. speciosa. This is the familiar gloxinia of nurserymen. It has basal clusters of softly hairy, deep green leaves and large velvety flowers, purple in the species, but now available in shades of red, pink, purple, and white as well as bicolors with a white margin to the petals, and both single and double forms.

S. s. 'Defiance'. A single, bright red form.

S. s. 'Emperor Frederick'. A long-established favorite with deep red flowers which are white-edged.

S. s. 'Mont Blanc'. A very beautiful, pure white cultivar.

S. s. 'Princess Elizabeth'. A form having lilac-blue flowers centered with white.

S. s. 'Tigrina'. An unusual form, the white tube speckled with purplish-red and opening at the mouth to show lobes of the same color.

Smithiantha

Temple bells. GESNERIACEAE. A genus of 8 tropical American plants with beautiful, rounded to heart-shaped leaves. The elegant, bell-shaped flowers are borne in long, erect clusters in shades of yellow, orange, pink, and red. Grow in light shade with a minimum temperature of 60°F (15°C), and water freely while growing, drying off when the foliage yellows, and keeping dry until late winter or early spring. Propagate by division or seeds.

S. cinnabarina. Syn. *Naegelia cinnabarina.* A very beautiful 1½–2 ft. plant from Mexico and Guatemala, having deep green, thickly velvety leaves which are flushed with red. They are borne on erect stems which are topped with a spire-like spike of scarlet flowers which are deep yellow inside. They open in summer and autumn.

S. multiflora. Coming from Mexico, this plant reaches 1 ft. in height, and has round, softly hairy leaves and spikes of creamy, bell flowers which open in summer.

S. zebrina. Syn. *Naegelia zebrina.* A 2–3 ft. Mexican species which has dark green leaves marked and mottled with brown, and 1½ in., bright red flowers, yellow inside and borne in erect, slender spikes. This species is the chief parent of the many hybrid cultivars now available.

S. z. 'Abbey'. A creamy-white flowered form with orange markings.

S. z. 'Elke'. A beautiful form, with golden flowers flushed with a lighter orange.

S. z. 'Exoniensis'. This form has bright orange-yellow flowers and red-flushed leaves.

S. z. 'Orange King'. A clear orange cultivar.
S. z. 'Pink Domino'. This form has pink bells, the inside pure white.
S. z. 'Rose Queen'. A most attractive, pink-flowered form, the blooms spotted with purple inside.
S. z. 'Scarlet Emperor'. This is a brilliant scarlet, with yellow inside each flower.

Sobralia

ORCHIDACEAE.
S. discolor. A large, clump-forming orchid from Mexico, one of 90 members of the genus. The leafy stems can reach 2 ft. in height, and the 3–4 in. blooms are creamy-white and pink-flushed with a reddish-purple, yellow-streaked lip. They open in spring and summer. Grow in an ordinary compost mixed with equal parts of fern fiber or shredded bark to improve the aeration and drainage. Keep in shade with a minimum temperature of 55–60°F (13–15°C), and water freely especially when growing. Propagate by division when repotting is necessary.

Solandra

SOLANACEAE. 10 climbing shrubs make up this tropical American genus. They have oval, shiny, dark green leaves, and long, trumpet-shaped flowers which open at the mouth to 5 lobes. They look well trained around a large window, needing plenty of light. Maintain a minimum temperature of 50°F (10°C). Water freely while growing, then give a dry resting period to initiate flower buds. Propagate by seeds or cuttings.
S. grandiflora. A tall, but little branching climber from Jamaica with oblong leaves and 6–9 in. long, fragrant flowers which change from pale green to a rich golden-brown as they mature. They open in spring.
S. longiflora. A 6 ft. climber from Jamaica which has long, oval leaves, and 9–12 in., white flowers with lilac and brown shading.

Solanum

SOLANACEAE. A very large genus comprising some 1700 species including the potato, of which a number make attractive pot plants. Grow in sun or light shade with a minimum temperature of 45°F (7°C), and water when the compost feels dry. Propagate by cuttings or seed.
S. capsicastrum. Winter cherry. A Brazilian shrub reaching several feet in the wild. It has long, narrow, pointed leaves borne in pairs, one larger than the other. The small, white, starry flowers open in summer, and are followed by shiny, scarlet fruits like ripe cherries. They remain on the plant

until well into winter. This plant is best raised annually from seed, and needs pinching to keep bushy. The flowers should be pollinated for a good setting of fruit, or insects will do this if the plants are kept outside when in bloom.

S. jasminoides. Potato vine. A Brazilian twining plant with variable leaves, some ovate and undivided, others cut into 3 or 5 leaflets. The bluish-white, starry flowers have a boss of yellow stamens and are very like those of the potato. They are borne in clusters through summer and autumn. **(illus.)**
S. j. 'Album'. This form has pure white flowers.
S. pseudocapsicum. Jerusalem cherry; Christmas cherry. A 4 ft. shrub from Madeira which is usually grown as an annual. It has narrow, deep green, soft leaves, and starry flowers in summer. These are followed by vermilion berries like cherries which hang on the plant over Christmas. There is also a form with yellow berries.

Solisia

CACTACEAE.
S. pectinata. Syn. *Mammillaria pectinata*. Lace bugs. A tiny cactus from Mexico, the only one of its genus. It makes a 1 in. globe and is covered with closely set, stiff, white starry spines. The relatively large flowers are yellow. Not the easiest of cacti to grow, but worth some trouble for its attractiveness. Grow in sun with a minimum temperature of 45°F (7°C), and water only when the compost feels dry. Propagate by seed, though purchased plants may be grafted.

Sonerila

MELASTOMATACEAE.
S. margaritacea. 175 species make up this southeast Asian genus of herbaceous and shrubby plants.

169

Some have beautifully patterned leaves and many also have showy flowers. This species has bright red stems up to 10 in. long, becoming straggly with age. The ovate, slender pointed leaves are a deep green and covered with tiny hairs and silvery spots. The reverse is purplish-red. Through summer and autumn, the small clusters of pinkish-purple flowers open.

S. m. 'Argentea'. A form with the spots coalesced to give a silvery surface to the leaf.

S. m. 'Marmorata'. In this form the spots have joined to form bands of silver. Grow in shade with a minimum temperature of 60°F (15°C), and water freely. These plants require additional humidity and are best grown under a glass or plastic cover. Propagate by seeds or cuttings.

Sophronites

ORCHIDACEAE.

S. coccinea. Syn. *S. grandiflora.* One of a small genus comprising only 6 epiphytic orchids, this species from Mexico has small pseudobulbs and narrowly oblong, 2–3 in. leaves. The flowers which are borne in autumn and winter are a brilliant scarlet and up to 3 in. across, the side petals broadly oval, the sepals narrower. Grow in light shade with a minimum temperature of 50°F (10°C), and water freely, maintaining a high humidity. Propagate by division.

Sparaxis

IRIDACEAE.

S. tricolor. Harlequin or Wand flower. Of the 4 bulbous plants which make up this South African genus, this species produces fans of narrow, strap-shaped leaves about 12–15 in. long. The 6-petalled

flowers open flat like a star. There are a number of color forms, the most frequent having orange petals with a yellow center, the two colors divided by a black blotch. Others have blooms in combinations of pinks, reds, and purples. The larger flowered, closedly related *S. grandiflora* is also grown. Grow in sun with a minimum temperature of 45°F (7°C), and water freely while growing, drying off when the leaves yellow, repotting in autumn. Propagate by offsets. *(illus.)*

Sparmannia

TILIACEAE.

S. africana. African or Window linden. One of a genus of 7 species of shrubs or trees from Africa. In the wild this plant can reach 10–20 ft., but as a pot plant is usually grown as an annual reaching no more than 3 ft. It has long, softly hairy leaves which are heart-shaped and taper to a slender point. The clusters of small, wide open flowers are borne in summer even on first-year plants, each bloom being centered with purple-tipped, golden stamens. Grow in sun or light shade with a minimum temperature of 45°F (7°C), and water freely. Propagate by seed or cuttings.

Spathiphyllum

ARACEAE. A genus comprising 27 species of evergreen perennials all except one from South America. They have long, oval leaves, and arum-like flowers. Grow in shade with a minimum temperature of 50–55°F (10–13°C), and water freely. Propagate by division.

S. cannifolium. This plant from Venezuela and Guyana has long, ovate, dark green leaves which can reach 20 in. in length, and a stiff, fleshy spathe, white on the inside and green on the outside. The spadix is also white.

S. cochlearispathum. This is a large plant from Mexico and Guatemala. It has 18–30 in., oblong leaves on a stalk equally as long, and a white spadix within a greenish-yellow spathe.

S. floribundum. This Columbian plant is usually less than a foot in height. It has 4–6 in. long, tapering leaves and a small green or white spadix with a pure white spathe.

S. f. 'Mauna Loa'. This hybrid is particularly floriferous, and has broad, almost triangular, white spathes.

S. patinii. Coming from Colombia, this plant has narrow leaves up to 10 in. long, and a white spadix and spathe, both with green markings.

S. wallisii. From Colombia and Venezuela, this small plant rarely exceeds 9 in. in height. The long, oval spathe is white and encloses a yellow spadix contrasting well with the very dark green leaves. *(illus.)*

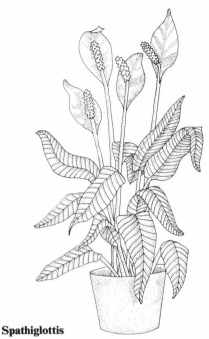

Spathiglottis

ORCHIDACEAE.

S. plicata. Belonging to a genus of 46 species, this ground-growing orchid from southeast Asia and the Pacific Islands has broad, bright green ribbed leaves up to 3 ft. in length, erect at first, then arching over. The dense clusters of purplish-pink flowers are borne at the top of a long stalk in spring and early summer. Grow in a compost mixed with osmunda or bark fiber in sun or light shade with a minimum temperature of 55–60°F (13–15°C). Water freely. Propagate by division.

Sprekelia

AMARYLLIDACEAE.

S. formosissima. Jacobean lily. This bulbous plant is the only one of its genus and comes from Mexico. It has narrow, strap-shaped leaves, usually occurring after the remarkably orchid-like flowers. These are bright scarlet, occasionally white, and have an erect, similarly colored bract, 2 spreading side petals and the 3 lower petals rolled together at the base to give the appearance of a lip. They can reach 5 in. across, and open in late spring or early summer. Dry off when the leaves yellow, bringing into growth in autumn. Grow in sun with a minimum temperature of 50°F (10°C), and water freely when in growth. Propagate by offsets.

Stapelia

Carrion flower. ASCLEPIADACEAE. 75 species make up this genus of African succulent plants which have thick fleshy stems but no proper leaves,

and 5-petalled flowers usually like a starfish in appearance, but with an unpleasant odor of bad meat which attracts pollinating flies. Grow in light shade with a minimum temperature of 45°F (7°C), and water when the compost feels dry, giving more in summer when hot, but keeping drier in winter. Propagate by division or cuttings.

S. flavirostris. This most attractive species has light green, 4-angled stems, and purple flowers with long, fine white hairs along the points of the petals. The blooms can reach 6 in. across, opening through summer into early autumn.

S. glandulifera. This small plant has softly hairy, dark green stems, the angles dotted with white teeth, and small, pinkish-white, glandular, hairy flowers, the hairs like tiny glassy projections. They open through summer and autumn.

S. hirsuta. A strong-growing plant with erect, fleshy, leafless stems up to 8 in. in height. The 5 in. flowers are pale yellow with purple bars and hairs. A number of color forms are grown, many of which are in fact hybrids.

S. nobilis. This plant has 4-angled, softly hairy stems with white teeth along the margins. The flowers are very large, up to 12 in. across, and pale yellow with reddish lines giving a salmony effect. The reverse side of the petals is purple. *(illus.)*

S. revoluta. A handsome plant with bluish-green, hairless, spiny stems, and red-brown flowers in which the joined petals are folded strongly back so that the bloom appears almost circular.

S. variegata. The most popular species, with slender, green or purple mottled, 4 in. stems, and 2–3 in., starry flowers which are yellow-green, barred with purple and having a ring-like central corona.

Stenocarpus

PROTEACEAE.

S. sinuatus. Fire-wheel tree. This Australian evergreen tree is one of a genus of 20 species. It can reach 100 ft. in the wild, but when young makes a good decorator plant with its distinctive juvenile foliage. It has large, shiny leaves which are up to 2 ft. in length and are divided into up to 4 pairs of oblong lobes when young. With age, these decrease in size and become almost entire. The striking, wheel-like, red and yellow flowers rarely occur on young plants. Grow in sun with a minimum temperature of 45°F (7°C). Water when the compost feels dry, and propagate by cuttings or seed.

Stenomesson

AMARYLLIDACEAE.

S. incarnatum. One of a genus of 20 species, this attractive bulbous plant from Peru and Ecuador grows to 2 ft. in height. It has small clusters of bright red, 3–4 in., tubular flowers, widening at the mouth showing the darker markings inside. They are borne on 2 ft. stems in summer, usually with or just before the leaves. When these yellow, the plant should be dried off until the following spring. Grow in sun with a minimum temperature of 45°F (7°C), and water freely in summer. Propagate by offsets.

Stenotaphrum

GRAMINEAE.

S. secundatum. St. Augustine grass. A small, creeping grass belonging to a genus of 20 species and coming from the warmer areas of Central and North America. It has 6 in., narrow leaves.
S. s. 'Variegata'. This is the form grown and is particularly good in a hanging basket, the leaves being striped lengthwise with ivory-white. Grow in sun with a minimum temperature of 50°F (10°C), and water freely. Propagate by cuttings.

Strelitzia

Bird of Paradise flower. STRELITZIACEAE. A genus comprising 5 species of perennials from South Africa. They have most striking flowers resembling a colorful bird's head. Grow in sun or light shade with a minimum temperature of 45–50°F (7–10°C), and water when the compost feels dry. Propagate by seeds or division.
S. parvifolia. This species makes a 4 ft. clump of slender stems bearing very narrow, flattened leaves and orange petals borne within boat-shaped bracts with a tongue-like, purple lower petal. They open in late spring.
S. p. juncea. This variety has the leaves either very small, or not developed at all, forming tall, rush-like clumps of stiff stems bearing the remarkable flowers.

172

S. reginae. This is the species most usually seen. It has 3 ft. clumps of bright green, long, narrow leaves. The orange upper petals and purple tongue are carried in red-edged, green bracts. A number of forms occur, mostly differing in size and leaf shape. The blooms open in spring.

Streptanthera

IRIDACEAE. Only 2 species belong to this South African genus of small, bulbous plants. They have narrow, strap-shaped leaves and colorful 6-petalled flowers. Grow in sun with a minimum temperature of 45°F (7°C), and water when in leaf and flower, drying off when the foliage yellows, repotting in late autumn. Propagate by offsets.
S. cuprea. Orange kaleidoscope flower. The wide open, 1½–2 in. flowers of this elegant plant are bright orange with a purple ring near the center of each bloom and a yellow spot at the base of the petals. They open in summer.
S. elegans. This attractive species has pink blooms with a yellow-marked, black ring and a purple zone at the center of each flower. They open in summer. *(illus.)*

Streptocarpus

Cape primrose. GESNERIACEAE. A genus comprising 132 species from Africa and southeast Asia. Most of the popular indoor plants have stemless rosettes of long, ovate to oblong leaves, sometimes only a single large leaf, from which arise the erect flowering stems. Others have leafy, branching stems and form small, shrubby plants. The tubular flowers open flat at the mouth to show 5 rounded petals. Grow in light shade with a minimum temperature of 50°F (10°C), and water when the compost feels dry. Propagate by division, by stem or leaf cuttings, or by seed.
S. caulescens. Violet nodding bells. An east African

species up to 2 ft. in height with stout, purplish, branched stems bearing pairs of roundly oval leaves, all softly white-hairy. The small, mauve-purple, nodding blooms are borne in erect clusters.

S. dunnii. A curious plant from South Africa, having a single silvery-gray hairy, strongly rib-veined leaf which can reach 3 ft. in length, and brick-red, tubular flowers $1\frac{1}{2}$ in. long and opening to rounded petal lobes. They are borne in clusters of 6–8 on 1 ft. stems. Some extra humidity is needed for this species.

S. holstii. This erect plant from East Africa has rather slender, branching fleshy stems and opposite pairs of deep green, wrinkled, ovate leaves. The small, purple flowers are borne in clusters through summer and autumn.

S. kirkii. This tropical African species has erect stems and pairs of hairy, ovate, heart-shaped leaves. The lilac flowers are borne in loose clusters on long stems in summer and autumn.

S. rexii. This South African species has tufted rosettes of neat, narrowly oblong leaves, and 4–6 in. stems bearing in summer, pale lilac to blue flowers, the throat striped with purple. The plants sold under this name are usually hybrids, sometimes known as *S. x hybridum*, and involve this and other species in their make up. They occur in a wide range of flower size and color. *(illus.)*

S. r. 'Constant Nymph'. This cultivar has slender, tubular flowers which are an attractive purplish-blue.

S. r. 'Merton Blue'. This cultivar has blue-purple, trumpet-shaped flowers.

S. r. 'Wiesmoor Hybrids'. This form has large flowers with frilled and patterned petals.

S. saxorum. A most attractive east African species having almost prostrate stems, bearing whorls of

1 in., rounded ovate, bright green leaves, and $1\frac{1}{2}$ in., lavender flowers which have 3 large, rounded, petal-like lobes and 2 small ones from a slender white tube. They are borne on long, slender stems through spring and summer. A good basket plant.

Streptosolen

SOLANACEAE.

S. jamesonii. Marmalade bush. This is the only species of the genus. It is a soft-stemmed, evergreen shrub from Colombia with 2 in. long, ovate, wrinkled leaves. The loose clusters of bell-shaped, orange flowers are abundantly borne in summer even on first-year plants. It can be grown as an annual in a pot, needing some form of support, or as a climber. Grow in sun or light shade with a minimum temperature of 45°F (7°C), and water freely. Propagate by cuttings.

Strobilanthes

ACANTHACEAE.

S. dyerianus. Persian shield. One of a genus of 250 species, this Malaysian plant has decorative, shining green leaves which are long, ovate, and taper to a slender point. The upper surface has a silvery-purple sheen and the reverse is flushed purple. The light blue, funnel-shaped flowers are borne in spikes from late winter, through spring and often into summer. Grow in light shade with a minimum temperature of 45°F (7°C), and water freely. Some extra humidity should be provided if possible. Propagate by cuttings.

Stylidium

STYLIDIACEAE.

S. graminifolium. Trigger plant. There are 136 species in this largely Australian genus. This plant has tufts of 3–10 in., grassy leaves, and $1\frac{1}{2}$ ft., erect flowering stems which bear in summer rose-purple blooms with 2 lips. They have a curious trigger mechanism in the center comprising the style and stamens which are joined in such a way that a visiting insect will spring the trigger and be showered with pollen. Grow in sun with a minimum temperature of 45°F (7°C). Water when the compost feels dry. Propagate by seeds or division.

Syagrus

PALMAE.

S. weddeliana. Syn. *Cocos weddeliana*. This palm is one of a genus of 50 species, all from South America. It is extremely elegant as a young plant with a slender stem and arching fronds which are divided into many narrow segments. Grow in light shade with a minimum temperature of 55°F (13°C), watering frequently. It requires extra humidity, and for this reason is a very good plant for growing in a planting under a glass cover. Propagate by seeds.

Synadenium

EUPHORBIACEAE.
S. grantii. Milk bush. Belonging to a genus of 15 species this very decorative East African succulent shrub has thick branches and round to oval, leathery, green leaves. The small flowers are dark red.
S. g. 'Rubra'. This striking form has deep red-flushed leaves. Grow in sun with a minimum temperature of 55°F (13°C), and water when the compost feels dry. Propagate by cuttings allowing the cut end to dry before insertion.

Syngonium

ARACEAE. A genus of 20 climbing or creeping plants from tropical America. They have two markedly different foliage phases, starting with arrow-shaped leaves but later divided into 3–9 leaflets. It is plants of the young stage that are usually grown as house plants. Grow in light shade with a minimum temperature of 55–60°F (13–15°C), and water freely. Propagate by cuttings.
S. hoffmannii. Goose foot. This creeping species has pointed, arrow-shaped leaves with a gray-green surface, patterned with silver veins and having a whitish patina over the center of the leaf.
S. podophyllum. African evergreen. This popular species is grown both as a young plant to show off its dark, glossy green, arrow-shaped leaves, and as a larger climber, trained onto some form of support, with its leaves divided into up to 9 plain green leaflets. Many forms are grown.
S. p. 'Albolineatum'. This form has a silvery-white central area and veins.
S. p. 'Albo-virens'. This form has the leaves overlain with white, except for the green margins.
S. p. 'Emerald Gem'. A more compact plant with brighter green, glossier leaves.
S. p. 'Green Gold'. *(xanthophilum)*. A particularly attractive form having light yellowish shading on the green leaves.
S. wendlandii. This Costa Rican species has 3-lobed leaves even when young. Each lobe is long and narrow, forming the arms of a letter T. They are dark green with white veins. This coloration goes as the plant matures.

T

Tacca

Cats whiskers; Devil flower. TACCACEAE. A genus of 30 species of evergreen perennials from the tropics. They are grown for their most curious flower clusters. Keep in shade with a minimum temperature of 55°F (13°C), and water freely in summer. In winter keep the compost barely moist. Propagate by division.
T. aspera. This 1½–2 ft. plant from southern Asia has long, slender leaves, and in summer strong, erect stems bearing dense clusters of purple, cup-shaped flowers with rounded petals. At the base of each cluster are 2 ovate bracts and several long, thread-like, pendant ones. They are borne in winter and spring.
T. chantrieri. A Malaysian species with long, dull green, wrinkled leaves, and almost black flowers surrounded by deep red-purple bracts, the large oval ones spreading sideways, the many narrow ones trailing downwards. They are borne in winter and spring.

Tavaresia

ASCLEPIADACEAE.
T. grandiflora. Syn. *Decabelone grandiflora*. Thimble flower. One of 3 species in this succulent genus from southern Africa. It has leafless, 3–8 in., cylindrical, green stems with white bristles borne in threes from the tubercles which occur on the stem angles. The 4 in., lemon-yellow blooms are purple-spotted, fancifully giving the appearance of giant thimbles. Grow in sun with a minimum temperature of 50°F (10°C), and water only when the compost feels dry. Propagate by cuttings.

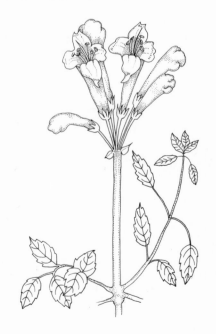

Tecomaria

BIGNONIACEAE.

T. capensis. Cape honeysuckle. Of the 2 species in this genus, the one described is an attractive evergreen shrub from South Africa. It can be grown as a climber, or kept bushy by pinching out the leading growths. The dark green, glossy leaves are divided into 6–8 leaflets and the tubular, 2 in., bright orange-scarlet flowers are borne in clusters from spring to autumn. Blooms are produced less freely on small specimens. Grow in sun with a minimum temperature of 50°F (10°C), and water when the compost feels dry. Propagate by cuttings or by layering. *(illus.)*

Tetranema

SCROPHULARIACEAE.

T. mexicana. Mexican foxglove. A genus containing 3 species of perennials from Central America of which this Mexican plant has dark green, oval leaves, and tiny, purple, foxglove-like flowers on erect 6–8 in. stems. It is best replaced annually or every 2 years. Grow in sun with a minimum temperature of 45°F (7°C), and water when the compost feels dry. Propagate by seeds.

Tetrapanax

ARALIACEAE.

T. papyriferus. Rice paper plant. The only species of its genus, this handsome plant makes a 10–20 ft. tree in its native China. As a pot plant it can be kept much smaller, though it soon demands several feet of space. It has large, gray-green, lobed leaves which are white-felted beneath when young and most decorative. Keep in light shade with a minimum temperature of 45°F (7°C), and avoid rooms hotter than 65–70°F (18–21°C). Water freely and propagate by seed or cuttings.

Tetrastigma

VITIDACEAE.

T. voinierianum. Syn. *Vitis voinieriana*. Chestnut vine. About 40 species make up this genus of climbers from southern Asia. This plant is a strong grower, but makes a good pot plant when young if given some support, and responds well to pruning. It has glossy-green leaves with 3, 5–6 in. leaflets which have a fine pelt of fawn hair beneath. Grow in light shade with a minimum temperature of 55°F (13°C), and water freely. Propagate by cuttings.

Thelocactus

CACTACEAE. A genus containing 17 species of cacti from Central America and the southern USA. They are small and usually globular, with large tubercles bearing spreading and straight spines. The large flowers open near the top of the plants. Grow in sun with a minimum temperature of 45°F (7°C), and water only when the compost feels dry. Propagate by seed.

T. bicolor. Glory of Texas. This globular species is remarkable for its many colorful, spreading spines which can be red, yellow, or white as can the 4 large, central ones. The large flowers are pinkish-purple.

T. nidulans. This small, globular plant is flattened on top. It has large tubercles which carry up to 15 spreading, gray spines and wide open, creamy-yellow flowers.

Thrinax

PALMAE.

T. parviflora. Florida thatch palm. One of a genus comprising 12 species, this palm can reach 25 ft. in its native Central America and southern USA. As a tub plant, it is very decorative having deeply dissected, fan-shaped fronds, the long leaflets forming an almost complete circle. Grow in light shade with a minimum temperature of 50°F (10°C), and water freely. Propagate by seeds.

Thunbergia

THUNBERGIACEAE. A genus of some 200 plants, mainly annual and perennial climbers. The annual sorts make good pot plants, the perennials provide bigger specimens and are only suitable for a large window or similar area where they can be given support. Grow in sun with a minimum temperature of 50°F (10°C) and water freely. Propagate by seed or cuttings.

T. alata. Black-eyed Susan. A twining species from South Africa with ovate, toothed leaves up to 3 in. long. The colorful, bright orange, funnel-shaped flowers open flat at the mouth to show a deep velvety-brown center. They bloom in late summer and autumn from spring-sown seeds.

T. coccinea. A tall climber from southern Asia which can reach 20 ft. in the wild. In pots it will remain smaller, but must not be pruned too hard as this may prevent flowers from forming. It has 5–8 in., heart-shaped, oval leaves, and hanging chains of small, red flowers in spring.

T. grandiflora. This Indian climber has 6 in., long, ovate leaves, and clusters of blue flowers with a 3 in. tube, opening wide at the mouth. They are borne in summer and autumn.

T. gregorii. From southeastern Africa, this species, which is sometimes incorrectly called *T. gibsonii*, makes an annual twiner having 3 in., ovate, toothed leaves, and deep orange, tubular flowers.

T. mysorensis. This Indian climber has long, oval,

pointed leaves and purplish, 1½ in. blooms opening to yellow lobes at the mouth. They are borne in hanging clusters in spring.

Tibouchina

MELASTOMATACEAE.

T. urvilleana. Syn. *T. semidecandra.* Glory bush. Belonging to a genus of 200 species from South America, this is a largely evergreen shrub, up to 10 ft. in its native Brazil, but less in pots. It has bright green, velvety, ovate leaves, and clusters of wide open, rich purple blooms, each 3–4 in. across, and borne in summer and autumn. Grow in sun or light shade with a minimum temperature of 45°F (7°C), and water freely. Propagate by cuttings.

Tigridia

IRIDACEAE.

T. pavonia. Peacock flower; Tiger flower. A genus of 12 bulbous plants from America. This species from Mexico and Guatemala has stalkless, sword-shaped leaves standing stiffly from the lower part of the stem, and 18–30 in., flowering stems carrying 6-petalled flowers up to 6 in. across. The outer petals are large and orange, the inner very small with red spotting on the orange background. Many colorful cultivars are now available. Grow in sun with a minimum temperature of 45°F (7°C), and water freely while in growth. When the foliage yellows in late summer, dry off and store the corms until spring. Propagate by offsets or seed.

Tillandsia

Silver birds; Wild pines. BROMELIACEAE. A large genus comprising 500 species of American bromeliads. Most are epiphytic in the wild, but with a few exceptions grow well in pots. In some species the flowers are colorful, in others it is the bracts that provide the attraction. Grow in a compost mixed with about a third part sphagnum, in shade, with a minimum temperature of 50–55°F (10–13°C). Water freely. Propagate by offsets or division.

T. bulbosa. Dancing bulb. A most curious epiphyte from Mexico south to Brazil. It has a basal rosette of narrow, twisted leaves, the sheaths forming a rounded bulb beneath. The spike of white-tipped, purple flowers is shorter than the leaves. They open in late autumn.

T. cyanea. Pink quill. An attractive rosette-forming plant from Ecuador. It has very narrow, 16 in. long leaves and a long, branched spike of blue-purple flowers, borne within pink and green bracts in summer.

T. fasciculata. Wild pine. An epiphytic species from Florida to Panama which grows well in a pot having a dense basal rosette of long, narrow, recurved leaves, and branched flower head with blue flowers protruding from the red-edged, green bracts.

T. flabellata. Red fan. A Guatemalan plant forming a rosette of arching, strap-shaped, light green leaves with a red flush which intensifies in good light. The red bracts enclose blue flowers in a spreading spike borne on an erect, 18–24 in. stem.

T. imperialis. Christmas candle. A dramatic species from Mexico, having a rosette of broad, leathery leaves, and a thick, brilliant red central spike like a bright candle, bearing small, purple flowers.

T. ionantha. Sky plant. From Mexico south to Nicaragua is found this tiny epiphytic plant. It has a minute rosette of narrow, pointed, silvery leaves rarely over 2 in. across, and flushing red in the center as the small purple flowers develop. Grow on pieces of bark or a branch.

T. lindeniana. Syn. *T. lindenii.* Blue torch. A very decorative species from Ecuador and Peru making 2 ft. rosettes of narrow, arching leaves. The bright blue-purple flowers are borne from a long, torch-like spike of rose-pink bracts.

T. pulchella. A small species from Brazil and Trinidad which forms tufts of 4–6 in., narrow leaves, and small, white flowers almost completely enclosed by the rose-red bracts.

T. recurvata. Ball moss. Widespread through the regions of North and South America, this small plant grows as an epiphyte, producing stiff, silvery-white leaves, curling round to form small, wiry balls. The pale mauve to white flowers are borne on small spikes.

T. stricta. Hanging torch. This South American plant forms rosettes of 6 in., narrow leaves, and has deep violet flowers which age to red, and are borne within reddish-brown bracts in pendant spikes.

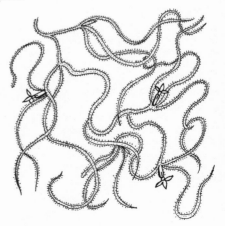

T. usneoides. Spanish moss; Old man's beard. A completely epiphytic plant growing on trees, or any other suitable perch, throughout the warmer parts of America. It is a true epiphyte having no roots, and should be grown on bark or a branch, without soil. It forms tufts of silvery, scaly stems many feet long, and small, yellowish-green flowers. Extra humidity is essential if this plant is kept in a warm room. *(illus.)*

T. wagneriana. Flying bird. A very handsome Peruvian species with a wide rosette of glossy green, strap-shaped leaves. The branched spikes of blue flowers are carried in glistening pink bracts and borne on stiffly erect stems.

T. xiphioides. The narrow, rolled leaves of this Central American species are borne in dense rosettes from which rise the flower spikes. These have large, pure white, fragrant blooms carried among short, green bracts.

Titanopsis

AIZOACEAE.

T. calcarea. Limestone mimic. Of the 8 species which make up this succulent genus from South Africa, this stemless plant has 1–1¼ in., thickened leaves like rather flat spoons. They are gray-green with a dense covering of white tubercles. The flowers are ¾ in. across and golden-yellow, opening in summer. Grow in sun with a minimum temperature of 45°F (7°C), and water only when the compost feels dry. In winter keep almost completely dry. Propagate by seed.

Tolmiea

SAXIFRAGACEAE.

T. menziesii. Piggy-back plant. Coming from Alaska south to California, this evergreen perennial plant is the only species in its genus. It has hairy, rounded, lobed and toothed leaves which are a soft green, and have the curious habit of producing plantlets from their junctions with the leaf stalk. The long, flowering stems produce small, purple-marked, green flowers in summer. Grow in light shade with a minimum temperature of 45°F (7°C), and water freely. Propagate by removing the plantlets, or division.

Torenia

SCROPHULARIACEAE.

T. fournieri. Wish-bone plant. This tropical Asian plant is one of a genus comprising 50 species. It is a 1 ft. perennial and has long, narrowly ovate, toothed leaves and very attractive tubular flowers. These are lilac, the upper petals rounded, the lower divided into 3 lobes, each a deep violet with a velvety texture and a central yellow patch. They

open almost throughout the year. The plant should be grown as an annual, sowing seeds in spring and autumn. Grow in light shade with a minimum temperature of 45°F (7°C), and water freely. Propagate by seed or cuttings.

Trachelospermum

APOCYNACEAE. 30 species make up this largely Asian genus of climbing shrubs. They have undivided, glossy green leaves, and clusters of small, tubular flowers opening to 5 recurved or twisted lobes. Grow in sun or light shade with a minimum temperature of 45°F (7°C), and water when the compost feels dry. Propagate by cuttings.

T. asiaticum. An evergreen climber from Korea and Japan, with 2 in., ovate leaves, and large, loose clusters of fragrant, yellow-white flowers in summer. The long shoots can be pruned to keep the plant a manageable size and shape.

T. jasminoides. Confederate jasmine; Star jasmine. This Chinese species has long, ovate, tapering leaves, and very fragrant, pure white flowers with narrow lobes, abundantly borne in summer. Will remain bushy if pruned.

Tradescantia

Spiderwort. COMMELINACEAE. A genus containing 60 species, all from America. Among them are a number of very popular and tough house plants, good for growing in pots or baskets. Grow in sun, or light shade for the variegated forms, and water when the compost feels dry. Propagate by cuttings.

T. albiflora. Wandering Jew; Inch plant. This trailing species from South America has bright, shining green, ovate, 1½ in. leaves, and small, 3-petalled, white flowers.

T. a. 'Albo-vittata'. A form with larger leaves, up to 4 in. in length, with blue-green and white bands. 'Tricolor' has cream and green striped leaves with a pinky flush.

T. blossfeldiana. Flowering inch plant. This Argentinian plant has semi-erect stems bearing dark green, oval leaves which are red-purple and hairy beneath. The small, rose-pink to purple flowers are white-centered and are very freely borne.

T. b. 'Variegata'. A form with creamy-white striping on the upper surface of the leaves.

T. fluminensis. Spreading Jenny; Wandering Jew. This trailing plant from South America has 2 in., long, ovate leaves, and small, white, 3-petalled flowers. 'Aurea' is a form with creamy-yellow striped leaves while 'Variegata' has a few wide, green and white stripes.

T. navicularis. Chainleaf or Boatleaf plant. An almost succulent, creeping plant from Peru, with long stems bearing clasping leaves which are folded upwards into a boat-shape, the central area being very thick and fleshy. The pinkish-purple flowers are borne in small clusters.

T. sillamontana. Syn. *T. pexata*. White velvet. An attractive erect Mexican plant, which is thickly covered with silvery-white hairs. The 1½–3 in. leaves are slightly waved along the edges and take on a pinkish tinge in strong light. The rose-purple flowers are 3-petalled and are borne in white hairy, boat-shaped bracts through summer and autumn. Keep dry over winter, letting the plant die back to ground level, then water again in early spring when the new, white furry shoots will emerge.

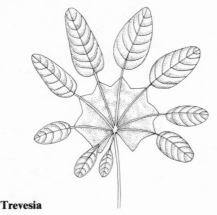

Trevesia

ARALIACEAE.

T. palmata sanderi. Vietnam snowflake plant. One of 10 species of shrubs and small trees from tropical Asia and the Pacific Islands. It has very large leaves, up to 2 ft. across and almost circular in outline, divided into about 8 leaflets which are joined together at the base. Each of these is divided and lobed giving the effect of a large, green snowflake. It is a good decorator plant for a not too dry atmosphere, and should be kept in shade with a minimum temperature of 60°F (15°C). Water freely, and propagate by cuttings. *(illus.)*

Trichantha

GESNERIACEAE.

T. elegans. Belonging to a genus of 12 species, this climbing shrub from Colombia has pairs of ovate, pointed leaves, and tubular flowers which are purple and hairy outside with narrow, yellow lines along the tube, opening to 5 bright yellow, spreading, rounded lobes. The 5 sepals are divided into fine, thread-like segments adding greatly to the attraction of the plant. Grow in light shade with a minimum temperature of 55°F (13°C), and water freely. Propagate by cuttings.

Trichocereus

CACTACEAE. This genus comprises 40 species of erect, columnar cacti from Central and South America. Although some will eventually become very large, they are slow growing and can be kept in pots for many years. They have most attractive, large flowers, but these are rarely produced on small plants of pot size. Grow in sun with a minimum temperature of 45°F (7°C), and water only when the compost feels dry. Propagate by stem tip cuttings or seeds.

T. coquimbensis. In its native Chile, this species reaches 3–4 ft. It has light green, erect stems lined with large areoles, each carrying 25–30 brownish-black spines, darkening from a yellow-brown when young. Black, hairy flower buds open to produce white flowers on large specimens.

T. pasacana. This species from Argentina and Bolivia can reach 15 ft. in the wild, but makes an interesting, rather barrel-shaped specimen when young. The stem is a mid-green, and the ribs bear well-spaced tubercles from which are borne long, red to yellow-brown spines.

T. spachianus. Torch cactus. This Argentinian species has branched, bright green stems, the ribs with short, yellow to brown spines. The white flowers, produced on mature specimens, open at night and are up to 8 in. in length.

Trichopilia

ORCHIDACEAE.

T. suavis. One of a genus of 30 species, this Central American orchid has oval pseudobulbs bearing long, leathery leaves. The creamy-white, fragrant flowers are up to 4 in. across and are sometimes marked with pink. The large lip is frilled, and has purplish-red markings with yellow in the throat. They are borne on short, arching stems, and open in winter and spring. Grow in fiber, in light shade, with a minimum temperature of 50°F (10°C), and water freely. Propagate by division.

Tropaeolum

TROPAEOLACEAE. A genus comprising 90 species of annual and perennial plants, some of which are suitable for home culture. They have showy flowers with short spurs. Grow in sun with a minimum temperature of 45°F (7°C) and water freely when in growth. Dry off the perennial species as the leaves yellow. Propagate these by division, or all sorts by seed.

T. majus. Nasturtium. This annual species from Peru is a rapid-growing, rather succulent plant with almost circular leaves, and red, yellow, or orange blooms.

T. m. 'Flore pleno'. A double form.

T. m. 'Tom Thumb'. A dwarf, non-climbing cultivar and the most suitable for pot culture.
T. tricolorum. Syn. *T. tricolor.* A small, dainty climber from Chile and Bolivia which grows from tubers. It requires small supports. The leaves are divided from the end of the stalk into 5 or 6 leaflets, and the small, pouch-like, scarlet and yellow flowers have long, upturned spurs. They open in spring. Dry off in summer.

Tulbaghia
ALLIACEAE.
T. fragrans. Syn. *T. pulchella.* Pink agapanthus. Belonging to a genus of 26 species, this South African plant has 12–15 in., strap-shaped leaves and clusters of 20–30 small, pinky-violet, fragrant flowers borne on 18 in. stems in winter. Grow in sun, with a minimum temperature of 50°F (10°C), keeping in a cool, airy place as much as possible in summer. Water freely, and propagate by division.

Tulipa
LILIACEAE. Many of the 100 species of tulips are in cultivation, and many more hybrids and cultivars have been raised. Most can be grown as short-term pot plants, bringing them into the house for flowering. Pot the bulbs in autumn, and keep cool until the flower buds begin to show color, then bring indoors. High temperatures while the plants are blooming will cause them to drop quickly, so if possible, keep them in a cool place overnight. Water sparingly, keeping the compost just moist. Propagate by offsets, but for indoor flowering it is best to use new, full-size bulbs each year.
T. 'Brilliant Star'. A bright scarlet form, centered with black and yellow.
T. 'Christmas Marvel'. A bright pinky-red form.
T. 'Diana'. This tulip has pure white flowers.
T. 'Joffre'. A very early sort with pure yellow blooms.
T. 'Makassar'. A deep yellow form for later forcing.
T. 'Prince of Austria'. This form has brilliant orange-scarlet flowers which are very fragrant.
T. 'Red Giant'. A good, late form which is bright red.
T. 'Van der Neer'. An unusual purple tulip.

U

Urceolina
AMARYLLIDACEAE.
U. peruviana. Syn. *Pentlandia miniata.* This Peruvian species is one of 5 belonging to the genus. It has narrow, strap-shaped leaves up to 6 in. long, and tubular, bright scarlet flowers, 1–1½ in. long,

and opening wide at the mouth. They are borne in autumn on erect, 1 ft. stems. Grow in sun with a minimum temperature of 45°F (7°C), and keep the soil moist after potting until the leaves appear. Then water freely until they yellow, when they should be dried off. Propagate by offsets removed when repotting every third year.

Urginea
LILIACEAE.
U. maritima. Sea onion. This bulbous plant is one of a genus of 100 species. It comes chiefly from the Mediterranean region and is found growing on sandy beaches. It has a large, brownish-red bulb which bears 12–18 in. long, sword-shaped leaves in spring. As these die off, the plant must be kept dry and warm until the flower spike appears in early autumn. The individual blooms are small and starry, the petals white with a narrow, green stripe. They are borne in dense tapering spikes on a 1–3 ft. stem. Grow in sun with a minimum temperature of 45°F (7°C). Propagate by seeds or offsets.

V

Vallota
AMARYLLIDACEAE.
V. speciosa. The only species of the genus, coming from South Africa. It has 8–24 in., strap-shaped leaves, and bright scarlet, funnel-shaped flowers which are 3 in. across and are borne on an erect 1–3 ft. spike in summer. Grow in sun in a minimum temperature of 45°F (7°C), and keep just moist throughout the year, watering more freely when growing. Propagate by seeds or bulblets.

Vanda
ORCHIDACEAE. A genus comprising 60 species of most attractive orchids from southern Asia and northern Australia. They are epiphytic in the wild, but have no pseudobulbs, producing an erect, woody stem. The blooms have 3 sepals and 2 petals of similar shape and color, the third petal forming a small lip. Grow in a fiber or bark based compost, in light shade, with a minimum temperature of 60°F (15°C), and water freely. Propagate by separating sections bearing aerial roots.
V. coerulea. Blue orchid. A strong-growing plant which can reach 4 ft. in height with many stiff, yellow-green leaves up to 10 in. in length. The pale blue flowers are 2–3 in. across and marked with darker purplish veins, the lip being a deeper blue. They are borne in arching spikes of up to 15 flowers, from late summer to late winter.

V. denisoniana. This spring-flowering species has 12 in., long, narrow leaves, deeply notched at the end, and very fragrant, greenish-white to ivory, waxy blooms, the lip having a yellow blotch. They are borne on short, arching stems of up to 6 flowers.

V. tesselata. Syn. *V. roxburghii*. The 1–2 ft. stems of this plant bear many stiff, 6 in. leaves with two notches at the ends. The 2 in. flowers are greenish-white with brown checker markings and the lip is 3-lobed, the central lobe purple, the outer white. They are borne on 6–12 in. stems in summer and autumn.

V. tricolor. Syn. *V. suaveolens*. This strong-growing species can reach 6 ft. in height, but flowers when much smaller than this. It has 15–18 in., arching, strap-shaped leaves, and 2–3 in., fragrant blooms very variable in color but usually light yellow with red-brown spots. They are borne in spikes of up to 12 flowers on a short stem in autumn and winter.

V. t. suavis. This form has white flowers with fewer markings, which are borne on longer, more floriferous spikes.

Veitchia

PALMAE.

V. merrillii. Christmas palm. One of a genus of 9 species, this small palm has a single erect trunk, and arching, deeply dissected fronds with bright green leaflets. Large specimens produce shining red fruits in winter. It makes a very good decorator plant in a tub and will stand considerable shade. Ideally, grow in light shade in a minimum temperature of 50°F (10°C), and water freely. Propagate by seed.

Veltheimia

LILIACEAE.

V. viridiflora. Forest lily. One of six species making up this South African genus of bulbous plants. This handsome lily has glossy green, strap-shaped leaves up to 1 ft. in length and dense clusters of pink, rarely red or yellow, tubular flowers, erect in bud, becoming pendant as they open. They are borne on 1–1½ ft. stems in spring. Grow in light shade with a minimum temperature of 45°F (7°C), and water freely when in growth, drying off when the leaves yellow. Propagate by offsets.

Viburnum

CAPRIFOLIACEAE. 216 species make up this genus, absent only from Australasia. Most are shrubs with pairs of undivided leaves and clusters of pink or white flowers. Those described below make good tub plants for a cool position. Grow in light shade with a minimum temperature of 45°F (7°C), and

water freely. Propagate by seed or cuttings.

V. odoratissimum. A large, evergreen species from southeast Asia which can reach 20 ft., but is easily kept to a manageable shape and size by pruning. It has 4–8 in. long, glossy green leaves, and erect heads of pure white, fragrant flowers in late summer.

V. rigidum. This 6–10 ft. shrub from the Canary Islands has rather rough, deep green leaves, 2–6 in. in length, and flattish heads of abundant white flowers, each with a pink stigma. They open in spring and are followed by blue-black berries.

V. suspensum. This shrub from Japan can reach 12 ft., and has broadly ovate, pointed leaves up to 5 in. in length, and long, dense clusters of pink-flushed, white flowers in spring. They are very fragrant.

V. tinus. Laurestinus. This shrub is native to southeast Europe, and makes a 10–12 ft. bush unless pruned. It has deep shining green, ovate leaves up to 4 in. long, and clusters of white flowers, pink on the reverse of the petals, the color showing in bud. They open through winter and early spring.

Vinca

Periwinkle. APOCYNACEAE. All the 5 species belonging to this genus are relatively frost hardy. Grow in sun with a minimum temperature of 45°F (7°C), and water freely. Propagate by cuttings or division.

V. major. Band plant. This European species has long, flexuous stems, and pairs of ovate, glossy green leaves. The large, blue-purple flowers open wide at the mouth to 5 somewhat angular petals. They open in spring. The plant is best cut back hard in autumn when it will sprout again.

V. m. 'Variegata'. This form has cream-edged leaves, and is more decorative for pot growth.

V. minor. A small, trailing evergreen species from Europe and western Asia with pairs of narrowly oblong leaves, and small, lilac-blue, tubular flowers, opening to 5 flat petals and white in the mouth. White, red, and purple forms are grown as are those with double flowers. 'Variegata' has creamy-yellow variegated leaves. A good ground cover for large plantings.

Vittaria

VITTARIACEAE.

V. lineata. Shoestring fern. One of a genus of 50 tropical ferns, this species is grown as a curiosity. It is found almost throughout the tropics and has very narrow, leathery fronds up to 18 in. long, but less than ⅛ in. wide. They hang from the rootstock and are best grown in light shade in a compost mixed with sphagnum, in pans or hanging baskets.

Keep a minimum temperature of 50°F (10°C), and water freely. Propagate by division.

Vriesea

BROMELIACEAE. This tropical genus contains 190 species, most of which are rosette-forming epiphytes with stiff, evergreen leaves, often with decorative markings. The flowers are borne in large spikes, each held within a colorful, long-lasting bract. Grow in shade with a minimum temperature of 55–60°F (13–15°C), and water freely, but do not allow the compost to become waterlogged. Propagate by offsets.

V. carinata. Lobster claws. A small-growing species from Brazil which has pale green, flattened leaves up to 8 in. long, and 2½ in., flat spikes of curved, red-based, yellow bracts from which the yellow flowers barely protrude. They are borne on an erect 6–8 in. stem and open in late autumn.

V. duvaliana. This 1 ft. species is native to Brazil and has thin textured, strap-shaped leaves up to 9 in. long, and flushed with red beneath. The tiny, yellow-green flowers are carried within scarlet bracts which have a narrow, yellow-green edge. They open in autumn and form a 6–8 in. spike borne on an erect, 1 ft. stem.

V. x erecta. Red feather. This hybrid makes a small, neat plant with soft, pale green leaves, and small flowers just visible within the deep, shining red bracts. The dense, oval flower spike is borne on an erect stem in autumn.

V. fenestralis. Netted vriesea. A very attractive Brazilian species grown as much for its decorative leaves as for its colorful flowers. The broad, flat, pale green leaves are up to 18 in. long, and arch over, showing the beautiful patterning of dark green veins. The fragrant, yellow flowers are borne within greenish-brown bracts, and open in summer.

V. heliconioides. This species occurs in the wild in Brazil and Colombia north to Guatemala. It has shining green leaves which are red-flushed beneath and up to 8 in. long, and wide spreading, red bracts, yellow at the tips and holding the creamy-white flowers. They open in autumn.

V. hieroglyphica. A large Brazilian species, the 18 in., broadly strap-shaped leaves marked with greenish-purple, hieroglyphic-like marks above, and flushed with a blackish-purple beneath. The yellow flowers are borne on stout, branching stems up to 3 ft. in height. 'Zebrina' has very dark blackish-purple markings and bands.

V. incurvata. A small plant from Brazil, only 1 ft. in height. It has soft, green, pointed leaves, and yellow flowers held within yellow-orange margined, scarlet bracts. They are borne in oval, flattened spikes on an erect stem.

V. psittacina. A Brazilian species with 12 in. long, narrowly strap-shaped leaves, thin and soft in texture, and somewhat wavy. The yellow flowers are spotted with green, and borne in summer in a loose 8 in. spike, each within a red bract and on a 12 in. stem. *(illus.)*

V. rodigasiana. Wax shells. Coming from Brazil, this species has narrow, dull green leaves with a few red-purple markings, and bright yellow flowers and bracts, the latter with red shading. They are borne in a branched spike of distinctive appearance.

V. saundersii. Silver vriesea. This Brazilian plant has broad, strap-shaped leaves up to 1 ft. long, and rather stiff in texture. They are a blue-gray with abundant red spotting. The yellow flowers and bracts are borne in loose, arching clusters. This species will withstand cooler temperatures than most vrieseas.

V. splendens. Syn. *V. speciosa.* Flaming sword. A species from Guyana with 12 in., green leaves, crossbanded with deep brown, and yellow flowers within brilliant orange-scarlet bracts in an erect, 15–18 in. spike. 'Major' is a strong-growing cultivar with purplish-brown banding, and bright coppery-red bracts.

W

Washingtonia

PALMAE. A genus comprising 2 species of fan palms from Mexico, California, and Arizona. They can be grown as tub plants while small but demand good light. Grow in sun with a minimum temperature of 50°F (10°C), and water freely. Propagate by seed.

W. filifera. Desert fan palm; Petticoat palm. In the wild, up to 75 ft. in height, this palm is very decorative when young, having rounded fronds, divided to halfway into narrow segments, the edges appearing frayed into fine threads.

W. robusta. Mexican fan palm. A fast-growing species with stiff fans of bright green leaves, cut for only about a ⅓ of their width, into slender segments with some thread-like fibers along their margins while young.

Watsonia

IRIDACEAE. A genus containing 70 species of South African plants growing from corms and having narrow, sword-shaped leaves, and spikes of handsome, colorful flowers. Grow in sun with a minimum temperature of 45°F (7°C). Water freely when in growth, drying off after flowering in summer, and keeping quite dry until autumn. Propagate by offsets and seeds.

W. coccinea. The flowers of this striking plant are brilliant red with a 2 in. tube opening to 6 rounded lobes, each 1 in. in length. It reaches 1 ft. in height. *(illus.)*

W. humilis. Growing up to 18 in., this species has very narrow leaves, and large, rose-pink flowers, the tube darker than the petal lobes.

W. h. maculata. This form has larger flowers, the petals with a purple marking in the throat.

Westringia

LABIATAE.

W. rosmariniformis. One of a genus of 22 evergreen shrubs from Australia, this species makes an attractive bushy plant which can be kept under 2 ft. by pinching. It has 1 in., narrow, rosemary-like leaves which are silvery beneath, and light blue, tubular flowers, opening to 2-lobed lips in summer. Propagate by cuttings.

Wittrockia

BROMELIACEAE.

W. superba. Syn. *Nidularium splendens*. A strong-growing, rosette-forming plant from Brazil, one of a genus of 6 species. It has long, waxy textured leaves which are light green with darker markings and red-toothed margins and tip. The flowers are small and blue, and are held within green sepals to form a cup at the center of the rosette. Grow in shade with a minimum temperature of 60°F (15°C), and water freely. Propagate by suckers.

X

Xanthosoma

Yautia. ARACEAE. A genus containing 45 species of herbaceous plants from tropical America. Most have arrow-shaped leaves and arum-like spathes. These however are not borne on pot plants. Grow in light shade with a minimum temperature of 60°F (15°C), and give additional humidity. Propagate by suckers or stem cuttings.

X. lindenii. This Colombian species has spear-shaped, deep green leaves up to 1 ft. in length and leathery in texture. 'Magnificum' has somewhat larger leaves with the veins and margins picked out in a clear, creamy-white.

X. violaceum. The arrow-shaped leaves of this West Indian species have violet-purple veins and margins, the color being stronger on the underside of the leaves.

Y

Yucca

Palm lily; False agave. AGAVACEAE. A genus of 40 species of evergreen trees and shrubs from Central America and the southern states of the USA. They bear dense clusters of stiff, narrow, sword-shaped leaves, sometimes borne on thick, trunk-like stems and spikes of attractive white, bell-shaped flowers which are borne only on large plants. Grow in sun, though they will tolerate some shade, with a minimum temperature of 45°F (7°C), and water when the compost feels dry. Propagate by suckers, stem cuttings, and seed.

Y. aloifolia. Spanish bayonet. A slender species with rosettes of stiff, strong pointed leaves 18–30 in. long and a bluish-green. With age it forms a slender trunk. 'Variegata' is variegated with white. 'Marginata' with yellow-cream.

Y. elephantipes. Syn. *Y. guatemalensis; Y. gigantea.* Spineless yucca. A large, strong-growing plant making a 45 ft. tree in its native Guatemala. The shining green leaves are tough but not stiff, and arch outwards making an elegant silhouette when young.

Y. gloriosa. Palm lily. Only 8 ft. in the wild, this species forms a short, rough trunk, and bears a rather loose rosette of leathery, blue-green leaves. The spikes of white flowers sometimes have purple striping and they are fragrant at night. 'Variegata' has creamy-white margined leaves.

Z

Zamia

ZAMIACEAE. 40 species make up this genus of cycads, which in appearance are rather like palms with fern leaves. They are native to tropical America. Grow in light shade with a minimum temperature of 45°F (7°C), and water freely. Propagate by division, offsets, and seed.

Z. floridana. Coontie; Seminole bread. A compact plant with its stem largely underground and 2 ft., dark shining green fronds divided into many narrow, stiff segments. A good decorator plant.

Z. furfuracea. Jamaica sago-tree. This plant has 3–4 ft. fronds which are largely erect and are divided into long, relatively broad segments which taper at both ends. A good, tough plant for indoor use.

Zantedeschia

Syn. *Richardia.* Calla lily. ARACEAE. A genus containing 9 species, all from Africa. They have fleshy arrow- or strap-shaped leaves, and showy blooms, the actual flowers comprising a tiny spadix or spike of petal-less flowers, but surrounded by a large spathe opening like a single, wide petal. They are borne on sturdy, erect stems. Grow in sun or light shade with a minimum temperature of 45°F (7°C), and water freely when in growth. After flowering, dry off when the foliage yellows, except for *Z. aethiopica,* which should be kept just moist. Propagate by offsets.

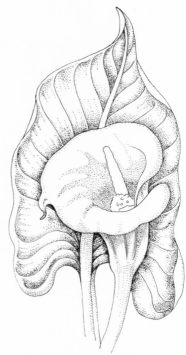

Z. aethiopica. Pig lily; White arum lily; Calla lily. A clump-forming species with dark green, arrow-shaped leaves which can reach 3 ft. in length, and an 8–10 in., glistening white spathe which encloses the yellow spadix. A favorite cut flower, it blooms in winter if given its dry resting period in summer, but normally is spring- to summer-flowering. 'Compacta', Syn. 'Godfreyana', is smaller in all parts and more suitable as a house plant. *(illus.)*

Z. albomaculata. Spotted calla lily. A slender species with narrow, deep green, arrow-shaped leaves which bear many oblong, translucent spots. The 4–5 in., white spathe is crimson-marked at the base, and appears in summer.

Z. elliottiana. Yellow calla; Golden calla. This species has bright green, ovate to heart-shaped leaves having the same straight-sided, translucent spots as *Z. albomaculata.* The 4–6 in. spathes are bright yellow, and open in summer.

Z. pentlandii. Yellow arum lily. This yellow-flowered species has arrow-shaped, unspotted, dark green leaves, the spathes having purple markings at the base.

Z. rehmannii. Pink calla. This neat growing species has 6–10 in. long, strap-shaped, dark green leaves, marked with narrow, light green, translucent spots, and small spathes which are variously colored from light pink to a pinkish-rose. They open in early summer.

Zebrina

COMMELINACEAE. This genus contains 4 species of small trailing plants from Central and North America, often confused with *Tradescantia*. They are strong-growing and look particularly well in hanging baskets. To keep them from becoming straggly, pinch out leading shoots. Grow in sun or light shade with a minimum temperature of 45°F (7°C), and water when the compost feels dry. Propagate by cuttings.

Z. pendula. Wandering Jew. A somewhat fleshy, trailing plant from Mexico, bearing 2 in., ovate leaves, which are purplish-green above with 2 wide, silvery bands, and deep purple beneath. The 3-petalled flowers are rose-purple and are borne within 2 leafy bracts. 'Discolor' has narrow silver bands on a coppery-green leaf, and a more purple flower. 'Quadricolor' is a cultivar with irregularly striped leaves in bands of purple-green, silver, pink, and red. It needs a little more care than other forms. *(illus.)*

Z. purpusii. Bronze wandering Jew. A strong-growing Mexican species having broadly ovate, green leaves, flushed on both surfaces with purple, but brighter beneath. The coloration deepens in bright light. The 3-petalled, lilac flowers open in autumn.

Zephyranthes

AMARYLLIDACEAE.
Z. grandiflora. Zephyr lily; Rain lily. This Central American lily is one of a genus containing 35 species. It has narrow, almost grassy, arching leaves up to 1 ft. in length, and clear pink, 2–4 in., funnel-shaped flowers opening wide to 6 starry petals, and borne on slender, 1 ft. stems in summer. Grow in sun with a minimum temperature of 45°F (7°C), and water freely while growing, drying off when the leaves turn yellow after flowering, and keeping dry until potting in late winter. Propagate by offsets. *(illus.)*

Zygopetalum

ORCHIDACEAE. A genus containing 20 species of orchids, all from South America. Many are epiphytic, but most of those suitable for indoor culture are clump-forming, ground species. They have egg-shaped pseudobulbs and arching, strap-shaped leaves. Grow in a compost mixed with fiber, in shade with a minimum temperature of 50°F (10°C), and water freely when growing, giving a short, drier resting period before flowering. Propagate by division.

Z. intermedium. Coming from Brazil, this species has narrow leaves up to 18 in. in length, borne on short pseudobulbs. The autumn- and winter-borne flowers are fragrant with green and brown marked, narrow, somewhat wavy, 1½ in. sepals and petals, and a wide, rounded, white lip with purple streaking. They are carried on arching, 12–30 in. stems.

Z. mackayi. This Brazilian plant has 15 in. stems which bear the 2 in. wide, fragrant flowers in autumn and winter. The narrow sepals and petals are red-brown and green, while the broad, rounded lip is white and streaked with violet-purple lines. The strap-shaped leaves can reach 20 in. in length.

Index

185

Buddhist pine: *Podocarpus macrophyllus*
Buchu: *Diosma ertcoides*
Buck bay daisy: *Dorotheanthus gramineus*
Bunny ears: *Opuntia microdasys*
Burro tail: *Sedum morganianum*
Bush acacia: *Acacia longifolia latifolia*
Bush violet: *Browallia speciosa*
Busy Lizzie: *Impatiens wallerana*
Butcher's broom: *Ruscus aculeatus*
Butterfly orchids: *Oncidium*
Butter plant: *Sedum adolphii*
Butterwort: *Pinguicula*
Button cactus: *Epithelantha micromeris*
Button fern: *Pellaea rotundifolia*
Button flower: *Centrantherum lntermedium*

Cabbage tree: *Cordyline australis*
Cactus vine: *Cissus cactiformis*
Calamondin: *Citrus mitis*
Calico flower: *Aristolochia elegans*
Calico hearts: *Adromischus maculatus*
Californian monkey: *Mimulus aurantiacus*
Californian pitcher plant: *Darlingtonia californica*
Calla lily: *Zantedeschia aethiopica*
Canary Island broom: *Cytisus canariensis*
Canary Island date palm: *Phoenix canariensis*
Canary Island ivy: *Hedera canariensis*
Candelabra plant: *Euphorbia ingens*
Candle plant: *Plectranthus coleioides*
Candle plant: *Senecio articulatus*
Candystick: *Senecio stapeliaeformis*
Cape cowslip: *Lachenalia*
Cape grape: *Rhoicissus capensis*
Cape honeysuckle: *Tecomaria capensis*
Cape jasmine: *Gardenia jasminoides*
Cape marigold: *Dimorphotheca ecklonis*
Cape plumbago: *Plumbago capensis*
Cape primrose: *Streptocarpus*
Cape sundew: *Drosera capensis*
Cape tulip: *Homeria*
Cardamon: *Elettaria cardamomum*
Cardamon ginger: *Amomum cardamon*
Cardinal flower: *Rechsteineria cardinalis*
Caribbean agave: *Agave angustifolia*
Caribbean spider lily: *Hymenocallis caribaea*
Caricature plant: *Graptophyllum pictum*
Carrion flower: *Stapelia*
Carrot fern: *Davallia canariensis*
Cast iron plant: *Aspidistra elatior*
Castor oil plant: *Ricinus communis*
Cathedral bells: *Cobaea scandens*
Cat's claw vine: *Bignonia unguis-cati*
Cat's jaws: *Faucaria felina*
Cat's whiskers: *Tacca*
Century plant: *Agave americana*
Chain cactus: *Rhipsalis paradoxa*
Chain-leaf plant: *Tradescantia navicularis*
Chain orchids: *Dendrochilum*
Chenille plant: *Acalypha hispida*
Chenille plant: *Echeveria pulvinata*
Cherry pie: *Heliotropium x hybridum*
Chestnut dioon: *Dioon edule*
Chestnut vine: *Tetrastigma voinerianum*
Chilean bell flower: *Lapageria rosea*
Chilean glory flower: *Eccremocarpus scaber*
Chilean jasmine: *Mandevilla suaveolens*
Chin cactus: *Gymnocalycium*
China berry: *Aechmea mertensii*
Chincherinchee: *Ornithogalum thyrsoides*
Chinese brake: *Pteris multifida*
Chinese evergreens: *Aglaonema modestum*
Chinese fan palm: *Livistona chinensis*
Chinese lantern: *Abutilon megapotamicum*
Chinese lantern: *Sandersonia aurantiaca*
Chinese lantern: *Hibiscus schizopetalus*
Chinese primrose: *Primula sinensis*
Chocolate plant: *Pseuderathemum elatum*
Cholla: *Opuntia bigelowii*
Christmas begonia: *Begonia x cheimantha*
Christmas cactus: *Schlumbergera x buckleyi*

Christmas candle: *Tillandsia imperialis*
Christmas cheer: *Sedum rubrotinctum*
Christmas cherry: *Solanum pseudocapsicum*
Christmas fern: *Polystichum acrosticoides*
Christmas orchid: *Cattleya labiata trianaei*
Christmas palm: *Veitchia merrillii*
Christmas pride: *Ruellia macrantha*
Christmas star: *Euphorbia pulcherrima*
Chrysamphora californica: *Darlingtonia californica*
Chufa: *Cyperus esculentus*
Cider gum: *Eucalyptus gunnii*
Cigar flower: *Cuphea platycentra*
Cineraria cruenta: *Senecio cruentus*
Cinnamon cactus: *Opuntia rufida*
Classic myrtle: *Myrtus communis*
Cliff brake: *Pellaea viridis*
Climbing aloe: *Aloe ciliaris*
Climbing butcher's broom: *Semele androgyna*
Climbing fern: *Lygodium japonicum*
Climbing fig: *Ficus pumila*
Climbing onion: *Bowiea volubilis*
Clipped window plant: *Haworthia truncata*
Clown orchid: *Odontoglossum grande*
Cluster cattleya: *Cattleya bowringiana*
Cluster fig: *Ficus glomerata*
Cockleshell orchid: *Epidendrum cochleatum*
Cockscomb: *Celosia argentea Cristata*
Cocktail orchid: *Cattleya intermedia*
Cocoon plant: *Senecio haworthii*
Cocos weddeliana: *Syagrus weddeliana*
Coffee: *Coffea arabica*
Column cactus: *Cereus peruviana*
Common ivy: *Hedera helix*
Common myrtle: *Myrius communis*
Cone plant: *Conophytum*
Confederate jasmine: *Trachelospermum jasminoides*
Coontie: *Zamia floridana*
Copihue: *Lapageria rosea*
Copperbranch: *Rhipsalis rhombea*
Copperleaf: *Acalypha wilkesiana*
Copperleaf: *Alternanthera versicolor*
Copper pinwheel: *Aeonium decorum*
Copper rose: *Echeveria multicaulis*
Coral aloe: *Aloe striata*
Coral bead plant: *Nertera granadensis*
Coral berry: *Aechmea fulgens*
Coral berry: *Ardisia crispa*
Coral cactus: *Rhipsalis cereuscula*
Coral gem: *Lotus bertholetii*
Coral plant: *Russelia juncea*
Coral vine: *Antigonon leptopus*
Corncob cactus: *Euphorbia mammillaria*
Cornish moneywort: *Sibthorpia europaea*
Corn lily: *Ixia viridiflora*
Cowhorn haworthia: *Haworthia coarctata*
Cradle orchid: *Anguloa virginalis*
Creeping Charlie: *Pilea nummularifolia*
Creeping fig: *Ficus pumila*
Crepe jasmine: *Ervatamia coronaria*
Crimson bottlebrush: *Callistemon citrinus*
Crocodile jaws: *Aloe brevifolia*
Croton: *Codiaeum variegatum pictum*
Crown beauty: *Hymenocallis americana*
Crown of thorns: *Euphorbia milii milii*
Crozier cycad: *Cycas circinalis*
Cub's paw: *Cotyledon ladismithensis*
Cup and saucer creeper: *Cobaea scandens*
Cup flower: *Nierembergia caerulea*
Cupid's bower: *Achimenes erecta*
Curley kidney begonia: *Begonia x erythrophylla 'Bunchii'*
Curly palm: *Howeia belmoreana*
Curtain plant: *Kalanchoe pinnata*
Cushion moss: *Selaginella kraussiana brownii*
Cyathea australis: *Alsophila cooperi*
Cypripedium: *Paphiopedilum*

Dainty rabbit's foot fern: *Davallia fejeensis plumosa*
Dancing bulb: *Tillandsia bulbosa*
Date palm: *Phoenix dactylifera*

Decabelone: *Tavaresia grandiflora*
Delta maidenhair: *Adiantum raddianum*
Desert barrel: *Ferocactus acanthodes*
Desert fan palm: *Washingtonia filifera*
Desert privet: *Peperomia magnoliifolia*
Desert rose: *Adenium obesum*
Devil flower: *Tacca*
Devil's ivy: *Scindapsus aureus*
Devil's tongue: *Ferocactus latispinus*
Dichorisandra albo-lineata: *Campelia zanonia*
Dinner plate aralia: *Polyscias balfouriana*
Diplacus: *Mimulus aurantiacus*
Doxantha: *Bignonia unguis-cati*
Dracaena australis: *Cordyline australis*
Dracaena congesta: *Cordyline stricta*
Dragon lily: *Dracaena*
Dragontree agave: *Agave attenuata*
Drejerella: *Beleperone guttata*
Drunkard's dream: *Hariota salicornioides*
Dumb cane: *Dieffenbachia*
Dutchman's pipe: *Aristolochia sempervirens*
Dwarf banana: *Musa acuminata*
Dwarf Chinese lemon: *Citrus x 'Meyeri'*
Dwarf fishtail palm: *Caryota mitis*
Dwarf kumquat: *Fortunella hindsii*
Dwarf lily turf: *Ophiopogon japonicus*
Dwarf mountain palm: *Chamaedorea elegans*
Dwarf myrtle: *Myrtus communis*
Dwarf rabbit's foot fern: *Davallia pentaphylla*
Dwarf sugar palm: *Arenga engleri*

Earthstars: *Cryptanthus*
Easter cactus: *Rhipsalidopsis gaertneri*
Easter lily: *Lilium longiflorum*
Easter orchid: *Cattleya labiata mossiae*
East Indian holly fern: *Polystichum aristatum*
Egyptian star cluster: *Pentas lanceolata*
Elegant philodendron: *Philodendron elegans*
Elephant bush: *Portulacaria afra*
Elephant's ear: *Philodendron hastatum*
Elephant's ear: *Kalanchoe beharensis*
Elephant's ear begonia: *Begonia haageana*
Elephant's foot: *Dioscorea elephantipes*
Elfin herb: *Cuphea hyssopifolia*
Elkhorn fern: *Platycerium grande*
Emerald ivy: *Hedera helix 'Chicago'*
Emerald ripple: *Peperomia caperata*
Emerald spiral ginger: *Costus malorticanus*
Episcia tesselata: *Nautilocalyx bullatus*
European fan palm: *Chamaerops humilis*
Everblooming acacia: *Acacia retinodes*
Eve's pin cactus: *Opuntia subulata*

Fairy castles: *Opuntia clavaroides*
Fairy primrose: *Primula malacoides*
False agave: *Furcraea*
False agave: *Yucca*
False heather: *Cuphea hyssopifolia*
False panax: *Pseudopanax lessonii*
Fan begonia: *Begonia rex*
Fan grass: *Reineckia carnea*
Fancy leaf geranium: *Pelargonium x hortorum*
Fat pork tree: *Clusia rosea*
Feather cactus: *Mammillaria plumosa*
Fern-leaf aralia: *Polyscias filicifolia*
Fern-leaf begonia: *Begonia foliosa*
Fern-leaf mimosa: *Acacia baileyana*
Fern-leaf philodendron: *Philodendron pinnatilobum*
Fern palm: *Cycas circinalis*
Ferocious aloe: *Aloe ferox*
Ferocious blue cycad: *Encepharlartos horridus*
Fiddle leaf: *Philodendron panduriforme*
Fiddle-leaf fig: *Ficus lyrata*
Fiery costus: *Costus igneus*
Fiery reed orchid: *Epidendrum ibaguense*
Fiery spike: *Aphelandra aurantiaca*
Fiji rabbit's foot: *Davallia fejeensis*
Fingernail plant: *Neoregelia spectabilis*
Fire barrel: *Ferocactus acanthodes*
Firebush: *Kochia scoparia triphylla*

Firecracker: *Brodiaea ida-maia*
Firecracker cactus: *Cleistocactus smaragdiflorus*
Firecracker flower: *Crossandra undulata*
Firecracker plant: *Manettia bicolor*
Firewheel tree: *Stenocarpus sinuatus*
Fishbone cactus: *Euphorbia polyacantha*
Fishhook barrel: *Ferocactus latispinus*
Fish-pole bamboo: *Phyllostachys aurea*
Fishtail fern: *Cyrtomium falcatum*
Flame of the woods: *Ixora coccinea*
Flame plant: *Anthurium scherzerianum*
Flame violet: *Episcia fulgida*
Flamingo flower: *Anthurium scherzerianum*
Flaming sword: *Vriesia splendens*
Flaming torch: *Guzmannia berteroniana*
Flask philodendron: *Philodendron cannifolium*
Flax lily: *Dianella*
Floppers: *Kalanchoe pinnata*
Florida silver palm: *Coccothrinax argentata*
Florida thatch palm: *Thrinax parviflora*
Flowering fern: *Aneimia phyllitidis*
Flowering inch plant: *Tradescantia blossfeldiana*
Flowering maple: *Abutilon*
Flowering oak: *Chorizema cordatum*
Fluted urn: *Billbergia macrocalyx*
Flying bird: *Tillandsia wagneriana*
Forest lily: *Veltheimia viridiflora*
Forster's sentry palm: *Howeia forsteriana*
Fox brush orchid: *Aerides fieldingii*
Foxglove gloxinia: *Rehmannia angulata*
Foxglove kohleria: *Kohleria digitaliflora*
Frangipani: *Plumeria rubra*
Friendship plant: *Billbergia x albertii*
Friendship plant: *Pilea involucrata*
Fuchsia begonia: *Begonia fuchsioides*
Fuzzy ears: *Cyanotis somaliensis*

Genista: *Cytisus*
German ivy: *Senecio mikanioides*
Giant dumb cane: *Dieffenbachia amoena*
Giant false agave: *Furcraea gigantea*
Giant maidenhair: *Adiantum trapeziforme*
Giant saguaro: *Carnegiea gigantea*
Giant spider lily: *Crinum giganteum*
Glory bower: *Clerodendron speciosum*
Glory bush: *Tibouchina urvilleana*
Glory lily: *Gloriosa*
Glory of Texas: *Thelocactus bicolor*
Glory pea: *Clerodendron formosum*
Glory tree: *Clerodendron fragrans*
Glossy privet: *Ligustrum lucidum*
Gloxinia: *Sinningia*
Goat's horn cactus: *Astrophyton capricorne*
Gold dust dracaena: *Dracaena godseffiana*
Golden ball: *Notocactus leninghausii*
Golden bamboo: *Phyllostachys aurea*
Golden barrel: *Echinocactus grusonii*
Golden brodiaea: *Brodiaea lutea*
Golden calla: *Zantedeschia elliottiana*
Golden ice plant: *Lampranthus aureus*
Golden jewel orchid: *Anoectochilus roxburghii*
Golden lace: *Mammillaria elongata*
Golden lily cactus: *Lobivia aurea*
Golden mimosa: *Acacia baileyana*
Golden pothos: *Scindapsus aureus*
Golden sedum: *Sedum adolphii*
Golden shower orchid: *Oncidium sphacelatum*
Golden spider lily: *Lycoris aurea*
Golden star: *Mammillaria elongata*
Golden trumpet: *Allamanda cathartica*
Goldfish bush: *Columnea x 'Vega'*
Goldfish plants: *Columnea*
Gold ivy: *Hedera helix 'Buttercup'*
Gold-rayed lily: *Lilium auratum*
Gold tooth aloe: *Aloe nobilis*
Golf balls: *Epithelantha micromeris*
Good luck plant: *Kalanchoe tubiflora*
Good luck plant: *Oxalis deppei*
Goosefoot: *Syngonium hoffmannii*
Granadilla: *Passiflora quadrangularis*

Grand Somali hemp: *Sansevieria grandis*
Grape ivy: *Cissus rhombifolia*
Grapeleaf begonia: *Begonia vitifolia*
Grass nut: *Brodiaea laxa*
Grass palm: *Cordyline australis*
Grecian laurel: *Laurus nobilis*
Grecian vase: *Quesnelia marmorata*
Green crown: *Euphorbia flanaganii*
Green earthstar: *Cryptanthus acaulis*
Green peppers: *Capsicum annuum*
Green rays: *Schefflera arboricola*
Green-tip Kaffir lily: *Clivia nobilis*
Green tongue: *Glottiphyllum linguiforme*
Grizzly bear: *Opuntia erinacea ursina*
Guava: *Psidium guajava*
Guernsey lily: *Nerine sarniensis*
Gum: *Eucalyptus*

Hanging torch: *Tillandsia stricta*
Hardy begonia: *Begonia evansiana*
Hare's foot fern: *Polypodium aureum*
Harlequin flower: *Sparaxis tricolor*
Hatiora salicornioides: *Hariota salicornioides*
Heart-leaf: *Philodendron oxycardium*
Heart of fire: *Bromelia balansae*
Heart of flame: *Bromelia serra*
Heart vine: *Ceropegia woodii*
Heath: *Erica*
Heather: *Erica*
Heavenly bamboo: *Nandina domestica*
Hedgehog agave: *Agave stricta*
Hedgehog aloe: *Aloe humilis*
Hedgehogs: *Echinocereus*
Heeria elegans: *Schizocentron elegans*
Hen and chicken fern: *Asplenium bulbiferum*
Heptapleurum arboricolum: *Schefflera arboricola*
Herald's trumpet: *Beaumontia grandiflora*
Heterocentron elegans: *Schizocentron elegans*
Hindustan gentian: *Chirita lavandulacea*
Hoary navelwort: *Cotyledon barbeyi*
Holly fern: *Cyrtomium falcatum*
Holly-leaved begonia: *Begonia cubensis*
Holly-leaved glory pea: *Chorizema cordatum*
Homalocladium: *Muehlenbeckia platyclada*
Honey bush: *Melianthus major*
Honey plant: *Hoya imperialis*
Hong Kong kumquat: *Fortunella hindsii*
Honolulu queen: *Hylocereus undatus*
Hookera coronaria: *Brodiaea coronaria*
Hop barleria: *Barleria lupulina*
Horsehead: *Philodendron panduriforme*
Howea: *Howeia*
Humble plant: *Mimosa pudica*

Imantophyllum miniatum: *Clivia miniata*
Impala lily: *Adenium obesum*
Inch plant: *Tradescantia albiflora*
Indian azalea: *Rhododendron simsii*
Indian day flower: *Commelina benghalensis*
Indian laurel: *Ficus microcarpa*
Indoor oak: *Nicodemia diversifolia*
Irish ivy: *Hedera helix hibernica*
Irish mittens: *Opuntia monacantha*
Irish moss: *Selaginella kraussiana*
Ironcross begonia: *Begonia masoniana*
Isolepis gracilis: *Scirpus cernuus*
Isolome: *Kohleria bogotensis*
Ithuriel's spear: *Brodiaea laxa*
Ivy arum: *Scindapsus*
Ivy-leaved geranium: *Pelargonium peltatum*
Ivy peperomia: *Peperomia hederifolia*
Ivy tree: *x Fatshedera lizei*

Jacobean lily: *Sprekelia formosissima*
Jade plant: *Crassula*
Jade plant: *Sedum platyphyllum*
Jamaica sago tree: *Zamia furfuracea*
Japanese glory tree: *Clerodendron fragrans pleniflorum*
Japanese ivy: *Hedera helix 'Conglomerata'*
Japanese painted fern: *Athyrium goeringianum*

Japanese pittosporum: *Pittosporum tobira*
Japanese privet: *Ligustrum japonicum*
Japanese spindle tree: *Euonymus japonicus*
Jasmine: *Jasminum*
Java glory bean: *Clerodendron fragrans*
Jelly beans: *Sedum rubrotinctum*
Jerusalem cherry: *Solanum pseudocapsicum*
Jewel orchid: *Anoectochilus*
Jewel plant: *Bertolonia hirsuta*
Josephine's lily: *Brunsvigia josephinae*
Joseph's coat: *Amaranthus tricolor*
Joseph's coat: *Opuntia monacantha 'Variegata'*
Jungle geranium: *Ixora javanica*

Kaffir lily: *Clivia miniata*
Kaka beak: *Clianthus puniceus*
Kangaroo ivy: *Cissus antarctica*
Kangaroo thorn: *Acacia armata*
Kangaroo vine: *Cissus antarctica*
Kentia: *Howeia*
Kimono plant: *Achimenes grandiflora, A. patens*
King agave: *Agave ferdinandi-regis*
King of the aerides: *Aerides crassifolium*
King of the forest: *Anoectochilus sikkimensis*
King pins: *Conophyllum grande*
Kiss-me-quick: *Brunfelsia latifolia*
Kitchingia uniflora: *Kalanchoe uniflora*
Kleinia: *Senecio*
Kohuhu: *Pittosporum tenuifolium*
Kola ears: *Kalanchoe millottii*
Kris plant: *Alocasia sanderiana*

Lace aloe: *Aloe aristata*
Lace aralia: *Polyscias guilfoylei*
Lace bugs: *Solisia pectinata*
Lace flower: *Episcia dianthiflora*
Lace orchid: *Odontoglossum crispum*
Lace trumpets: *Sarracenia drummondii*
Lacquered pepper tree: *Piper magnificum*
Lacy leaf philodendron: *Philodendron selloum*
Lady fern: *Athyrium filix-foemina*
Lady of the night: *Brassavola nodosa*
Lady of the night: *Brunfelsia americana*
Lady palm: *Rhapis excelsa*
Lamp flower: *Ceropegia caffrorum*
Lance copper leaf: *Acalypha godseffiana*
Lantern flowers: *Ceropegia*
Large-flowered butterwort: *Pinguicula grandiflora*
Latania borbonica: *Livistona chinensis*
Laurestinus: *Viburnum tinus*
Lawyer cane: *Calamus ciliaris*
Leaf flower: *Breynia nivosa 'Roseo-picta'*
Leather dracaena: *Dracaena hookerianum*
Leather fern: *Acrostichum aureum*
Leather fern: *Rumohra adiantiformis*
Leather leaf: *Rumohra adiantiformis*
Ledebouria socialis: *Scilla violacea*
Lemon: *Citrus limon*
Lemon-scented gum: *Eucalyptus citriodora*
Leopard begonia: *Begonia manicata 'Aureo-maculata'*
Leopard leaf: *Drimiopsis kirkii*
Leopard orchid: *Ansellia gigantea*
Leopard plant: *Ligularia tussilaginea 'Aureo-maculata'*
Leucophyta brownii: *Calocephalus brownii*
Libonia floribunda: *Jacobinia pauciflora*
Lilac bells: *Lachenalia lilacina*
Lilac shower: *Homeria lilacina*
Lilliput agave: *Agave striata nana*
Limestone mimic: *Titanopsis calcarea*
Lipstick vine: *Aeschynanthus lobbianus*
Little banana: *Chirita micromusa*
Little man orchid: *Gomesa*
Little princess agave: *Agave parviflora*
Little suns: *Mammillaria microhelia*
Living rock cactus: *Pleiospilos bolusii*
Living stones: *Lithops*
Lobster claws: *Vriesia carinata*
Lollipop plant: *Pachystachys lutea*
Lomarea ciliata: *Blechnum moorei*

Lophomyrtus bullata: *Myrtus bullata*
Lorraine begonia: *Begonia x cheimantha*
Love plant: *Anacampseros rufescens*

Madagascar cactus: *Didieria madagascariensis*
Madagascar dragon tree: *Dracaena marginata*
Madagascar periwinkle: *Catharanthus roseus*
Maguey: *Agave americana*
Maidenhair fern: *Adiantum*
Mallee: *Eucalyptus*
Mammillaria clava: *Coryphantha clava*
Mammillaria desertii: *Coryphantha desertii*
Mammillaria pectinata: *Solisia pectinata*
Mammillaria longimamma: *Dolichothele longimamma*
Manuka: *Leptospermum scoparium*
Marbled rainbow plant: *Billbergia x 'Fantasia'*
Marmalade bush: *Streptosolen jamesonii*
Maroon chenille plant: *Echeveria 'Set-oliver'*
Mauritius hemp: *Furcraea gigantea*
Medusa's head: *Euphorbia caput-medusae*
Mescal: *Lophophora williamsii*
Mesembryanthemum cordifolium: *Aptenia cordifolia variegata*
Metal-leaf begonia: *Begonia metallica*
Mexican fan palm: *Washingtonia robusta*
Mexican foxglove: *Tetranema mexicana*
Mexican pincushion: *Mammilaria magnimamma*
Mexican rose: *Dombeya cayeuxii*
Mexican snowball: *Echeveria elegans*
Mickey Mouse plant: *Ochna*
Mignonette peperomia: *Peperomia resediflora*
Milk bush: *Synadenium grantii*
Milkwort: *Polygala myrtifolia grandiflora*
Mimosa: *Wattle*
Ming aralia: *Polyscias fruticosa*
Miniature bulrush: *Scirpus cernuus*
Miniature croton: *Codiaeum variegatum pictum*
Miniature eyelash begonia: *Begonia boweri*
Miniature gardenia: *Gardenia jasminoides radicans*
Miniature grape ivy: *Cissus striata*
Miniature holly: *Malpighia coccigera*
Miniature maple-leaf begonia: *Begonia dregei*
Miniature marble plant: *Neoregelia tristis*
Miniature pine tree: *Crassula tetragona*
Miniature rose stripe star: *Cryptanthus bivittatus minor*
Miniature slipper plant: *Sinningia pusilla*
Miniature sweet flag: *Acorus gramineus*
Miniature wax plant: *Hoya bella*
Mind your own business: *Helxine soleirolii*
Miniature silver fern: *Athyrium goeringianum*
Mint bush: *Prostanthera rotundifolia*
Miracle leaf: *Kalanchoe pinnata*
Mirror plant: *Coprosma baueri*
Mistletoe cactus: *Rhipsalis cassutha*
Mistletoe fig: *Ficus diversifolia*
Molded wax: *Echeveria agavoides*
Monarch of the east: *Sauromatum guttatum*
Mondo grass: *Ophiopogon japonicus*
Monkey apple tree: *Clusia rosea 'Aureo-variegata'*
Monk's hood: *Astrophytum ornatum*
Moon cereus: *Selenicereus urbanianus*
Moreton Bay fig: *Ficus macrophylla*
Morning glory: *Ipomoea purpurea*
Mosaic plant: *Fittonia verschaffeltii*
Moses in the cradle: *Rhoeo spathacea*
Moss bamboo: *Phyllostachys purpurea*
Moss fern: *Selaginella emmeliana*
Mother fern: *Asplenium bulbiferum*
Mother-in-law's tongue: *Sansevieria trifasciata*
Mother of hundreds: *Mammillaria compressa*
Mother-of-pearl plant: *Graptopetalum paraguayense*
Mother of thousands: *Saxifraga stolonifera*
Mother's tears: *Achimenes candida*
Moth king: *Plectranthus purpuratus*
Moth orchid: *Phalaenopsis*
Mountain aralia: *Oreopanax peltatus*
Mountain ebony: *Bauhinia variegata*
Mouse thorn: *Ruscus hypoglossus*
Myrtle-leaf eugenia: *Eugenia myrtifolia*

Myrtle-leaf orange: *Citrus aurantium myrtifolia*
Mystacidium: *Angraecum*

Naegelia: *Smithiantha*
Nasturtium: *Tropaeolum majus*
Natal plum: *Carissa grandiflora*
Neanthe bella: *Chamaedorea elegans*
Needle vine: *Ceropegia debilis*
Netted vriesia: *Vriesia fenestralis*
Nerve plant: *Fittonia verschaffeltii*
Nidularium splendens: *Wittrockia superba*
Norfolk Island pine: *Araucaria heterophylla*
Norse fire plant: *Columnea x 'Stavanger'*
Northern pitcher plant: *Sarracenia purpurea*
Notonia petraeus: *Senecio jacobsenii*
Nutmeg geranium: *Pelargonium x fragrans*

Oak-leaf croton: *Codiaeum variegatum pictum*
Oak-leaf fig: *Ficus quercifolia*
Oak-leaf geranium: *Pelargonium quercifolium*
Oak-leaved velvet plant: *Gynura bicolor*
October plant: *Sedum sieboldii*
Octopus plant: *Aloe arborescens*
Old lady cactus: *Mammillaria hahnii*
Old man cactus: *Cephalocereus senilis*
Old man of the Andes: *Oreocereus celsianus*
Old man's beard: *Tillandsia usneioides*
Old man's head: *Rhipsalis capilliformis*
Oleander: *Nerium oleander*
Opal lachenalia: *Lachenalia glaucina*
Opopanax: *Acacia farnesiana*
Orange jasmine: *Murraya exotica*
Orange kaleidoscope: *Streptanthera cuprea*
Orange lipstick vine: *Aeschynanthus x splendidus*
Orange star: *Guzmannia lingulata 'Minor'*
Orchid cactus: *Epiphyllum*
Orchid tree: *Bauhinia variegata*
Ornamental birthwort: *Aristolochia leuconeura*
Oxtongue lily: *Haemanthus coccineum*
Oxtongue plant: *Gasteria x hybrida*

Pachystachys coccinea: *Jacobinia coccinea*
Painted leaf begonia: *Begonia rex*
Painted blood-leaf: *Iresine herbstii*
Painted drop-tongue: *Aglaonema crispum*
Painted kohleria: *Kohleria tubiflora*
Painted lady: *Echeveria derenbergii*
Painted lady: *Gladiolus carneus*
Painted nettle: *Coleus blumei*
Painted tongue: *Salpiglossis sinuata*
Palm bromeliad: *Pitcairnia corallina*
Palm grass: *Curculigo capitulata*
Palm-leaf begonia: *Begonia luxurians*
Palm lily: *Yucca*
Panama hat plant: *Carludovica palmata*
Panda plant: *Kalanchoe tomentosa*
Pansy orchid: *Miltonia*
Paper-flower: *Bougainvillea glabra*
Paper-spine cactus: *Opuntia turpinii*
Parachute plant: *Ceropegia sandersonia*
Paradise palm: *Howeia forsteriana*
Parlor ivy: *Philodendron oxycardium*
Parlor palm: *Aspidistra*
Parlor palm: *Chamaedorea elegans*
Parrot bill: *Clianthus puniceus*
Parrot leaf: *Alternanthera amoena*
Parsley moss: *Selaginella apus*
Partridge-breasted aloe: *Aloe variegata*
Passion flower: *Passiflora*
Patient Lucy: *Impatiens wallerana*
Peacock flower: *Moraea villosa*
Peacock flower: *Tigridia pavonia*
Peacock plant: *Calathea mackoyana*
Peanut cactus: *Chamaecereus silvestri*
Pearl acacia: *Acacia podalyriaeflora*
Pearl anthurium: *Anthurium scandens*
Pearl plant: *Haworthia margaritifera*
Pearly dots: *Haworthia papillosa*
Pearly moonstones: *Pachyphytum oviferum*
Pebbled tiger jaws: *Faucaria tuberculosa*

Peepul: *Ficus religiosa*
Pelican flower: *Aristolochia grandiflora*
Pentlandia miniata: *Urceolina peruviana*
Pen-wiper plant: *Kalanchoe marmorata*
Peppermint geranium: *Pelargonium tomentosum*
Periwinkle: *Vinca*
Persian shield: *Strobilanthes dyerianus*
Peruvian candle: *Borzicactus humboldtii*
Peruvian daffodil: *Pamianthe peruviana*
Peruvian foliage plant: *Nautilocalyx bullatus*
Peruvian old man: *Espostoa lanata*
Petticoat palm: *Washingtonia filifera*
Peyote: *Lophophora williamsii*
Pheasant leaf: *Cryptanthus forsterianus*
Phyllocactus: *Epiphyllum*
Piggyback plant: *Tolmeia menziesii*
Pig lily: *Zantedeschia ethiopica*
Pigmy bowstring: *Sansevieria intermedia*
Pigmy date palm: *Phoenix roebelenii*
Pincushion cacti: *Mammillaria*
Pineapple: *Ananas comosus*
Pineapple flower: *Eucomis*
Pineapple-scented sage: *Salvia rutilans*
Pine cone bromeliad: *Acanthostachys strobilacea*
Pink agapanthus: *Tulbaghia fragrans*
Pink ball: *Dombeya cayeuxii*
Pink calla: *Zantedeschia rehmannii*
Pink cissus: *Cissus adenopoda*
Pink ice plant: *Lampranthus roseus*
Pink jasmine: *Jasminum polyanthum*
Pink quill: *Tillandsia cyanea*
Pink spot angel-wing: *Begonia serratipetala*
Pinuela: *Bromelia balansae*
Pinwheel: *Aeonium haworthii*
Pistol plant: *Pilea microphylla*
Pitcher plant: *Nepenthes*
Pitcher plant: *Sarracenia*
Platyclina: *Dendrochilum*
Plover eggs: *Adromischus cooperi*
Plume asparagus: *Asparagus densiflorus 'Meyersii'*
Plush plant: *Echeveria x 'Pulv-oliver'*
Plush rose: *Echeveria x 'Doris Taylor'*
Plush vine: *Mikania ternata*
Poet's jasmine: *Jasminum grandiflorum*
Poinsettia: *Euphorbia pulcherrima*
Polka dots: *Opuntia microdasys albispina*
Pomegranate: *Punica granatum*
Poor man's orchid: *Schizanthus pinnatus*
Popinac: *Acacia farnesiana*
Porcelain flower: *Hoya australis*
Potato vine: *Solanum jasminoides*
Pothos argyraeus: *Scindapsus pictus argyraeus*
Powder puff: *Mammillaria bocasana*
Prayer plant: *Maranta*
Pretty face: *Brodiaea lutea*
Prickly tufts: *Mammillaria densispina*
Primrose jasmine: *Jasminum mesnyi*
Prince's feather: *Amaranthus hypochondriacus*
Princess Astrid's peperomia: *Peperomia orba*
Prism cactus: *Leuchtenbergia principis*
Propellor plant: *Crassula falcata*
Prostrate coleus: *Plectranthus oertendahlii*
Puka: *Griselinia lucida*
Purple cape cowslip: *Lachenalis purpuo-caerulea*
Purple granadilla: *Passiflora edulis*
Purple guava: *Psidium cattleianum*
Purple robe: *Nierembergia caerulea*
Purple scallops: *Kalanchoe fedtschenkoi*
Pussy ears: *Cyanotis somaliensis*

Queen agave: *Agave victoriae-reginae*
Queen anthurium: *Anthurium warocqueanum*
Queen cattleya: *Cattleya labiata dowiana*
Queen lily: *Phaedranassa carmioli*
Queen of the dracaenas: *Dracaena goldieana*
Queen of the night: *Cestrum nocturnum*
Queen of the night: *Epiphyllum oxypetalum*
Queen of the night: *Selenicereus grandiflorus*
Queen of the orchids: *Laelia purpurata*
Queensland umbrella tree: *Brassaia actinophylla*

Queen's spiderwort: *Dichorisandra reginae*
Queen's tears: *Billbergia nutans*

Rabbit's foot: *Maranta leuconeura*
Rabbit's tracks: *Maranta leuconeura*
Radiator plant: *Peperomia maculosa*
Ragwort vine: *Othonna capensis*
Rainbow bush: *Portulacaria afra*
Rainbow fern: *Selaginella uncinata*
Rainbow kalanchoe: *Kalanchoe fedtschenkoi 'Marginata'*
Rainbow orchid: *Epidendrum prismatocarpum*
Rainbow pincushion: *Mammillaria rhodantha*
Rainbow plant: *Billbergia saundersii*
Rain lily: *Zephyranthes grandiflora*
Rangoon creeper: *Quisqualis indica*
Rat's tail cactus: *Aporocactus flagelliformis*
Rattlesnake plant: *Calathea insignis*
Rattlesnake tail: *Crassula teres*
Red aglaonema: *Aglaonema rotundum*
Red bird cactus: *Pedilanthes tithymaloides*
Red box gum: *Eucalyptus polyanthemos*
Red bristle philodendron: *Philodendron squamiferum*
Red calico plant: *Alternanthera bettzickiana*
Red Christmas pride: *Ruellia amoena*
Red earthstar: *Cryptanthus acaulis rubra*
Red fan: *Tillandsia flabellata*
Red feather: *Vriesia x erecta*
Red heath: *Erica cerinthoides*
Red herringbone: *Maranta leuconeura*
Red-hot catstail: *Acalypha hispida*
Red ice plant: *Lampranthus spectabilis*
Red-leaf philodendron: *Philodendron x mandaianum*
Red peppers: *Capsicum annuum*
Red spray: *Ruellia amoena*
Red-tipped dog's-tail: *Harrisia tortuosa*
Red-veined prayer plant: *Maranta leuconeura*
Red yucca: *Hesperaloe parviflora*
Reed palm: *Chamaedorea siefrizii*
Regal pelargonium: *Pelargonium x domesticum*
Renealmia: *Alpinia*
Renga lily: *Arthropodium cirrhatum*
Resurrection plant: *Selaginella lepidophylla*
Rex begonia vine: *Cissus discolor*
Rhaphidophora aurea: *Scindapsus aureus*
Rhoicissus rhombifolia: *Cissus rhombifolia*
Ribbon aglaonema: *Aglaonema commutatum*
Ribbon bush: *Hypoestes aristata*
Ribbon bush: *Muehlenbeckia platycladum*
Rib fern: *Blechnum brasiliense*
Rice paper plant: *Tetrapanax papyriferus*
Richardia: *Zantedeschia*
Rock lily: *Arthropodium cirrhatum*
Rooting fig: *Ficus radicans*
Rose geranium: *Pelargonium graveolens*
Rose grape: *Medinilla magnifica*
Rose heath: *Erica gracilis*
Rose mallow: *Hibiscus*
Rose moss: *Portulaca grandiflora*
Rose of China: *Hibiscus rosa-sinensis*
Rose of Jericho: *Selaginella lepidophylla*
Rose stripe star: *Cryptanthus bivittatus*
Rosy moth orchid: *Phalaenopsis schilleriana*
Rouge plant: *Rivina humilis*
Royal red bugler: *Aeschynanthus pulcher*
Rubber plant: *Ficus elastica*
Ruffled fan palm: *Licuala grandis*
Rusty fig: *Ficus rubiginosa*

Saccolabium: *Ascocentrum miniatum*
Sacred bo tree: *Ficus religiosa*
Sacred lily of Japan: *Rohdea japonica*
Saffron spike: *Aphelandra squarrosa*
Sago palm: *Cycas revoluta*
Saint Augustine grass: *Stenotaphrum secundatum*
Salmon blood lily: *Haemanthus multiflorus*
Sand dollar cactus: *Astrophyton asterias*
Sapphire flower: *Browallia speciosa*
Satin leaf: *Philodendron gloriosum*
Saucer plant: *Aeonium tabulaeforme*

Scallop echeveria: *Echeveria crenulata*
Scarlet banana: *Musa coccinea*
Scarlet Indian shot: *Canna coccinea*
Scarlet leadwort: *Plumbago rosea*
Scarlet magic flower: *Achimenes antirrhina*
Scarlet plume: *Euphorbia fulgens*
Scarlet spike: *Aphelandra aurantiaca*
Scarlet star: *Guzmannia lingulata*
Scarlet trompetilla: *Bouvardia ternifolia*
Scarlet trumpets: *Datura sanguinea*
Schefflera macrostachys: *Brassaia actinophylla*
Screw pine: *Pandanus*
Sea coral: *Opuntia clavarioides*
Sea daffodil: *Pancratium maritimum*
Sea grape: *Coccoloba uvifera*
Sea lavender: *Limonium suworowii*
Sea onion: *Urginea maritima*
Sea urchin: *Astrophytum asterias*
Sea urchin cactus: *Echinopsis*
Seminole bread: *Zamia floridana*
Senegal date palm: *Phoenix reclinata*
Sensitive plant: *Biophytum*
Sensitive plant: *Mimosa pudica, M. sensitiva*
Sentry palm: *Howeia belmoreana*
Setcreasea striata: *Callisia elegans*
Seville orange: *Citrus aurantium*
Shell ginger: *Alpinia speciosa*
Shining broad-leaf: *Griselinia lucida*
Shoestring fern: *Vittaria lineata*
Show geranium: *Pelargonium x domesticum*
Showy bamboo palm: *Chamaedorea costaricana*
Showy billbergia: *Billbergia vittata*
Shrimp cactus: *Schlumbergera russelliana*
Shrimp plant: *Beleperone guttata*
Shrub verbena: *Lantana camara*
Sidney golden wattle: *Acacia longifolia*
Silk oak: *Grevillea robusta*
Silver ball: *Notocactus scopa*
Silver birds: *Tillandsia*
Silver bracken: *Pteris quadriaurita*
Silver calathea: *Calathea argyraea*
Silver chirita: *Chirita sinensis*
Silver coral: *Senecio scaposus*
Silver dollar: *Crassula arborescens*
Silver dollar tree: *Eucalyptus polyanthemos*
Silver garland ivy: *Hedera helix 'Marginata'*
Silver heart: *Peperomia marmorata*
Silver jade plant: *Crassula arborescens*
Silver jaws: *Argyroderma aureum*
Silver leaf: *Euonymus japonicus*
Silver princess vine: *Cissus albo-nitens*
Silver queen: *Euonymus japonicus*
Silver ruffles: *Cotyledon undulatum*
Silver vase: *Aechmea fasciata*
Silver vriesia: *Vriesia saundersii*
Silver wattle: *Acacia dealbata*
Silver worms: *Anacampseros buderiana*
Silvery patience plant: *Impatiens marianae*
Sky plant: *Tillandsia ionantha*
Sleepy mallow: *Malvaviscus penduliflorus*
Slender dog's-tail: *Harrisia gracilis*
Slender lady palm: *Rhapis humilis*
Slipper orchids: *Paphiopedilum*
Slipperworts: *Calceolaria*
Small-leaved goldfish vine: *Columnea microphylla*
Smilax asparagoides: *Asparagus medeoloides*
Snake plant: *Sansevieria trifasciata*
Snakeskin plant: *Fittonia verschaffeltii*
Snowball pincushion: *Mammillaria candida*
Snow bush: *Breynia nivosa*
Snow on the mountain: *Euphorbia marginata*
Snowy mint bush: *Prostanthera nivea*
Snowy pincushion: *Mammillaria celsiana*
Soap aloe: *Aloe saponaria*
Song of India: *Pleomele reflexa*
South American blue column: *Cereus hexagonus*
Spanish bayonet: *Yucca aloifolia*
Spanish jasmine: *Jasminum grandiflorum*
Spanish moss: *Tillandsia usneoides*
Spear sansevieria: *Sansevieria cylindrica*

Spider aloe: *Aloe humilis*
Spider lily: *Hymenocallis*
Spider lily: *Lycoris*
Spider orchid: *Brassia*
Spider plant: *Chlorophytum comosum*
Spiderwort: *Tradescantia*
Spiked cabbage tree: *Cussonia spicata*
Spiked clubs: *Caralluma neobrownii*
Spindle kalanchoe: *Kalanchoe x kewensis*
Spineless yucca: *Yucca elephantipes*
Spiny aloe: *Aloe africana*
Spiny Kaffir bread: *Encephalartos latifrons*
Spiral ginger: *Costus speciosus*
Spironema: *Callisia fragrans*
Spotted angel-wing begonia: *Begonia corallina*
Spotted calla lily: *Zantedeschia albomaculata*
Spotted dumb cane: *Dieffenbachia picta*
Spotted evergreen: *Aglaonema costatum*
Spotted laurel: *Aucuba japonica*
Spotted spindle: *Adromischus tricolor*
Spreading Jenny: *Tradescantia fluminensis*
Spruce cones: *Opuntia strobiliformis*
Spurge: *Euphorbia*
Squill: *Scilla*
Stag's horn fern: *Platycerium bifurcatum*
Star acacia: *Acacia verticillata*
Star cactus: *Astrophytum myriostigma*
Star cactus: *Astrophytum ornatum*
Star jasmine: *Jasminum simplicifolium*
Star jasmine: *Trachelospermum jasminoides*
Star of Bethlehem orchid: *Angraecum sesquipedale*
Starry ball: *Coryantha bumamma*
Stenocactus zacatecasensis: *Echinofossulocactus
  zacatecasensis*
Sticky moonstones: *Pachyphytum brevifolium*
Stonecrops: *Sedum*
Strawberry geranium: *Saxifraga stolonifera*
Strawberry guava: *Psidium cattleianum*
String of beads: *Senecio rowleyanus*
Striped bird's nest: *Nidularium innocentii*
Striped dracaena: *Dracaena deremensis*
Striped inch plant: *Callisia elegans*
Sultana: *Impatiens wallerana*
Summer cypress: *Kochia scoparia*
Summer torch: *Billbergia pyramidalis*
Sun cactus: *Heliocereus*
Sundew: *Drosera*
Sun hemp: *Crotalaria juncea*
Sun plant: *Portulaca grandiflora*
Swamp lily: *Crinum moorei*
Swan flower: *Aristolochia grandiflora*
Swan orchid: *Cycnoches*
Sweet bouvardia: *Bouvardia longifolia*
Sweetheart peperomia: *Peperomia verschaffeltii*
Sweet potato: *Ipomoea batatas*
Sword fern: *Nephrolepis*
Sycamore fig: *Ficus sycomorus*

Taffeta plant: *Hoffmannia*
Tailed butterwort: *Pinguicula caudata*
Tail flower: *Anthurium andreanum*
Tailor's patch: *Crassula lactea*
Tapeworm plant: *Muehlenbeckia platyclada*
Tasmanian tree fern: *Dicksonia antarctica*
Tea tree: *Leptospermum scoparium*
Teddy bear: *Opuntia bigelowii*
Teddy bear vine: *Cyanotis kewensis*
Telegraph plant: *Desmodium gyrans*
Temple bells: *Smithiantha*
Temple tree: *Plumeria rubra*
Testudinaria elephantipes: *Dioscorea elephantipes*
Thatch leaf: *Howeia forsteriana*
Thick plant: *Pachyphytum compactum*
Thimble cactus: *Mammillaria gracilis*
Thimble flower: *Tavaresia grandiflora*
Thorny cactus: *Acanthocereus pentagonus*
Thread agave: *Agave filifera*
Thread-leaf sundew: *Drosera filiformis*
Tiger aloe: *Aloe variegata*
Tiger flower: *Tigridia pavonia*

Tiger nut: *Cyperus esculentus*
Tiger orchid: *Odontoglossum grande*
Tiger's jaws: *Faucaria tigrina*
Tiger urn plant: *Billbergia horrida*
Tiled spurge: *Euphorbia bupleurifolia*
Tom Thumb cacti: *Parodia*
Tongue fern: *Pyrrosia lingua*
Toog tree: *Bischofia javanica*
Torch cactus: *Cereus*
Torch cactus: *Trichocereus spachianus*
Torch plant: *Aloe x spinosissima*
Totem pole: *Euphorbia ingens*
Toy cypress: *Crassula lycopodioides*
Tradescantia dracaenoides: *Callisia fragrans*
Tradescantia reginae: *Dichorisandra reginae*
Transvaal daisy: *Gerbera jamesonii*
Tree aralia: *Dendropanax chevalieri*
Tree gloxinia: *Kohleria*
Tree of kings: *Cordyline terminalis*
Tree oxalis: *Oxalis ortgiesii*
Tree philodendron: *Philodendron bipinnatifidum*
Trembling brake: *Pteris tremula*
Trichosporum: *Aeschynanthus*
Tricolor cape cowslip: *Lachenalia aloides*
Trigger plant: *Stylidium graminifolium*
Tropical tree opuntia: *Opuntia braziliensis*
Trumpet lily: *Brodiaea coronaria*
Tuberose: *Polianthes tuberosa*
Turkish temple: *Euphorbia obesa*
Turks' cap: *Malvaviscus penduliflorus*
Turks' cap: *Melocactus bahiensis*
Twelve apostles: *Neomarica northiana*
Twin-leaved sundew: *Drosera binata*

Umbrella plant: *Cyperus alternifolius*
Umbrella tree: *Schefflera actinophylla*
Urbinia agavoides: *Echeveria agavoides*
Unicorn plant: *Martynia louisiana*

Variegated ginger: *Alpinia sanderae*
Vegetable sponge loofah: *Luffa cylindrica*
Velour philodendron: *Philodendron andreanum*
Velvet cissus: *Piper porphyrophyllum*
Velvet leaf: *Kalanchoe beharensis*
Velvet leaf: *Philodendron verrucosum*
Velvet leaf vine: *Philodendron micans*
Velvet peperomia: *Peperomia velutina*
Velvet plant: *Gynura aurantiaca*
Venus fly trap: *Dionaea muscipula*
Victory plant: *Cheiridopsis candidissima*
Vietnam snowflake plant: *Trevesia palmata*
Vinca rosea: *Catharanthus roseus*
Violet bush: *Iochroma tubulosum*
Violet nodding bells: *Streptocarpus caulescens*
Virgin palm: *Dioon edule*
Vitis rhombifolia: *Cissus rhombifolia*
Vitis voinieriana: *Tetrastigma voinierianum*

Walking fern: *Adiantum caudatum*
Walking iris: *Neomarica northiana*
Walnut orchid: *Bulbophyllum pulchellum*
Wandering Jew: *Tradescantia albiflora*
Wandering Jew: *Zebrina pendula*
Wand flower: *Sparaxis tricolor*

Wart plant: *Haworthia reinwardtii*
Watermelon peperomia: *Peperomia argyreia*
Wattle: *Acacia*
Wax begonia: *Begonia semperflorens*
Wax ivy: *Senecio macroglossus*
Wax plant: *Hoya carnosa*
Wax privet: *Peperomia glabella*
Wax shells: *Vriesea rodigasiana*
Wax torch: *Aechmea bromeliifolia*
Weeping fig: *Ficus benjamina*
Western aloe: *Hesperaloe parviflora*
West Indian laurel fig: *Ficus jacquinifolia*
Whirlpool begonia: *Begonia x erythrophylla*
White arum lily: *Zantedeschia aethiopica*
White fluff post: *Eulychnia floresii*
White lily turf: *Ophiopogon jaburan*
White paintbrush: *Haemanthus albiflos*
White rain tree: *Brunfelsia undulata*
White velvet: *Tradescantia sillamontana*
White wax tree: *Ligustrum lucidum*
Whitey: *Mammillaria gemispina*
Whorled peperomia: *Peperomia pulchella*
Wild coffee: *Polyscias guilfoylei*
Wild pineapple: *Ananas bracteatus*
Wild pines: *Tillandsia*
Window linden: *Sparmannia africana*
Wine glass vine: *Ceropegia haygarthii*
Winged pea: *Lotus bertholetii*
Winter cherry: *Solanum capsicastrum*
Winter jewel: *Begonia bartonea*
Wishbone plant: *Tourenia fournieri*
Woody leaf flower: *Phyllanthus speciosus*
Wonga-wonga vine: *Pandorea pandorana*
Woolly bear: *Begonia leptotricha*
Woolly kohleria: *Kohleria lanata*
Woolly rose: *Echeveria x 'Doris Taylor'*
Woolly tree fern: *Dicksonia antarctica*

Xeranthemum: *Chameranthemum*

Yam: *Dioscorea*
Yautia: *Xanthosoma*
Yellow arum lily: *Zantedeschia pentlandica*
Yellow blood-leaf: *Iresine lindenii*
Yellow calla: *Zantedeschia elliottiana*
Yellow cape cowslip: *Lachenalia aloides*
Yellow flax: *Reinwardtia trigyna*
Yellow hook cushion: *Mammillaria aurihamata*
Yellow pitcher plant: *Sarracenia flava*
Yellow sage: *Lantana camara*
Yerba linda: *Peperomia rubella*
Yesterday, today and tomorrow: *Brunfelsia calycina*

Zebra basket vine: *Aeschynanthus marmoratus*
Zebra haworthia: *Haworthia fasciata*
Zebra plant: *Aechmea chantinii*
Zebra plant: *Aphelandra squarrosa*
Zebra plant: *Calathea zebrina*
Zebra plant: *Cryptanthus zonatus*
Zebra urn: *Billbergia zebrina*
Zephyr lily: *Zephyranthes grandiflora*
Zonal pelargonium: *Pelargonium x hortorum*
Zygocactus truncatus: *Schlumbergera truncata*